Louise Brooks, The Persistent Star: Articles, Essays, Blogs and Interviews

Louise Brooks, The Persistent Star: Articles, Essays, Blogs and Interviews

THOMAS GLADYSZ

Cover design by site bilder

A publication of the Louise Brooks Society

www.pandorasbox.com

All images from the collection of
Thomas Gladysz / Louise Brooks Society
unless otherwise indicated

Copyright © 2018 Thomas Gladysz

All rights reserved, including the right of
reproduction in whole or in part in any form

ISBN-13: 978-0-692-15102-0

ISBN-10: 0692151028

DEDICATION

To Barry Paris, who inspired this quest

And to Christy Pascoe, companion in my life & work

CONTENTS

	Acknowledgments	11
1	Introduction	13
2	The Star	17
3	The Films	53
4	The Legend	117
5	The Society	157
	Photo Insert	190
6	Related Reading	205
7	Further Reading	283
	About the Author	293

ACKNOWLEDGMENTS

These pieces first appeared in the following publications and on the following websites: Brattle Theater blog, examiner.com, *Film International*, Huffington Post, Louise Brooks Society blog, Open *Salon*, Patch.com, PopMatters, *Publishers Weekly*, *San Francisco Chronicle*, San Francisco Silent Film Festival blog, SFGate.com, Starts Thursday!, SiouxWire, and the University of Wisconsin Cinematheque blog. My thanks go to the editors and publishers. A few pieces appear here for the first time.

For their friendship, encouragement, support, and assistance I would like to thank: John Baxter, John Bengtson, Kevin Brownlow, Frank Buxton, Robert Byrne, Gianluca Chiovelli, Dwight Cocke, Bruce Conner, Peter Cowie, Emily Freitag, Jack Garner, Paul Gladysz, Donna Hill, Stephen Horne, Amanda Howard, Pamela Hutchinson, Roland Jaccard, Nancy Kaufman, Meredith Lawrence, Emily Leider, Paul McGann, Tim Moore, Laura Moriarty, Hugh Munro Neely, Stuart Oderman, Barry Paris, Becca Pascoe, Christy Pascoe, James and Ethel Pascoe, Ira Resnick, Stephen Salmons, Camille Scaysbrook, Judith Sheldon, Frank Thompson, Michael T. Toole, Philip Vorwald, Jan Wahl, Lynne Watson and the members of the worldwide Louise Brooks Society.

1 INTRODUCTION

The Internet, it turns out, is an ephemeral archive.

I began writing online articles about early film in 2009. At first, I wrote for the once well-trafficked, now defunct news site called examiner.com, where I contributed pieces under the moniker San Francisco Silent Film examiner. The Bay Area and silent film were my beat, so to speak, and my first piece was a write-up of an event with film historian Cari Beauchamp for her book, *Joseph P. Kennedy Presents: His Hollywood Years*.

I considered myself an online journalist. And though the pay was negligible, (I had a full time job and didn't depend on compensation from writing), I took my position seriously. Having written for my college newspaper and later a regional wire service, and having free-lanced for various newspapers including the *San Francisco Chronicle*, I knew what to do—and intended to cover local goings-on as a real journalist might, which meant writing about screenings and film festivals, interviewing notable individuals, reviewing books and DVDs, and covering anything newsworthy related to early film. Over the next few years, I wrote some three hundred pieces. And though the pay was negligible, I considered writing for examiner.com good practice, and even fun. I liked what I was writing about.

Soon enough, my perspective broadened, and so did my desire to write more about Louise Brooks, as well as silent film. I was aware of Brooks' films being shown in Hollywood, and was able to contribute pieces to the Los Angeles examiner.com. I also heard about screenings elsewhere, but, not having access to an outlet with which to cover them, I became frustrated in my desire to write about happenings outside "my beat." Noticing other examiner.com contributors were writing about individual celebrities, like Madonna or the Kardashian Sisters, it occurred to me to take on another role at this quasi news site, that of celebrity correspondent, albeit a long dead celebrity. As the national "Louise Brooks Examiner," I wrote about screenings in Brooklyn and Atlanta and elsewhere across the United States, and covered other news related to the silent film star. As such, I was amused to think I was one of the first silent film or "dead celebrity" correspondents for this (or any?) news site.

My interest in the actress was long standing. I had founded the Louise Brooks Society in 1995, and as the group's Director, I felt it was my "job" to spread the word; as an online journalist, I worked in a similar fashion to get the news out about the actress and her films. Not only did I preview screenings, but I also wrote about and reviewed new books and DVDs, interviewed individuals including a few celebrity admirerers, and on an occasion or two, helped break a news story about the actress.

I make no great claims, but over the years, I believe I wrote a few articles that mattered, or at least are still worth reading. For example, my 2010 article about Jan Wahl's *Dear Stinkpot: Letters from Louise Brooks* was one of the first to consider the book, an important addition to the Brooks' bookshelf. In 2018, I still come across film buffs that refer to it, passing along links to their friends.

I also wrote one of the first articles about the opening of a Brooks' archive at the George Eastman House, now the George Eastman Museum, in Rochester, New York. One of my 2010 examiner.com articles, "Louise Brooks' private journals to be revealed," received a great deal of traffic and even a few celebrity readers. Remarkably, film critic Roger Ebert and bestselling novelist Neil Gaiman both tweeted my article.

ebertchicago October 4, 2010
Louise Brooks' private journals to be revealed after being sealed for 25 years after her death. I'm there.
http://www.examiner.com/louise-brooks-in...

Neil Gaiman @neilhimself   5 Oct 10
Louise Brooks' private journals to be released... http://exm.nr/cle2ZD

Despite acknowledgement and a small readership, after four or five years I began to weary of writing for a single outlet. While there was little compensation, I had the satisfaction of knowing my work was getting out there, and that I was being read by at least a few of those interested in early film. I found my articles linked to on film message boards, and even plagiarized by bloggers and students. However, a turning point came when Google made the decision that examiner.com content was no longer considered news, and thus was no longer indexed as such. My readership fell off. And so did my interest in writing for examiner.com.

I looked around for other writing opportunities. And soon enough, I began contributing to Huffington Post, SFGate (the news / blog site for the *San Francisco Chronicle*), Open Salon (the blogger arm of Salon), and Patch.com (another open contributor / quasi news site). For these sites and others, I wrote a few hundred pieces—more reviews, event coverage, interviews and even a few obituaries. Some of it was related to silent film, some of it was related to Louise Brooks.

All along, I also contributed to blogs run by the likes of the San Francisco Silent Film Festival (which I started), University of Wisconsin Cinematheque and others, as well as websites like PopMatters. Meanwhile, my program notes were published by the likes of the Telluride festival, Syracuse Cinefest, Ebertfest, and the Brattle Theater in Cambridge, Massachusetts.

This writing coincided with my keeping the Louise Brooks Society blog. I started the LBS blog on LiveJournal in the summer of 2002, when blogs and blogging were all the rage. For the first decade or so, many entries were given over to notices of screenings of Brooks' films, the appearance of interesting items on eBay, the publication of newspaper or magazine articles mentioning the actress, or reports on my ongoing research. In 2009, I moved the LBS blog over to Blogger, which I considered a better platform. I also sought to improve the blog, to make it more substantial. The LBS blog is still going strong, and in the spring of 2018 it surpassed its 3000th entry.

As mentioned at the beginning of this introduction, the Internet is an ephemeral archive. In the years since I started publishing on the web, examiner.com has ceased operations, and my contributions (along with the work of others) have disappeared. Open Salon has also been discontinued, and gone are the dozen or so articles (a few editor's picks) which I posted there. In 2012, SFGate closed its blogger platform. And in early 2018, Huffington Post announced it was closing its contributor platform, cutting me off from yet another outlet for my writing. (As of now, my dozens of articles about Louise Brooks, as well as silent film, books & authors, music, art, etc… are still available on SFGate and HuffPo.)

With so much of my work disappearing, it occurred to me to gather some of my online journalism into a book. I had written a lot, and at least some of it, I believed, was worth preserving in the pages of a bound volume. That's how *Louise Brooks, the Persistant Star*, a selection of my best work on the actress, came into being.

While compiling this book, I decided to extend its range—beyond my online articles and essays, and include pieces I wrote for print publications as well as my Louise Brooks Society blog. There was a lot of material, but not all of it was worth preserving.

I wrestled with how to organize this book. At first, I envisioned a chronological gathering of my best work. *Louise Brooks, the Persistant Star*, which at first I rather plainly titled *About Louise Brooks*, was to be a mass of text. I gathered together some 150,000 words about the silent film star. However, as the editing process went on, themes began to emerge, as did the relationship of one article to another, as did the need to cut pieces which I found repetitive or of little real interest. Unintended themes, which form the chapters of this book, became The Star (biographical or historical pieces), The Films, The Legend (the actress' continueing influence), The Society (about The Louise Brooks Society), and Related Reading (more-or-less tangential articles).

Louise Brooks, the Persistant Star is not the definitive book about the actress. That, I feel, is the Barry Paris' biography. But, it does contain some interesting information and opinions which I hope, in book form, will make their way into a library or archive.

I have not included any material on Brooks' time with Denishawn, as I am working on a rather detailed book on that phase of Brooks' career. Nor have I emphasized Brooks' filmwork, as I am also writing a comprehensive, illustrated work on Brooks' films which I hope to finish in a couple of years. I expect the latter to run well more than 500 or 600 pages, and survey all there is to know about Brooks' brief film career.

I have excised from the pieces collected in this book much of the dated information, like the bits related to screenings which note ticket availability, venue location, etc…. And except for cleaning up typos and grammatical errors, I have, generally speaking, remained faithful to the original text of each piece—though the writing now seems a little poor in some instances. Links and embedded video clips have been cut out of necessity, as have some images due to space consideration.

Otherwise, here is selection of 15 years of my writing about Louise Brooks.

2 THE STAR

Galley Talk • Louise Brooks as the bride of Tom Thumb, and other early performances • First known advertisement to name Louise Brooks • Louise Brooks stars in a two-act comedy, Mr. Bob • Posing Regretted by Louise Brooks, Erstwhile "Friend" of Charlie Chaplin • Louise Brooks first radio appearance, in 1926? • Lulu in Detroit • Louise Brooks stars in Los Angeles series • Louise Brooks mentioned in Nazi era publication • Making Personas: Transnational Film Stardom in Modern Japan • Louise Brooks on stage in the 1930s • Louise Brooks Journals to be Revealed, and Perhaps Published • Dear Stinkpot: Letters from Louise Brooks by Jan Wahl • Notes on Louise Brooks' notebooks • Louise Brooks, Lost Girl

I fell in love with Louise Brooks twice. The first time was after viewing *Pandora's Box* one weekend a long time ago. I was wowed, confronted by the cinematic presence of a woman and an actress the likes of which I had never seen before. I have seen that film, as well as Brooks' other films, many times since. And each time I am smitten.

The second time was after reading the Barry Paris biography. In that 'swonderful book, I entered Brooks' world and found myself at the center of an exploding nexus of new interests and passions (silent film, the Jazz Age, 20th century popular culture, history, etc…). Paris' comprehensive biography, first published in 1989, is thoroughly researched, thoughtfully contextualized, and empathetic in a way that makes me think he really "gets" his subject.

I read a lot of biographies. It's my favorite genre. The Paris biography is the best biography I have ever read and the best biography I ever will read. I know that for sure. It is a book I have read more than a few times, refer to often, and expect to read from throughout my life. I can't recommend it enough, and have been known to buy extra copies which I pass along to friends.

If all this sounds a little like a "road to Damascus" conversion, then so be it. My twice-inflamed passion for Brooks changed my life in ways both trivial and profound. Not only did I acquire a life-long hobby (which some have called an "obsession"), I also found a life partner, my wife, Christy. A mutual interest in Brooks brought us together nearly 25 years ago.

Brooks, I would argue, is an important cultural figure. She was also a complicated, even mercurial individual. Academy Award honoree Kevin Brownlow, who knew her as well as any in her later years, described Brooks as "One of the most remarkable personalities to be associated with film."

My desire to learn more about this actress, dancer, and writer has led me to research and write about Brooks for more than two decades. The pieces in this chapter represent my "striving to understand."

Galley Talk

This piece appeared in Publisher's Weekly on July 28, 2006. It is a short write-up of Peter Cowie's 2006 book, Louise Brooks: Lulu Forever. I was able to meet the author a few months after it appeared, when I put on an event to mark the publication of Cowie's exceptional book.

Louise Brooks (1906-1985) is best known for playing Lulu in the silent 1929 German film *Pandora's Box*. Critics called her "an astonishing actress endowed with an intelligence beyond compare" and "the most seductive, sexual image of woman ever committed to celluloid." Peter Cowie's new book, *Louise Brooks: Lulu Forever* (Rizzoli, Oct. 31), emphasizes the dual nature of the actress's brains and beauty appeal. In telling the story of her rise, fall and eventual rediscovery, Cowie quotes from the witty and often frank letters he received from the actress and writer. Equally alluring are the dozens of beautifully printed portraits and film stills that fill the book. To mark Brooks's centenary, there are new DVDs, museum exhibits, a silent stage play and screenings taking place. Cowie's new book is a fitting, even fascinating literary tribute to an actress whose popularity today rivals that of her more celebrated contemporaries. It is a valuable addition to film history. It is also what the actress's many fans have long waited for.

Louise Brooks as the bride of Tom Thumb, and other early performances

This piece appeared on the Louise Brooks Society blog on February 2, 2016. It and the pieces that follow reveal some little known incidents in Brooks' early life.

Many fans of Louise Brooks, at least those who have read Barry Paris' outstanding biography, will be familiar with the image of Louise Brooks as the bride of Tom Thumb. It was the first ever role for the pint-sized performer, who was just 3 years old.

What else do we know about the image and the circumstances behind its making? Very little, it turns out, until now. Recent research has revealed that . . . this photograph of little Louise Brooks was taken ahead of a September 2, 1910 production of *Tom Thumb Wedding* at the Christian Church in Cherryvale, Kansas. Admission to this Friday evening event, a benefit, was 15 and 25 cents.

Despite bad weather around the state, many turned out. The following day, a newspaper article stated there was "good attendance," and that the "program pleased the audience, and netted the sum of $30 for the church." Doing the math, that means the audience numbered around 100.

Here is a picture of the venue for Brooks' first performance, the Christian Church in Cherryvale. This postcard image dates to right around the time that Brooks appeared as the bride of Tom Thumb.

Over the eight years, Brooks would dance and perform in public on a number of occasions in Cherryvale. For example, Brooks took piano lessons from a woman named Bertha Nusbaum, and on August 6, 1915 as one of Nusbaum's piano students, an eight year old Brooks performed the "Little Fairy Waltz Op. 105, No. 1" by Ludovic Streabbog at the home of a neighbor.

Another early documented performance took place on March 7, 1917 when the ten year old Brooks performed "Anitra's Dance" (from the *Peer Gynt* ballet by Edvard Grieg) at the Cherryvale Arts Festival. Cherryvale resident Reba Randolph accompanied on piano.

On January 18, 1918 a then eleven year old Brooks, who was referred to as "Mistress Mary, Quite Contrary" in the local newspaper, lead a "Dance of the Flowers" with 12 other Flower Maidens in a Mother Goose Pageant at the local High School. This event, held while the war in Europe was still raging, was a benefit for the local Red Cross fund.

Below is a picture of the Cherryvale High School, where on May 9 and 10, 1918 Brooks performed as the Fairy Queen in "On Midsummer's Day," a benefit to raise money to purchase Victrolas for the school.

First known advertisement to name Louise Brooks
This piece appeared on the Louise Brooks Society blog on February 3, 2016.

Pictured here is what I believe to be the first newspaper advertisement to name Louise Brooks. This ad from May, 1919 states that Brooks—then only 12 years old—would appear in "The Progress of Peace," an allegorical pantomime featuring 50 characters. The ad notes that Brooks will perform a solo dance.

The event, held under the auspices of the local Y.W.C.A. under the direction of the women's committee of the Victory loan, was a benefit to further the sale of Liberty bonds, or what were known as war bonds. Vivian Jones, a childhood friend and the future actress known as Vivian Vance (of *I Love Lucy* fame), also took part. Jones played one of the "peoples of the world." Music was supplied by local Paul O. Goepfert and His Orchestra. Eva Rude (Brooks' aunt) helped with costumes.

While living in Independence, Brooks studied gymnastics and aesthetic dancing with Mrs. May Argue Buckpitt, who wrote, directed and organized the pantomime. Brooks' contribution to "The Progress of Peace" was "The Gloating Dance of Destruction," arranged by Mrs. Milburn Hobson, also from Independence. According to press accounts from the time, a "large audience" turned out at the local Beldorf theater (pictured below).

According to the local newspaper, "The play dealt with Progress, rallying the peoples of the world to righteousness and truth, blesses them and gives them happiness. She is greatly perturbed by the coming of Destruction and Death" (played by Brooks). "Then the Peoples of the world are driven back and Progress is overcome. There is a call to arms and the Nations are mobilized. Belgium enters the fray and is backed by the Allies, one by one. Columbia is supported by the Seven Assisting Organizations and the Red Cross. The coming of Peace is represented in pantomime by the Allies and the Dance of the Dawn of Peace."

At the conclusion of the event, all of the cast as well as five older soldiers (Civil War, or the Spanish American War?) and eight veterans of the then concluded world war came on the stage.

This war & peace-themed event took place just 5 months after the end of the First World War, the "War to End All Wars." Admission to the benefit was 10 and 20 cents, which included an admission tax. I assume the admission tax was left over from the war, when movie theaters were taxed to raise funds for the war. (That tax continued into the early 1920s; I have come across advertisements noting a "war tax" on performances by the Denishawn Dance Company while Brooks was a member of the company.)

It's worth noting the ways in which the war in Europe impacted Brooks' youth—both directly (like the two benefits she participated in), and indirectly (like the tax on movie theater admissions). As a bright youngster, she must have been aware of the war and the many ways it affected daily life.

As a youngster in Cherryvale, for example, Brooks had friends who came down with German measles, which during the war were renamed "Liberty measles."

More importantly, Brooks knew a few men who served in the armed forces, among them her neighbors in Cherryvale, as well as her cousin, Robert Rude; he belonged to the 137th U.S. infantry, Company H., which was stationed at Camp Doniphan in Oklahoma. Rude once visited the Brooks' family home while on a furlough.

Tomorrow's blog will look at another little known early Brooks' performance, and will include a rare image of Brooks not seen in nearly 100 years.

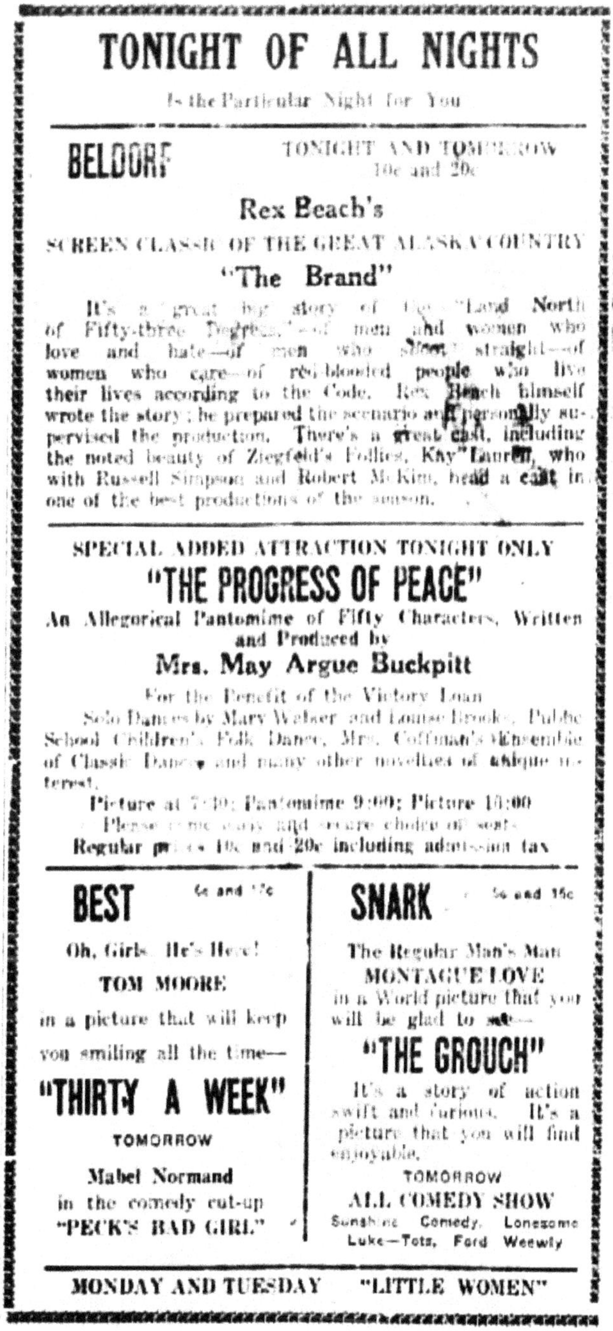

TONIGHT OF ALL NIGHTS

Is the Particular Night for You

BELDORF — TONIGHT AND TOMORROW — 10c and 20c

Rex Beach's

SCREEN CLASSIC OF THE GREAT ALASKA COUNTRY

"The Brand"

It's a great big story of the "Land North of Fifty-three Degrees"—of men and women who love and hate—of men who shoot straight—of women who care—of red-blooded people who live their lives according to the Code. Rex Beach himself wrote the story; he prepared the scenario and personally supervised the production. There's a great cast, including the noted beauty of Ziegfeld's Follies, Kay Laurell, who with Russell Simpson and Robert McKim, head a cast in one of the best productions of the season.

SPECIAL ADDED ATTRACTION TONIGHT ONLY

"THE PROGRESS OF PEACE"

An Allegorical Pantomime of Fifty Characters, Written and Produced by

Mrs. May Argue Buckpitt

For the Benefit of the Victory Loan

Solo Dances by Mary Walker and Louise Brooks, Public School Children's Folk Dance, Mrs. Coffman's Ensemble of Classic Dances and many other novelties of unique interest.

Picture at 7:30; Pantomime 9:00; Picture 10:00

Please come early and secure choice of seats

Regular prices 10c and 20c including admission tax

BEST — 6c and 17c

Oh, Girls, He's Here!

TOM MOORE

in a picture that will keep you smiling all the time—

"THIRTY A WEEK"

TOMORROW

Mabel Normand

in the comedy cut-up

"PECK'S BAD GIRL."

SNARK — 5c and 15c

The Regular Man's Man

MONTAGUE LOVE

in a World picture that you will be glad to see—

"THE GROUCH"

It's a story of action swift and furious. It's a picture that you will find enjoyable.

TOMORROW

ALL COMEDY SHOW

Sunshine Comedy, Lonesome Luke—Tots, Ford Weewly

MONDAY AND TUESDAY "LITTLE WOMEN"

"Tonight of All Nights Is the Particular Night for You." Pictured here is the first newspaper advertisement which I've come across which names Louise Brooks. She is listed, along with another girl, Mary Walker, as one of two solo dancers who would appear in "The Progress of Peace."

Louise Brooks stars in a two-act comedy, *Mr. Bob*
This piece appeared on the Louise Brooks Society blog on February 4, 2016.

On May 20, 1921, fourteen year old Louise Brooks played a lead role in a two-act comedy, *Mr. Bob*, which was staged in the auditorium of the Horace Mann intermediate school in Wichita, Kansas. Brooks played the role of Catherine Rogers.

Some 600 students attended the event. On the following page is a picture of the cast, which includes a seated, smiling Louise Brooks. She certainly stands out, at least in my eye, in the way she holds herself—confident, relaxed.

I wasn't able to find much on *Mr. Bob*, except that it was royalty free and performed in a number of schools in the first few decades of the 20th century. I did a quick search, and managed to purchase an inexpensive copy from the turn of the last century. Here is a synopsis of the play which I found online.

Mr. Bob. By Rachel E. Baker. (Baker.) Comedy, in two acts. Three men, four women. One and one-half hours.
    Mr. Bob, a girl, visits her chum whose brother is expecting a man. Very humorous mistakes of identity follow as she takes a lawyer for the brother. An amusing light comedy, much played for years. Always "goes." No literary pretensions.

What follows the picture of the cast is a postcard of the Horace Mann School, where the play was performed. The postcard dates from around 1920.

Posing Regretted by Louise Brooks, Erstwhile "Friend" of Charlie Chaplin
This piece appeared on the Louise Brooks Society blog on June 26, 2014.

Here is one of the rarest bits of Brooksiana and Chapliniana you are likely to see. . . a four panel comic strip "history" of the summer long affair between Louise Brooks, a then little known showgirl and Charlie Chaplin, the international film star. It ran in a New York City newspaper. Tongues were certainly wagging in 1925.

Gossip was news in the Fall of 1925. This feature photo was syndicated to newspapers across the United States. I have found a number of instances of this captioned image in various papers, from Pennsylvannia and South Carolina to Nebraska and Oregon. Some ran under the headline "Chaplin, Living with Wife, Brands Rumors of Follies Romance False," other under the more concise "Rumors of Follies Romance False."

No matter what the headline, the caption below the picture uniformly read, "Stories linking the names of Charlie Chaplin, screen comedian, and Louise Brooks, Follies beauty, in a romance, are being indignantly denied in Los Angeles, where Chaplin is living with his wife and their son. Charles Spencer Chaplin jr. It is stated, however, that Miss Brooks may be the comedian's leading woman in his next picture."

[The source for this news bit is unknown, as Brooks was not known to be one to kiss-and-tell. Chaplin likely never mentioned the affair either, as he was married at the time. Only in later years did the comedian comment on Brooks, when he told composer David Diamond that she had breasts "like little pears."]

POSING in the "almost altogether." Louise Brooks, then a Follies girl, had many scantily draped photos of herself made as an aid to publicity. These have brought about her suit against John de Mirjian, photographer.

LOVELINESS of this new budding actress held Charlie Chaplin enthralled on the comedian's recent visit to this city. Night after night he watched her dazzling beauty behind the footlights.

MEETING of the famous Charlie and the fair Louise was "arranged" at a party. Thereafter they were constant companions at the night clubs. And the "Roaring Forties" lowered their tone to whispers.

YESTERDAY Louise, very much in the limelight because of her startling suit, denied that she had ever, ever envisioned anything more than friendship with Mr. (he's sometimes called that) Chaplin.

Louise Brooks first radio appearance, in 1926?

*This piece appeared on the Louise Brooks Society blog on May 28, 2016.
In 2018, I came upon an incomplete cache of Brooks' 1962 radio broadcasts.*

Editor, VARIETY:

The claims and counter-claims of several gentlemen in Hollywood that they were the pioneers of movie commentator radio programs must be amusing to a number of film stars who were my guests on WIP, WPG and WGBS way back in 1924 and 1925. With all due respect to Tamar Lane and even Mr. Brown on KMTR may I suggest that they peruse these figures and facts.

'Emo's Movie Broadcast' was inaugurated as regular Tuesday night feature on WIP, Sept. 23, 1924. On Saturday night, Jan. 24, 1925, I conducted the first movie star's party ever broadcast in which the following participated: Ben Lyon, the late Milton Sills, Doris Kenyon, Hobart Bosworth, Viola Dana, the late John Bowers, Marguerite De LaMotte, Dorothy MacKaill, the late Gladys Brockwell, Myrtle Stedman, etc. Fred Stanley, then with First National, with Lambert Hillyer, Earl Hudson headed the contingent. On individual broadcasts I presented the late Rudolph Valentino, Richard Barthelmess, Doug Fairbanks, Jr.; the late Ernest Torrence, Lupe Velez, Gilda Gray, Flora Finch, Kane Ricmond, Ben Turpin, Josef Swickard, Adolphe Menjou, the late Marie Prevost, Marian Nixon, Ethlyne Claire, Madeline Hurlock, linor Fair, George K. Arthur, Mary McAllister, Anne Cornwall, the late Walter Hiers, Dorothy Phillips, Cullen Landis, Betty Francisco, Jacqueline Logan, Louise Brooks, Buddy Rogers, Jackie Coogan, the late Barbara LaMar, the late Marcus Loew, Madge Kennedy, Sidney Blackmer, Louise Glaum, Pedro DeCordoba, and a score of others.

Discontinued the broadcasts in 1928 to head the advertising, publicity and exploitation department for RKO theatres but resumed broadcasting in 1932. That year we inaugurated movie broadcast material in continuity form and have been servicing over 80 radio stations continuously in the United States and in Canada. In New York our material is presented on CBS twice weekly and fed to a number of eastern stations for a sponsor. Furthermore, the names of all the film players listed above cover the period prior to the advent of talkies. It was a novelty to the ear to hear the voices of silent film stars.

E. M. Orowitz,
EMO Movie Club.

In the 1940s, Louise Brooks worked in radio. That's known. Her film career had come to an end, and she found work writing bits for Walter Winchell's broadcasts; she also found voice work while appearing on a small handful of radio soaps on CBS network.

The question arises, where these her earliest radio appearances?

I am certain the answer is no. According to a letter to the editor published in *Variety* in 1937, Brooks and many other noted silent stars appeared on the radio in the mid-1920, most likely in 1926 while she was still resident in New York City. (It's possible she appeared on the radio in 1927, or even 1928, as she was known to criss-cross the country during that time. However, no search of radio listing from the time has mentions Brooks; the usual description of any given show is as unrevealing as "variety.")

I feel the claims of E.M. Orowitz, (who was also the associate editor of *The Exhibitor*, a Philadelphia trade journal), can be believed. In the past, I have found radio listings and newspaper articles which corroborate his claim.

One article I came across, for example, stated that while the Brooks film, *A Social Celebrity*, was playing at the Rivoli in New York in April, 1926, Adolphe Menjou appeared on WGBS, the Gimbel Brothers radio station in NYC. According to this newspaper report, Menjou spoke about the film and the scenes shot locally on Long Island.

The 1937 *Variety* letter is a significant discovery, at least in terms of Brooks' biography. Should there be any surviving records, documents or even (unlikely) recordings, then its significance grows. The search goes on….

[….As it does for recordings of Brooks' 1962 radio broadcasts on WHAM in Rochester, New York.. As it does for her appearances on the CBC in the early 1970s. And as it does for recordings of the radio broadcasts made by Ruth St. Denis and Ted Shawn while Brooks was part of Denishawn.]

Lulu in Detroit

These introductory remarks were given prior to a screening of Pandora's Box at the Detroit Film Theatre in Detroit, Michigan on December 8, 2006. Located within the Detroit Institute of Arts, this historic theatre was the first museum theater in the United States to screen film as art, prior to similar screenings at the Museum of Modern Art in New York City.

Good evening, and on behalf the Detroit Institute of Arts—thank you all for coming. My name is Thomas Gladysz.

I am the Director of the Louise Brooks Society, an online archive and fan club devoted to the actress. Established in 1995, the Louise Brooks Society is the largest, most comprehensive, and most visited website in the world devoted to any silent film star. Reflecting her world wide appeal, the Louise Brooks Society claims more than 1500 members in 50 countries on five continents. I would encourage everyone to visit the Society's website, which is located at the easy to remember URL www.pandorasbox.com. There, you'll find information about the actress and her films, suggestions for further reading, links, event listings, a blog, and even RadioLulu—a Louise Brooks-themed online radio station featuring music of the twenties through today.

I live in San Francisco, but grew up in the Detroit area. Thus, I am pleased to return to my hometown to say a few words about the actress and to introduce this special screening of what is certainly her best-known film. If you've never seen *Pandora's Box*, I know you're in for a treat.

This year marks the Louise Brooks centenary. The actress, dancer and writer was born on November 14th, 1906 is the small town of Cherryvale, Kansas. And this year, the world is celebrating her birth with the release two new books, three new DVD's, a couple of museum exhibits, a touring stage play, major film retrospectives in Los Angeles, New York, Berlin, Vienna and London—as well as dozens of screenings across Europe and the United States—including this one here at the Detroit Institute of Arts.

I might mention that *Pandora's Box*—the film we will be seeing tonight has just been released *for the first time ever* on DVD in the United States. Criterion has put together a two disc package which includes lots of bonus material as well as four different musical scores—including one by Ann Arbor composer Gillian Anderson. Also just out, from Rizzoli, is a lovely new coffee table book by film historian Peter Cowie titled *Louise Brooks: Lulu Forever*. If, after seeing tonight's film, you become obsessed with Louise Brooks as I did—you'll want check out these two new releases. Also recommended is the actress' 1982 book, *Lulu in Hollywood*, as well as the great 1989 biography by Barry Paris' titled *Louise Brooks*. Each is still in print.

Before I say something about *Pandora's Box*, I thought I might speak a little bit about Louise Brooks and her relationship with the Motor City. Yes, the gods do sometimes walk among us.

Before she became an actress, Louise Brooks was a dancer. For more than two years, Brooks was a member of—and toured with—Denishawn, the leading modern American dance company of the teens and twenties. Led by Ruth St. Denis and Ted Shawn, the company included a who's who of those who would shape modern dance in America. During the 1922-23 and 1923-24 seasons, the future actress—then still a teenager—danced alongside such legendary figures as Martha Graham, Charles

Weideman, and Doris Humphrey.

The company came to Detroit twice—first in March of 1923, and then again in March of 1924. As a member of Denishawn, Louise Brooks performed at Orchestra Hall, the current home of the Detroit Symphony Orchestra. According to contemporary accounts, the company enjoyed large crowds and received favorable reviews.

Dance would play an important part in Brooks' life. In the opening scene in *Pandora's Box*, the actress performs a short dance—something Brooks had recalled from an earlier Denishawn routine. Later in life she would remark, "I learned to act by watching Martha Graham dance, and I learned to dance by watching Charlie Chaplin act."

Ultimately, however, it was an actress that Louise Brooks made her greatest impression on the Motor City—*especially* its film critics. In the 1920's, Detroit was a three paper town. There was the *Detroit News* and *Detroit Free Press*, as well as the now defunct *Detroit Times*. Also covering the local arts and entertainment scene—including motion pictures—was a weekly called *Detroit Saturday Night*. Each of these publications reviewed new films, and each usually went out of its way to say something good or interesting about Louise Brooks.

For example, Charles J. Richardson of the *Detroit Times*, in reviewing *The American Venus*—a somewhat risqué 1926 comedy which first brought Louise Brooks to public notice as a film actress—stated "Louise Brooks, the former Follies chorine, makes her film debut in the production and does well in a small role. This Miss Brooks just now is the patron saint of all chorus girls seeking admittance into the sacred ranks of screen players." That's not a bad write-up for a first screen credit.

Harold Hefferman, writing in the *Detroit News*, had also noticed the young actress in her first big role. He wrote "Louise Brooks, a black-haired boyish-bobbed entry . . . cuts quite a figure." Indeed, throughout the 1920's, Harold Hefferman would lavish praise on the actress. The *Detroit News* critic nearly gushed while reviewing her next film, *A Social Celebrity*. "Louise Brooks, possessing one of the most striking and expressive faces ever to come to the screen, plays the heroine in a saucily successful manner."

Meanwhile, Hefferman's journalistic rival, Charles J. Richardson, continued to express similar sentiments in his reviews for the *Detroit Times*. In writing about the 1927 comedy, *Rolled Stockings*, Richardson stated bluntly "Louise Brooks, as usual, is delightful to gaze upon." Back then, critics sometimes wore their hearts on their sleeves.

Admiration for the actress was not limited to the city's male critics. During the 1920's, Ella H. McCormick of the *Detroit Free Press* also repeatedly singled out the actress. "Louise Brooks is the nifty stepper" she would write in May, 1926. A month later, reviewing *It's the Old Army Game*, McCormick observed "W. C. Fields scored a splendid triumph in this picture. A great part of the success of the offering, however, is due to Louise Brooks, who takes the lead feminine part." At year's end, in her review of the December 1926 release, *Just Another Blonde*, McCormick would state "Miss Brooks is one of the best brunette contradictions to the lighter hypothesis that can be found on the silver screen."

In the mid-1930's, as her film career began fade, Louise Brooks returned to dance—and once again returned to Detroit. With a partner, Brooks performed as a ballroom dancer in night clubs, theaters, and other Midwest and East Coast hotspots. In August of 1934, Louise Brooks danced at the Blossom Heath Inn on Jefferson Avenue. Today, that venue—which is located between 9 and 10 mile road—hosts weddings and bridal fairs, but back then the Blossom Heath Inn was a well known road-house which hosted prominent touring acts.

At the time of her month-long engagement in what would become St. Clair Shores, both the *Free Press* and *News* ran the following notice in the night-club column of their respective papers. "Edward Fritz, proprietor of the Blossom Heath Inn, announces the engagement of the season's greatest floor show, headed by Louise Brooks, motion picture star, and Dario, creator of the Bolero from the motion picture *Bolero*. Several other new acts are included." It was an unimpressive dénouement to a remarkable career. Within a few years, Louise Brooks would appear in her last film, leave Hollywood, and sink into decades of obscurity.

But things changed. Louise Brooks and her great European films—*Pandora's Box*, *Diary of a Lost Girl*, and *Prix de beauté*—were rediscovered. And today, the actress is best known for the role as Lulu in G.W. Pabst's 1929 masterpiece. In his rather thoughtful article in this week's *Metro Times*, Michael Hastings noted: "Has there ever been a more perfect, more tragic, more mythic fusion of actor and character than Louise Brooks' Lulu in *Pandora's Box*? The girl with the "black helmet" hairdo may not have been German, and she certainly didn't go on a date with Jack the Ripper, but just about everything else in Brooks" life leading up to and following her signature 1929 role became, in some weird, extrasensory way, the blueprint for director G.W. Pabst's masterpiece of sexual suggestion."

Despite Louise Brooks' now legendary status, there are those who have questioned her art. In her classic book about German expressionist film entitled, *The Haunted Screen*, historian Lottie Eisner asked, "Was Louise Brooks a great artist—or only a dazzling creature whose beauty leads the spectator to endow her with complexities of which *she herself* was unaware?" That's a good, provocative, question—as it lies at the heart of the debate still surrounding the actress.

When a heavily censored *Pandora's Box* made its American debut in December of 1929, the critic for the *New York Times* wrote "Miss Brooks is attractive—and she moves her head and eyes at the proper moment, but whether she is endeavoring to express joy, woe, anger or satisfaction—it is often difficult to decide." The N.Y. *Herald Tribune* added, "Louise Brooks acts vivaciously but with a seeming *blindness* as to what it is all about." Other reviews were just as damning.

Critics then—and critics today—call her talent into question. Is Louise Brooks a great actress?—or only someone who kind-of *fools* the audience and gets by on her looks?

Admittedly, Louise Brooks is something of a problem in film history. She is unique among movie icons in that no other actress has made such an impact with so few films. Part of the problem is that a quarter of her films are lost. And today, Brooks' reputation rests almost *unfairly* on one role—that of Lulu, a prototypical femme fatale in this 77-year-old film by G.W. Pabst.

When a revised edition of *The Haunted Screen* was published in 1957, Lottie Eisner answered the question she had posed just a few years before. Then, in writing about the two films Brooks made with Pabst, Eisner asked if Brooks was a great artist. Now, revising her text, Eisner wrote something just as provocative: "Her gifts of profound intuition may seem purely passive to an inexperienced audience, yet she succeeded in stimulating an otherwise unequal director's talent to the extreme. Pabst's remarkable evolution must thus be seen as an encounter with an actress who needed no directing, but could move across the screen causing the work of art to be born¹ by her mere presence. Louise Brooks, always enigmatically impassive, overwhelmingly exists throughout these two films. We know *now* that Louise Brooks is a remarkable actress endowed with uncommon intelligence, and not merely a dazzlingly beautiful woman."

This screening, featuring a beautiful new 35mm print, gives us the chance to see for ourselves. Thank you. I hope you enjoy the film.

Louise Brooks stars in Los Angeles series
This piece appeared on examiner.com on April 29, 2009. This was the first article I wrote for the site covering a screening outside the San Francisco Bay Area.

Los Angeles has long had a love affair with Louise Brooks. That relationship continues with a series of Wednesday night screenings at the Silent Movie Theatre on North Fairfax Avenue. Throughout May, the quirky cinema showcase will screen four films featuring the legendary silent film star.

It all began with what might be Brooks' first film review. On August 31, 1925 the *Los Angeles Times* commented on the actress' appearance in *The Street of Forgotten Men* (1925). Brooks' bit part was a brief, uncredited role as girlfriend to a gangster. Nevertheless, an anonymous critic for the paper went out of their way to write, "And there was a little rowdy, obviously attached to the 'blind' man, who did some vital work during her few short scenes. She was not listed."

The *Los Angeles Times* was the only newspaper in the country to take notice of the 18 year old showgirl making her film debut.

Over the years, most every Los Angeles newspaper would sing the praises of the actress. And sometimes, they would even swoon. When the now lost *Evening Clothes* (1927) had its world premiere at the Metropolitan Theater, the *Daily Illustrated News* gushed, "Louise Brooks - yes, the one you dream about—is as alluring and pert as ever." The *Los Angeles Evening Express* echoed the competition when it found Brooks' "haunting vivacity has necessitated the restringing of more than one male's heartstrings."

It wasn't only male newspaper critics struck by the actress. Eleanor Barnes stated in her *Daily Illustrated News* review of *Rolled Stockings* (1927), "Louise Brooks, judging by this film, is destined to go a long way. She has some of Colleen Moore's qualities with a dash of Florence Vidor thrown in, and a lot of her own distinctive personality."

If you've never seen a Brooks' film, expect to be bowled over by her charisma and otherworldly beauty.

On successive Wednesdays throughout May, Brooks takes center stage at the Silent Movie Theatre (611 N Fairfax Avenue) in Los Angeles. On May 6th at 8 pm, the theater will screen *Pandora's Box* (1929), a film considered not only Brooks' best but one of the great masterpieces of the silent era. In truth, the film (heavily censored in its time and still incomplete today) is only just above average. However, because of Brooks' truly sensational performance as Lulu the film has achieved its stellar reputation. In ways, it is riveting.

Pandora's Box was based on two turn-of-the-last-century plays by the German writer Frank Wedekind (who also authored the text behind the recent Broadway smash *Spring Awakening*). In it, Brooks reveals a unique persona—that of an unknowing femme fatale whose "sinless sexuality hypnotizes and destroys the weak, lustful men around her." *Pandora's Box* features the screen's first lesbian. Brooks' magnetism had few limits..

On May 13th at 8 pm, the theater will screen *Diary of a Lost Girl* (1929). Both it and *Pandora's Box* were directed by G. W. Pabst—one of the great German directors of the interwar period. In *Diary of a Lost Girl*, a film in some ways more satisfying than *Pandora's Box*, Brooks plays a not dissimilar role, that of a beautiful young innocent raped, abandoned, and sent to a brutal reformatory from which she escapes to a brothel in search of revenge and redemption. It's a morality play, really.

Brooks' two German films are not infrequently screened in the Unites States. What is shown less frequently are the American silent films of this Kansas-born actress.

On May 20th at 8 pm, the Silent Movie Theatre will screen *It's The Old Army Game* (1926). A comedy, the film stars W.C. Fields as a wacky druggist who gets mixed up in a real-estate scam. Brooks plays his assistant. When the film opened at the Metropolitan Theater in Los Angeles, Jimmy Starr wrote in the *Los Angeles Record*, "Louise Brooks is evidently very proud of her comely figure. This is the third picture in which she has worn that black bathing suit. However, Louise is a clever little actress."

And on May 27th at 8 pm, the theater will screen the rarely shown minor masterpiece *Beggars of Life* (1928). This is the film the great director William Wellman made just after *Wings*, the first movie to win an Academy Award. Based on a book of the same name by the once popular hobo writer Jim Tully, *Beggars of Life* tells the story of a wronged girl who commits murder and, disguised as a boy, runs from the law and rides the rails into a threatening hobo underworld.

When *Beggars of Life* played at the Metropolitan in October 1928, the *Los Angeles Times* commented, "Richard Arlen and Louise Brooks also capture honors for their sincerity and a poignant, moving quality they infuse into their roles without seeming to act at all. Miss Brooks, who has hitherto qualified as a particularly provocative figurante, now establishes herself as a real actress."

However, the character of an androgynous wronged girl did not sit well with everyone. The role, though convincingly played, was quite different from the mostly charming characters with which the actress had long been associated. Louella Parsons expressed her discomfort in the *Los Angeles Examiner*. "I was a little disappointed in Louise Brooks. She is so much more the modern flapper type, the Ziegfeld Follies girl, who wears clothes and is always gay and flippant. This girl is somber, worried to distraction and in no comedy mood. Miss Brook is infinitely better when she has her lighter moments."

With its dark mood, in its air of pastoral malevolence—*Beggars of Life* prefigures the more sophisticated roles the actress would play in her two German films and in the French *Prix de beauté* (1930). Though her work on the Continent marked the beginning of the end of her American career, these European films would gain Brooks film immortality.

Fans that miss the Silent Movie Theatre screenings in May will be able to catch Brooks on the big screen when the Los Angeles Conservancy presents *Pandora's Box* as part of their 23rd Annual Last Remaining Seats series. That screening will take place on Wednesday, July 1st at the Orpheum Theatre. Acclaimed organist Robert Israel will accompany the film on the Orpheum's Mighty Wurlitzer. Hosting the evening is Hugh Munro Neely, film historian and director of the superb documentary *Louise Brooks, Looking for Lulu* (1998). The sponsor for the Los Angeles Conservancy event is Hugh Hefner, a longtime fan of the actress.

Louise Brooks mentioned in Nazi era publication
This piece appeared on the Louise Brooks Society blog on March 9, 2013.

I recently came across this short piece in a German magazine. It caught my attention because it referenced Louise Brooks and G.W. Pabst and *Pandora's Box*. I ran it through a couple of translation programs (see the results below), but its meaning escapes me. I am guessing that it is meant to be a joke, or perhaps to ridicule the Pabst film. I think the meaning of this brief piece is found somewhere between the lines.

> **Der Jagdfilm**
> Lange bevor man beschloß, Wedekinds „Büchse der Pandora" mit Louise Brooks zu drehen, kam ein Schriftsteller zu einem Münchner Filmproduzenten und sagte: „Herr Direktor, ich habe eine ausgezeichnete Idee. Könnte man nicht mal ‚Die Büchse der Pandora' verfilmen?"
> Der große Filmmann sah ihn an, wiegte den Kopf hin und her, dann meinte er: „Büchse der Pandora? Gar nicht schlecht. Jagdfilme gehen bei uns in Baiern immer!"

Der Jagdfilm (original text)
Lange bevor man beschloss, Wedekinds "Buchse der Pandora", mit Louise Brooks zu drehen, kam ein Schriftsteller zu einem Munchner Filmproduzenten und sagte: "Herr Direktor, ich habe eine ausgezeichnete Idee. Konnte man nicht mal "Buchse der Pandora" verfilmen?"

Des grosse Filmmann sah ihn an, wiegte den Kopf hin und her, dann meinte er: "Buchse der Pandora? Gar nicht schlecht. Jagdfilme gehen bei uns in Baiern immer!"

The Film Search (a translation)
Long before it was decided to shoot Wedekind's Pandora's Box with Louise Brooks, a writer came to a Munich film producer and said, "Sir, I have an excellent idea. Could you not make a movie of Pandora's Box?"

The great movie man looked at him, shook his head back and forth, then said: Pandora's Box? Not bad at all. Hunting movies are always welcome in Bavaria!"

What's interesting about this otherwise ephemeral piece of magazine filler is that it is from 1943. That's during the second World War, and at a time when Wedekind's and Pabst's works were viewed with a suspect eye and Brooks herself had fallen far into obscurity both in Germany and America.

"Der Jagdfilm," attributed to S.S., was published in *Kladderadatsch*, a satirical humor publication begun in 1848. With the rise of the Nazi Party, it's politics turned conservative. It was a favorite in Berlin, and supported the Nazi ideology. For something like this to run in a German periodical in 1943 suggests to me that *Pandora's Box* was still a remembered if not familiar film in Germany.

I would appreciate hearing from anyone who could shed some light or parse the meaning of this bit of text. Please post your comments or translation in the comments field to this post.

[On March 5, 2013, a reader using the handle Vlad Tepes left a comment: "There's another meaning of the German word büchse. Büchse = rifle, not only box."]

Making Personas: Transnational Film Stardom in Modern Japan
This piece blends entries which appeared on the Louise Brooks Society blog on December 18, 2013 and February 13, 2014.

Lately, I've been reading *Making Personas: Transnational Film Stardom in Modern Japan*, by Hideaki Fujiki (Harvard University Asia Center). It is a scholarly work that looks at the way movie stars were "made" in Japan in the Teens, Twenties, and Thirties.

"Made" is meant to mean the way their personas were presented and copied by those both in and outside the film world. This book covers Japanese stars of the time, as well as American stars and how they helped shape Japanese youth culture. It girl Clara Bow figures prominently as a leading type of "modern girl" (the Japanese term for a flapper). Louise Brooks also figures in this a fascinating book.

Fujiki's book is a detailed look at film star culture. According to the publisher, "The film star is not simply an actor but a historical phenomenon that derives from the production of an actor's attractiveness, the circulation of his or her name and likeness, and the support of media consumers. This book analyzes the establishment and transformation of the transnational film star system and the formations of historically important film stars—Japanese and non-Japanese—and casts new light on Japanese modernity as it unfolded between the 1910s and 1930s."

One chapter, "Modern Girls and Clara Bow," strongly suggests that the It girl was the subject of an intense following in Japan. And not far behind was Louise Brooks.

In Japan in the late 1920s, the two actresses were compared and contrasted. Both were considered "modern girls," another term for flappers, and each influenced the way young Japanese women dressed and acted. (Colleen Moore was also considered a modern, though less so than Bow and Brooks, and in opposition to Mary Pickford and Lillian Gish, who were considered "old fashioned.")

Bow and Brooks were each the subject of articles, which the author cites, in the Japanese press. Fujiki also notes that Akira, a film critic, historian, and producer who helped introduce German experimental film in Japan, once penned a story called "Clara Louise."

In *Making Personas*, Fujiki "illustrates how film stardom and the star system emerged and evolved, touching on such facets as the production, representation, circulation, and reception of performers' images in films and other media."

In Japan, Bow and Brooks were considered Moga (short for modan gāru, or "modern girl"). The term first appeared in 1923, and wasn't connected with any particular star. Soon enough, however, critics began to associate the "modern girl" type with certain American stars such as Bow and Brooks.

The fame these American actresses enjoyed in Japan was such that young women were reported to have modeled themselves after each. Critics in the late 1920s even remarked that Japanese youth knew more about the two actresses than they did about classic literary figures or contemporary politicians. The two actresses were also compared and contrasted.

Picking through the footnotes and bibliography of *Making Personas* led me to Kimio Uchida's *Eigagaku nyūmon* (1928), whose title translates as *Introduction to Film Study*. The book, pictured previously, was published in Toyko in 1928. Remarkably, its frontis image (I am not sure I can call it a frontis piece, as it does not face a title page) depicts Louise Brooks in a still from *Love Em and Leave Em* (1926).

I obtained this scan by borrowing, via interlibrary loan, one of the very few vintage copies of this book in the United States.

As such, this inclusion of Brooks marks the actress's first appearance in a book of film criticism. It precedes by a few years both Cedric Osmond Bermingham's *Stars of the Screen 1931* and C.A. Lejeune's *Cinema*, each of which were published in England in 1931.

Louise Brooks on stage in the 1930s

This piece appeared on the Louise Brooks Society blog on April 10, 2018. It breaks new ground in revealing little known details regarding Brooks' stage work in the 1930s.

In the 1930s, Louise Brooks attempted—or was seen to attempt—a series of comebacks. Hoping to relaunch her sputtering film career, the actress kept her name in gossip columns and made it known she was interested in working; she tested with a few studios, took the occasional role in films for which she was poorly suited (namely westerns), and even worked on the stage.

Recently, I have been researching Brooks' life for material to ad to the "Louise Brooks: Day by Day 1906-1985" page on the Louise Brooks Society website when I came across a couple of little known occurrences regarding Brooks" work on the stage.

It is known, for example, is that in the Fall of 1931, while living in New York City, Brooks was under consideration for the ingenue role in Norma Krasna's *Louder Please*, a comedy about Hollywood press agentry. Replacing Olive Borden at the end of October, Brooks appeared in a pre-Broadway staging of Krasna's play at Brandt's Boulevard Theater in the Jackson Heights neighborhood in Brooklyn. Within a few weeks, however, the actress left the cast and was replaced by Jane Buchanan. Here is a rare newspaper advertisement of that production which mentions Brooks. Tickets were only 50 cents.

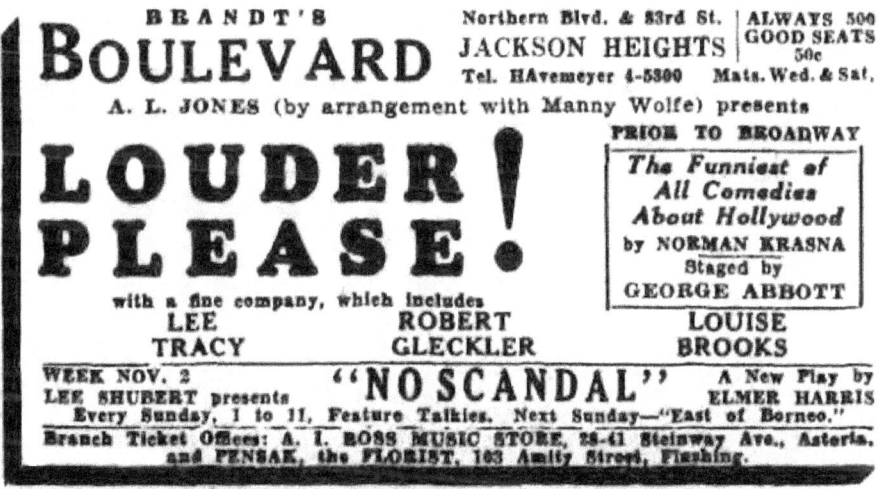

What is not known is that earlier in the year, while living in Los Angeles, Brooks was under consideration for the role of Poppy in an upcoming stage production of *The Shanghai Gesture* at the Music Box theater in Hollywood. The production was being staged by no less a person than Mrs. Leslie Carter, the red-haired American silent film and stage actress known as "The American Sarah Bernhardt." Brooks did not get the role, despite being under serious consideration for three weeks. Because of a disagreement over billing, Brooks and Mary Duncan were passed over for a young actress named Isabel Dawn, a former Indiana newspaper reporter.

Over the next few years, mentions would appear in various newspapers noting

Brooks come back. On New Year's Eve in 1936, the *New York Times* wrote "Louise Brooks, star of the silent screen, is making her screen comeback as a member of the ballet in Grace Moore's forthcoming Columbia production, *When You're in Love*." Nothing came of it.

In June of 1938, the *Los Angeles Times* columnist Read Kendall reported "Louise Brooks, under the name Linda Carter, is essaying a comeback through the Bliss-Hayden Miniature Theater. Her first appearance is in the play *Miracle for Two* by Stanley Kaufman and Effie J. Young. Others in the cast include Beverly Holden, William Stelling, Margaret Meri, Harry Hayden, Howard Johnson, Walter Murray, Nell Keller, Michael Stuart, Mary Rains, Geraldine Gorey and Franco Corsaro." A couple of days later, Louella Parsons reported in her syndicated column that "Louise Brooks has changed her name to Carrington [Carter], dyed her hair black and opened in a play at the Bliss-Hayden Theater. It is the first step in her new career." The following day, in its review of *Miracle for Two*, which the *Los Angeles Times* thought "zestful," the newspaper coyly remarked "Linda Carter used her every artifice to give an interesting portrayal."

Brooks seemed to have stuck with it, despite the fact that her part was only a supporting role. In early July, syndicated columnist Paul Harrison reported that Brooks, under the stage name Linda Carter, has been appearing in a play in Los Angeles. "A 20th-Fox talent scout spotted a girl called Linda Carter in a little-theatre play and offered her a screen test. It turned out that 'Linda Carter' really is Louise Brooks, who's aiming at a screen comeback under a different name." I don't think the production ran much more than a month, perhaps five weeks, as other productions were announced in mid-July.

The *Miracle for Two* actress who did get some attention was the star of the production, Beverly Holden (who seemingly replaced Margo Bennett just before opening?). Despite a bit of press, I wasn't able to find any other screen credits for Holden. Nor could I find any other stage credits for Linda Carter. In early August, production work began on *Overland Stage Raiders*, a film which would turn out to be Brooks' last.

I was able to learn a little more about the Bliss-Hayden Miniature Theater. The building still stands, and is now known as the Beverly Hills Playhouse, an acting school with theaters and training facilities in Beverly Hills. From the pictures I found online, it's stage is indeed a small one. The Bliss-Hayden School of Acting was founded and run by a husband and wife team of motion picture actors—actress Lela Bliss with over 45 credits stretching from 1915 to 1965, and her husband actor Harry Hayden with over 260 credits from 1936 to 1955. Veronica Lake, Mamie Van Doren and many other professional actors later studied there. I contacted the Beverly Hills Playhouse asking if they had any archives or records from 1938, and they responded that they did not. Might any reader of this blog know if any sort of regional theater archives cover this historic little theater exists?

[In 1954, the Bliss-Hayden Theatre was acquired by Douglas Frank Bank and Jay Manford, and renamed The Beverly Hills Playhouse. Many actors had performed there including Anne Baxter and Louella Parsons. Bank and Manford owned the theatre until 1959. Later stars that studied and performed under later owners include George Clooney, Alec Baldwin, Tom Selleck, Michelle Pfeiffer, Tyne Daly, James Cromwell, and others.]

A footnote to Brooks' 1930s stage work was her work as a ballroom dancer and her curious appearance at the Racquet Club of Palm Springs. On November 4, 1939, Brooks and dance partner Barrett O'Shea (pictured left) performed at a Saturday night party at the Racquet Club in support of headliner Rudy Vallee. (Actor Ralph Bellamy, one of the founders of the Racquet Club, actor Charles Butterworth, director Edmund Goulding, and singer Judy Starr were also present, and took their turn on the Racquet Club's "stage.") According to a report in the Palm Springs *Desert Sun*, O'Shea, and "his charming partner Louise Brooks, did a very clever mask dance, imitating Mrs. Roosevelt and [English Prime Minister] Chamberlain, doing an old time square dance."

The Racquet Club in Palm Springs was a Hollywood hot spot. Reportedly, Mr. and Mrs. Humphrey Bogart had their own table near the dance floor, and Harry Cohn, Howard Hawks, Franchot Tone, Peter Lorre, and others were occasional visitors.

A week after Brooks did her mask dance, *The Desert Sun* reported that O'Shea and Brooks had been hired as staff dance instructors at the Racquet Club. "They will teach Saturday and Sunday afternoons until the middle of the season and then every afternoon for the rest of the season. Rhumba and La Conga classes, as well as ordinary ballroom dances and private lessons, will be their feature."

Louise Brooks Journals to be Revealed, and Perhaps Published

This piece appeared on Huffington Post on October 11, 2010. It was a rewrite and slightly longer version of a piece I published on examiner.com a few days earlier. That prior piece drew considerable attention, and was tweeted about by the likes of film critic Roger Ebert and bestselling author Neil Gaiman, both acknowledged fans of the actress.

John Updike once told me that Louise Brooks was the finest writer to have ever come out of Hollywood. That was his long-held opinion when I met him in 2006. Updike had reviewed the silent film star's book of autobiographical essays, *Lulu in Hollywood*, for the *New Yorker* in 1982.

A similar opinion is held by another Pulitzer Prize winner. In his 1997 anthology, *Roger Ebert's Book of Film: From Tolstoy to Tarantino, the Finest Writing From a Century of Film*, the Chicago critic describes *Lulu in Hollywood* as "one of the wittiest and most truthful books ever written about the movies."

Last week, word broke that the George Eastman House has unsealed Brooks' private journals. Before her death, she had bequeathed them to the famed Rochester, New York museum with instructions they remain sealed for 25 years. Brooks—Kansas-born and long a resident of New York City and Los Angeles—had lived in Rochester during the last few decades of her life. She was drawn there by the Eastman House film collection. Brooks liked watching movies, and writing about them.

A quarter century has now passed since the actress' death. And, as David S. Cohen reported in *Variety*, Brooks' private notebooks have been unsealed and "Eastman staffers have been poring over the journals before making them available to the public." Everyone is wondering what they will reveal.

Brooks kept journals from 1956 until her death in 1985. According to an Eastman House archivist, there are 29 research journals—which contain her notes and thoughts while she conducted research for her book and other writing projects—ranging in size from 20 to 120 pages. All together, these working journals approach 2000 pages of hand-written text. Notably, Brooks went back and reworked material in various notebooks over the years. She also added a table of contents to the cover of each volume.

As fans of the actress are well aware, she was more than just a pretty face—she was considered "smart" by her Hollywood peers. In a 1967 reminiscence, the German film critic Lotte Eisner recalled a 1928 visit she made to the set of *Pandora's Box* in which she observed Brooks, between takes, reading Schopenhauer. Eisner would later describe Brooks as an "An astonishing actress endowed with an intelligence beyond compare."

Long a reader, Brooks was also a gifted writer, and later in life authored a number of well received articles for various film magazines including *Sight and Sound, Film Culture, Positif,* and *Cahiers du Cinema*. Many of these essays were collected in *Lulu in Hollywood*. Brooks last published piece during her lifetime was a single sentence statement in the *New York Times Book Review*: "I have been reading Proust all my life, and I'm still reading him."

What's in the journals isn't yet publicly known. A spokesperson for the George Eastman House had an idea—but wouldn't say. According to the article in *Variety*, which was leaked a few choice tidbits, the journals do include observations and comments by the actress about cinematic contemporaries like Garbo ("She strains terribly"), Marlene Dietrich ("a puzzled bloodhound"), Humphrey Bogart ("beyond any man I know, he loved women"), and others. Brooks also comments on herself and her efforts before the camera. She was always her own worst critic.

Near the end of Barry Paris' Pulitzer worthy biography, Paris quotes a letter from Brooks to her brother written a decade before her death: "I have been taking stock of my 50 years since I left Wichita in 1922 at the age of 15 to become a dancer with Ruth St. Denis and Ted Shawn. How I have existed fills me with horror. For I failed in everything—spelling, arithmetic, riding, swimming, tennis, golf, dancing, singing, acting, wife, mistress, whore, friend. Even cooking. And I do not excuse myself with the usual escape of 'not trying.' I tried with all my heart."

The spokesperson for the George Eastman House said there were no plans at present to publish the journals—but suggested that could change. "It's under consideration" is the way one archivist put it. Brooks' smarts and natural talents as a writer suggest her journals could be something remarkable—or at least an interesting read to film buffs. Her rabid cult following suggests there would be considerable interest.

Fans and the curious wishing to sample Brooks' singular personality should check out the 1989 biography by Paris—or the recently released *Dear Stinkpot: Letters from Louise Brooks* (BearManor Media, 2010). The latter was edited by Jan Wahl, the acclaimed children's book author and the person to whom the letters in this new book are addressed.

According to the Paris biography, Brooks wrote hundreds if not thousands of letters to individuals all over the world—to other writers, film historians, critics, and actors. Along with abortive attempts at fiction and her various articles, writing is what she did in the last decades of her life.

When Brooks died in 1985, James Card, the first and legendary curator of film at the Eastman House as well as her on-and-off again friend for many year, said of her, "She was an enormously powerful individual, thinker, and searcher for the absolute essence of things. I think she'd like to be remembered for her writing rather than for her films."

Dear Stinkpot: Letters from Louise Brooks by Jan Wahl
This piece appeared on Huffington Post on October 13, 2010. It would lead to an exchange of letters and telephone calls between Wahl and myself.

The George Eastman House in Rochester, New York announced last week that they have unsealed the journals of actress Louise Brooks. The actress kept journals from 1956 until her death in 1985. According to an Eastman House archivist, there are 29 journals with approximately 2000 pages of hand-written text. She bequeathed them to the photography and film museum with instructions they remain sealed for 25 years.

The announcement has everyone wondering what they will reveal, and what sort of literary talent was this now iconic silent film star.

The answer may well lie in a book published earlier this year, *Dear Stinkpot: Letters from Louise Brooks* (BearManor Media). The recipient of the letters, and the editor of the book, is the celebrated contemporary children's book author Jan Wahl.

Brooks was a lot of things to a lot of people. To some, including the British theater critic Kenneth Tynan, "She was the most seductive, sexual image of woman ever committed to celluloid." Beauty, yes, and also brains.

To the noted German film writer Lotte Eisner, Brooks was "An astonishing actress endowed with an intelligence beyond compare." To the film historian and Academy Award honoree Kevin Brownlow, Brooks was "One of the most remarkable personalities to be associated with films."

To Wahl, Brooks was a kindred soul with whom he corresponded for more than 20 years. Their roller-coaster friendship is documented in *Dear Stinkpot*. The title comes from Brooks' nickname for the author.

Wahl met Brooks in 1957. At the time, he was a poor graduate student and aspiring writer. Brooks, nearly twice his age, was then a mostly forgotten silent film star. The aspiring writer and the forgotten actress struck up an intense friendship, as well as a correspondence that spanned more than two decades. What drew them together was the desire to write.

The craft of writing, as well as books, authors, and the actress' current reading, are the dominant theme in *Dear Stinkpot*. There are, for instance, a handful of letters regarding Vladimir Nabokov. Wahl had taken classes with the Russian émigré at Cornell University and was an advocate of his fiction, including *Lolita*.

At the time, Brooks was working on a never published essay titled "Girl Child in Films." The actress read Nabokov's then (in)famous novel—and disliked it, at first. Eventually, however, Brooks changed her mind about "Naby's" fiction. She came to appreciate his use of language and sense of satire. Brooks even hoped Wahl might be able to pass along to Nabokov her 1951 autobiographical short story, "Naked on My Goat." Brooks described it as her own version of *Lolita*.

As with Nabokov, Brooks at first disliked then came to appreciate the work of another contemporary writer. "The dialogue in Beckett is marvelous," she would write in one letter. Other writers, including Hemingway, take her punches, as would F. Scott Fitzgerald for other reasons. There is admiration for earlier authors like Thackery and Dickens. There are gossipy anecdotes about the Algonquin Roundtable writers who hung out in her Ziegfeld Follies dressing room. And there is a consideration of Leslie Fiedler's once seminal *Love and Death in the American Novel*.

Despite a continuous exchange of letters, it wasn't easy being Brooks' friend.

(Elsewhere, she once famously wrote, "I have a gift for enraging people, but if I ever bore you, it'll be with a knife.") And here she admits, "The MAD AT BROOKS CLUB is a seething kettle."

The first letter in this collection begins, "If you care to be my pen pal, I'll thank you not to write on both sides of that thin paper." In later letters, Brooks' pointedly challenges Wahl's early efforts at getting published (his first book, *Pleasant Fieldmouse*, with illustrations by Maurice Sendak, was published in 1964), knocks his literary heroes, and occasionally comes off somewhat snarky. Apologies would follow, as would Brooks' homemade fudge.

But along with the challenges were the rewards. Brooks could be witty, whimsical, profound, and endearing. And fascinating. What movie lover (and Wahl was that, as well as a collector of vintage films) wouldn't want to receive letters detailing meeting Jean Harlow, how Lillian Gish acted with her hair, personal observations of Chaplin, Garbo, Buster Keaton and Clara Bow, critiques of films and film makers, critiques of film historians, and the admission that her favorite actor was Ronald Colman.

Only occasionally would Brooks reference her own work, her now immortal performance as Lulu in G.W. Pabst's *Pandora's Box*, and her still highly regarded roles in *Diary of a Lost Girl*, *Beggars of Life* and other films.

There were other epistoltory discussions. About her finances: CBS founder William S. Paley gave her a monthly allowance, in remembrance of their brief affair decades earlier. About religion: Brooks converted to Catholicism for nearly a decade and read various mystical texts including works about Saint Teresa of Ávila.

And about dance: especially Isadora Duncan. Apparently, Brooks saw the legendary dancer perform, most likely in the early 1920's when she was still a teenage member of the Denishawn Dance Company alongside Martha Graham and under the tutelage of Ruth St. Denis and Ted Shawn. In the early 1960's, Brooks was considering the subject of dance while working on a never finished essay on women and movement. One of Brooks' singular observations was regarding Duncan's large flopping breasts.

Wahl has written about his friendship with Brooks in earlier articles scattered in various newspapers and magazines. There is also a substantial piece about the actress in Wahl's engaging book of autobiographical essays, *Through a Lens Darkly* (BearManor Media, 2008).

However, Wahl's new book, *Dear Stinkpot: Letters from Louise Brooks*, is the most detailed and telling portrait yet of their friendship. The story of their friendship as revealed through these letters—and in Wahl's worthwhile commentary interspersed throughout—is the story of two writers developing their craft. It is a revealing look at the later years of one of the remarkable personalities of the 20th century, and it suggests the kind of material which might be found in the newly unsealed journals.

Notes on Louise Brooks' notebooks
This piece appeared on the Louise Brooks Society blog on December 9, 2015.

I recently took the opportunity to visit Rochester, NY and its world famous George Eastman Museum. The purpose of my visit—a trip five years in the planning—was to spend time at the museum with which Louise Brooks was closely associated for many years.

Back in October of 2010, I published a piece titled "Louise Brooks Journals to be Revealed, and Perhaps Published". My piece was occasioned by the announcement by the then George Eastman House that it had unsealed Brooks' private notebooks. Before her death, the actress had bequeathed her notebooks to the museum with instructions they remain sealed for 25 years. That was five years ago. This was my first opportunity to check out the notebooks for myself.

As my 2010 article stated, "Brooks kept journals from 1956 until her death in 1985. According to an Eastman House archivist, there are 29 research journals—which contain her notes and thoughts while she conducted research for her book and other writing projects—ranging in size from 20 to 120 pages. All together, these working journals approach 2000 pages of hand-written text. Notably, Brooks went back and reworked material in various notebooks over the years. She also added a table of contents to the cover of each volume."

I enlisted the help of Rochester resident Tim Moore, and allotted myself two and one-half days to read / skim / survey the material—which literally was nearly 2000 pages of mostly handwritten, sometimes difficult to read material. There was also some typewritten material inserted into binders or pasted onto the pages of the notebooks. After I was done, I felt I barely scratched the surface.

The author inside the George Eastman Museum

The material in the notebooks is largely just that—notes. More than anything, Brooks compiled filmographies of many of the leading movie personalities of her time (this was in the day before IMDb, as well as before many of the film books we know were even published—think the ubiquitous "The Films of ....." series). One almost gets the impression that Brooks had the idea to write some sort of grand history of film as a way of understanding her small part.

Brooks also listed and took notes from the books she was reading. Often times she would transcribe passages out of biographies, memoirs, and film histories. Brooks recorded the titles of many if not most of the films she viewed and where she saw them, either at the Eastman House or on television. (Back in the late 1950s and early 1960s, silent films and films from the early 1930's turned up on broadcast TV more often than they do today.) The actress also recorded key information about each film— year of release, director, actor—along with her thoughts on what she had seen.

There are passages on the Talmadge sisters, Garbo, Pola Negri, Clara Bow, Marion Davies, Tallulah Bankhead, Leni Riefenstahl, Humphrey Bogart, Grace Moore, Shirley MacLaine and Warren Beatty, and numerous others—along with encounters with director Jean Renoir (at a party in Paris in the 1950s) and Roddy McDowell (when the actor came to her apartment to photograph her). In the margin, Brooks" recorded the fact that G.W. Pabst had called her on the telephone while she was living in New York City in 1948.

Brooks watched films by D.W. Griffith and Erich von Stroheim (her opinion on the director changed over time), as well as those starring Marlene Dietrich, like *The Blue Angel* and *I Kiss Your Hand Madame*. She also saw *Dinner at Eight*, William Wellman's *The Public Enemy*, and G.W. Pabst's *Threepenny Opera*. On October 29, 1959 she saw *Empty Saddles*, a 1936 B-western in which she had a supporting role. Brooks wrote "First film I ever heard my voice." Brooks was also taken with John Barrymore's performance in *Maytime* (1937). There were others, many others.

Brooks watched television programs and listened to the radio. If something stood out, she noted it. On September 28, 1960 she recorded watching Fred Astaire on NBC. Brooks also noted having seen the poet W.H. Auden on television in 1958 (two pages of her commentary on Auden followed), or listening to a local radio program on the critic H.L. Mencken. She also seemed to have a liking for Mitch Miller, and recorded hearing him on the radio at least a couple of times.

On occasion, Brooks was also a list maker. There was one listing the twelve painting she had completed up to that time. There was another listing books she intended to read about the 1920s. There was one noting "geniuses I have known: Chaplin, Gershwin, Graham, Thalberg, Gish, Garbo". There was another from the early 1970's listing where she had lived and for how long:

18 Kansas
21 New York
9 Hollywood
16 Rochester
1 Europe - Chicago

The notebooks also contain a number of clipping, which most often were obituaries of individuals she had known, including actor Addison (Jack) Randall, NYMoMA film curator Iris Barry, dancer Ruth St. Denis, and others. Usually, these clipping came from either *Variety* or *TIME* magazine, which she seems to have had regular access to. (Brooks also seems to have had access to a run of past issues of *Photoplay* magazine, as she often cites it.)

Brooks read a book about the composer George Gershwin, someone she first met and flirted with during her brief time with the George White Scandals, and recorded and dated an impressionistic memory: "at Scandals 1924 rehearsals George took off coat—played in vest—sometimes with a cigar in his mouth LB 1968". In her notebooks, she took notes on Gershwin's upbringing, on his many compositions, and on his early death on July 11, 1937, adding in parenthesis "[Two weeks before at the Clover Club George asked me to dance and seemed brilliantly healthy.]"

There was a good deal of surprising material. For a while, Brooks was deeply interested in existentialism, which was in vogue in the 1960s. She recorded reading a couple of books on the subject, as well as one or two by Jean Paul Sartre. She disliked Simone de Beauvoir, and said so in the pages of her notebooks. [Curiously, Sartre records in his own journals that one of his very first dates with de Beauvoir was when he took her to see *A Girl in Every Port*, which co-starred Brooks.]

Brooks also wrote her observations on Elizabeth Taylor and on Marilyn Monroe, thoughts on George Raft, and pasted in a clipping on Andy Warhol. She watched television coverage of Queen Elizabeth's 1957 visit to the United States and Canada, and wrote pages and pages about it. She also wrote many pages of material on Henry Kissinger, the Kennedys, and Zen thinker Alan Watts (which tied into her interest in existentialism). English writers John Ruskin and Lewis Carroll, and American novelists F. Scott Fitzgerald and Ernest Hemingway are also referenced time and again.

Outside the Rochester Public Library, which Brooks often visited.

One of the binders which the Eastman House inherited from Brooks contains even earlier notes, loose leaf pages dating from as early as the 1940s. There are pages and pages of notes on the French philosopher Henri Bergson from 1941, on the English writer George Meredith from 1943, on Lord Byron and the qualities of great poetry from 1948, on Gandhi's *Autobiography* from 1949, on the letters of Marcel Proust from

1955. There are also scattered notes on art, and on modern painters.

Considering Brooks never have achieved her high school degree (she left to join Denishawn after her sophomore year in school), these notebooks reflect an intellectually curious mind. Brooks was striving to understand. She was fascinated by authority figures—either spiritual or political or literary or cinematic or romantic. George Bernard Shaw was a major obsession.

Brooks attempted to understand the world and herself through the pages of literature, and in the biographies and histories of great individuals and momentous times. Her notebooks are a record of her striving to understand.

During my two and a half days reading Brooks' notebooks, I took lots of notes, and transcribed a few passages. That is all researchers may do. (Recording devices like scanners or cameras are not allowed.) The material above represents a summation of my notes. There is all kinds of material in the notebooks. I also came across this recipe: "Brooks' cookies 18 March 1973"

1 stick butter
1 cup brown sugar
2 eggs
1 table spoon milk
2 cups flour
2 tsp baking powder
1/4 tsp salt
dates and nuts. lemon rind
350 degrees 45 minutes cut to squares

Louise Brooks and Denis Marion: a correspondence
This piece appeared on the Louise Brooks Society blog on May 1, 2018. To me, the need for a volume or two of Brooks' letters is all the more apparent.

Just recently, I acquired a French-language book, *Denis Marion; pleins feux sur un homme de l'ombre* (LE CRI). It is about the French-speaking Belgian writer, lawyer, journalist, chess player, literary critic, film critic, playwright, and university professor Denis Marion. I did so because the book contains a 17-page chapter about Marion's long correspondence with Louise Brooks. And though I don't read French, I was able to pick through the chapter (by Muriel Andrin and Caroline Pirotte) and gleam some fascinating material. Happily, for me, bits of some of their letters are presented in their original English.

Marion is only mention in passing in the Barry Paris biography, but from what I was able to find out, Marion (whose real name is Marcel Defosse) was born in 1906, the same year as Brooks. He began a career as a lawyer while indulging in his passion for chess (he participated in six championships in Belgium). In 1928, he published a laudatory article on a novel by André Malraux, which earned him the friendship of the famed author. In the early 1930s, he was one of the founders of the Screen Club (the precursor of the Belgian Royal Cinematheque), and was involved in the making of various documentary films. In 1945, he left his law firm to become the correspondent in Paris of the Belgian daily newspaper *Le Soir*. He signed his articles under the pseudonym Denis Marion. As such, he wrote books on literature (on Daniel Defoe, Edgar Allen Poe), and the cinema (including titles on Erich von Stroheim, and Igmar Bergman), a novel published by Gallimard, two plays, a couple of screenplays (both films were directed by Albert Valentin), and gave classes at the Université Libre de Bruxelles on the history of cinema.

Marion knew many cultural personalities in France, as well as in the post-WWII film world. I don't think Marion and Brooks ever met. But, they did strike up a seven-year correspondence with Brooks that began in 1962 and lasted until 1969.

Chapter VII of *Denis Marion; pleins feux sur un homme de l'ombre*, titled "Louise Brooks/Denis Marion, fragments d'une correspondence (1962-1968)" offers a glimpse of what I gather to have been a vigorous meeting of minds. At one point in the exchange of letters, there was much discussion regarding Erich von Stroheim. Marion was writing a book on the director, and was pleased to be in contact with someone who had met him.

According to a Brooks' letter from 1964, the actress met von Stroheim at G.W. Pabst's Hollywood apartment in 1935. "I shall never forget him sitting tense, separate, flashing me a quick, ugly look and saying not a word as we were introduced. He made not even a gesture of rising. In that look, we knew each other—why pretend?" Brooks goes on to discuss silent era actors who made up a past.

In 1966, the French film journal *Etudes Cinematographiques* published its "von Stroheim" issue, edited by Denis Marion (and dedicated to Brooks). The actress contributed one page of notes about the director excerpted from her 1964 contribution to the Montreal journal *Objectif*. Brooks' name also appears on the cover alongside Rene Clair, Lillian Gish, Jean Renoir and others.

Here are some highlights which I gathered from "Louise Brooks/Denis Marion, fragments d'une correspondence (1962-1968)," which only quotes snippets from their correspondence. All together, this is fascinating material, and well worth publishing in its entirety.

August 27, 1962
Begins corresponding with Denis Marion.

August 28, 1962
Writes to Marion, "Yesterday when I wrote to you I was so busy—reading your article, feeding the cat, checking my notebook, making a cake, writing to Lotte [Eisner], clipping the ivy and reading a letter from William Inge."

November 20, 1962
Marion writes to Brooks offering to translate her book *Women in Film* into French and to help find a publisher in France.

November 25, 1962
Writes to Marion in which Brooks states her reluctant admiration for Mae Murray.

December 8, 1962
Writes a letter to Marion offering to help research Erich von Stroheim. Brooks also writes that she will acquire a copy of Daniel Defoe's *Moll Flanders*, which she plans to

read again.

August 26, 1963
Writes a letter to Denis Marion, who notes she often spent nights in Chez Florence in Montmartre while in Paris.

September 18, 1963
Writes a letter to Marion in which Brooks says "Perhaps I never would have had courage to write had you not told me to read novels."

October 3, 1963
Writes a letter to Marion asking which Balzac novels he suggests she read. "I reread *Manon Lescaut*. It is just as silly to me now as 35 years ago.... Another book I read again was [Flaubert's] *Madame Bovary*."

March 27, 1967
Writes a letter to Marion stating she gave up sex in 1958. "But right up to my retirement from sex in 1958, I always had some pretty lesbians on a string -- flattering and fun. So if I am known as a lesbian it is my own doing, and I don't mind, I like it."

May 10, 1967
Writes to Marion which states she has "fallen in love with Stroheim—as a person now."

November 13, 1967
Writes a letter to Marion, "Tomorrow I shall be 61, knowing no more about myself or why I do anything then I did at 6. Except this—all my life I have been a learner. That is why I write. As Dylan Thomas put it... 'My poetry is the record of my struggles from darkness to some measure of light'."

July 10, 1969
Writes last letter to Marion.

Louise Brooks, Lost Girl
This piece appeared on the Brattle Theatre blog on August 27, 2017 in conjunction with the screening of two of Brooks' films. The historic Brattle is located in Cambridge, Massachusetts.

On first glance, the silent films *Beggars of Life* and *Diary of a Lost Girl* appear to have little in common, except that each stars the luminous actress Louise Brooks. Yes, should you need to be reminded, that Louise Brooks, the actress equally famous for her beauty and bobbed hair as well as for her role as Lulu in the sensational 1929 film, *Pandora's Box*.

Brooks, once described by a surrealist critic as "The only woman who had the ability to transfigure—no matter what the film—into a masterpiece," appears on the Brattle screen in early September. Recently, both *Beggars of Life* and *Diary of a Lost Girl* were digitally restored and released on home video by Kino Lorber. In fact, the restored *Beggars of Life* has just come out on DVD / Blu-ray for the first time.

Beggars of Life (1928) is an American film. It has a rural setting, and is dry, earthy, and hot. Based on the bestselling memoir by the celebrated "hobo author" Jim Tully, *Beggars of Life* was directed by the multiple Academy Award winner William Wellman the year after he directed *Wings* (the first film to win the Oscar for Best Picture). It is a rough and humble story about an orphan girl (Brooks) who kills her abusive step-father and flees the law, dressing as a boy and riding the rails through a hobo underground ruled over by future Oscar winner Wallace Beery. Danger, and the threat of danger, is always close at-hand.

Diary of a Lost Girl (1929) is a German film. It has an urban setting, and is damp (it sometimes rains), ordered, and cool. Based on the controversial book by the feminist author Margarete Böhme, *Diary of a Lost Girl* was directed by G.W. Pabst less than a year after he worked with the actress on *Pandora's Box*. Just as sensational as that earlier film, *Diary* is a disturbing story about a naive teenager (Brooks) who is seduced by her Father's business associate. Pregnant, she is forced to give up the baby, and is sent to live in a kind of reform school ruled over by a sadistic couple (one of whom is played by the legendary avant-garde dancer Valeska Gert). She escapes, and wanders the streets among the down and out before ending up in a house of prostitution.

These two films are different in many ways, but share a few similarities below their surface. Essentially, in each, Brooks plays a vulnerable young woman who is sexually assaulted, and is then "cast out" as a consequence. Made worlds apart (though not in time), these two films reflect not dissimilar attitudes towards women and women's sexuality.

It should be mentioned that Brooks herself, as a young girl, was a victim of sexual abuse. A certain neighbor named "Mr. Flowers" lured the then 9-year-old Brooks into his home where he abused her. When Brooks told her mother, the child was asked what she did to provoke the incident.

Beggars of Life author Jim Tully too experienced a difficult childhood. After his mother died in 1892, Tully's father was unable to care for his children, and the six year old boy was sent to a Catholic orphanage in Cincinnati, Ohio. At age 12, Tully's father removed him from the orphanage and gave the child to an abusive farmer who employed the boy as a laborer. Within a couple of years, Tully ran away, and was quickly lured into life on the road. *Beggars of Life*, his 1924 novelistic memoir, tells the story of his early days, with certain characters changed for the 1925 stage adaption and later film. (The 2012 biography of Tully is a terrific read.)

Diary of a Lost Girl author Margarete Böhme also had a secret, one which I feel was submerged in her 1905 book, originally titled *Tagebuch einer Verlorenen*. It purportedly tells the true story of Thymian, a young woman forced by circumstance into a life of prostitution. When it was first published, it was said to be a genuine diary, and Böhme claimed only to be its editor. The book's wild popularity (it was filmed twice, adapted for the stage, parodied, and was the subject of scorn, censorship, and lawsuits) led to ongoing speculation as to its actual authorship. As such, it anticipates the "falsified memoirs" of today.

By 1929, when Pabst came to make his film of Böhme's book, *Diary of a Lost Girl* had sold more than 1,200,000 copies, making it what one contemporary scholar has called "Perhaps the most notorious and certainly the commercially most successful autobiographical narrative of the early twentieth century." Up until the early 1930's, when right-wing groups in Nazi Germany drove it out of print, Böhme denied authorship of this lost girl's diaries.

The question is why. What was the secret, or the shame, hidden in the pages of Böhme's book? My 2010 "Louise Brooks edition" of Böhme's *Diary of a Lost Girl* attempts to answer the question.

Does Brooks' own experience as a victim / survivor of sexual abuse appear on the screen? It is hard to say. But then, in some oblique way, how could it not have? The actress seldom saw her own films—some she only saw for the first time late in life; others she claimed not to know what they were about, as was the case with *Pandora's Box*, where again her character is sexually manipulated and coerced.

What we do know is that Brooks' experience as a child marked her entire life. She said so. It certainly contributed to her lack of self esteem and self-destructive ways. It also isolated the actress. Writing about *Diary of a Lost Girl* in 1938, an Italian critic commented, "She suffers and remains unmoved. And precisely this is what counts most: with an almost total lack of acting, she has created around herself a dense atmosphere of intense emotions."

Ultimately, Brooks' story is one of redemption. She spent the last half of her life out of the limelight, virtually forgotten for decades, striving to understand what had happened to her life and aborted career. She experienced an emotional and spiritual tumult before settling into a kind of gin-soaked intellectual understanding late in life. The result of her striving is her 1982 bestseller, *Lulu in Hollywood*. To find out more about Brooks, be sure and check out Barry Paris' beautifully empathetic 1989 biography of the actress, titled *Louise Brooks*.

Brooks never made it to Cambridge, as far as I know. But she did appear in Boston on a couple of occasions as a teenage member of Denishawn, then the leading modern dance company in America. This was before her film career, and before she appeared in the Ziegfeld Follies. On January 17 and then again on March 2, 1923, the Denishawn company (which included the 16-year-old Brooks, Martha Graham, founders Ruth St. Denis and Ted Shawn, and others of note) performed at the Boston Opera House. Touring the country, Denishawn returned to the Opera House one year later, performing again on April 11 and 12, 1924. Late in life, the one–time actress stated all she ever wanted to be was a dancer. [Brooks' entrance into Denishawn is a plot point in the forthcoming film of Laura Moriarty's bestselling novel, *The Chaperone*, from PBS Masterpiece. It is currently in production.]

Beggars of Life, as with all of Brooks' American films, was shown in Boston when first released. It played at the Metropolitan theater in late September, 1928, where it was well received in the pages of the *Boston Post* and *Boston Herald*. In its pages, Harvard's *The Crimson* simply noted, "Tramp, Tramp, the hoboes are coming to town." More than a few years later, in 1989, critic Jay Carr described *Beggars of Life* in the *Boston Globe* as "Louise Brooks' best American film before she went to Germany."

Diary of a Lost Girl was not as fortunate. The film debuted in Berlin on October 15, 1929. And by December 5, it had been banned by the state censor and was withdrawn from circulation. After cuts were made, the ban was lifted and the film re-released on January 6, 1930. However, *Diary of a Lost Girl* was poorly received, not only because sound was coming in and there was diminishing interest in the silent cinema, but because the film continued to be censored and cut (according to local standards) wherever it was shown, leaving its already problematic story in shambles. Rudolph Leonhardt, the film's screenwriter, wrote that he saw it in Paris at the time and stayed in his seat at the end because he thought the film had broken.

The many negative reviews the film received sometimes had little to do with the movie. Some German critics, no doubt disliking the pointed social critique found in the film, instead devoted their columns to savaging Böhme's then 25 year old book! Siegfried Kracauer, a critic at the time, was among them. In his famous 1946 book, *From Caligari to Hitler: A Psychological History of the German Film*, Kracauer wrote about the Pabst film and its literary source—"the popularity of which among the philistines of the past generation rested upon the slightly pornographic frankness with which it recounted the private life of some prostitutes from a morally elevated point of view."

Diary of a Lost Girl was not shown in the United States until the 1950s, and it did not receive a theatrical release in America until the 1980s. Such were the fortunes of silent film in the age of talkies. Recent restorations, however, have brought renewed attention, and in the eyes of some critics including myself, *Diary of a Lost Girl* is considered the near equal of the better known *Pandora's Box*.

Fortunately, the Kino Lorber print of *Diary of a Lost Girl* restores just about as much footage as possible, bringing the film back into a broad semblance of what it was like when initially released. The same can be said for the Kino Lorber *Beggars of Life*, which was digitally restored from 35mm film elements held at the George Eastman Museum in Rochester, New York.

Both films, I suggest, are worth witnessing—not only for what is on the screen, but for what can be seen below their surface.

3 THE FILMS

Louise Brooks' first film review on this day in 1925 • Strange Silent Film Screens in Syracuse • The original Lassie, canine thespian • Louise Brooks and The American Venus • A movie herald: what it can tell us • Louise Brooks, at the corner of Brooklyn Avenue and 16th Street • The Show-Off, with Louise Brooks, screens July 10 • Rare Louise Brooks film to screen in Niles • Louise Brooks in Fairbanks, Alaska - better late than never • Long Missing Louise Brooks Film Found • A little something about Now We're in the Air • A Girl in Every Port: The Birth of Lulu? • Beggars of Life Screens Under the Stars August 15 • Six questions with . . . the Dodge Brothers • A World Turned Over: Wellman's Beggars of Life • A significant find? • Did small pox kill The Canary Murder Case? • Louise Brooks is Lulu in Pandora's Box • Lulu by the Bay: Louise Brooks is legend in Pandora's Box • Lulu in New York: Pandora's Box at Film Forum • The Lost History of Pandora's Box in the United States • The BFI Re-Opens Pandora's Box • Diary of a Lost Girl, with Louise Brooks, screens in Brooklyn • A dense atmosphere of intense emotions • What a trippple bill of classic silent films! • Stephen Horne interviewed about the Prix de beauté • Eureka - Hélène Caron • Louise Brooks, product placement and the 1931 film It Pays to Advertise • A double bill featuring Louise Brooks on this day in 1937 • getTV Premieres Rare Cary Grant film • Louise Brooks at a drive-in and other firsts from the 1950s • First Louise Brooks television broadcast

In her day, Louise Brooks was never considered a major star. Her career, relatively speaking, was brief. The actress appeared in 24 films between 1925 and 1938—a period spanning 13 years, four of which she was absent from the screen. By comparison, her celebrated contemporary Clara Bow (the "It" girl) appeared in 57 films over 11 years, while another contemporary, silent era star Colleen Moore, appeared in 48 films over 18 years.

Of Brooks' 24 films, she received top billing in only three productions. Notably, these were the three films she made in Europe. In the United States, Brooks was usually given second or third billing to the film's male stars. In only one of her American films, *Rolled Stockings*, was she considered the lead—though just as often, this 1927 film was promoted as starring not Brooks, but the Paramount junior stars.

As film historians have pointed out, few actors have attained such a large reputation through so few films. The Surrealist French film critic Ado Kyruo once said Brooks was "The only woman who had the ability to transfigure—no matter what the film—into a masterpiece." While I appreciate his sentiment, I don't think Kyrou had seen *The Canary Murder Case* or *Windy Riley Goes Hollywood* or *Empty Saddles*. Each are middling films that even Brooks' presence couldn't "transfigure" beyond mediocrity.

Beyond their individual worth as films, almost each of Brooks' movies has an interesting backstory, an interesting production, or an interesting critical history. There is more to them than meets the eye, as the pieces in this chapter intend to show.

Louise Brooks' first film review on this day in 1925

This piece appeared on examiner.com on August 31, 2010. Four years earlier, I was fortunate to have seen The Street of Forgotten Men in a viewing cubicle at the Library of Congress, where I hand-cranked this little seen film through a small projector.

On this day in 1925, Louise Brooks received her first critical notice as an actress.

The *Los Angeles Times* took note of Brooks' brief appearance in *The Street of Forgotten Men* when its anonymous critic wrote, "And there was a little rowdy, obviously attached to the 'blind' man, who did some vital work during her few short scenes. She was not listed." The paper was referring to Brooks, whose brief appearance in the Herbert Brenon-directed film was uncredited. It was her first role, and she played the bit part of a moll (the girlfriend of a gangster) whose companion feign's blindness. Her screen time lasts less than five minutes.

Prior to August 31, 1925—Brooks had been mentioned in newspapers and magazine reviews largely in connection with her appearances as a Denishawn dancer or as showgirl with the George White Scandals and Ziegfeld Follies. (She also had a knack for showing up in various New York City gossip columns.) This *Los Angeles Times* review was her first notice in connection with a film.

The article, titled "Marmont Metropolitan Star," stands out not only as the first review to reference Brooks but as the only review of *The Street of Forgotten Men* to note her appearance. One wonders who that anonymous though prescient critic might have been?

The Street of Forgotten Men is an underworld romance set among professional beggars in New York's Bowery. It is a singular film, and received uniformly good reviews when first released. Leading man Percy Marmont was singled out for his exceptional performance and director Brenon was praised for his realistic depiction of Bowery life.

The National Board of Review named it one of the 40 best pictures of 1925, and it was picked as one of the best films of the year by the *Houston Chronicle*, *Pittsburgh Gazette Times*, *Tacoma Times*, and Topeka *Daily Capital*. In many reviews and advertisements, *The Street of Forgotten Men* was compared to *The Miracle Man*, a similarly themed 1919 Lon Chaney film about a gang of criminals.

The Street of Forgotten Men was long thought lost. However, six of seven reels were later found at the Library of Congress. Among the surviving footage (the second reel is missing) is the scene that includes Brooks. Part of that scene is excerpted in the outstanding documentary, *Louise Brooks: Looking for Lulu*.

Eighty-five years ago today, Louise Brooks received her first film review. It was a tentative beginning to a comet-like career.

Strange Silent Film Screens in Syracuse

This piece appeared on Huffington Post on March 15, 2012. It was adapted from the program notes I wrote for a Cinefest screening in Syracuse, New York. Admittedly, I am partisan for this little known and somewhat unusual film, and not just because it includes Brooks. Film historian Kevin Brownlow once told me he thinks highly of it as well.

Silent films have enjoyed a good deal of attention lately, thanks to the Academy Award-winning efforts of Michel Hazanavicius (*The Artist*) and Martin Scorsese (*Hugo*).

Each took the silent era as the subject of their recent work, and each of their films took home five Oscars. New fans to early film have a world to explore.

Cinefest, an annual movie convention held in Syracuse, New York, is set to screen one of the more unusual films from the silent era, Herbert Brenon's *The Street of Forgotten Men* (1925). Long thought lost, this "underworld romance" has seldom been seen since its debut 87 years ago. The Library of Congress holds one of the only surviving prints, and representatives of the LOC will bring their copy to Cinefest for this rare screening.

Described at the time as "strange and startling" and "a drama of places and of people you have never seen before," *The Street of Forgotten Men* tells the story of a gang of professional beggars whose underworld headquarters is known as a "cripple factory." Led by the colorfully named Easy Money Charlie (played by Percy Marmont), the gang preys on public sympathy by disfiguring themselves and feigning various disabilities.

The Street of Forgotten Men also tells the story of Mary Vanhern, played by winsome Mary Brian, whose life is linked to these con artists as well as to a young millionaire, played by handsome Neil Hamilton. (Yes, that Neil Hamilton—Commissioner Gordon from the 1960's television series, *Batman*.)

Set on the Bowery and shot in part on the streets of New York City, the film is a mix of old-fashioned melodrama and gritty realism. It was based on a short story by George Kibbe Turner, a muckraking journalist and novelist of the time. In its review of the film, New York's *Daily News* stated, "*The Street of Forgotten Men* dips into the dark pools of life. It shows you the beggars of life—apologies to Jim Tully—and in showing them, it shows them up." On the other coast, the *San Francisco Bulletin* noted, "For fine dramatic detail, for unusualness, for giving us a glimpse into a world we never see and into the other sides of characters we simply pass in pity on the streets, *The Street of Forgotten Men* is a photoplay revelation."

The film's most unusual scenes occur when this band of beggars check into work and are fitted with bandages, artificial arms and legs, high-heeled shoes and other trick paraphernalia for the luring of sympathetic coins into battered tin cups. Canes and crutches along with signs that read "I Am Blind" and "Please help a cripple" lend atmosphere to the group's "changing room." According to studio press sheets, a mendicant officer and 20-year veteran of the Brooklyn Bureau of Charity served as adviser for scenes shot inside the dingy cripple factory.

Though the film and its source material was a look back at the Bowery and the then practices of the disreputable down-and-out, a 1926 article in the *New York Times* reported that the film may have inspired a group of fake beggars. "The police are investigating the speakeasy. It was recalled that several months ago a motion picture, *The Street of Forgotten Men*... showed just such an establishment for equipping 'cripples' as that described by Williams, and the police thought the movie idea might have been put to practical use."

Aside from its strange subject matter, there is much to recommend in *The Street of Forgotten Men*. The film was shot in the Astoria studios on Long Island, as well as on location in 1925 New York City. One memorable scene—when Marmont and Brian come across the character known as Bridgeport White-Eye—was filmed on a busy Fifth Avenue near Saint Patrick's Cathedral. Shot with a concealed camera, unaware crowds passing on the street along with images of shops and businesses from long ago—including a vegetarian restaurant—prove striking. According to press reports from the time, which should be taken with a grain of salt, the appearance of pathetic-looking actors dressed in disheveled attire drew spontaneous donations from passers-by not realizing a motion picture was being filmed. Another memorable scene with a good deal of local color takes place at the still standing Little Church Around the Corner on East 29th.

Two performers not listed in the film's credits also made their mark in *The Street of Forgotten Men*. One was a dog named Lassie. (This bull terrier-cocker spaniel mix predated the more famous Collie.) A 1927 *New York Times* article about the canine stated, "It is said that the death of Lassie in *The Street of Forgotten Men* was so impressive that persons were convinced that she must have been cruelly beaten. Her master, Emery Bronte, said that the dog seemed to enjoy acting in the scenes, and that after each 'take' she went over to Mr. Brenon and cocked her head on the side, as if asking for a pat or two." Regrettably, one of the reels of *The Street of Forgotten Men* is missing, and not all of Lassie's scenes are extant.

The other performer who made an impression was Louise Brooks, who was dancing with the Ziegfeld Follies when she agreed to play a bit part in *The Street of Forgotten Men*. Though not credited, the film marked her screen debut. As a moll, Brooks' role was slight—she appears on screen for only about five minutes. Nevertheless, her brief role drew the attention of an anonymous *Los Angeles Times* reviewer who singled out the actress when they wrote, "And there was a little rowdy, obviously attached to the 'blind' man, who did some vital work during her few short scenes." This was Brooks' first film review.

Like the film, the director of *The Street of Forgotten Men* has fallen into the shadows of history. Herbert Brenon enjoyed a long career which lasted from 1912 to 1940, but today, he is one of those early directors who is largely forgotten though deserving of greater recognition. *The Street of Forgotten Men* was made shortly after Brenon made the film for which he is best remembered, *Peter Pan* (1924). His other notable efforts include *The Spanish Dancer* (1923) with Pola Negri, *Dancing Mothers* (1926) with Clara Bow, *Beau Geste* (1926), *The Great Gatsby* (1926), *God Gave Me Twenty Cents* (1926), and *Laugh, Clown, Laugh* (1928) with Lon Chaney. All were major hits.

Though little known today, *The Street of Forgotten Men* was especially well regarded in its day. Marmont, a leading star of the silent era, was singled out for his exceptional Lon Chaney-like performance, and director Brenon was praised for his realistic depiction of Bowery life. The National Board of Review named the film one of the best pictures of 1925, and it was picked as one of the best of the year by newspapers around the country. This rare screening gives Cinefest 32 attendees an opportunity to see a film which should be better known, and on DVD.

The original Lassie, canine thespian
This piece appeared on the Louise Brooks Society blog on March 17, 2012.

I have received an email asking about Lassie, the canine actor in *The Street of Forgotten Men*. That film was shown on March 15th at Cinefest 32 in Syracuse, New York.

A 1927 *New York Times* article about the canine stated, "It is said that the death of Lassie in *The Street of Forgotten Men* was so impressive that persons were convinced that she must have been cruelly beaten. Her master, Emery Bronte, said that the dog seemed to enjoy acting in the scenes, and that after each 'take' she went over to Mr. Brenon and cocked her head on the side, as if asking for a pat or two." Apparently, this notable scene—her best scene, her death scene—is missing from the surviving six reels (of this seven reel film).

This Lassie, a contemporary of Rin-Tin-Tin, was bull terrier-cocker spaniel mix who predated the more famous Collie which later starred in movies and television. The *New York Times* describes her as an "intelligent animal" and a "clever screen actress." And according to that 1927 article, she was then earning a remarkable $15,000 a year as a canine actor / performer. That was a lot of money.

Lassie, a Clever Screen Actress.

Some of the other films in which Lassie appeared include *Tol'able David*, *Knockabout Riley*, *The Beautiful City* and *Sonny*. Her fellow actors included Mabel Normand, Viola Dana, Richard Barthelmess, Marion Davies, Richard Dix, Tom Moore and George Walsh, among others.

On the following page is an April, 1926 Mexican newspaper advertisement for *The Street of Forgotten Men* (and two other films) depicting a character from the Herbert Brenon-directed film holding Lassie. (In Spanish, *The Street of*

Forgotten Men is titled *La Calle del Olvido*.) Here is another depiction of Lassie, who looks like a pretty cute dog. Watch out Uggie!

Louise Brooks and *The American Venus*
This piece appeared on the Starts Thursday on August 3, 2010.

The coming attraction slide for *The American Venus* heralded the arrival of a major new release in early 1926. The film, from Paramount (then known as Famous Players Lasky), was a romantic comedy set at a beauty pageant. Typical for its time, the film featured plenty of pretty girls in bathing suits and even less, as certain groups in the American Midwest were to complain.

The film was billed as a "novel and magnificent beauty-comedy special." What made it special was not only its all-star cast, but also the fact that some scenes were filmed in Technicolor. *The American Venus* was one of the earlier films to feature the then new color process.

Parts of *The American Venus* were shot at the 1925 Miss America contest in Atlantic City, New Jersey—where Oakland, California resident Fay Lanphier was crowned that year's Miss America. It's her image that's depicted on the coming attraction slide.

As the winner of the beauty contest, Lanphier was given a movie contract and starring role in *The American Venus*. The film was directed by reliable Frank Tuttle, and was based on a story by Townsend Martin (a Princeton friend of F. Scott Fitzgerald). And, according to the *New Yorker* and other publications, humorist Robert Benchley wrote the inter-titles.

The cast includes lovely Esther Ralston (nicknamed the "American Venus"), San Francisco-born leading man Lawrence Gray, comedian Ford Sterling, and up-and-comer Louise Brooks in her second film. Renowned artist W.T. Benda, character actor Ernest Torrence, and Douglas Fairbanks Jr. also have supporting roles.

In the 1920's, national beauty contests were a phenomenon. And in this age of ballyhoo, considerable press coverage was given over to just about every facet of any contest. That's why Lanphier—then enjoying the peak of her celebrity—was featured on the glass slide pictured here. This was the nation's chance to see moving pictures of the current Miss America!

As with other films, the coming attraction slide was only one aspect of the studio's overall promotional campaign. In the Paramount press book for *The American Venus*, the "announcement slide" is shown along with window and lobby cards. Such materials were made available through the studios and local film exchanges, which supplied exhibitors with an array of promotional materials. The glass announcement slide costs 15 cents, the same price as a one sheet poster.

Lanphier enjoyed considerable fame after winning the 1925 Miss America contest; she wrote articles, judged local beauty contests, and made personal appearances around the country—some in conjunction with the screening of *The American Venus*. However, her movie career never developed. Lanphier appeared in only one other film, a Laurel and Hardy short entitled *Flying Elephants* (1928). Later, the honey-blond beauty worked as a stenographer in Hollywood.

Today, *The American Venus* is considered a lost film. All that remains are its ephemeral material culture—like glass slides, lobby cards, movie heralds, and a couple of movie trailers uncovered in the late 1990's.

A movie herald: what it can tell us
This piece appeared on the Louise Brooks Society blog on June 12, 2010.

On eBay, there is an *American Venus* movie herald for sale. Just about any movie herald from the silent era is uncommon. Some are rare. What makes this particular herald a bit unusual are its hand written annotations. They have a story to tell.

The American Venus was released in early 1926. This herald is dated 1927, apparently by someone who saw the film. That suggests that the two theaters which showed the film in May of that year, one in Petersburg and one in Blissfield (located less than 9 miles apart in Monroe County in Michigan), showed it late in the exhibition life of the film. That was not usual for small towns, which usually but not always got major films later than the bigger cities and towns.

The film's plot revolved around a beauty contest, and as I have found out, many theaters sponsored their own beauty contests or fashion shows in connection with the showing of the film. Such was the case with the Petersburg and Blissfield Theaters.

Beauty contests, and to a lesser degree this film, helped "define" the notion of beauty. The film's star, Fay Lanphier, was named Miss America in 1925, and as press coverage at the time indicates, she was considered an ideal beauty. I have found many newspapers advertisements which detailed Lanphier's physical attributes, including her measurements. She is shown, arms outstretched, in the interior of the herald. Esther Ralston, another renown beauty, is pictured on the cover of the herald.

On the back of the herald is a custom message from the sponsoring theaters which reads "The lady turning in measurements nearest to the AMERICAN VENUS will be given—ten tickets to this theatre. Measurements must be turned in on playing date—at box office."

What's interesting are the herald's handwritten notations. They record one woman's measurements in comparison to Lanphier's. On the back, that same someone recorded their weight throughout the 1930's. This woman, who weighed 169 pounds in 1939, held onto this herald for more than 12 years. *The American Venus* must have made an impression. This battered herald, this scrap of paper, tells their story.

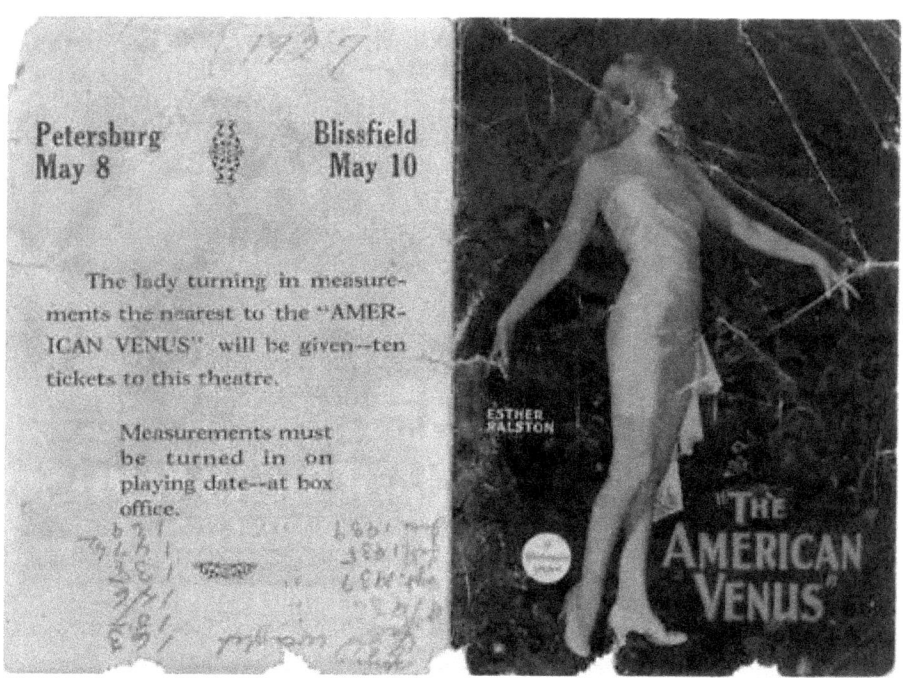

Louise Brooks, at the corner of Brooklyn Avenue and 16th Street
This piece appeared on the Louise Brooks Society blog on November 5, 2016.

In the 1920s, movies were advertised in all manner of ways—in newspapers and magazines, on posters and handbills, in window displays, and even by individuals walking down the street wearing a sandwich board. And like today, they were also advertised on billboards.

In the past, I have seen only one image of a billboard promoting a Louise Brooks' film, namely *The Canary Murder Case*, as it appeared in a distant and grainy photograph in a 1929 Winnipeg, Manitoba newspaper.

Recently, I came across something special—a photograph of a billboard promoting *A Social Celebrity* in Kansas City, Missouri. To me, it is a remarkable image, as it is not in a downtown setting (as in *The Canary Murder Case* image I had seen), but rather, in a city neighborhood.

What's more, I found the image on an African-American history website—the Black Archives of mid-America, which leads me to guess but not know for sure that the neighborhoods depicted below were African American neighborhoods. [It's not surprising that Brooks' films were advertised in Black neighborhoods, as Paramount films were popular and Brooks' youthful manner gained her many fans. In fact, I have come across a handful of instances when Brooks' films were shown in theaters that catered to African Americans, one in Harlem, and one in Baltimore. I know this because I have found advertisements for Brooks' films in African American newspapers which served those communities. Other of Brooks' films, especially *Beggars of Life*, which featured an African American actor, Edgar 'Blue' Washington, were written up in African American newspapers of the time.]

What follows is the first close-up image I have found which depicts an outdoor billboard featuring a Brooks' film; it is followed by an even greater close-up of the billboard itself.

This billboard depicted promotes a showing of *A Social Celebrity* at the downtown Newman Theater in Kansas City, commencing the week of May 1.

Released by Famous Players-Lasky Corporation, this Malcom St. Clair-directed film stars Adolphe Menjou (who is featured on the billboard), along with two more-or-less generic flappers. Also credited, by name, are actors Chester Conklin and Louise Brooks. Menjou was a major star at the time (thus his prominence in the ad), Conklin less so, and Brooks even more less so. *A Social Celebrity* was officially released on March 29, 1926.

One might ask or wonder why was this picture taken? Most likely, I would guess, was to prove to Famous Players-Lasky or the film's local distributor or exhibitor that the film was in fact advertised as per an agreement.

I also happened to come upon another photograph from the time (all of which were credited to the Merritt Outdoor Advertising Co.) which depicts another billboard promoting *A Social Celebrity* in Kansas City! This photo is set at Broadway and 35th Street.

Just as I began to wonder it there had been a city wide campaign to promote the film, I came across another image of a billboard promoting *A Social Celebrity*. This one is located at 15th and Holmes Streets in Kansas City.

And here is another, where the billboard is on the left of the three billboard construct. This picture was shot 4025 Troost Avenue

I found four more images of billboards promoting *A Social Celebrity*, including the picture below. Unfortunately, this photograph, which is typical of the others, shows the billboard either distant or obscured (here behind a tree at the corner of Independence Avenue and Maple Boulevard). Nevertheless, that makes eight photographs of eight billboards promoting the same showing of *A Social Celebrity*.

Incidentally, the Newman showed many of Brooks' films when they were first released. The Newman was a major first run theater in a major metropolitan area. In fact, it was the "largest motion picture theater to be built in the downtown district and the most costly theater of any sort" erected at the time in Kansas City. Seating capacity was 2,000. There was also a big organ installed.

Named after Frank L. Newman and opened in 1919, the Newman theater was later sold to and operated by Paramount Pictures starting in 1925, when Newman left to manage theaters in Los Angeles for the Famous Players-Lasky Film Corporation. After another change of name and a renovation in 1969, the theater was closed for good and later demolished in 1972.

These historic billboard images got me wondering. If they exist for one film in one city, where are others like them from other major cities? The search continues....

I wasn't able to find much about Frank Cambria's Garden Festival, which was the opening act for *A Social Celebrity* at the Newman in Kansas City. Seemingly, he/it was a traveling act, turning up in 1926 in Buffalo, Detroit, St. Louis and elsewhere. When Cambria's Garden Festival was staged that same year in Brooklyn ahead of the Richard Dix's film, *Let's Get Married*, the *Brooklyn Daily Eagle* described it as "a lovely presentation, staged in good taste and has as its theme song Schubert's *Serenade*."

Incidentally, I did find a few other images depicting billboards for other silent films starring the likes of Norma Shearer, Zasu Pitts, Helen Chadwick and others. Here is one of them, for the Priscilla Dean, Lon Chaney film *Outside* the Law at the Liberty theater.

The Show-Off, with Louise Brooks, screens July 10.
This piece appeared on examiner.com on July 8, 2010.

Today, Louise Brooks is best known for her *heavy* dramatic roles in films like *Pandora's Box* and *Diary of a Lost Girl* (both 1929). However, she got her start—and really blossomed as an actress—in lighter fair like *The American Venus* and *It's the Old Army Game* (both 1926).

Perhaps her best work in a light comedy-drama is in *The Show-Off*, also from 1926. It will be screened under the stars on July 10 at the Heritage Square Museum in Los Angeles.

This rare screening is part of a double bill celebrating the talents of noted actresses who came to fame during the early years of Hollywood. Also on the bill is *A Fool There Was* (1915), starring the legendary vamp, Theda Bara.

The Show-Off is an ensemble effort. Besides Brooks (who makes the best of a smaller role), the film stars Ford Sterling, Lois Wilson, and Gregory Kelly. Sterling plays an insufferable braggart named Audrey Piper who disrupts the lives of his middle-class family by pretending to be much, much, much more than he really is. The film was directed by Malcolm St. Clair for Famous Players-Lasky.

The Show-Off was based on a stage play by George Kelly (no relation to actor Gregory—though George is the uncle of actress and later princess Grace Kelly). In its day, the stage version of *The Show-Off* was a huge popular and critical success. Heywood Broun dubbed it "the best comedy which has been written by an American." In 1924, it was to have been awarded the Pulitzer Prize in Drama, but was controversially denied. Kelly won the prize the following year for *Craig's Wife*.

As a satire on American manners, *The Show-Off* is both brilliant and typical. Its story was made into a film again in 1934 with Spencer Tracy, and in 1946 with Red Skelton. By common consensus, the first version is best.

The film did good box office in mid-1926. Robert E. Sherwood, writing in LIFE, stated that Malcolm St. Clair has "taken a simple play of average American life and made a genuinely tender, touching, sympathetic picture of it. . . . a worthy reproduction of a great comedy."

Similarly, John S. Cohen Jr., writing in the *New York Sun*, noted "the film boasts of exceptional naturalistic acting on the part of Ford Sterling, Lois Wilson, Claire McDowell, C. W. Goodrich, Gregory Kelly and—in one sequence—Louise Brooks. . . . Miss Brooks is best in the scene where she burlesques the pantomime employed by Mr. Sterling to describe his automobile experience."

When the film opened at the Metropolitan Theater in Los Angeles, it and Louise Brooks drew favorable reviews. The city's dailies ran reviews with headlines describing it as a "cure for ailments" and "riot of fun."

Herbert Moulton, writing in *Los Angeles Times*, noted "The sweetheart of the brother is played by Louise Brooks, who does well in a negligible role." The *Los Angeles Evening Herald* echoed the sentiment with "The cast includes Louise Brooks, who does a bit of excellent acting." Go see for yourself. The film is seldom shown on the big screen and is hard to find on VHS or DVD.

The Heritage Square Museum double bill of *A Fool There Was* / *The Show-Off* is set for Saturday, July 10. It is part of a month-long series of Silent and Classic Movie Nights. (Clara Bow will be featured on July 24.)

Rare Louise Brooks film to screen in Niles

This piece appeared on examiner.com on September 21, 2010.
I had the honor to introduce the film when it showed at the Niles film museum.

Love 'Em and Leave 'Em, a charming fast-paced romantic comedy featuring Bay Area favorite Louise Brooks, will be shown at the Niles Essanay Silent Film Museum in Fremont, California on October 9th. It's a rare screening (in 16mm) of one of the actress' best American silent films.

This Frank Tuttle-directed feature tells the story of two sisters—one good (the always sultry Evelyn Brent) and one bad (the devilish Brooks)—who share a boyfriend (San Francisco-born Lawrence Gray) while all are employed at a big-city department store. Of note, in a supporting role, the film features Osgood Perkins, the father of actor Anthony Perkins.

Love 'Em and Leave 'Em is a charming slice-of-life portrayal of the loves and misadventures of typical young people of the 1920s. There is much to recommend.

The film showcases Brooks in a made-to-order role as an attractive bad girl, a Flapper on the make for any male that crosses her path. Though only in a supporting role, Brooks has no trouble stealing the picture as well as her sister's boyfriend, even though Brent puts up a noble fight on both fronts. And for the verisimilitude it lends, the location scenes inside a real New York City department store are also notable.

Despite a somewhat negative review in *The New York Times*, the movie proved to be a hit wherever it showed.

The critic for the *New York Sun* wrote, "The real surprise of the film is Louise Brooks. With practically all connoisseurs of beauty in the throes of adulation over her generally effectiveness, Miss Brooks has not heretofore impressed anyone as a roomful (as Lorelei says) of Duses. But in *Love 'Em and Leave 'Em*, unless I too have simply fallen under her spell, she gives an uncannily effective impersonation of a bad little notion counter vampire. Even her excellent acting, however, cannot approach in effectiveness the scenes where, in 'Scandals' attire, she does what we may call a mean Charleston."

Echoing that sentiment, the *Chicago Tribune* named it one of the six best movies of the month. Mae Tinee wrote, "*Love 'Em and Leave 'Em* is one of the snappiest little comedy dramas of the season. Full of human interest. Splendidly directed. Acted beautifully."

Locally, the *San Francisco News* noted, "With Evelyn Brent as the wisecracking Mame, Louise Brooks as Janie, her younger sister, to whose net all was fish, and Lawrence Gray as Bill Billingsley, in love with Mame, but ensnared by Janie, and the other roles in very capable hands, the piece has been excellently cast."

The film was adapted from the stage play by John Van Alstyne Weaver and George Abbott. The film's screenplay is by Townsend Martin, a silent era scenario writer whose credits include *The American Venus* (1926) and *A Kiss for Cinderella* (1925).

Martin, a college friend of F. Scott Fitzgerald and a well-to-do writer of some talent but little ambition, specialized in light, frothy films. And in *Love 'Em and Leave 'Em* he delivers. Martin also figures in the Brooks' legend as having once put-off the actress and as a consequence was slashed across the face and bloodied by a dozen roses.

Love 'Em and Leave 'Em was officially released on December 6, 1926. It made its Bay Area debut at the California Theater in Pittsburg on December 14, 1926. It went on to show in San Jose, Oakland, Mill Valley and elsewhere in the following months. The last time *Love Em and Leave Em* was publicly screened in the Bay Area was on November 21, 2006 at the San Francisco Public Library.

Louise Brooks in Fairbanks, Alaska - better late than never
This piece appeared on the Louise Brooks Society blog on January 25, 2013.

I am continuously researching Louise Brooks and her films. And recently, I came across a couple of clipping which merit mentioning. These findings are notable on a few accounts.

In January, 1930 two of Louise Brooks' silent films—*The City Gone Wild* and *Now We're in the Air*—were shown in Fairbanks, Alaska. The paper's "Screen Life" column detailed the events. These screenings are not the first instances of Brooks' films showing in Alaska, then an American territory. (Alaska did not gain statehood until 1949.) For example, *A Social Celebrity* (1926), was shown at the Empress theater in Fairbanks in April, 1927.

What is notable about these particular screenings is that each took place long after the films were released. Both films debuted in the Fall of 1927, and these two screenings took place more than two years later. That is a long time for a film to be in circulation during the silent era. Notably, they are also the very last American screenings that I have come across for these two now lost films.

What is also notable is that theaters in Fairbanks were still screening silent films well after the sound era had started. For the record, a 1929 sound film featuring Brooks, *The Canary Murder Case*, was shown in Fairbanks in April, 1930, about 14 months after it first debuted. And another, *It Pays to Advertise*, also with Brooks, was shown in Fairbanks only nine months after its release in November, 1931.

I have also come across a handful of screenings of Louise Brooks' films in Honolulu during the 1920s, decades before Hawaii gained statehood. Notably, Hawaii seems to have gotten films sooner than Alaska. Better late than never.

Long Missing Louise Brooks Film Found
This piece appeared on Huffington Post on March 30, 2017. It was the first to break the news of the discovery of this once lost Brooks film, which I played a part in preserving.

Approximately 23 minutes of a long missing 1927 Louise Brooks film, *Now We're in the Air*, has been found in an archive in the Czech Republic. The discovery is significant, not only because of Brooks' widespread popularity, but because it helps fill a gap in the legendary actress' body of work. Until now, each of the four films Brooks made in 1927—at the peak of her American career—have been considered lost.

The San Francisco Silent Film Festival revealed the existence of the film while announcing the lineup of works to be shown at its upcoming event. The newly restored partial film will be shown at the Festival, which is set to take place June 1 through June 4 at the Castro Theater in San Francisco.

Now We're in the Air will be paired with *Get Your Man* (1927), a Dorothy Arzner directed film starring Clara Bow. The Library of Congress has reconstructed *Get Your*

Man from recovered materials, filling in missing sequences with stills and intertitles. Festival Executive Director Stacey Wisnia noted that the pairing brings together not only two recovered films, but also the era's two "It" girls, Bow and Brooks.

The discovery of *Now We're in the Air* came about, in part, through the efforts of film preservationist Robert Byrne, president of the Board of Directors of the San Francisco Silent Film Festival. Byrne has made a name for himself of late, having helped in the recovery and restoration of a handful of important films over the last few years. Prominent among his discoveries were two films identified in the collection of Cinematheque Francaise, *Sherlock Holmes* (1916), and *Silence* (1926). The latter, a Cecil B. DeMille production directed by Rupert Julian, will also debut at the June event. Another of Byrne's efforts, *Behind the Door* (1919), is due out on DVD / Blu-ray from Flicker Alley.

In a recent interview, Byrne related how he mentioned to English film historian and Academy Award honoree Kevin Brownlow that he would be going to Prague to visit the Czech Národní filmový archiv (the Czech Republic's National Film Archive). It's known they have an extensive collection of silent era material, including the only remaining nitrate copies of a number of American silent films. Unsure as to what might be found, Brownlow provided Byrne with a list of about a dozen titles he should ask to see. That list included *Now We're in the Air*. Though popular in its time, the 1927 film is little known today except for the fact it includes Brooks in a supporting role.

When Byrne inspected the elements for *Rif a Raf, Piloti* (the Czech title for *Now We're in the Air*), he found the film had only partially survived in a state which also showed nitrate decomposition. Additionally, the surviving scenes were found to be out of order, and there were Czech-language titles in place of the original American titles. Byrne spent more than eight months reconstructing the surviving material, including restoring the film's original English-language inter-titles and original tinting.

"As is often the case, the most challenging aspect was not the technical work of cleaning up the image," Byrne stated, "but rather the research that ensured we were making a faithful restoration, especially when it came to replacing the Czech language inter-titles with the original English versions."

Byrne was especially appreciative of the help given by the Národní filmový archive. "They were incredibly gracious and generous with their time and resources; in addition to granting access to their nitrate print, they are responsible for the color-dye tinting of our new 35mm print. This is the first San Francisco Silent Film Festival restoration where we have used the traditional dye-tinting process to restore a film's original color. In prior projects, we have used a modern method that utilizes color film stock." Byrne added, "This is what an American audience would have seen when the film was released in 1927."

Byrne said he was "thrilled" to find a missing Brooks film. "The shame is that so many of her American films are lost. Seeing *Now We're in the Air* projected for the first time was pretty amazing. I have seen stills of her in the black tutu a million times, but actually seeing the sequence where she is wearing it was like watching a still photograph magically come to life." Byrne's excitement for the newly found Brooks' film was matched by Judy Wyler Sheldon, a longtime Brooks' fan and the daughter of legendary director William Wyler. Festival Artistic Director Anita Monga was likewise excited, and thought the fragment was "revelatory."

Directed by Frank Strayer, *Now We're in the Air* is a World War One comedy starring future Oscar winner Wallace Beery and the once popular character actor Raymond Hatton. The film, released by Paramount, also features Brooks in two supporting roles. The actress plays twins, one raised French, one raised German, who are the love interest of two goofy fliers. The surviving footage of Brooks only includes her in the role of the French twin, a carnival worker dressed in a short, dark tutu.

In the 1920s, Beery and Hatton were teamed in a number of popular *Dumb and Dumber*-like comedies. With its aviation-theme, *Now We're in the Air* was one of the pair's "service comedies," following similar themed movies like *Behind the Front* (1926) and *We're in the Navy Now* (1926).

Notably, the film's cinematographer is Harry Perry, who worked on two other significant aviation pictures, *Wings* (1927), and *Hell's Angels* (1930). Perry was nominated for an Academy Award for his work on the latter. Interestingly, a notation in the script for *Now We're in the Air* uncovered during its restoration calls for the use of left-over footage from the William Wellman-directed *Wings*, another WWI movie, and the first film to win an Academy Award for Best Picture. That footage can be seen during the Armistice scene in *Now We're in the Air*, near the end of the surviving footage.

Though some winced at its crude humor (not evident in the surviving material), the Beery-Hatton film proved to be one of the more popular comedies of 1927. Generally liked by the critics, the film did big box office where ever it showed. In New York City, it enjoyed an extended run, as it did in San Francisco, where it proved to be one of the year's biggest hits. At a time when most new releases played only one week, *Now We're in the Air* ran for a month in San Francisco, according to local newspaper listings. In Boston, the film also did well, opening simultaneously in five theaters. At the time, the *Boston Evening Transcript* noted the audience at one screening "was so moved by mirth that they were close to tears."

The recovery of *Now We're in the Air* comes 90 years after its first release, and 100 years after the United States formally entered what became known as the First World War, on April 6, 1917. Though a comedy, *Now We're in the Air* was one of a number of silent films from the time—including *Behind the Door* (1919), *The Four Horsemen of the Apocalypse* (1921), *The Big Parade* (1925), *What Price Glory?* (1926), and *Wings* (1927), which depict the conflict.

Byrne and others involved in the restoration of *Now We're in the Air* believe the surviving footage lives up to the promise of its original reviews. In June, Festival goers and Louise Brooks fans will have the chance to see for themselves.

A little something about *Now We're in the Air*
This piece appeared on the Louise Brooks Society blog on April 7, 2017.

As you should know by now, a chunk (*a technical terms meaning partial*) of the 1927 Louise Brooks film *Now We're in the Air* has been found in Prague at the Czech Republic's Národní filmový archive (National Film Archive). The restored, 23 minute fragment will be shown June 2 at the San Francisco Silent Film Festival. In the meantime, here is a little background on the film.

Now We're in the Air is a comedy about two fliers (a pair of "aero-nuts" also called "looney Lindberghs") who wander on to a World War I battle field near the front lines. The film was one of a number of aviation-themed stories shot in 1927 (following Lindbergh's historic solo flight across the Atlantic), as well as one in a popular series of "service comedies" pairing Wallace Beery and Raymond Hatton. Louise Brooks plays the unusual role of twin sisters, one raised French and one raised German, named Griselle & Grisette, who are the love interest of the two fliers.

Arguably, *Now We're in the Air* was the most popular American silent in which Brooks appeared. Generally liked by the critics, the film did big box office where ever it showed. In New York City, it enjoyed an extended run, as it did in San Francisco,

where it proved to be one of the biggest hits of the year. At a time when most new releases played only one week, *Now We're in the Air* ran for more than a month in San Francisco, where it was extended due to robust ticket sales. In Boston, it also did well, opening simultaneously in five theaters in the area. The *Boston Evening Transcript* noted, "most of the audience at the Washington Street Olympia this week were so moved by mirth that they were close to tears. Presumably the experience has been the same at the Scollay Square Olympia, the Fenway, the Capitol in Allston and the Central Square in Cambridge." Newspapers in other large cities like Atlanta, Georgia and St. Louis, Missouri reported a similar reception.

The *New Orleans Item* noted, "The added feature of *Now We're in the Air* is the presence of Louise Brooks as the heroine. One of the cleverest of the new stars, she has immense ability to appear 'dumb' but like those early Nineteenth Century actresses, commended by Chas. Lamb, she makes the spectators realize that she is only playing at being dumb." Radie Harris of the New York *Morning Telegraph* wrote, "Louise Brooks is seen as the feminine lead. She essays the role of twins. Which, if you know Louise, is mighty satisfactory. She is decorative enough to admire once, but when you are allowed the privilege of seeing her double, the effect is devastating." The *Boston Post* added, "You see there are pretty twin sisters, Grisette and Griselle, both played by the fetching Louise Brooks, who marry Wally and Ray, who cannot tell their wives apart except by their dogs, one a poodle, one a daschund."

The dual role played by Brooks made the film for many critics. Curran D. Swint of the *San Francisco News* stated, "Both the hulking and ungainly Beery and the cocky little Hatton give goofingly good accounts of themselves. Then there is Louise Brooks. She's the girl—or the girls—in the case, for Louise is twins in the story, and about this fact much of the comedy is woven." Across town, A. F. Gillaspey of the *San Francisco Bulletin* added, "Louise Brooks is the leading woman of this picture. She appears as the

twin sisters. This results in some remarkable and very interesting double exposures."

Mae Tinee, the *Chicago Tribune* critic who seemed to always champion Brooks, put it this way, "Louise Brooks as twins, is—are—a beautiful foil for the stars and if you think she doesn't marry both of them before the picture ends, why, cogitate again, my darlings."

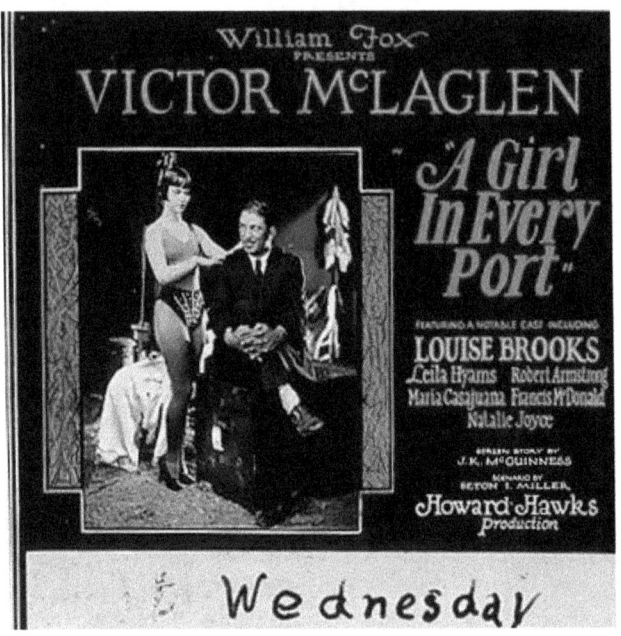

A Girl in Every Port & The Birth of Lulu?
This piece appeared on the University of Wisconsin Cinematheque blog on December 2, 2013.

Howard Hawks' *A Girl in Every Port* is a well-crafted and entertaining "buddy film" widely considered the director's best silent. It's also a film with a special legacy.

A Girl in Every Port features a romantic triangle—a reoccurring motif in many of Hawks' later works. It tells the story of two sailors (Victor McLaglen and Robert Armstrong) and their adventures in various ports of call around the world. Louise Brooks plays Marie (Mam'selle Godiva), a high diver and sideshow siren and the love interest of both sailors. Other girls in other ports of call include Myrna Loy, Sally Rand, Leila Hyams, and Maria Casajuana (the future Maria Alba).

Released by Fox in February of 1928, *A Girl in Every Port* debuted at the 6,000 seat Roxy Theater in New York City. For days on end, the film played to a packed house. Ads placed by the studio in trade publications claimed it set a "New House Record—and a World Record—with Daily Receipts on February 22 of $29,463." Considering ticket prices of the time, that's a lot of money.

Popular as well as critically acclaimed, the film received good reviews in New York's daily newspapers. *The New York Times* described it "A rollicking comedy," while the *New York Telegram* called it "a hit picture." *The Morning Telegraph* pronounced it a "winner."

The *Daily News* noted, "Director Howard Hawks has injected several devilish touches in the piece, which surprisingly enough, got by the censors. His treatment of the snappy scenario is smooth and at all times interesting. Victor's great, Armstrong's certainly appreciable, and Louise Brooks is at her loveliest."

Reviewing the premiere, *TIME* magazine stated, "There are two rollicking sailors in this fractious and excellent comedy. . . . *A Girl in Every Port* is really *What Price Glory?* translated from arid and terrestrial irony to marine gaiety of the most salty and miscellaneous nature. Nobody could be more charming than Louise Brooks, that clinging and tender little barnacle from the docks of Marseilles. Director Howard Hawks and his entire cast, especially Robert Armstrong, deserve bouquets and kudos."

A number of critics singled out Brooks. The *New York American* stated, "Then comes THE woman. She is Louise Brooks, pert, fascinating young creature, who does high and fancy diving for a living. . . . Miss Brooks 'takes' our hero in somewhat the manner that Grant took Richmond. . . . Louise Brooks has a way of making a junior vamp and infantile scarlet lady seem most attractive."

A reviewer for the *English Kinematograph Weekly* echoed American reviews of the film, and picked up on the film's somewhat different bromance. "Louise Brooks made a charmingly heartless vamp. . . . It has the novelty of a love interest that does not materialize, which is replaced by the friendship between two men."

The film made a bigger splash in France. Writing in 1930 in his "Paris Cinema Chatter" column in the *New York Times*, Morris Gilbert noted ". . . there are a number of others—mostly American—which have their place as 'classics' in the opinion of the French. . . . They love *A Girl in Every Port*, which has the added distinction of being practically the only American film which keeps its own English title here." The film enjoyed an extended run in the French capitol, and lingered for decades in the French consciousness.

Writing in *Cahiers du Cinéma* in 1963, French film archivist Henri Langlois stated, "It seems that *A Girl in Every Port* was the revelation of the Hawks season at the Museum of Modern Art in New York. For New York audiences of 1962, Louise Brooks suddenly acquired that 'Face of the century' aura she had had, many years ago, for spectators at the Cinema des Ursulines. . . . That is why Blaise Cendrars confided a few years ago that he thought *A Girl in Every Port* definitely marked the first appearance of contemporary cinema. To the Paris of 1928, which was rejecting expressionism, *A Girl in Every Port* was a film conceived in the present, achieving an identity of its own by repudiating the past."

Brooks, under contract to Paramount, was loaned to Fox for her role in *A Girl in Every Port*. Anticipating the female types cast by Hawks in later works, the bobbed-hair actress stands as what might well be the first "Hawksian woman." Years later, the director stated, "I wanted a different type of girl. I hired Louise because she's very sure of herself, she's very analytical, she's very feminine, but she's damn good and sure she's going to do what she wants to do."

Film histories note that *A Girl in Every Port* ranks as the most significant of Hawks' silent films; additionally, historians claim, it seemingly persuaded G.W. Pabst to cast Louise Brooks in *Pandora's Box*. Such a claim was likely first made by James Card of the George Eastman House in his 1956 article, "*Out of Pandora's Box: Louise Brooks on G. W. Pabst.*" It was repeated by others, including Brooks herself in filmed interviews in the 1970's.

In Germany, Pabst came to cast Brooks as Lulu only after a well publicized nationwide search which concluded months after *A Girl in Every Port* premiered in New York City. Not quite content with a German actress (including, legend has it, Marlene Dietrich), Pabst wrote to Paramount asking after Brooks, then an American starlet. The German director was also in search of a "different type."

Chronologically, the assumption that Pabst saw his Lulu in Hawks' Marie makes sense—Brooks plays a temptress in both films. Records show, however, that *Blaue jungens, blonde Madchen* (the German title for Hawk's film) was not shown in Germany until December, after production on *Pandora's Box* was finished.

Could Pabst have seen *A Girl in Every Port* well prior to its release in Germany? Or, might Pabst have noticed Brooks in one of her earlier American films, like *Die Braut am Scheidewege* (*Just Another Blonde*) or *Ein Frack Ein Claque Ein Madel* (*Evening Clothes*)? Each were shown in Berlin while Pabst was looking for Lulu, and each received press which highlighted Brooks.

Whatever the answer to this small mystery, *A Girl in Every Port* remains an entertaining film worthy of greater recognition—not only because it stars Louise Brooks, and not only because it may or may not have led Pabst to cast the actress as Lulu in *Pandora's Box*. It's deserving because it is an early work by great director which introduces the themes and characters Hawks would continue to explore throughout his long and distinguished career.

Beggars of Life Screens Under the Stars August 15
This piece appeared on Huffington Post on August 12, 2010.

Beggars of Life is a film whose critical reputation is picking up steam—pun intended.

Shot by William Wellman the year after he made *Wings* (the first film to win a Best Picture Oscar), *Beggars of Life* is a gripping melodrama about a girl (Louise Brooks) dressed as a boy who goes on the run after killing her abusive stepfather. Fleeing the law, she rides the rails through a threatening, male dominated, hobo underworld.

The film was based on the 1925 novelistic memoir by Jim Tully, a once celebrated "hobo author" whose own reputation is also on the rise. Kent State University Press in Kent, Ohio (Tully's one-time hometown) has started an ambitious program of reissuing many of the author's books, including *Beggars of Life*, his best remembered work.

Though shot as a silent, *Beggars of Life* is considered Paramount's first sound film. Now lost talking sequences, a song, and sound effects were added while the film was in production. Early advertisements for the 1928 film boasted "Come here Wallace Beery sing!" The memorable character actor and a future Oscar winner plays Oklahoma Red, a tough hobo with a soft heart. Richard Arlen, who the year before had starred in *Wings*, plays Brooks' romantic interest. Much of the film was shot near Jacumba, California, near the Mexican border.

Beggars of Life is a film about the desperate and the downtrodden. And, in some ways, it anticipates the films of the Depression. Among them is Wellman's own not dissimilar *Wild Boys of the Road*, from 1933.

Beggars of Life was named one of the six best films for the month of October by the *Chicago Tribune*, and it made the honor roll for best films of 1928 in an annual poll conducted by *The Film Daily*. Nevertheless, its grim tale set among disheveled tramps drew mixed reviews. One Baltimore newspaper said it would have limited appeal, while quipping "Tully tale not a flapper fetcher for the daytime trade."

Louella Parsons, writing in the *Los Angeles Examiner*, echoed the sentiment when she stated, "I was a little disappointed in Louise Brooks. She is so much more the modern flapper type, the Ziegfeld Follies girl, who wears clothes and is always gay and flippant. This girl is somber, worried to distraction and in no comedy mood. Miss Brooks is infinitely better when she has her lighter moments."

Harrison Carroll, writing in the *Los Angeles Evening Herald*, stated, "Considered from a moral standpoint, *Beggars of Life* is questionable, for it throws the glamour of adventure over tramp life and is occupied with building sympathy for an escaping murderess. As entertainment, however, it has tenseness and rugged earthy humor.... It is a departure from the wishy-washy romance and the fervid triangle drama."

Norbert Lusk of the *Los Angeles Times* added "Richard Arlen and Louise Brooks also capture honors for their sincerity and a poignant, moving quality they infuse into their roles without seeming to act at all. Miss Brooks, who has hitherto qualified as a particularly provocative figure, now establishes herself as a real actress."

The Afro-American (a newspaper based in the Baltimore-Washington D.C. area) also took note. "In *Beggars of Life*, Edgar Blue Washington, race star, was signed by Paramount for what is regarded as the most important Negro screen role of the year, that of Big Mose. The part is that of a sympathetic character, hardly less important to the epic of tramp life than those of Wallace Beery, Louise Brooks and Richard Arlen, who head the cast."

Pastoral life gone wrong, girls dressed as boys, blacks and whites mingling, desperation among the glitz and glamour of the Twenties—there is a lot going on in *Beggars of Life*. It's a worthwhile film well worth watching. And, until just a few years ago when the George Eastman House enlarged its sole surviving 16mm print to 35 mm, *Beggars of Life* had been a seldom screened film.

William Wellman made a lot of great movies—*Wings* (1927), *The Public Enemy* (1931), *A Star is Born* (1937), *Beau Geste* (1939), *Roxie Hart* (1942), *The Ox Bow Incident* (1943), and *Battleground* (1949) are all on the short list. Actor and author William Wellman Jr., who has nearly completed a biography of his father for a major publisher, stated via email, "*Beggars of Life* was one of my Father's favorite silent films. He loved it. He talked about it a great deal with appreciation and GUSTO." *Beggars of Life* has it.

Beggars of Life will be screened as part of The Hollywood Heritage "Silents Under the Stars" series on August 15 at the Paramount Ranch in Agoura, northwest of Los Angeles. Michael Mortilla will provide live musical accompaniment.

Six questions with . . . the Dodge Brothers
This piece appeared on exaimner.com on May 23, 2010.

The Dodge Brothers are renowned for playing the hell out of classic American music. Described as "wonderful stuff" on British radio, the UK-based group plays an exuberant hybrid of American country blues, jug band and skiffle. In current American lingo, they might be termed "roots music"—but with a strong feel for rock-a-billy.

Last month, the Dodge Brothers performed their original score for the 1928 film, *Beggars of Life*. That movie, and the book it was based on, are fast becoming classic works of Americana. The Dodge Brothers musical accompaniment is a natural fit.

Beggars of Life was directed by William Wellman and based on the acclaimed book by "hobo-author" Jim Tully. The film stars future Academy Award winner Wallace Beery and silent film stars Richard Arlen and Louise Brooks. It tells the gritty story of a girl who dresses as a boy and goes on the run and rides the rails in pre-Depression America.

That screening, as well as their musical accompaniment to it, was by all accounts well attended and just as well received. The screening was part of the British Silent Film Festival held in the UK.

The Dodge Brothers have released two albums to date. The group is made up of Mike Hammond (lead guitar, lead vocals), Mark Kermode (bass, harmonica, vocals), Aly Hirji (rhythm guitar, mandolin, vocals) and Alex Hammond (washboard, snare drum, percussion).

Recently, Hammond—the group's singer (and silent film expert) took time out to answer a few questions on behalf of the band about their score, their music, Louise Brooks, and silent film.

TG: The Dodge Brothers accompanied the Louise Brooks' film, *Beggars of Life*, on April 18th. For those not familiar with the Dodge Brothers, what can you tell us about the group?

MH: Well here is the short version. The Dodge Brothers are a four-piece band modeled on the skiffle and jug bands of the 20s and 30s. Each of us plays more than one instrument, Aly plays acoustic guitar and mandolin, Alex plays washboard, snare and wine bottle, I play guitar, banjo, piano and tap dance while Mark plays double bass, harmonicas, accordion and is soon to unveil his prowess on the bag pipes. We started from a love of the music that leads up to Elvis, which ranges widely from railroad songs, murder ballads to ragged street blues. We got going learning ten songs ('Frankie and Johnny' and 'Stagger Lee' among others) and over the years we have amassed about 150 songs. A couple of years ago we started to write our own songs that resulted in our album *Louisa and the Devil*. Mark started this by bringing in 'Church House Blues' and saying it was by an old jug band. We still do that; if it fools the rest of us into believing its authentic then we play it. (Did I say short version?)

TG: With that said, what can one expect—musically speaking, from your score?

MH: The score for the film will draw from those old songs from the period. I am a silent film scholar and I know that Paramount had the most film theatres in the rural areas so it was not uncommon for them to release different versions of films, one for the big cities and one for the rural towns. I have kept this in mind when thinking about the score. The lovely Troubadors version of 'Beggars of Life' was meant as a theme for the film and we will be incorporating a version of that but combining it with motifs which call up railroad songs that were popular during the period, particularly those by Jimmie Rogers. Lots of those songs are really about hobos riding the rails and they have a wonderful wistfulness about them, a mixture of loneliness and humor that both fits the film and the way we play.

TG: *Beggars of Life* is unlike any of Brooks' earlier American films. Had you seen it before? And what were your impressions?

MH: You're so right about it being an exceptional Brooks film. Most people associate her with the Jazz Age flapper-type but in this film she plays a girl on the run, dressed as a boy! None of us had seen the film before and it was our fifth member, the fabulous pianist and silent film composer Neil Brand, who drew it to our attention. Brooks really 'pops' out of the screen and holds her own with Wallace Beery, which is no mean feat. The tension that is generated by her masquerade as a boy amongst a lot of rough hobos is tight as a drum. There is a real sense of menace and danger from the beginning where 'The Girl' (Louise) takes matters into her own hands with a firearm. She reminds me of Louisa in our song 'The Ballad of Frank Harris'. Maybe that's what I really like about this film, she is self-sufficient and an equal partner with Arlen. And she can shoot a gun!

TG: Do you consider yourself a fan of Louise Brooks?

MH: Oh yes and not only because of the fact that she is the most compelling of screen stars. She is intuitive as an actress and gives the sense that she is being rather than acting. I do think Pabst understood that best. However, I am as big a fan of her writing. She is incisive and brutal in her analysis of Hollywood and, perhaps most touching, of herself.

TG: When did you first come across the actress?

MH: I can't speak for the rest of the guys. I first saw her in an undergraduate film class in the 80s. It was *Pandora's Box*. I remember thinking; of course these guys are giving away everything for her, who wouldn't?

TG: Louise Brooks has been getting the musical treatment of late. Rufus Wainwright, who will be touring the UK in the coming months, just released a musical tribute to Brooks titled *All Days Are Nights: Songs For Lulu*. And of course, it was preceded by earlier rock and pop musical tributes by the likes of Orchestral Manuevers in the Dark (OMD), Marillion, Jen Anderson, Soul Coughing, and others—even the cartoonist Robert Crumb. Where might your score fit into this history?

MH: Well all of these tributes are really great and it's nice to be in their company. I haven't heard Rufus Wainwright's but I guess in this history we will probably be closer to R. Crumb's. We are trying to bring a flavour of the kind of music that might have been played in the rural areas of the US to this film. Remember that the orchestras in most of those theatres at the time would have been as small as a quartet. They also played to their audience who would have known the railroad songs as well as the popular tunes of the day so they would mix them up. We'll be doing something similar and hopefully support the wide-ranging emotions in this film, from lonesome and sad, to tender, to fast action and gunplay. Louise does it all here and, come to think of it, that's a good description of The Dodge Brothers' music too.

A World Turned Over: Wellman's *Beggars of Life*

This piece appeared on the University of Wisconsin Cinematheque blog on November 28, 2017. It's preface read: "These notes on William Wellman's Beggars of Life by film scholar Thomas Gladysz are adapted from his new book, Beggars of Life: A Companion to the 1928 Film, as well as his audio commentary to the movie, which can be heard on the recent Kino Lorber release. A recently restored DCP, featuring a score by the Mount Alto Motion Picture Orchestra, will screen as part of our Silents Please! Series."

In 1928, thirty-two year old director William Wellman was at the top of his profession. He was still basking in the critical and commercial triumph of *Wings* when his latest production, *Beggars of Life*, hit screens in the fall. Considered one the studio's most important dramatic productions of the season, *Beggars of Life* was a film which couldn't help but provoke. Wellman was already developing a reputation as a maverick director. And this film's gritty realism stood at odds with the otherwise carefree glitz and glamour of the Jazz Age.

Beggars of Life was loosely based on a bestselling book of the same name by Jim Tully, a celebrated, rough-and-tumble, two-fisted "tramp writer of Hobohemia." In Tully's book—a kind of novelistic memoir, the author gave a grim account of the nearly seven years he spent wandering America as a "road kid." It is a book not only about Tully's journeys (many of them made jumping trains), but also about the colorful and sometimes unsavory characters he met along the way—in jails, bars, hobo camps and small towns across the Midwest.

Though cut from the same rough cloth, Wellman's movie tells a different story. *Beggars of Life* is a tersely filmed drama about an orphan girl (Louise Brooks) dressed as a boy who flees the law after killing her abusive stepfather. With the help of a young tramp (Richard Arlen), the two hop a freight train, ending up at a hobo camp ruled by Oklahoma Red (future Oscar winner Wallace Beery). In this male-dominated underworld, with the police on their trail, danger is always close at-hand.

Wellman's artfully photographed, morally dark tale of the down-and-out stars Beery. He receives top billing, and gives an especially vital performance. Arlen, an otherwise indifferent actor, is also good. However, it is Brooks (the only woman in the film) who dominates the screen in what is arguably her best role in her best American film. Brooks stands out, and not just for her appealing, androgynous appearance. Rather, she captures our attention through her authentic performance. As a young girl in Kansas, Brooks was sexually abused. It marked her life. In *Beggars of Life*, she plays a vulnerable young woman who is sexually assaulted.

In Wellman's film, Brooks seemingly reached down inside herself to give an authentic performance. She would do so again in *Pandora's Box* and *Diary of a Lost Girl*, two 1929 films where she once again plays a character who is sexually abused. Too what degree Brooks' childhood experience affected her performance in these films we can never know, but, in all likelihood, it's there in ways the camera could only record superficially. Watch Brooks' face.

Beggars of Life is a film filled with transgression, acts that go against a law, rule, or code of conduct. In the film, Brooks plays a character identified only as "The Girl." Her abuse at the hands of a farmer who has "adopted" her, and the assault that leads to his manslaughter, in turn causes this orphan to flee disguised as a boy.

On the run, this cross-dressing young woman descends into a desperate social stratum even lower than her standing as an orphan. Brooks' and Arlen's characters enter a "hobo jungle"—a camp of homeless men where criminal activity is rampant. We see fighting, theft, drinking (this was during prohibition), trespassing, attacks upon the police, and the suggestion that Brooks' character would be claimed by another and in all-likelihood again sexually assaulted. Set in America's heartland, this is pastoral life gone awry. And too, there is race mixing at a time when black and white characters were seldom shown as equals. In fact, the sole African American actor in the film, Edgar "Blue" Washington, plays one of its very few noble characters.

The late 1920's marked a period of transition in the film industry, as the studios came to grips with emerging sound technologies. At the time, Wellman was resistant to using sound: according to film historian and Wellman authority Frank Thompson, Wellman felt its intrusion into his carefully constructed drama would prove disturbing to the mood of the film. The director, however, was overruled, and Paramount instructed special effect engineer Roy Pomeroy to supervise a scene that would feature a bit of dialogue and a song sung by Beery.

At the time, the use of sound equipment was notorious for slowing down a film's action. Actors had to stand still in order to be heard in near proximity to hidden microphones. And that was a problem in the making of *Beggars of Life*, which was all about movement. Throughout the film, its many colorful characters are frequently in motion, either walking down a road or across a field or riding on trains, automobiles, or even a slow-moving bread-cart. When Wellman wants to indicate a character's mood, he will show us their feet.

A bit of dialogue (song lyrics actually) was first heard well into the sound version of the movie, in the scene when Oklahoma Red first enters the story. Paramount executives wanted the stout actor to arrive, stand in the midst of the hobo camp, and sing a hobo song. Wellman thought such a scene would prove too static, and the director asked Beery to instead walk into the camp while singing and carrying a barrel of moonshine. The soundman insisted it couldn't be done, and that the microphone couldn't be moved.

The director's near obsession with movement led to a solution, and something of an innovation. Others have been credited with first moving a microphone during the making of a film, but according to David O. Selznick, Wellman did it first for Paramount. Selznick made his claim to Kevin Brownlow, who included it in his 1968 book, *The Parade's Gone By*. "I was also present on the stage when a microphone was moved for the first time by Wellman, believe it or not. Sound was relatively new and at that time the sound engineer insisted that the microphone be steady. Wellman, who had quite a temper in those days, got very angry, took the microphone himself, hung it on a boom, gave orders to record—and moved it."

Though a few earlier Paramount releases had also utilized music and sound effects, *Beggars of Life* was notably the first studio release to include spoken dialogue. The film was released in September of 1928 as both a silent and sound film (the latter with added music, sound effects—including the dramatic sounds of a locomotive, and a bit of dialogue, all of which are now considered lost). The sound version played in larger markets like Madison and Milwaukee, while the silent version played in smaller towns and those markets not yet "wired for sound." Despite not being a full-fledged talkie, *Beggars of Life* remained in circulation for nearly two years, as both sound films and the Depression overtook the country.

Beggars of Life has long been a somewhat little known and little seen film. Within the last few years, however, things have begun to change. A rare surviving 16mm print of *Beggars of Life* (owned by the George Eastman Museum in Rochester, New York) was optically enlarged to 35mm, making it available to festivals and other special screenings. And earlier in 2017, *Beggars of Life* enjoyed its first real commercial release when Kino Lorber issued the George Eastman print on DVD/Blu-ray.

According to Wellman's son, *Beggars of Life* was the director's favorite among his silent movies. Not as grand in scope as *Wings*, *Beggars of Life* is, rather, a small masterpiece. It is also a film which speaks to our troubled times.

A significant find?
This piece appeared on the Louise Brooks Society blog on August 24, 2009.

The other day, I was scrolling through newspaper microfilm when I happened to notice a petite portrait of Louise Brooks. It wasn't something I was looking for, but there it was. It caught my eye. I suppose I've become trained to notice Brooks' image wherever it appears.

What I came across surprised me. It was something I had not seen before or even known about. And, as far as Brooks and film history is concerned, I think it may be a significant find.

What I came across was an item in a column by Louella Parsons. The clipping is dated February 1, 1929. At the time, Hollywood studios were undergoing the transition from silent films to talkies. Also undergoing change were the careers of many actors and actresses. Some, with weak voices or heavy accents, failed to make the transition to talking pictures.

According to the clipping I came across, Brooks sent a telegram to the famous, nationally syndicated columnist Louella Parsons asking her to help put out the word that her voice was not bad, and that the reason her voice was dubbed in the then just released *The Canary Murder Case* was that she was simply unavailable to do the job. (The film, released in 1929, was originally shot as a silent in 1928 and was adapted as a sound film.)

The column reads, "Louise Brooks sends a wire to this desk begging me to say that the reason Famous Players-Lasky used a voice substitute was because she could not leave New York when *The Canary Murder Case* was being synchronized. 'Please,' asks Louise, 'deny that they used a substitute because my voice was bad. I was tied up in New York and could not come to the coast. That is the real reason.' We are big minded and are not going to get Louise in bad if we can help it. So please heed the contents of her telegram."

What revelatory about this brief piece is that 1) it suggests Brooks was aware of the poor notices her voice was receiving in early reviews of *The Canary Murder Case*, and 2) it supports Brook's long held contention (debated by some film historians) that some studios knowingly wrecked the careers of actors—often using the "bad voice" gambit during this turbulent period in the industry's history.

Seemingly, Brooks' considered herself a victim of studio sabotage as far back as 1929. What's also interesting is that Brooks is here attempting to make her case in the court of public opinion. That's unusual. I don't think she ever did anything as proactive again—or at least until she turned to writing about film in the 1950's and 1960's.

Interestingly, in her own review of *The Canary Murder Case* which ran on February 8th, Parson commented "He was handicapped by no less a person than Louise Brooks, who plays the *Canary*. You are conscious that the words spoken do not actually emanate from the mouth of Miss Brooks and you feel that as much of her part as possible has been cut. She is unbelievably bad in a role that should have been well suited to her. Only long shots are permitted of her and even these are far from convincing when she speaks."

Brooks' part in *The Canary Murder Case* marked her last important role in an American silent film. With her career in turmoil, Brooks worked in Europe. (There, she made what many consider to be her three best films. Each was a silent.) When Brooks eventually returned to work in America in 1931, some newspapers and magazines referred to her attempted "comeback." A few mentioned her last starring role in *The Canary Murder Case*. All that would be available to the once popular actress were supporting roles in largely B-movies.

Did small pox kill *The Canary Murder Case?*
This piece appeared on the Louise Brooks Society blog on December 30, 2009.

I come across a lot of unusual things while researching Louise Brooks and her films. Here is one more example.

In the same June, 1929 issue of the *North Sacramento Journal* that carried an advertisement for a local showing of *The Canary Murder Case* at the Del Paso theater, the newspaper also ran an informational advertisement concerning a supposed small pox infestation at the same theater. Here is that advertisement.

> **READ THIS! — IMPORTANT!!**
>
> Some uninformed person has circulated the report that your theatre, the Del Paso, is infested with smallpox.
>
> There is nothing further from the truth and no better proof of this is that the theatre is open and doing business as usual.
>
> The Del Paso is one of the most sanitary theatres in the state.
> Your health is always guarded.
> Thank you.
>
> **BLUMENFELD THEATRE CIRCUIT**

According to Wikipedia, "Transmission of smallpox occurs through inhalation of airborne variola virus, usually droplets expressed from the oral, nasal, or pharyngeal mucosa of an infected person. It is transmitted from one person to another primarily through prolonged face-to-face contact with an infected person, usually within a distance of 6 feet, but can also be spread through direct contact with infected bodily fluids or contaminated objects (fomites) such as bedding or clothing. Rarely, smallpox has been spread by virus carried in the air in enclosed settings such as buildings, buses, and trains."

Apparently, it was believed by some back in 1929, one could become infected by sitting in a theater seat.

I didn't notice any later articles mentioning that people stayed away from the Del Paso and its June 7-8 screening of *The Canary Murder Case*, which starred William Powell and Louise Brooks. But, if the Del Paso was concerned enough to place a newspaper advertisement, I could imagine many individuals did not go the movies at a certain theater in north Sacramento in 1929. The Del Paso theater, located at 2120 Del Paso Blvd, burnt down on January 15, 1942. Due to wartime restrictions, the Blumenfeld circuit did not build a replacement until 1946, and the brand new Del Paso Theatre opened January 23, 1947. That theater closed in 1972, sat vacant for years, and was gutted by fire in July, 1990.

Louise Brooks Is Lulu in *Pandora's Box*

This piece appeared on Huffington Post on March 22, 2012. In 2018, I was pleased to see it quoted in a trailer for the film made by the British Film Institute.

These days, Frank Wedekind is best known as the author of *Spring Awakening*. His 1891 play about teenage sexuality was turned into a smash-hit by Duncan Sheik and Steven Sater. Their long running Broadway musical won eight Tony awards and has been staged all over the world.

Before *Spring Awakening*, Wedekind (1864-1918) was best known for his Lulu plays.

Those two "Lulu" plays, *Earth Spirit* (1895) and *Pandora's Box* (1904), were originally conceived of as a single work. Called a "monster tragedy," the Lulu plays tell the story of an alluring, somewhat petulant show-girl who rises in society through her relationships with wealthy, lustful men—like "moths around a flame." Eventually, after a series of unfortunate events, she falls into poverty and prostitution. The play's frank depiction of sexuality and violence, including lesbianism, murder and an encounter with Jack the Ripper, pushed the boundaries of what was considered acceptable literature.

Despite their provocative subject matter, the Lulu plays are among the most performed and adapted early 20th century dramas. There were two silent films, and as many as a dozen later movies and TV films based on *Pandora's Box* alone. Alban Berg's acclaimed opera, *Lulu* (1937), was based on Wedekind's work. As were the works of numerous other writers, poets, performance artists, comic artists, and rock musicians who found inspiration in the German playwright's words. Rufus Wainwright's *All Days Are Nights: Songs for Lulu* (2010) and the Lou Reed-Metallica collaboration, *Lulu* (2011), are two recent examples.

On Sunday, March 25th the Callanwolde Fine Arts Center in Atlanta, Ga. along with the Atlanta Chapter of the American Theatre Organ Society will screen the second film version of *Pandora's Box*, which stars Louise Brooks as Lulu. Ron Carter, silent film accompanist and Callanwolde House Organist, will accompany the film on Callanwolde's 60-rank Aeolian organ using the instrument as a symphony orchestra.

Pandora's Box is a film which can still shock and enthrall, even 80-plus years after its release. It is also a film whose reputation has ridden a roller-coaster of scorn and acclaim.

Pandora's Box made its world premiere in February of 1929 at the Gloria-Palast in Berlin; German reviews of the time were mixed. When *Pandora's Box* opened at a small art house in New York City in December of that same year, American newspaper and magazine critics were also ambivalent, even hostile.

Photoplay, one of the leading fan magazines of the time, noted "When the censors got through with this German-made picture featuring Louise Brooks, there was little left but a faint, musty odor. It is the story, both spicy and sordid, of a little dancing girl who spread evil everywhere without being too naughty herself. Interesting to American fans because it shows Louise, formerly an American ingénue in silent films, doing grand work as the evil-spreader."

Mordaunt Hall, critic for the *New York Times*, famously wrote, "Miss Brooks is attractive and she moves her head and eyes at the proper moment, but whether she is endeavoring to express joy, woe, anger or satisfaction it is often difficult to decide." Quinn Martin, critic at the New York *World*, echoed Hall's remarks when he stated, "It does occur to me that Miss Brooks, while one of the handsomest of all the screen girls I have seen, is still one of the most eloquently terrible actresses who ever looked a camera in the eye."

Variety put the nail in the coffin when its critic opined "Better for Louise Brooks had she contented exhibiting that supple form in two-reel comedies or Paramount features. *Pandora's Box*, a rambling thing that doesn't help her, nevertheless proves that Miss Brooks is not a dramatic lead."

Lulu has been described as a vamp or femme fatale, but in fact, she is a kind of naive, almost innocent character. As Brooks biographer Barry Paris put it, her "sinless sexuality hypnotizes and destroys the weak, lustful men around her." And not just men... Lulu's sexual magnetism knows few bounds, and this once controversial film features what may be the screen's first lesbian character.

At times, this G.W. Pabst-directed film—heavily censored in its day and still incomplete—can come off a little heavy handed, almost like a melodrama. In *Pandora's Box*, Brooks nevertheless reveals her considerable gifts as an actress through an individualized interpretation of her otherwise archetypical character. And largely because of Brooks' sensational performance, this more than 80 year-old film now enjoys a large reputation. Today, *Pandora's Box* is widely considered not only Brooks' best work, but one of the great masterpieces of the silent film era.

What is it that continues to attract contemporary viewers to *Pandora's Box*, and to its singular star? Perhaps, the answer lies in our ability to see beyond the film's melodramatic trappings, and to appreciate qualities found beneath its celluloid skin.

Lottie Eisner, the great German film critic, once described Brooks as "An astonishing actress endowed with an intelligence beyond compare." While Kevin Brownlow, the Academy Award-winning British film historian, described the actress as "One of the most remarkable personalities to be associated with films." Louise Brooks is certainly both of these, and more.

Those who catch the film Sunday night in Atlanta will be able to judge for themselves.

Music in *Pandora's Box*: Sid Kay's Fellows
This piece appeared on the Louise Brooks Society blog on April 29, 2012.

If you have seen *Pandora's Box*, then you may have noticed the musical group playing during the wedding reception. The name of the group, at times cut off by the camera or somewhat obscured by the movements of various characters, can be spotted on the group's drum kit. They are Sid Kay's Fellows.

As it turns out, they were a real musical act of the time. Founded in 1926 and led by Sigmund Petruschka ("Sid"—pictured center) and Kurt Kaiser ("Kay"), Sid Kay's Fellows were a popular ten member dance band in Berlin. This jazz ensemble performed at the Haus Vaterland (a leading Berlin night-spot) between 1930 and 1932. And in 1933, they accompanied the great Sidney Bechet during his recitals in the German capitol. Sid Kay's Fellows also accompanied various theatrical performances and played in Munich, Dresden, Frankfurt, Vienna, Budapest, Barcelona and elsewhere.

From what I have been able to find out, the group's depiction in *Pandora's Box* (filmed in late 1928) predates their career as recording artists. In 1933, when the Nazis came to power, Sid Kay's Fellows were forbidden to perform publicly. They disbanded, and transformed themselves into a studio orchestra and made recordings for the Jewish label Lukraphon. Most all of their recordings seem to date from around the early to mid-1930s. [Some of these scattered recordings, issued on 78rpm records, can now be found on an out-of-print multi-disc set called *Beyond Recall: A Record of Jewish Musical Life in Nazi Berlin, 1933-1938* (Bear Family Records, 2001).]

Not all that much is known about Sid Kay's Fellows. Under the name "John Kay," band leader Kurt Kaiser had also, at one time, been a member of the famous Weintraubs Syncopators (founded 1924), whose members included Friedrich Holländer. That group appeared in *The Blue Angel* (1930) starring Marlene Dietrich, a film for which Holländer wrote the music including the famous hit song, "Falling in Love Again." I'm uncertain if Kaiser was still playing with the group when they appeared in *The Blue Angel*. His fate from the early 1930s onward is little known.

Sigmund Petrushka (1903-1997) was born Sigmund Leo Friedmann in Leipzig, Germany and grew up in a Jewish orthodox family. In 1933, Sid Kay's Fellows disbanded and he, under the name Shabtai Petrushka, founded a new musical group while playing with The Orchestra of the Jewish Cultural Society and composing music for various plays. Using pseudonyms to disguise his Jewish background (as noted, there was a ban on Jewish musicians), Petrushka worked as a music arranger for Deutsche Gramophone and UFA films. In 1934, his fox-trot number, "Flying Hamburger," was recorded by James Kok for the Deutsche Gramophone label. In 1938, Petrushka was allowed to immigrate to Palestine, where his sister had been living since the 1920s.

Petrushka went on to a distinguished career: he joined the Palestine Broadcasting Service as composer, conductor and arranger of its orchestra. And, in the first decade of the independent State of Israel, Petrushka served as Deputy director of the Music Programs Department of "Kol Yerushalaym" ("Voice of Jerusalem"). In 1958, he was appointed the Director of Music Section in "Kol Israel" ("Voice of Israel"), a post he held until his retirement. Some of Petrushka's recordings from the mid-1930's can be heard on webpages devoted to Yiddish music.

If you are interested in finding out more, be sure and check out Michael H. Kater's *Different Drummers: Jazz in the Culture of Nazi Germany* (Oxford University Press, 1992). There are also many available CDs of music from the time, including *Berlin By Night* (EMI, 1991), *TanzSzene Berlin 1930* (Bob's Music, 2004), and *German Tango Bands 1925-1939* (Harlequin, 1999). I have each of them, and like each a lot. Some of their tracks can be heard on RadioLulu, the online radio station of the Louise Brooks Society.

When *Pandora's Box* debuted in Berlin in February of 1929, an orchestra playing a musical score accompanied the film. The score was reviewed in at least one of the Berlin newspapers. The score, however, seemingly does not survive. What is also not known is if the music of Sid Kay's Fellows, or any sort of jazz, played a part in the music of *Pandora's Box*.

More on Sid Kay's Fellows
This piece appeared on the Louise Brooks Society blog on October 20, 2012.

Earlier this week, I received an extraordinary email. It was from Israel, and it came from Dr. Uriel Adiv, the grandson of Shabtai Petrushka (Sigmund Petruschka), the noted German musician and composer and a co-founder of the Sid Kay's Fellows. That is the jazz combo seen in the Louise Brooks' film, *Pandora's Box* (1929).

Dr. Uriel Adiv wrote in response to an earlier LBS blog, "Music in *Pandora's Box*: Sid Kay's Fellows." He sent images and information, and promised to send more.

Here are a couple of the scans which he sent, the front and reverse of a vintage flyer promoting the group. Dr. Uriel Adiv wrote, "You can see my grandpa playing the trumpet on the upper right side as well as playing the accordion on the middle of the right side."

Not only does its collage design (by Umbo, a noted Bauhaus artist) reflect a modernist aesthetic, but it also contains valuable bits of information about the widespread popularity of this group (which I hadn't known) who performed for various stage, film, and dance productions. Also of note is the fact that the group was managed by impresario Hanns Wollsteiner, who early on helped promote Marlene Dietrich.

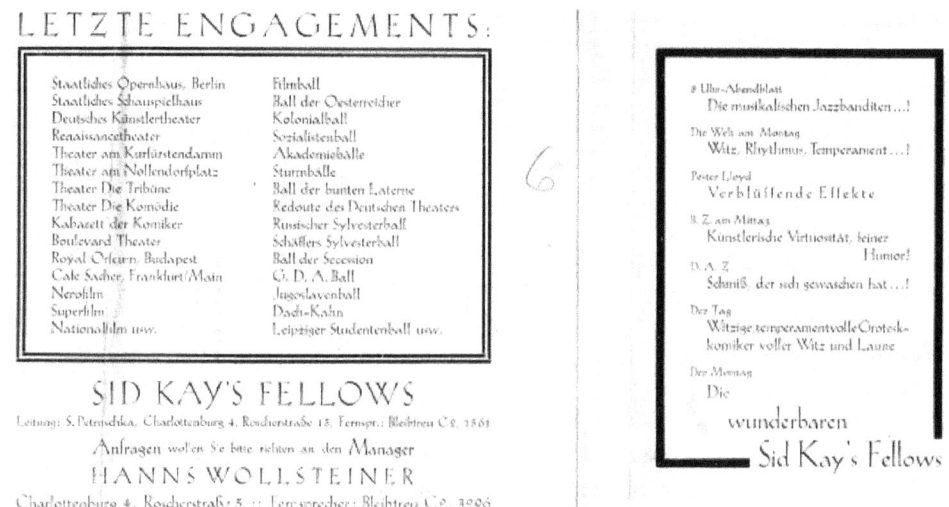

Lulu by the Bay: Louise Brooks is legend in *Pandora's Box*
This piece appeared on SFGate on July 12, 2012.

On Saturday July 14th, the San Francisco Silent Film Festival will show *Pandora's Box*. Today, it is considered one of the great films of all time, largely in part because of the stunning performance given by Louise Brooks in the role of Lulu. Saturday's event marks the second time in the Festival's 17 year history that G.W. Pabst's 1929 masterpiece has been shown. However, it is the first time that this very special version of the film has been seen anywhere in the San Francisco Bay Area.

For locals, and for Louise Brooks fans everywhere, this San Francisco screening is a must attend event. That's because the San Francisco Silent Film Festival is showing a new and true, frame-by-frame, digital restoration of *Pandora's Box*. And by all reports, it is gorgeous. Not available on DVD, this restoration has only been shown twice before anywhere in the world. And what's more, the team responsible for the restoration are local residents Angela Holm, David Ferguson and Vincent Pirozzi. They will be introducing the event at the Castro theater.

Controversial, censored, cut, and critically disregarded when it first debuted, *Pandora's Box* is today considered one of great silent films. This restoration, the Festival's centerpiece event, was funded by silent movie enthusiast and Louise Brooks partisan Hugh Hefner. It may come as close as we will ever get to director Pabst's original vision—and Brooks' original luminescence.

This screening is also significant as it marks something of return for the character of Lulu, whose creator was almost born in San Francisco. As most filmgoers know, *Pandora's Box* is based on two plays, *Earth Spirit* (1895) and *Pandora's Box* (1904), by the German writer Frank Wedekind (1864–1918). Today, he is best known as the author of *Spring Awakening* (1891), which six years ago was turned into a hugely popular Broadway musical.

What's little known is that Wedekind's parents were European immigrants resident in San Francisco in the years following the 1849 Gold Rush. His German father was a physician and progressive democrat whose participation in the Revolutions of 1848 (in the German states) led him to exile in America. Wedekind's Swiss mother was an attractive singer and actress twenty-three years his junior. This unlikely and unconventional union has led some scholars to speculate that the relationship between Wedekind's parents could have served as a model for the similar, unconventional relationship between the older and respected Dr. Schon and the much younger showgirl Lulu in *Pandora's Box*.

Of course, such things are open to interpretation. However, what we do know is that Friedrich Wedekind and Emilie Kammerer's second child—the future writer—was conceived in San Francisco, and born in what is now Hanover, Germany. According to Wedekind's biography, early in the pregnancy the homesick couple risked a return to their homeland, and stayed. And that's where Benjamin Franklin Wedekind, named for the free-thinking American writer, was born in 1864.

To mark the occasion of the first ever showing of the restored *Pandora's Box* in San Francisco, what follows is a brief, discursive history of the film's reception in the United States and the greater Bay Area.

Pandora's Box had its world premiere in February of 1929 at the Gloria–Palast theater in Berlin. German reviews of the time were mixed, even dismissive. (See the essay in the Festival program for a fuller account.) Some months later, when *Pandora's Box* opened at a single theater in New York City, American newspaper and magazine critics were similarly ambivalent, and even hostile.

In its now infamous review, the *New York Times* critic stated, "In an introductory title the management sets forth that it has been prevented by the censors from showing the film in its entirety, and it also apologizes for what it termed 'an added saccharine ending'." Adding salt to the wound, the *Times* critic noted, "Miss Brooks is attractive and she moves her head and eyes at the proper moment, but whether she is endeavoring to express joy, woe, anger or satisfaction it is often difficult to decide." Ouch.

Despite poor reviews, the film drew crowds. The *New York Sun* reported that *Pandora's Box* " . . . has smashed the Fifty-fifth Street Playhouse's box office records," and was held over for another week. With its brief run completed, *Pandora's Box* fell into an obscurity from which it barely escaped.

Things have changed since the late 1920s, and the reputation of *Pandora's Box* has continued to grow. The film has been screened numerous times in the last few decades, and perhaps nowhere more often than in the San Francisco Bay Area. Chances are if you are still reading this article you saw an earlier print at the Castro Theater in San Francisco or the Pacific Film Archive in Berkeley, where between those two venues the film has been shown nearly two dozen times since the mid-1970s.

As far as I have been able to document, the first screening of *Pandora's Box* in the City of San Francisco took place at the old Surf Theater in January of 1974, as part of a double bill with *The Last Laugh*. A couple of years earlier, in October of 1972, the Pacific Film Archive had screened it in Berkeley in what could have been one of the film's earliest East Bay screenings.

One of those early East Bay screenings was likely prompted by film critic Pauline Kael, who was then living in the Bay Area and had a hand in local film exhibition. At that time, Kael was also corresponding with Louise Brooks, who was living in Rochester, New York. On at least one occasion in their exchange of letters, Kael implored Brooks to come to the Bay Area to be present at a screening of *Pandora's Box*. But Brooks, who was reclusive, wouldn't budge.

In all likelihood, the very first screening of *Pandora's Box* in the Bay Area took place in 1962, when the Monterey Peninsula College in Monterey screened a print of *Pandora's Box* as part of its Peninsula Film Seminar. The event was organized around a visit by Brooks' early champion and friend James Card, who brought with him a small collection of rare films, including a messy, unrestored version of the Pabst masterpiece.

Card's print of *Pandora's Box* was probably one of the very few prints of the film in the United States. And in all likelihood, *Pandora's Box* and the other films shown at the Seminar were works the attendees had only heard of but not seen.

According to newspaper reports of the time, the Peninsula Film Seminar was a big deal in local film circles. And notably, it was attended by Bay Area cognoscenti like Pauline Kael, future San Francisco poet Laureate Jack Hirschman, a few East Bay film promoters involved with the Berkeley Film Guild, and others.

And there, in Monterey, the seeds were first sown for the film's now large reputation in the Bay Area.

Lulu in New York: *Pandora's Box* at Film Forum
This piece appeared on Huffington Post on March 16, 2016.

Today, *Pandora's Box* is considered a classic, a masterpiece of the silent era and a landmark work in the history of world cinema. Its reputation is due largely to the riveting, red hot performance given by its star, Louise Brooks, in the role of Lulu.

Few can match Brooks' intensity and erotic allure. Pauline Kael called her Lulu "The archetype of the voracious destructive women." Brooks is that, and more. In fact, she's stunning—and those who see the film for the first time often say they can't take their eyes off the actress.

Pandora's Box and its star, however, have not always enjoyed the reputation they do today. When the film first showed in New York—back in December of 1929—it received mostly negative reviews. Just about everyone, including its star, thought it stunk.

On March 19th, New Yorkers will have a chance to judge for themselves when Film Forum screens a 35mm print of *Pandora's Box* as part of "*It Girls, Flappers, Jazz Babies & Vamps.*" The series showcases some of the silver screen's provocative early sex symbols.

Pandora's Box, a German-made film directed by the highly regarded G.W. Pabst, premiered in Berlin in February of 1929; reviews were mixed, even dismissive. Some months later, when *Pandora's Box* opened at a single theater, the 55th Street Playhouse in New York, American newspaper and magazine critics were similarly ambivalent, and sometimes hostile.

Photoplay, one of the leading fan magazines of the time, wrote "When the censors got through with this German-made picture featuring Louise Brooks, there was little left but a faint, musty odor." *Billboard* had a similar take, "This feature spent several weeks in the censor board's cutting room: and the result of its stay is a badly contorted drama that from beginning to end reeks with sex and vice that have been so crudely handled as not even to be spicily entertaining. Louise Brooks and Fritz Kortner are starred, with Miss Brooks supposed to be a vampire who causes the ruin of everyone she meets. How anyone could fall for la belle Brooks with the clothes she wears in this vehicle is beyond imagination."

The *New York Times* went further, "Miss Brooks is attractive and she moves her head and eyes at the proper moment, but whether she is endeavoring to express joy, woe, anger or satisfaction it is often difficult to decide." The critic for the *New York World* echoed the *Times*, "It does occur to me that Miss Brooks, while one of the handsomest of all the screen girls I have seen, is still one of the most eloquently terrible actresses who ever looked a camera in the eye."

The critics, it seemed, were ganging up. The *New Yorker* dismissed the film. As did the *New York Post*, who described it as "a rather dull underworld offering which makes very little sense." *Film Daily* thought the film "too sophisticated for any but art theater audiences." And the *New York Herald Tribune* said "Louise Brooks acts vivaciously but with a seeming blindness as to what it is all about."

Variety put the nail in the coffin when its opined "Better for Louise Brooks had she contented exhibiting that supple form in two-reel comedies or Paramount features. *Pandora's Box*, a rambling thing that doesn't help her, nevertheless proves that Miss Brooks is not a dramatic lead."

2ND BIG WEEK PANDORA'S BOX
With LOUISE BROOKS—FRITZ KORTNER
55th ST. PLAYHOUSE Just East of 7th Ave.
Continuous 2 to Midnight

Despite such poor reviews, the film managed to draw an audience, albeit a modest art-house crowd. After the *New York Sun* reported *Pandora's Box* "has smashed the Fifty-fifth Street Playhouse's box office records," the film was held over for another two weeks.

With its New York run ended, *Pandora's Box* fell into an obscurity from which it would take decades to overcome. By then, sound had come in and poorly reviewed silent films from abroad were little in demand. Though exhibition records are fragmentary, the film was seldom if ever shown in the United States.

In fact, in the decades that followed, only one other screening is known to have taken place—in 1931 in New Jersey at a second-run house not above showing sensational or exploitative fare. Newspaper ads for the Little Theater in Newark warned "Adults Only," and *Pandora's Box*, synchronized with "thrilling" sound effects and English titles, was promoted as "The German sensation that actually reveals most of the evils of the world" offering "Raw reality! A bitter exposé of things you know but never discuss."

With its reputation in ruins, the film was little seen and little regarded, even by film curators. In 1943, Iris Barry, head of the Museum of Modern Art's film department, met with Brooks, who was then living in New York. Barry's opinion carried considerable weight (and did so for decades to come) in the film world; she told Brooks the museum would not acquire a copy of *Pandora's Box* for its collection, because "it had no lasting value."

Times change, and so do reputations. In the mid-1950s, *Pandora's Box* was rediscovered by a handful of European archivists and historians. Their enthusiasm would cross the Atlantic, and in the United States, the film was almost single-handedly championed by James Card, the founding film curator at the George Eastman Museum in Rochester. Year by year, screening by screening, a new and positive critical consensus grew around the once much maligned film.

Cut to 2006, the year which marked the Brooks' centenary. New York's Film Forum marked the occasion by screening a 35mm print of the film; remarkably, during its short run, *Pandora's Box* was reported to be the second highest grossing independent film in the United States.

In his acclaimed 1989 biography of Brooks, Barry Paris wrote: "A case can be made that *Pandora's Box* was the last of the silent films—not literally, but aesthetically. On the threshold of its premature death, the medium in *Pandora* achieved near perfection in form and content."

It's that "near perfection"—dark and riveting, that draws audiences time and again. *Pandora's Box* will be shown at Film Forum in New York (209 West Houston St. west of 6th Ave.) on Saturday, March 19 at 7:20 p.m. Steve Sterneron will accompany the film on piano.

The Lost History of *Pandora's Box* in the United States

This piece appeared on the Louise Brooks Society blog on June 25, 2018. Two days later, in a German-language newspaper of the time, I found the record of another screening of Pandora's Box; this one took place May 10-12, 1930 at the Acme Theater in New York City

It is widely believed that *Pandora's Box* was first shown in the United States at the 55th Street playhouse in December of 1929. It is also long been believed that the first post-1929 American screening of the Louise Brooks' film took place on June 9, 1958 at the Eastman House in Rochester, New York.

The long, almost 30 year gap in the film's American exhibition record is explained by a couple of widely held assumptions. One is that the film was poorly received when it debuted in New York City in late 1929, and, with sound films dominating American screens at the time, there was little if any demand for silent films from Germany. The second is that prior to 1960 the Eastman House had the only known American print of the film.*

Both assumptions are incorrect.

Just a few days ago I uncovered new information which adds a number of previously unknown details to the film's otherwise sparse exhibition history in America.

My first discovery was a clipping and a listing for what could be or was the first public screening of *Pandora's Box* in the United States. A brief item in the *Jersey Journal* on November 1, 1929 states the film would open the following day, on Saturday,

November 2 at the 55th Street Playhouse in New York City. That's nearly a month before it was believed to have opened. I also came across a November 3 listing (shown below) in the New York *Daily News* suggesting the film, under the title *Box of Pandora*, was playing that day.

But then the records stopped, as if the film had stopped showing after just a day or two (if it did in fact show at all). The 55th Street Playhouse—an art house which specialized in foreign films—replaced *Box of Pandora* with *Secrets of Nature*, second series, an UFA Production.

Broadway Movies

NEW FILMS.

CAMEO—"The Dancer of Barcelona," with Lily Damita.

CENTRAL—"Paris," with Irene Bordoni. Thursday night.

FILM GUILD—"Arsenal," with foreign cast.

55TH STREET—"Box of Pandora," with foreign cast.

In all likelihood, the reason *Box of Pandora* stopped showing just after it had reportedly opened was censorship. As is well known and documented elsewhere, this once controversial film was subject to censorship not only in Europe, but also in the United States. By the time the film (re)premiered on November 30th (or December 1 or 2—I have found newspaper clippings suggesting each date as the probable new opening date), nearly a third of it, by various accounts, was missing. The 55th Street Playhouse, the theater that debuted and widely advertised the film (including to NYC's non-English speaking population), projected a statement lamenting the film had been cut. The theater also apologized for the "added saccharine ending" in which Lulu joins the Salvation Army.

Nevertheless, *Pandora's Box*, or *Box of Pandora* as it was sometimes titled in advertisements and listing from the time, enjoyed an extended run. Despite its incomplete state and the generally poor reviews, the film did well, so much so the *New York Sun* reported *Pandora's Box* ". . . has smashed the Fifty-fifth Street Playhouse's box office records. It will therefore be held for another week." In fact, the film played about two weeks (at a time most films only played one), with the last known screening taking place on December 13, 1929, according to a listing in the Brooklyn *Standard Union*. (As newspapers didn't list every film showing every day, and some theaters—especially smaller theaters—didn't advertise every day, these records may not be exact, with exhibition records sometimes needing to be pieced together through various sources.)

94

After that, it has long been believed, *Pandora's Box* fell into obscurity and was not shown again in the United States until James Card screened the film in 1958 at the Eastman House's Dryden Theater in Rochester, New York.

Some ten or so years ago, and quite by chance, I stumbled across a few clippings related to a 1931 screening of *Pandora's Box* in Newark, New Jersey. I had been scrolling through microfilm looking for material on *It Pays to Advertise* or *God's Gift to Women* (both 1931 releases) when I came across a brief article and a couple of advertisements for a screening of the G.W. Pabst film at Newark's Little theater, starting May 16.

These two advertisements contain some interesting details. They note, for instance, that the film was shown with English titles and synchronized, "thrilling sound effects"! While the nature of these sub-titles and sound effects is unknown—they suggest there was at least one print prepared sometime after 1929 for American exhibition. Just as interesting is the fact that the film was advertised for "Adults Only." Like the 55th Street Playhouse in NYC, the Little theatre in Newark was a rep-house or art house which typically showed foreign films and travel films; however, it was not above showing what some considered sensational fair.

As mentioned earlier, a few days ago I found three more instances of the exhibition of *Pandora's Box* in the United States. One predates the 1931 Newark screening mentioned above, while the other two follow it.

On January 26, 1930, as *Box of Pandora*, the film opened at another Little Theater, this one in Baltimore, Maryland. The film, a silent version which was promoted as an "Ultra-Sophisticated Drama," ran for one week, until February 1, 1930. In writing about the film, a critic for one of the Baltimore newspapers thought it worthwhile and well handled, though felt it suffered from cuts made by the Maryland Board of Motion Picture Censors.

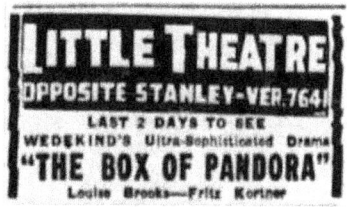

Four years after it debuted in New York City, *Box of Pandora* returned to the Big Apple, this time to the 5th Ave. Theater (Broadway at 28th St.) starting on December 5, 1933. Again billed as an "adults only" film and tagged with the words "Sin Lust Evil!"—it ran (continuously between 9:30 am to 11:00 pm) for three days, through December 7. This time (see below), the film, seemingly, has fallen into near exploitation fair. And notably, neither Brooks' nor Pabst's names are mentioned.

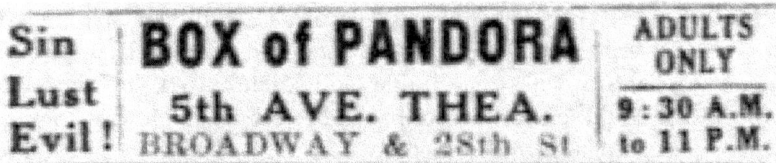

The third instance of a screening of *Pandora's Box* which I came across is one of the most fascinating! I didn't find an advertisement, only this passing reference in the *Wisconsin State Journal*, which was published in Madison.

Remarkably, this Sunday playhouse program took place on May 6, 1934 at Taliesin, the one-time home, studio, school, and country estate of Frank Lloyd Wright. Built by the famed architect and located in southwestern Wisconsin near Spring Green (about 50 miles from Madison), Taliesin served as Wright's home at the time, with its playhouse acting as a local rep-house which showed foreign and art films. (I found listings for other movies shown there in 1934, but no specific mention as to whether or not Wright attended these screenings.) This version of the Pabst film, termed "an outstanding German production," was shown with English subtitles.

> The playhouse program Sunday will consist of a G. W. Pabst film, "The Box of Pandora", an outstanding German production (English subtitles); "Old King Cole", color Silly Symphony and short subjects.

Evidently, from the newly uncovered records noted above, there was one or possibly two or more prints of *Pandora's Box* (one silent with English subtitles, another with synchronized sound effects?) in circulation in the United States in the early 1930s. If I were to guess, I would suggest that this print or these prints were likely circulated by a distributor which served the art-house or rep-house circuit. (One such distributor was Moviegraphs—the exchange that handled distribution of *Pandora's Box* in New York state in 1929; in 1932, as surviving records indicate, it applied for a new exhibition license for the film.)

Admittedly, there was little interest in *Pandora's Box* in the United States after 1929. Compared to most other films, it was rarely exhibited. The four records I've uncovered may be the only instances of screenings of the film in America in the 1930s. Or, perhaps, there are others, like an undocumented one-off screening at a university.

Someday, additional records may be found, and the remarkable, lost history of *Pandora's Box* in the United States will be further revealed.

* (This assumption, that there was only one print of *Pandora's Box* in the United States prior to 1960, begs the question as to what happened to the copy of the film which Iris Barry deemed of little value and infamously rejected adding to the collection of the New York Museum of Modern Art in 1943.)

The BFI Re-Opens *Pandora's Box*
This piece appeared on PopMatters on December 12, 2017.

Pamela Hutchinson thinks *Pandora's Box* is a confounding film. The German melodrama, which stars Louise Brooks as Lulu, is now considered one of the great films of the silent era. However, it wasn't always so. As Hutchinson states in her just published book, *Pandora's Box* (BFI Film Classics), the 1929 film failed commercially at first, then soared to popularity long after it might have been forgotten. "It is a masterpiece that has been mistreated and misunderstood," the author notes in her introduction.

Hutchinson, a London-based film critic who edits the Silent London website and writes on early film for the *Guardian* newspaper and *Sight & Sound*, has recently penned a book on this now iconic work. While exploring the history of its making, Hutchinson also challenges many of the assumptions around its legend. This is a book full of historical detail—but as much as it is scholarly, it's also lots of fun. As Hutchinson wryly notes in her introduction, "Exploring the film entails a journey back and forth between Europe and America, and occasionally into the gutter."

According to Hutchinson, Pandora's Box (*Die Büchse der Pandora*) is the result of a "creative tension between two of film history's most unusual characters." Louise Brooks (1906-1985) was an American actress, "a reckless hedonist, a dancer turned movie actress with a riotous love life." The Austrian-born G.W. Pabst (1885–1967) was "a serious and diligent actor turned director with a passion for the cinema and social justice." Their working relationship while making *Pandora's Box* (as well as in their subsequent 1929 film *The Diary of a Lost Girl*) was "dominated by conflict and a toxic sexual frisson."

As Hutchinson observes, Brooks and Pabst are linked in other ways as well. "Each knew both the warm critical acclaim and the cold shoulder of the industry. They were fiercely opposed to censorship and artistic timidity, and yet the films they made together were mutilated in the name of morality."

Hutchinson's book looks back to place *Pandora's Box* in its historical context; it also looks forward and investigates how this still popular old film speaks to new audiences. Already out in England, *Pandora's Box* (BFI Film Classics) is released in the US in December.

TG: You've just authored a new book on the 1929 film *Pandora's Box*. How did the project come about?

PH: The BFI Film Classics list is quite a well-known series, over here in Britain at least. One day someone asked me which film I would write one on if I ever had the chance and it just occurred to me – *Pandora's Box*. Sometimes you backtrack on these spur-of-the-minute ideas, but the more I thought about it, the more I realised that this film needed a monograph of its own, that there was so much to say about it, that it was a film that still resonated with audiences, and that writing a book on it would be fascinating.

TG: Was it challenge to write an entire book on a single film? I suppose some might wonder how much there is to say.

PH: There is far more to say about *Pandora's Box* than I could fit into this book! I had to edit judiciously. The book combines history and criticism, as well as talking about how the film endures. I wanted to give as full a picture as possible of how the film came to be made, from Frank Wedekind writing his plays to the careers of G.W. Pabst and his crew and actors.

Also, I walk through *Pandora's Box* act by act, drawing out more of the film's meaning. There were so many questions about the film that intrigued me—and I wanted to answer them all. Why does Dr Schön drop his cigarette? Why is there a menorah in Lulu's apartment? What does the letter K stand for? Then I gave over some space to talking about the film's legacy, and what the image of Louise Brooks as Lulu stands for now.

TG: The book's description states that you "revisit and challenge many assumptions made about the film, its lead character and its star." How so?

PH: Louise Brooks is the voice of *Pandora's Box*—she has written about the film and been interviewed about it more than anyone else involved in the production. This delights me, and I have a huge respect for her intellect, and her analysis of the film. But I wanted to dig deeper. Much of what she has said about the film has been taken as gospel, but there is often another side to the story.

I'm especially thinking about the character of Countess Geschwitz, and Alice Robert's performance. I wanted to reclaim the Countess as a passionate, heroic character. And there's a lot of criticism from elsewhere that I think confuses what Pabst is trying to do in his adaptation and he and Brooks are doing in the portrayal of Lulu. It's always good to look at an old film with fresh eyes, but still with an understanding of the circumstances in which it was made.

TG: What did you discover in writing the book that surprised you, or might surprise readers?

PH: Well, there's a credit on the film that always looked wrong to me, and I wanted to investigate that. In the end I discovered quite a lot about the man credited with editing the film—including the fact that he almost definitely had nothing to do with cutting *Pandora's Box*. He was a fascinating character, though, and while he didn't edit the film, he did have an important role to play in its reception. In America, at least.

TG: What does your book reveal that someone who has seen the film might not realize?

PH: Lots, I hope! For example, did you know that Pabst nearly made the film with Lili Damita as Lulu in 1926? I tried to cram as much information and informed critical thinking into the book as possible. I have covered the production history, and looked at the contribution of each actor and each key member of the crew, but I have trawled the imagery, too. It's almost impossible to tear your eyes away from Brooks when watching *Pandora's Box*, but if you do, Pabst is telling you the whole story in his design for the film, from the lighting, to all those ominous objects in the background.

TG: You are an English critic. What standing does *Pandora's Box* have in the

UK? And what standing does Louise Brooks have as well?

PH: Put it this way, the BFI Southbank (what used to be called the National Film Theatre), screened *Pandora's Box* four times last January, and then they showed it again in November, on its biggest screen, to coincide with the release of the book. I'm introducing the film at screenings up and down the country too. It's very well liked here – I mean, it's even set in London.

Pandora's Box is considered one of the greats of silent film, and taught in several university film studies departments. Louise Brooks is every bit as popular here as she is in America I think – you see her image in magazines and in posters all the time. Thanks to *Pandora's Box*, she'll always be a European star as well as an American one. She both defines the Roaring Twenties and stands outside it—she is timeless.

TG: The book's description states that your book "investigates how the film speaks to new audiences." How so?

PH: *Pandora's Box* will always feel modern—Lulu will always shock and enthral. And the image of Brooks as Lulu has been repeated and homaged so many times that the film is not confined to 1929, or "the silent era" or "Weimar Cinema". Lulu, this particular Lulu, is everywhere. How wonderful for each person who discovers the film, to then discover the scintillating character of Brooks herself and her intelligent, provocative writing.

TG: *Pandora's Box* contains a lot of great moments. What is your favorite scene in the film?

PH: This is a very difficult question. I think it has to be the backstage scene. Not so much for the confrontation in the prop room, but for the way Pabst manipulates all that complex action in the wings, and Brooks being so very Brooks, fighting the management with all her might. It's a fiery sequence, full of humour as well as foreboding, and the seething emotions of the main players. And that moment when Lulu and Dr Schön first see each other? Electric.

TG: Do you consider yourself a "fan" of Louise Brooks?

PH: Of course. She was a wonderful actress, and an intelligent and perceptive writer. She lights up the screen even in her smaller roles. In her Pabst films she's incandescent. I think she had a lot of sadness in her life, but she was full of fire and sexuality and she was so independent. She stood up for herself, and for other women.

In every word of hers that you read you sense her passions as well as her contradictions. She deserved better from her life in many ways, but she left us something, a fierce independence of spirit to aspire to.

TG: When did you first become aware of Louise Brooks?

PH: I was far too young to understand a word of it really, but I saw a snippet of a BBC documentary about Brooks (see below) — it must have been when I was six years old. I thought she looked like Betty Boop, who I thought was just brilliant, but the voiceover said that she had come from Hollywood to Europe and then she had been forgotten about. I thought that was so sad, as if she had left home and got lost.

But the image of Brooks, of her big eyes framed by that dinky bob, and her wide smile, that really stayed with me. I didn't take an interest in silent films until a decade later, but Brooks was always special to me.

TG: What's next for you?

PH: Well I always seem to be busy, writing about film as well as lecturing. I'm introducing *Pandora's Box* at lots of screenings around the UK to promote the book, which is bound to be fun. I have lots of small projects on the go, including a small book on cinema that I'm editing. I'd love to write another book some day, so fingers crossed I get to do that in the not-too-distant future.

A dense atmosphere of intense emotions
This piece appeared on the Fandor website in November, 2015.

By the time G.W. Pabst came to make *Diary of a Lost Girl* in 1929, the film had already picked-up a lot of baggage.

Diary of a Lost Girl is based on a bestselling book by Margarete Böhme, a popular German writer of the time. First published in 1905 as *Tagebuch einer Verlorenen, Von einer Toten* (or *The Diary of a Lost Girl, by One Who is Dead*), the book tells the story of a naive teenager who is seduced by her father's assistant, conceives a child, is disowned by her family, and has her baby taken away. This "lost girl"—named Thymian in the book and played by Louise Brooks on screen—is placed in a repressive home for wayward girls, from which she escapes and eventually finds refuge in prostitution.

To describe *Tagebuch einer Verlorenen* as melodramatic, sensational, or notorious would be something of an understatement. A bestseller, the book was translated into 14 languages and published around the world. It inspired not only a cult following (thought to be a genuine diary, teenage girls wrote to Böhme asking where Thymian was buried), but also a popular sequel, a parody, a stage play which was censored, and a genre's worth of imitators. There were pirated editions, and even a lawsuit (Böhme sued for slander after a newspaper wrote that only a whore could have written such a book). Not surprisingly, there were two prior film adaptions, one in 1912 and one in 1918. The latter was censored, as was the film (also released in 1918) made from the book's sequel.

Advertisements for Pabst's film proclaimed its literary origins, with some noting Böhme's book had sold more than 1,200,000 copies. In making his film, Pabst took the opportunity to turn the book's familiar story and more lurid moments into a work of social criticism. Pabst updated the story, bringing it from the corseted turn-of-the-century Wilhelmina Germany to the present day—wild Weimar Germany in the late Twenties. (Brooks' observations of Weimar Berlin and of working with Pabst are featured in Richard Leacock's revealing *Lulu in Berlin*.)

In *Diary*, as in the earlier *Pandora's Box* (also 1929 and also with Louise Brooks), Pabst was focused on the role of sex in society. The seduction scene (cut from most prints, it survives in the restoration but looks the worst for wear) was conceived as a kind-of ballet and directed, according to Brooks, as "a series of subtle, almost wordless manoeuvres between an 'innocent' young girl and a wary lecher." The reformatory scene—which Brooks referred to as the "orgasm scene"—features a sadistic headmistress (played by Valeska Gert) who beats a gong to which the wayward girls are made to exercise. And the brothel scene—considered shocking in 1929—show the actress at her most erotic, dancing and arching her swanlike neck in sexual submission. One critic even called *Diary* a "fictionalized documentary" on the moral and social climate of the country.

For some, it was all too much. Groups that objected to Böhme's book now objected to Pabst's film. The German Evangelical Church, a German morality association, a national organization of Protestant girl's boarding schools, a national organization for young women, and others all voiced their complaints.

Diary debuted in Vienna (Pabst was Austrian) on September 27th, and opened in Berlin on October 15, 1929. By December 5th, the film had been banned by the German state censor and withdrawn from circulation. Censors objected to the death of the housekeeper at the hands of an abortionist, the scene of Thymian's seduction, the removal of her baby in a tiny coffin, the portrayal of the girl's reformatory, sexual activity at the brothel, and more. Only after cuts were made was the ban lifted; on January 6, 1930 the film was rereleased.

Diary of a Lost Girl went on to play across Europe, but was additionally cut to satisfy the demands of local censors where ever it did show. The film's screenwriter noted ". . . entire filmed sequences were cut without mercy . . . . In one version, if I remember rightly, they cut 450 meters, and either in this or another version, they made another 54 further cuts. . . . The film comes to an end shortly after the middle of our script, inconclusively and incomprehensively. I once saw it myself at a cinema in Paris and stayed in my seat at the end because I thought the film had broken."

In a sense, *Diary of a Lost Girl* was broken. To critics and viewers, the censored film made little sense. And what meaning they could draw from the film they didn't like. *Diary* received poor reviews—but for reasons which sometimes had little to do with the movie itself. Some critics instead devoted their columns to attacking Böhme's novel. Among them was Siegfried Kracauer, a critic at the time of the film's release. In his famous 1946 book *From Caligari to Hitler: A Psychological History of the German Film*, he reflected on the Pabst film and its literary source—"the popularity of which among the philistines of the past generation rested upon the slightly pornographic frankness with which it recounted the private life of some prostitutes from a morally elevated point of view."

Brooks claimed to be unaware as to what *Diary* was all about. However, the actress brought to her role something of which Pabst was unaware. When Brooks was 9 years old, she was molested by a neighbor, and then blamed for provoking the incident. It was then that Brooks became what she admitted to being later in life, one of the "lost".

Despite the emotional intensity the actress brought to her role, publications generally gave Brooks poor reviews. In 1929, *Variety* described her as "monotonous in the tragedy which she has to present." In 1930, however, future French director Marcel Carné praised her in *Cinèmagazine*, as would the Surrealist poet Philippe Soupault, who described Brooks as an actress of the first rank in the pages of *L'Europe nouvelle*. In 1938, an Italian critic wrote, "She suffers and remains unmoved. And precisely this is what counts most: with an almost total 'lack of acting,' she has created around herself a dense atmosphere of intense emotions."

Without Brooks, *Diary* might be little regarded today. Its melodrama, leavened by a lightly drawn social message, bits of visual poetry, and suggested eroticism, all hang on Brooks' presence. Released as it was in a heavily censored form and as a silent at the beginning of the sound era—and with poor reviews trailing it, *Diary* failed to make much of a splash. It quickly faded from view. The film was not shown in the United States until the mid-1950s, and didn't have a theatrical release in America until the 1980's.

It would take time for audiences to catch-up with Brooks' remarkable performance, as well as with the film's still relevant message. This new reconstruction and restoration (remastered in a 2K high-definition video transfer from archival 35mm elements) released by Kino Lorber gives viewers a chance to see the film anew—almost as Pabst intended.

What a trippple bill of classic silent films!
This piece appeared on the Louise Brooks Society blog on January 20, 2016.

Over the years, I have found hundreds if not thousands of newspaper advertisements for Louise Brooks' films. Many of them are of little interest beyond the record of a Brooks' film having shown in a particular place on a particular date. But some stand out, especially if they note a premiere, or include unusual graphics or an usual opening act (like bandleader John Philip Sousa, pianist Art Tatum, or dancer turned actor George Raft), or.

Others stand out if they promote a Brooks' double bill—a somewhat rare occurrence back in the 20's and 30s. Over the years, I have found a few vintage advertisements promoting *Love Em and Leave Em* with *Just Another Blonde*, or *Now We're in the Air* together with *The City Gone Wild*. In both instances, these paired films were likely shown together because they were released around the same time (not because Brooks was in both films).

Another double bill I once came across, dating from 1931, featured the Brooks' talkie *It Pays to Advertise* (1931) with G.W. Pabst's *The White Hell of Pitz Palu* (1929), starring Leni Reifenstahl. One could only guess what movie patrons thought of that odd pairing?

Here is one of the most distinguished advertisements I have ever found, a rather brilliant trippple bill. From the LBS archive comes this November 1930 newspaper advertisement for the Ursulines theater in Paris. The evening's program begins with G.W. Pabst's *Joyless Street* (1925), starring Greta Garbo, followed by Howard Hawk's *A Girl in Every Port* (1928), starring Louise Brooks, followed by Pabst's *Diary of a Lost Girl* (1929), also starring Louise Brooks. What a line-up!

I wish I could have been there. . . . and through the magic of the internet, I can—at least in my imagination. Below is an exterior view of its rather famous facade. Today, the Ursulines theater survives, and thrives. In fact, it has an illustrious history as well as its own Wikipedia page.

According to Wikipedia, "It is one of the oldest cinemas in Paris to have kept its facade and founder's vision" as a "venue for art and experimental cinema." (And according to the Cinema Treasures website, "This little theatre with a balcony has a very charming facade looking like a romantic country house.") The historic cinema opened on January 21, 1926, and over the years, was a cinematic home to the Surrealist and other members of the Parisian avant-garde.

In fact, between 1926 and 1957, a numbered of now-classic films premiered or opened at the theater, such as René Clair's *Le Voyage Imaginaire* and Erich Von Stroheim's *Greed*. Hawk's *A Girl in Every Port* also premiered in Paris at the Ursulines. As did Josef von Sternberg's *Blue Angel* at the beginning of the sound era, where the Dietrich classic ran 14 months.

Stephen Horne interviewed about the *Prix de beauté*
This piece appeared on the Louise Brooks Society blog on July 11, 2013. On July 18, Horne accompanied a historic screening of the silent Prix de beauté at the Castro Theater in San Francisco. Horne's accompaniment on piano (mostly), as well as flute, accordion, and guitar, was well received by the more than 1200 people who turned out to see this rare screened version of the film.

On Thursday, July 18th the San Francisco Silent Film Festival will screen the rarely shown silent version of the 1930 Louise Brooks' film, *Prix de beauté*. Made as European cinema was converting to sound, the film marks Louise Brooks' last starring role in a feature.

Less well known than her work with G.W. Pabst (*Pandora's Box*, *Diary of a Lost Girl*), *Prix de beauté* is an otherwise very good film marred, in ways, by its foray into sound. Brooks' voice was dubbed, not always effectively, and sound effects were added.

The San Francisco Silent Film Festival will screen the silent version recently restored by the Cineteca di Bologna in Italy. The film's running time is given as approximately 108 minutes. (By comparison, the running time found on the KINO DVD is 93 minutes.) Accompanying the July 18th screening is British musician Stephen Horne.

Stephen has long been considered one of the leading silent film accompanists. Based at London's BFI Southbank, he has performed at all the major UK venues including the Barbican Centre and the Imperial War Museum; he has also recorded music for DVDs, BBC TV screenings, and museum installations of silent films. Although principally a pianist, he often incorporates flute, accordion and keyboards into his performances, sometimes simultaneously. Stephen performs internationally, and in recent years his accompaniments have met with acclaim at film festivals in Pordenone, Telluride, San Francisco, Cannes, Bologna and Berlin. Most recently, he accompanied some of the Hitchcock 9 silent films which have played around the United States.

Stephen answered a few questions about his upcoming accompaniment to *Prix de beauté*.

TG: How did the assignment to accompany *Prix de beauté* come about?

SH: I think the film was already in the minds of the festival team, because of the amazing response to Louise Brooks' films at earlier festivals. I mentioned to [SFSFF Director] Anita Monga that I'd played for the film a couple of times, so maybe that's why I was asked to accompany it.

TG: What were your impressions of the film?

SH: I did watch the sound version before the silent screenings that I accompanied. Normally I wouldn't consider this necessary, but on this occasion it was invaluable. I'm not sure that this restoration is truly the original silent version - I suspect that this doesn't actually survive intact and what we have is a recreation, using the sound version as a starting point and working backwards, so to speak. I think that both versions have their problems - they're imperfect gems - but for me the silent version works much better. And there are certain sequences that are sublime.

TG: What is your approach to composing for a silent film?

SH: My approach varies from event to event, depending on many variables - some of them quite prosaic, such as how much time I have! On occasion I'll be commissioned to compose a fully notated score, either to perform solo or with other musicians. Most often my approach is improvisatory, but 'planned'. By which I mean that I'll watch the film and prepare certain musical elements, along with certain specific effects, such as when I'll switch between instruments (for those that don't know, I'm something of an instrumental multi-tasker). I like the elastic quality of an improvised performance, which I think can sometimes respond from moment-to-moment in a way that is hard to do with a fixed score. But equally I recognize that people like a good tune! So I try to thread melodic elements throughout, which I guess creates something of a hybrid: an improvised score.

TG: Were there any special challenges in composing the score for a silent film that is today best known as a sound film?

SH: I think it's simplest to assume that the audience hasn't seen the sound version. Obviously several people will have done, but the event should ideally stand on its own terms, as a silent film / live music event. However, there are some challenges that this silent version presents, particularly all the images that specifically reference sound effects: the repeated close-ups of loudspeakers, etc. One has to make a decision about whether to acknowledge them musically, or 'play through' them instead.

TG: Music, song and sound are integral to certain passages in the film, especially the film's climatic ending. Did that prove a challenge?

SH: Unless you're playing an instrument that can produce comparable sound 'effects', I think it's best to approach these things in a slightly abstract way. In the tango song scene I've chosen to focus on a couple of specific elements within the scene - rather than trying to create an impression of vocalizing, for instance. However, the song in the final scene is inescapably important, so I think that I have come up with a rather clever solution to the problem. But you'll have to wait to find out what that will be!

TG: Were you able to integrate the two songs used in the sound version into your score? If so, how?

SH: See above! But again, I'm largely gearing the performance to people who are coming to this film without having seen the sound version. The songs are not generally known now, so while it's important that I play a tango when they're dancing / singing a tango, I don't think that it has to be the one sung in the sound version. But just wait until the climax...

TG: What can those who attend the Festival screening look forward to?

SH: A lovely but flawed film, elevated to near-classic status by the transcendence of Louise Brooks. On a musical note, I've noticed that the music I'm preparing often starts in a major key, before resolving to the minor. I think this is the influence of the Brooks persona: full of joy, but with a lingering note of melancholy.

TG: Louise Brooks fans will want to know.... Is there any chance the silent version and your score will be released on DVD?

SH: I would imagine that there's a good chance a DVD will be released, unless there are some copyright issues of which I'm unaware. But whether my music will be included is a question that is in the laps of the Gods of film restoration!

Eureka - Hélène Caron

This piece appeared on the Louise Brooks Society blog on June 19, 2006. In 2018, after uncovering a 1930 French newspaper clipping stating Hélène Regelly was Brooks' voice double in Prix de beauté, I am now less than 99% confident Hélène Caron sang the popular theme song. Did Regelly, a noted operetta singer, both speak Brooks' lines and sing the films's theme? Over the years, I have collected nearly a dozen 78 rpm recordings of the song, though none name Regelly.

I found it! And at long last, a minor Louise Brooks mystery has been solved . . . . In the early sound film *Prix de beauté*, Louise Brooks is seen singing "Je n'ai qu'un amour, c'est toi," a charming chanson of love and jealousy. As she did not speak French, Brooks' dialogue is dubbed. And the song she is seen singing at the end of the film is actually sung by someone else.

There has been some speculation as to whom that performer might be. The film itself does not credit anyone. And, in his detailed biography, Barry Paris does not state who sings. Some have suggested Edith Piaf. Now, I am 99% sure that Hélène Caron is the singer who performs "Je n'ai qu'un amour, c'est toi" in *Prix de beauté*.

In December of last year, while searching the internet, I came upon a compact disc of French music from the Thirties. I ordered a copy from Europe, and it arrived today. The disc contains "Je n'ai qu'un amour, c'est toi" by Hélène Caron, and it is a match for the version found in *Prix de beauté*. Additionally, the linear notes state the song is from the film (as well it indicates that this recording was released on the Parlaphone label). "Je n'ai qu'un amour, c'est toi" is a truely charming song. And, as this is one of three versions I have found recordings of, a perhaps popular song in France in 1930.

Louise Brooks, product placement & the 1931 film *It Pays to Advertise*

This piece appeared on the Louise Brooks Society blog on September 26, 2015. It was part of a series of four blogs detailing past controversy around product placement in films. Though the least regarded of Brooks' films, It Pays to Advertise enjoyed a life of its own throughout the 1930s due to the rise to stardom of Carole Lombard. As I found in researching the film, this Paramount programmer was revived during the 1930s to meet demand for more Lombard films; it was shown as late as August 21, 1940 at the Del Mar theater in Los Angeles.

The 1931 film *It Pays to Advertise* is a farce about rival soap companies, an advertising agency, and a ne'er do-well playboy who attempts to make good. Louise Brooks plays Thelma Temple, a dancer appearing in a musical entitled *Girlies Don't Tell*.

It Pays to Advertise was based on a popular stage play of the same name from 1914. Updated and set in the advertising and business worlds, the film referenced a number of actual products and their slogans. As a result, one trade journal took exception.

Harrison's Reports, which billed itself "a reviewing service free from the influence of film advertising," objected to product placement in film—be it verbal or visual. Over the course of four months (in articles titled "The Facts About Concealed Advertisements in Paramount Pictures," "This Paper's Further Efforts Against 'Sponsored' Screen Advertisements," and "Other Papers That Have Joined the Harrison Crusade Against Unlabelled Screen Advertising") editor P. S. Harrison railed against this business world farce in particular and product placement in films in general.

Harrison wrote, "The Paramount picture, *It Pays to Advertise*, is nothing but a billboard of immense size. I have not been able to count all of the nationally advertised articles that are spoken of by the characters." In the next issue, Harrison stated "In last week's issue the disclosure was made that in *It Pays to Advertise* there are more than fifteen advertisements in addition to the main advertisement, '13 Soap Unlucky for Dirt,' which Paramount is accused of having created as a brand for the purpose of selling it."

> **AS TO ADVERTISING IN THE MOVIES**
>
> THE amusing Paramount picture, "It Pays to Advertise," recently shown in Medford calls attention to a recent important development in the moving picture industry,—namely, an attempt to increase profits by injecting paid advertising into regular entertainment films.
>
> In this picture a trademark, "13 Soap, Unlucky for Dirt," is exploited and, according to Harrison's Reports, a motion picture reviewing service, edited by a former exhibitor, devoted exclusively to the interests of exhibitors, Colgate has offered $250,000 for it. The following nationally advertised articles are also given a boost: Boston garters, Arrow collars, Manhattan shirts, Colgate cream, Gillette razors, Victor phonographs, Murad cigarettes, Florsheim shoes, Dobbs hats, Forhan's tooth paste, and others.
>
> P. S. Harrison, the editor, comments as follows:
>
> It should be an education if the leaders of the motion picture industry go to these theatres to get the reaction of the public; they should save millions of dollars, for unless they discontinue the practice the box office receipts will dwindle to such a point that what profits they make out of the advertising reels and the subtle advertisements that are put into the features as well as the shorts will not make up the losses.
>
> Many of them point to the radio; they say that the public has become accustomed to it and do not protest. This is not so; they protest, by shutting off the radio or by switching to some other station.
>
> But even if it were not so, the motion picture industry cannot be compared with the radio, because, although the radio entertainment costs thousands of dollars, they get it free; but they pay an admission price to see motion pictures.
>
> This paper will advise its subscribers and all independent exhibitors to keep their screens clean of advertisements of this kind; they should feel proud of them. There was a time when big producers felt proud of their screens, too, but the circuit idea has warped their minds to the point of permitting a change of policy. Two years ago, who would have believed the Paramount theatre would turn its screen into a billboard?
>
> Mr. Harrison, we believe, is absolutely correct. Mr. Carl Laemmle, president of Universal, and one of the oldest and most successful producers in the industry, has the same view, and a few weeks ago issued the following public statement:
>
> I appeal to every exhibitor not to prostitute his screen with paid advertising!
>
> I appeal to every producer not to release "sponsored" moving pictures—meaning pictures which contain concealed or open advertising of some one's product!
>
> This kind of profit is a false one.
>
> It is temporary profit at best, for in the long run it will degrade the movies and earn a bad will which will drive millions from attending the movies.
>
> It is a serious mistake to figure that because the radio broadcasts contain advertising it is all right for the movies to do it. They are as far apart as the two poles.
>
> The millions who listen to fine radio entertainment do not pay for it. Therefore, they have no real right to object to injection of advertising blurbs by the announcers.
>
> But the millions who attend the movies are on a different footing. They pay at the box office for entertainment. They pay the price you fix. They are entitled to get what they pay for.
>
> When they buy a newspaper which contains advertising, they are not compelled to read the advertising if they don't want to. If they don't like the radio advertising, they can shut off the radio. But when they pay to enter your theatre, they can't turn a page nor turn off a dial. They can only look and listen to whatever is on your screen.
>
> Believe me, if you jam advertising down their throats and peck their eyes and ears with it, you will build up a resentment that will in time damn your business.
>
> The screen in all its years of existence has been kept free from propaganda, with only one exception—and that was during the war. In those black days we all did what we could to arouse the fighting and Liberty-bond-buying spirit of the people. It was for a real cause. But outside that, the screen has been kept free from propaganda—whether religious, political, advertising or otherwise.
>
> Your screen is a sacred trust. It is not actually yours. It belongs to the people who pay to see what is on it. In heaven's name don't prostitute it!
>
> We quote these two opinions, one from the standpoint of the exhibitors and one from that of the producers, to disabuse our readers of the assumption that the opposition of this newspaper to such advertising proceeds from the fact that it represents competition with newspaper advertising, and that our view is therefore biased and the product of self interest.
>
> Such an impression is incorrect.
>
> Newspapers would, no doubt, welcome a monopoly in advertising as keenly as any other business men would welcome a monopoly in their particular line. But monopolies can't be attained, and can only be approached by achieving a marked superiority in product in what must be, by the nature of things, a highly competitive field.
>
> Our opposition proceeds solely from the standpoint of the movie industry, and what effect the adoption of such a policy will have upon it.
>
> • • •
>
> WE AGREE with Messrs. Harrison and Laemmle absolutely that the moment the movie industry injects paid advertising into its entertainment, it kills the goose that lays the golden eggs.
>
> The success of the movie industry, like every other industry, depends essentially upon good will and public support. Once let the movie public become convinced that they can't attend a performance without running the risk of having some free advertising jammed down their throats, and this great industry, with its billions invested, is doomed.

Taking the high moral ground, *Harrison's Reports* spurred a campaign against "sponsored moving pictures—meaning pictures which contain concealed or open advertising of some one's product." Harrison wrote to the studios—and *Harrison's Reports* noted that a handful responded with pledges to not include verbal or visual product placement. The crusading editor also wrote to more than 2,000 newspapers, and a number published articles and editorials decrying the practice.

Among those papers that joined Harrison's cause were four of the New York dailies, the Gannett chain, scores of small town papers, as well as the *Denver Post*, *Detroit Free Press*, *St. Louis Globe-Democrat*, and *Tulsa Tribune*. The *Christian Science Monitor* added to the chorus of complaint when it remarked, "Paramount should have been well paid for the large slices of publicity for trade-marked products that are spread all through this artificial story."

Because of tepid reviews and negative publicity, *It Pays to Advertise* did poorly at the box office. At best, most exhibitors reported only fair business. In Los Angeles, according to one report, the film "set a new low."

And what of "13 Soap — Unlucky for Dirt"? The name of this fictional brand originated with the original story. I don't know that such a brand actually existed when the 1931 film was released, but according to news reports from the time (and this could be ballyhoo), an offer of $250,000 was made to secure the trademark for "13 Soap — Unlucky for Dirt".

Sometime in the last number of years, a company called LUSH manufactured a hand-made soap called "13 Soap — Unlucky for Dirt". (This product has been discontinued.) According to the company's website, the soap was named for the fictitious product in the 1931 film, *It Pays to Advertise*.

Yesterday's blog post discussed the 1931 Louise Brooks' film *It Pays to Advertise* and the controversy stirred up by the film's prolific product placement. The post also discussed the campaign against product placement initiated by *Harrison's Reports*, a motion picture industry trade journal. Reproduced below is one of a few newspaper editorials about the issue, this from a West Coast newspaper.

A double bill featuring Louise Brooks on this day in 1937
This piece appeared on the Louise Brooks Society blog on June 20, 2016.

On this date in 1937, the Lincoln Theater in San Francisco presented a double bill, *When You're in Love* together with *Empty Saddles*, starring Buck Jones and L. Brooks. I wish I could have been there!

This listing is one of a handful of Louise Brooks' "double bills" that I have come across over the years. I have also come across as many instances where one Brooks' films followed another at a local theater, or different Brooks' films played in different theaters at the same time and in the same town (as in the Omaha, Nebraska advertisement pictured below).

It's coincidental, but notable as Brooks made relatively few films. Her films got around.

getTV Premieres Rare Cary Grant film
This piece appeared on Huffington Post on May 4, 2016.

If you're not familiar with the 1937 film When You're in Love, you are not alone. These days, it's little known. It's one of those "old movies" few people have heard of, and even fewer have seen. Nevertheless, it is a charming and entertaining film deserving a wider audience.

If you like Cary Grant or have interest in the films of Frank Capra, enjoy opera or know of the once famed singer Grace Moore, or appreciate musicals or screwball comedies, then you'll want to tune in for the network premiere of the newly-restored film. When You're in Love airs Friday on getTV.

The draw for many will be the young Cary Grant, who shines in support of Moore in this not-quite screwball romantic musical. Grant's best known early films, the ones that helped make him a star - like Topper and Bringing Up Baby, were still a year off. Nevertheless, the actor's charm, witty delivery, and suave demeanor are all evident.

The film has other attractions; chief among them is its star, Grace Moore. She was a major name in her day, both as operatic singer and film actress. *When You're in Love* is one of nine in which Moore appeared, and it was seen as a worthy successor to her earlier triumph in *One Night of Love* (1934), for which Moore was nominated for the Academy Award for Best Actress.

The film features a fast-moving plot which turns on high-spirits and high-notes. Grant plays Jimmy Hudson, a care-free American artist who can't leave Mexico until he can pay his hotel bill. Caught in a similar conundrum is Louise Fuller (played by

Moore), a career-driven Australian opera singer deported to Mexico after her American visa expires. Desperate to re-enter the States - which she can only do married to an American, the singer's lawyer offers the impoverished artist $2,000 to marry - with the understanding the two divorce back in the States. Things get complicated when a real romance blossoms between the mismatched pair.

When You're in Love was scripted and directed by Robert Riskin, Frank Capra's Oscar-winning longtime collaborator. This was the only film Riskin would direct, and it contains plenty of delightful Capra-*esque* (or rather Riskin-*esque*) touches. Among them is a stellar supporting cast of character actors, which includes Henry Stephenson, future Oscar nominee Aline MacMahon, and future Oscar winner Thomas Mitchell, among others.

When You're in Love was promoted as featuring music "From Schubert to Swing." The film's eclectic score boasts a number of breezy song-and-dance numbers, including a couple of gems written by legendary composer Jerome Kern and famed lyricist

Louise Brooks' face is obscured by Grace Moore's left hand in *When You're in Love*.

Dorothy Fields. Though an operatic soprano who regularly performed at the Met, Moore even takes on two of the popular hits of the day, "Siboney" and "Minnie the Moocher." (Grant helps out on the latter, which was lightly censored and then cut from the film when first released. It has now been restored.)

When You're in Love was a big money maker, and the film proved especially popular with audiences. It was held over in New York (where it premiered at the Roxy City Music Hall), as well as in Atlanta, Baltimore, Seattle, Detroit, Hartford, New Orleans,

Trenton, Tacoma, and Springfield (Massachusetts and Illinois).

Critics also liked it. The *Hollywood Reporter* got it right when it stated, "With a more substantial story than the last two Grace Moore vehicles, *When You're in Love* is a signal triumph for the foremost diva of the screen, for Cary Grant who should soar to stardom as result of his performance in this, and for Robert Riskin, here notably handling his first directorial assignment."

If this is not enough to intrigue, note that *When You're in Love* also contains one of the last screen appearances by film legend Louise Brooks. The trouble is, it is hard to spot her. Brooks, then down and out and attempting yet another comeback, agreed to an uncredited bit part with the understanding she would be given the feminine lead in another Columbia film. (It never happened.)

To generate press, the studio put out the word that Brooks was willing to do anything to get back into pictures. "Louise Brooks is certainly starting her come-back from the lowest rung of the ladder," wrote the *Oakland Tribune*. "She is one of a hundred dancers in the ballet chorus of Grace Moore's *When You're in Love*." Brooks' bit is brief. She appears as a masked torch bearer in the film's finale, with Moore descending the stairs and passing within a few feet of the fallen star.

When You're in Love airs on getTV on Friday, May 6 at 8pm ET / 5pm PT, with a repeat later in the day. The film will be shown again on May 31 at 8pm ET.

Louise Brooks at a drive-in and other firsts from the 1950s
This piece appeared on the Louise Brooks Society blog on August 3, 2016.

I come across a lot of unusual material while researching Louise Brooks. Here are the latest items, each related to the 1938 film *Overland Stage Raiders*, a western from Republic Studios which featured Brooks alongside John Wayne.

Would you believe that in 1954 *Overland Stage Raiders* was shown at a drive-in in Carbondale, Illinois? The film was part of a Friday-Saturday triple bill, along with another Wayne film, *Lady from Louisiana* (1941) and a crime drama called *Million Dollar Pursuit* (1951). Both films were from Republic. The following day, the drive-in was showing the more recent *The Wild One* (1953), starring Marlon Brando.

Pictured left is an advertisement for the Waring Auto drive-in near Carbondale. This venue opened in July, 1948 as the Waring Auto Theatre, with space for 500 cars. It was later renamed the Campus Drive-In, after its proximity to Southern Illinois University. During the 1970's, it played mostly horror and adult movies, before closing towards the end of that decade. The drive-in has since been demolished and a hog farm s(h)its on the site today.

And that's not all....

Overland Stage Raiders had been reissued in 1953, and that same year it was shown as part of a double bill alongside *Zombies of the Stratosphere* in Kokomo, Indiana! The film was also screened on various bills in small towns and large cities across the United States, from Paris, Texas to Detroit, Michigan, from Green Bay, Wisconsin to St. Louis, Missouri.

Zombies of the Stratosphere, for those not familiar, was a 1952 black-and-white Republic Studios serial that was the second to feature Commando Cody. Today, it is best

remembered as one of the first screen appearances of a young Leonard Nimoy (Mr. Spock), who plays one of the three Martian invaders.

Overland Stage Raiders was also shown on television numerous times between 1953 and 1959. I found listings from across the United States. It was shown in Los Angeles, California and Phoenix, Arizona and Asbury Park, New Jersey and Rochester, New York (just before Brooks moved there) and elsewhere.

Certainly, *Overland Stage Raiders* was the first film featuring Louise Brooks to be shown either on television or at a drive-in. The earliest television listing I came across for the film was from March 8, 1953 in Hazelton, Pennsylvania as part of "John Wayne Theater." The film then showed two days later in Los Angeles. As far as television goes, 1953 is pretty early. Pictured below is a June, 1953 advertisement for "Sunday Televiewing" in Los Angeles. KTTV is now known as Fox 11 in Southern California.

First Louise Brooks television broadcast
This piece appeared on the Louise Brooks Society blog on August 4, 2016.

Yesterday, I wrote "Certainly, *Overland Stage Raiders* was the first film featuring Louise Brooks to be shown either on television or at a drive-in. The earliest television listing I came across for the film was from March 8, 1953 in Hazelton, Pennsylvania as part of "John Wayne Theater." The film then showed two days later in Los Angeles. As far as television goes, 1953 is pretty early."

I was wrong.

Yesterday, I couldn't imagine finding an earlier television broadcast of a film in which Louise Brooks appeared. Until today. . . , when I found *Windy Riley Goes Hollywood* was broadcast on TV in 1948, five years before *Overland Stage Raiders*. Wow, as far as television goes, 1948 is very early. The film was shown under the title *Windy Riley Goes to Hollywood* on November 18, 1948 on WJZ (Channel 7) in Asbury Park, New Jersey.

FOR SUNDAY TELEVIEWING

STARTS TONIGHT!
BLIND DATE
with Jan Murray
6:30 p.m.
Presented by Hazel Bishop

KTTV 11
Ed Reimers
your man-about-words on
Haven MacQuarrie's
NOAH WEBSTER SAYS
7:00 p.m.

KTTV 11
Thrilling action adventure
"Overland Stage Raiders"
John Wayne Westerns
7:30 p.m.

KTTV 11
Dr. Arthur Peters
and the 140-voice Victory
Baptist Church Choir bring you
VOICES OF VICTORY
8:30 p.m.
Presented by Gold's Department Store

That good-looking channel eleven!

I found the above listing while I was researching *Windy Riley Goes to Hollywood*, under which the 1931 Fatty Arbuckle-directed film was listed a few times in the early 1930s. Most times, exhibitors and advertisers got the title, *Windy Riley Goes Hollywood*, right. But sometimes they didn't. Here is a screen capture of the film's title. Following it is a 1931 advertisement from East Liverpool, Ohio for the Gloria Swanson film *Indiscreet*, with which the incorrectly named *Windy Riley Goes to Hollywood* was paired.

This mistake wasn't a one-off. The East Liverpool ad named *Windy Riley* incorrectly three times in three different ads over the course of three days. Others made the same mistake. So did the *Hamilton Evening Journal* in Hamilton, Ohio in 1931, and the *Rhinelander Daily News* in Rhinelander, Wisconsin in 1932, and the *Medford Mail Tribune* in Medford, Oregon also in 1932. As did the *Asbury Park Press* television listings in Asbury Park, New Jersey in 1948.

Out of curiosity, I searched for television listings for Louise Brooks' other talkies. I found that *God's Gift to Women* was shown on TV in Cincinnati in September, 1958, and again in 1959 in Bennington, Vermont and Sandusky, Ohio and elsewhere. It was also shown in Tucson, Arizona in 1960. The earliest television listing I could find for *Empty Saddles* was in March 1957 in Long Beach, California, and then Pittsburgh, Pennsylvania in November, 1957 and June, 1958, followed by St. Louis, Missouri in September, 1959. [*King of Gamblers* was shown in Portsmouth, New Hampshire in October 1960 and Pittsburgh, Pennsylvania on Christmas Day in 1960.]

[In preparing this entry in 2018, I searched once again for early television listings of Brooks' films, and found TV listings for *Empty Saddles* in Los Angeles, California in May, 1957, *God's Gift to Women* in Marion, Ohio in May 1957, *When You're in Love* in the San Francisco Bay Area in June, 1959, and a listing for *King of Gamblers* in Racine, Wisconsin in October, 1959. I couldn't find listings for *It Pays to Advertise*, which suggests its television debut may have taken place in the early 21st century.

No doubt, as more databases become available online, more listings will become available and the dates for the earliest television showings of Brooks' films will be pushed back.]

TODAY'S TELEVISION

WCBS—TV—Channel 2
12:30—Music; Program Review
12:45—Film Shorts
1:00—Vanity Fair
6:15—Music; Program Preview
6:30—Lucky Pup
6:45—Bob Howard Show
7:00—Film Shorts
7:30—Television News
7:45—Face the Music
8:00—Cooking Program
8:30—Film: The Ghost and the Guest
9:45—Film Shorts
9:55—Newsreel

WNBT—Channel 4
5:30—Howdy Doody
7:15—Cavalcade of Fashions
7:30—Film
7:45—Sportswoman of Week
8:00—Film: Princess Sagaphi
8:15—Nature of Things
8:30—Lanny Ross
9:00—Bob Smith Show
9:30-10:00—Dunninger

WABD—Channel 5
12:00 M.—Clock; Weather
12:45—Stan Shaw
1:00—Okay Mother
1:30—News; Films
2:30—The Needle Shop
2:45—Spare Room
3:00—Women's Club
3:15—Vincent Lopez
3:45—Society Page
4:00—Maxine Barratt
4:30—Wendy Barrie
5:00—Clock; Weather
6:00—Small Fry Club
6:30—Russ Hodges
6:45—Film Shorts
7:00—Oky-Doky
7:30—Camera Headlines
7:45—Jack Eigen Show
8:00—Film Shorts
8:30—Charade Quiz
9:00—Sports Film
9:05—Wrestling

WJZ—TV—Channel 7
7:00—News—Gordon Fraser
7:15—Film: Story of Wheat
7:30—Film: Windy Riley Goes to Hollywood
8:00—Fashion Story
8:30—Critic at Large
9:00—Film: Coming of Amos

WPIX—Channel 11
5:00—News and Music
5:45—Comics on Parade
6:00—Records
7:00—Record Rendezvous
7:30—Newsreel
7:40—Jimmy Jemail
8:00—Gloria Swanson
9:00—Wrestling
10:45—Newsreel

WATV—Channel 13
5:00—Junior Frolics
5:30—Film Serial
5:50—Camera Highlights
7:00—Film
8:00—Film

Windy Riley Goes to Hollywood aired on WJZ (Channel 7) on November 18, 1948.

4 THE LEGEND

Louise Brooks, the Persistent Star • Rick Geary's New Comic, Louise Brooks: Detective • Louise Brooks - Cover Girl and Secret Muse of the 20th Century • Author of Louise Brooks' novel, The Chaperone, comes to Bay Area • Downton Abbey – the Louise Brooks Connection • Doctor Who and Louise Brooks • Loving Louise Brooks: A Student Film You Must Watch • Remembering Richard Leacock • Louise Brooks stars in new music videos • Natalie Merchant's 'Lulu' Latest Pop Tribute to Silent Film Icon Louise Brooks • Louise Rutkowski, Diary of a Lost Girl • A Glastonbury First • Rufus Wainwright pens tribute to silent film star Louise Brooks • "I Am the Victim of Such a Lascivious Beauty": Rufus Wainwright on Louise Brooks • Rufus Talks Lulu - Plays Denver • Run You Luscious Lesbian • Lou Reed, Frank Wedekind, Metallica and Lulu • Lou Reed and Metallica dream a nightmare called Lulu • Louise Brooks, William Kentridge and the Making of Lulu • Lulu-mania Sweeps New York City • Opera with Louise Brooks inspired character debuts, and it's not Lulu • Louise Brooks' Star Shines Brighter Than Ever • Anthony Bourdain and Louise Brooks • Interview with Thomas Gladysz

Compared to most her more illustrious contemporaries, Louise Brooks has had a disproportionate influence late 20th and early 21st century culture. Why is hard to say. Perhaps it has something to do with Brooks' potent combination of beauty (defined by her striking hairstyle, a sharp bob) with her rebellious nature and self-destructive story. Brooks makes for an appealing anti-star. What's certain is that while many personalities of the silent era have faded from memory, Brooks is more popular today than she was in the 1920s.

It all started with Dixie Dugan. That was the name of the character modeled after Brooks who starred in J.P. McEvoy's popular 1928 comic novel, *Show Girl*. That book spawned sequels, as well as a stageplay, films, and a comic strip which ran until the 1960s. Dixie Dugan helped keep the memory of Brooks' alive.

Over the years, numerous artists and individuals have paid homage to Louise Brooks and Lulu, the character Brooks played in *Pandora's Box*. From characters in movies to novels, short stories, plays, comics, and graphic novels—to poems, songs, art, fan art and fashion—Brooks has been the subject of numerous tributes.

These many tributes to Brooks extend throughout popular culture and even include a character in an online computer game, street art from around the world, shop window displays, and a tattoo worn by a well known rock musician.

Aside from Charlie Chaplin, no silent film star—and few actors or actresses of today — have received so much cultural and creative recognition. Arguably, Brooks has become a 20th century icon, and even something of a muse.

Louise Brooks, the Persistent Star
This piece appeared on Huffington Post on August 22, 2017.

Louise Brooks, the silent film star best known for her bobbed hair as well as for her charismatic performance as Lulu in *Pandora's Box*, is once again enjoying the spotlight. This year, 2017, promises to be a big year in the actress' afterlife.

The American-born actress made relatively few films—24 in total, and most movie goers have likely seen only one or two of her European films. That should change now that Brooks' best American film, *Beggars of Life* (1928), has been released on DVD and Blu-ray by Kino Lorber.

Digitally restored from film elements held at the George Eastman Museum in Rochester, New York, this new DVD marks the film's first real release. For classic film buffs, it is a must see. [As the author of a new book on the film, *Beggars of Life: A Companion to the 1928 Film*, I am enthusiastically biased.]

Chances are, even if you are a film buff, you haven't seen *Beggars of Life*—at least not like this. Though widely acclaimed when first released, the film fell between the cracks of movie history and was considered lost for decades. Only recently, since its digital restoration, has this once-obscure film returned to general circulation. The new print is bright and detailed and a thrill to watch.

Based on the bestselling novelistic memoir by the celebrated "hobo author" Jim Tully, *Beggars of Life* was directed by multiple Academy Award winner William Wellman the year after he directed *Wings* (the first film to win the Oscar for Best Picture). It is a rough and tumble story about an orphan girl (Brooks) who kills her abusive step-father and flees the law, dressing as a boy and riding the rails through a hobo underground ruled over by future Oscar winner Wallace Beery. The film also includes leading man Richard Arlen, as well as the pioneering African-American actor Edgar "Blue" Washington.

Movie goers will have a chance to see *Beggars of Life* on the big screen in the coming months. The Brattle Theater in Cambridge, Massachusetts is set to screen *Beggars of Life* on September 5. The historic movie house will also screen *Diary of a Lost Girl* (1929), another digitally restored film starring the actress, on September 6. And on September 7, the Brattle reprises both films with special double bill.

The Cambridge screenings take place just before a larger Louise Brooks series at Film Forum in New York City. The famous repertory house is set to screen *Diary of a Lost Girl* on September 17, *Beggars of Life* on September 19, *Pandora's Box* on October 1, followed by a reprise of *Diary of a Lost Girl* on October 14. Each film will feature live musical accompaniment by silent film pianist Steve Sterner.

Brooks is also the focus of a multi-film series in Helsinki, Finland. That country's National Audiovisual Institute, KAVI, is set to show Beggars of Life on October 12 and 15, *Diary of a Lost Girl* on October 19 and 21, *Prix de beauté* on October 27 and 29, and *Pandora's Box* on November 27 and December 1. Elsewhere, *Pandora's Box* will be shown in Manila, Philippines on September 3 as part of the 11th annual International Silent Film Festival Manila.

In the United States, other screenings of *Beggars of Life* are set to take place in Cleveland, Ohio at the Cinematheque at the Cleveland Institute of Art on September 23 (with an introduction by Tully biographer Paul Bauer), and in Madison, Wisconsin at the University Cinematheque on December 1.

The new Kino Lorber *Beggars of Life* is a deluxe package. Besides being digitally restored, the Kino Lorber release has a fine audio commentary by actor William Wellman, Jr., the son of the film's director; an audio commentary by yours truly, Thomas Gladysz; a booklet essay by film critic Nick Pinkerton; a graceful musical score by The Mont Alto Motion Picture Orchestra; and swell, original cover art by artist Wayne Shellabarger.

All this Louise Brooks activity (the DVD release, my book, and the subsequent screenings) comes after two major announcements earlier in the year.

In March, the San Francisco Silent Film Festival revealed that film preservationist Rob Byrne had found a 23-minute fragment of the long missing 1927 Brooks film, *Now We're in the Air*, in an archive in the Czech Republic. Newly restored, the film made a well received world premiere at the San Francisco Festival in June, followed by a showing before archivists and historians at the Library of Congress in Washington D.C. Next up for the once lost work is the prestigious Le Giornate del Cinema Muto | Pordenone Silent Film Festival in Italy in October, where *Now We're in the Air* will be shown as part of the Festival's "Rediscoveries and Restorations" program.

That's not all the news from Europe. The British Film Institute recently announced the forthcoming publication of a new book on *Pandora's Box* by Pamela Hutchinson, a London critic who writes on early film for the *Guardian* newspaper and *Sight & Sound* magazine. Hutchinson's book, an illustrated study of the once controversial film, will be published as part of the BFI's familiar Film Classics series. The book will be released in Europe on November 21, and in the United States on December 19. Screenings of *Pandora's Box* around England are in the works.

But wait, there's more! In February, an opera with a Louise Brooks inspired character and with music by Stewart Copeland (the co-founder and drummer for the Police) opened in Chicago. *The Invention of Morel* will be staged in Long Beach, California in March 2018.

And in August, PBS announced that *Columbus* and *Split* star Haley Lu Richardson will play Louise Brooks in *The Chaperone*, joining Elizabeth McGovern in a period drama from PBS Masterpiece. *The Chaperone*, based on Laura Moriarty's best-selling novel from 2013, is scripted by Julian Fellowes and directed by Michael Engler. PBS announced principal photography has started on the film, which will air on PBS stations nationwide after its initial theatrical run in 2018.

McGovern, who is also a producer, optioned the novel and worked with Fellowes (both were involved with the popular PBS series *Downton Abbey*) to adapt the story for the big screen. In *The Chaperone*, McGovern portrays a woman whose life is changed when she escorts a teenage and soon to be famous Brooks to New York in the early 1920s.

Notably, *The Chaperone* is the first film from PBS Masterpiece, and, it's the first film to feature Brooks as a central character. That's not bad for an actress whose last film was shot more than 80 years ago.

Rick Geary's New Comic, *Louise Brooks: Detective*
This piece appeared on Huffington Post on July, 2015.

Comic book author Rick Geary is a longtime fixture at Comic-Con International.

Back in 1980, he took home their Inkpot Award given to individuals for their contributions to the world of comics. And this year, as it has in the past, his artwork (The Toucan) adorns the cover of the official events guide and "Reader" t-shirt.

Geary is at the 2015 Comic-Con International, which starts this week in San Diego. He is taking part in a panel, signing books, and celebrating the release of a new hardbound work, *Louise Brooks: Detective* (NBM Publishing).

This new comic is something of departure for Geary. Of the last number of years, he has been engaged in an ongoing non-fiction series, *A Treasury of XXth Century Murder* — a follow up to his popular and well regarded *A Treasury of Victorian Murder* which launched 20 years ago with *Jack the Ripper*. Both series are true-to-life comic book accounts of sensational death.

Geary's new comic is a departure because its fiction, though it is based on the life of a real person, the iconic Kansas-born silent film star Louise Brooks.

The story centers on the actress' return to Wichita after quitting Hollywood. It was one of the low points of her life, though she was still just in her early thirties. Living at home, she becomes intrigued by a murder involving a new friend, her friend's shady beau, and a famous reclusive writer. Not before she gets herself into trouble will Brooks emerge with the solution the local police have failed to grasp. It's a taut page turner, and an intriguing story that might make for a clever screenplay.

Publishers Weekly calls *Louise Brooks: Detective*, "A fun, twisty mystery for both film buffs and crime fiction lovers."

Geary is an Eisner award-winning cartoonist and illustrator with a distinctive visual style. He is the author and illustrator of several books, and has worked for Marvel Entertainment Group, DC Comics, Dark Horse Comics, and the revived Classics Illustrated series. For thirteen years, Geary was a contributor to *National Lampoon*. His work has also appeared in *Heavy Metal* magazine, *MAD*, *Spy*, *Rolling Stone*, and the *New York Times Book Review*. In 1994, the National Cartoonist Society awarded Geary its Magazine and Book Illustration Award.

Recently, Geary answered a few questions about the bobbed-hair actress and his new work, *Louise Brooks: Detective*.

TG: Your ongoing multi-volume true crime series, "A Treasury of Murder", is a great achievement in comic art. You done a number that center on historic mysteries, and few of which focus on old Hollywood. How did you come to

write one about Louise Brooks?

RG: After about 25 years of producing true murder books, my publisher Terry Nantier of NBM Publishing, suggested I do a work of fiction. I had long had an idea in my head for a murder mystery set in Kansas in the 1930s, so from there I made the leap of casting Louise Brooks as the detective. It seemed just outrageous enough to work.

TG: In *Louise Brooks: Detective*, you take a little documented time in the actress' life—after she quits Hollywood and returned home—and imagine her getting involved in a murder. Was there room then in Brooks' real life story to "make something up"?

RG: By fortuitous coincidence, my idea of setting the story in Kansas fit in with Louise's return there in 1940, after her Hollywood career had dissolved away. She was definitely at loose ends and, it would seem, ripe for any new kind of adventure.

TG: I've heard that you're related to Louise Brooks? Is it true?

RG: Yes, Louise was my mother's second cousin, and they both hailed from the same area of southeastern Kansas. My mom's maiden name was Brooks and it's also my middle name.

TG: We've also heard that you are friends with Barry Paris, who wrote the biography of actress published in 1989.

RG: Yes, Barry and I go back a long way. We're both from Wichita, and we've worked on various projects together since our high school days.

TG: When and how did you first become aware of Brooks as an actress and silent film star?

RG: I had been dimly aware of her as an image and icon, but knew very little about her until the early 1980s. That's when I first found out that we were related. I read her memoir *Lulu in Hollywood* and began to seek out her movies and find as much information on her as I could.

TG: There is an impressive amount of detail, both in the text and in the images, which suggests you did your research. What you do to prepare?

RG: I envisioned the book as a kind of tribute to Wichita and the little town of Burden, where both my mother's and Louise's branches of the Brooks family converged. This involved many trips there and many photos taken. Luckily the buildings and other locations in both towns are still there.

TG: For example, you mention the philosopher Schopenhauer - a favorite of Brooks, her affair with Charlie Chaplin, that she scrubbed floors at home as a kind of repentance after quitting Hollywood, and, as well, the name of the building in which she opened a dance studio in Wichita. Your attention to detail is remarkable.

RG: I put to use many of the biographical details I had learned over the years, from Barry's biography and other sources, to fill in the details of this period in her life. I've always loved it that she was such a voracious reader.

TG: There is the matter of Brooks' hair. She is famous for her bobbed hair — yet you chose to draw it a bit longer. Why so?

RG: I based her look on photos I had seen of her during this period in her life. The bangs were still there, but her hair had grown to shoulder-length.

TG: The crime at the center of the story seems quite real — like it could have happened. It's complex, and believable. Was it based on an actual event?

RG: No, the crime is pretty much all made up.

TG: What about the writer Thurgood Ellis, a key character in the story. Was he real?

RG: Thurgood Ellis wasn't real, but I based him on the kind of writer, *a la* J.D. Salinger, who develops a dedicated following with groundbreaking work and then vanishes from the cultural landscape.

TG: There have been a handful of comic strips and graphic novels based on Brooks, going back all the way to the late 1920's. I am thinking of *Dixie Dugan*, which ran for decades in American newspapers, as well as *Valentina* — the long-running Italian erotic comix by Guido Crepax that appeared in *Heavy Metal* magazine. There are other European works based on Brooks by Floc'h, Hugo Pratt, Marion Mousse and others. Kim Deitch has also drawn her. Brooks even appears in Dr. Who comic, and inspired a character in the Sandman series. Why do you think so many artists have drawn Brooks?

RG: I remember the *Dixie Dugan* strip, which ran in the Wichita paper for years. There's something about the eternal image of Louise Brooks that captures the imagination of artists worldwide.

TG: Were you aware of these earlier efforts? How does your work fit into theirs?

RG: I've been vaguely aware of those European versions of Louise, but I was never a regular follower. I'm not sure if my work fits in with theirs at all.

TG: Louise Brooks makes a great detective. And the final page suggests she might even write a mystery novel. Any chance she will return in your work?

RG: My hope is that she will return in a second volume someday.

More about Rick Geary and his work can be found on his website at www.rickgeary.com.

Louise Brooks - Cover Girl and Secret Muse of the 20th Century

This piece appeared on Huffington Post on June 6, 2012. About a week later, the Public Library in Arlington, Virginia posted a piece on its blog titled "Who was Louise Brooks, Anyway?" which showed a half dozen book covers related to the actress sourced from this piece. That was followed by a similar short write-up in Shelf Awareness, a publishing industry newsletter, which discussed my article.

She appears on, and in, a surprising number of books. The latest, which was just released and is set to be one of the big books of the summer, is Laura Moriarty's *The Chaperone*. The striking photo on the cover depicts Louise Brooks, the silent film star. Brooks (1906 - 1985) is also a supporting character in Moriarty's finely told novel.

F. Scott Fitzgerald once said there were no second acts in American life. Brooks is an exception. Back in the 1920s, at the height of her fame, Brooks was somewhat popular but never a top-ranked star. By the mid-1930s, when her career bottomed-out, she fell into an obscurity which lasted decades. Only since the 1970s has her celebrity reemerged and grown from small cult following to near mainstream recognition. Those that do not recognize her name almost certainly know her look.

Brooks has become a kind of a 20th-century icon, shorthand and symbol for the Jazz Age, flappers, femme fatales, wild women, and the modern woman. Adding fuel to the fire of her fame is the fact that she played an archetypal and oh-so-seductive character, Lulu, in the film for which she is best remembered, *Pandora's Box* (1929). Even more so, the extraordinarily beautiful Brooks is known for her distinct black bob — a hairstyle copied by women all over the world. Just ask *Vogue* magazine editor Anna Winotaur.

In publishing, her iconic image has graced the covers of an ever increasing number of books — many of which, notably, are not about the actress or the movies, Hollywood, acting, etc.

This slide show highlights just some of the many covers which feature Louise Brooks — including works of fiction, poetry, and other unrelated works of non-fiction.

Besides appearing on books, Brooks also shows up in others — either as a minor character or in the form of a literary allusion or shout-out. You will find her name-checked in works by the likes of everyone from Neil Gaiman and Paul Auster (*Lulu on the Bridge*) to Lemony Snicket, Salmon Rushdie and Clive Barker.

Other contemporary writers who have included Brooks in novels or short stories are Janet Fitch (*White Oleander*), Ann-Marie MacDonald (*Fall on Your Knees*), Jerry Stahl, Gary Indiana, Audrey Niffenegger, Roddy Doyle, Kim Newman, Peter Straub and a few dozen more. Another is Elizabeth Hand, an acknowledged fan of the actress, as was the late Theodore Roszak (Brooks is an important character in his brilliant 1991 novel, *Flicker*). Somewhat earlier, in the 1960s and 1970s, Brooks was referenced in works by admirers like S. J. Perelman and Fritz Leiber, Jr.

Homages to the actress go all the way back to the late 1920s and early 1930s. When J.P. McEvoy's popular novel, *Show Girl*, and its sequel, *Showgirl in Hollywood*, where first serialized in magazines of the day, they were illustrated with look-alike drawings of the actress. Their main character, Dixie Dugan, was directly based on Brooks, and was even spun-off into a long running comic strip of the same name. (A few early panels of the "Dixie Dugan" strip actually mimic Brooks' film stills.)

There have also been poems "written about" Brooks — by Frank O'Hara ("F.Y.I. Prix de beauté") and Bill Berkson ("Bubbles") and others, as well as a handful of dramatic works, including a staged but never published work by Kathy Acker, *Lulu Unchained* (c. 1985). Another is Hanna Schygulla's one person piece, *Elle! Louise Brooks*, which the renowned actress wrote and staged in Europe in the year 2000. There are others.

In the realm of non-fiction, Brooks shows up more than once in the works of Angela Carter, Kenneth Tynan, Greil Marcus, Jerome Charyn and others. As well as in various works (essays, memoirs, published letters) by the late Carlos Fuentes, Guillermo Cabrera Infante, Christopher Isherwood, Carl Sandburg, and even Robert Howard (author of *Conan the Barbarian*).

***

If you're intrigued by Brooks' literary legacy and want to learn more, start with Barry Paris' Pulitzer-worthy biography, *Louise Brooks*. First published by Knopf in 1989, it is still in print through the University of Minnesota Press. Paris' book is full of literary and cultural context, and is truly a great read. There is also Brooks' own collection of autobiographical essays, *Lulu in Hollywood*. Both John Updike and Roger Ebert, both Pulitzer Prize winners, describe it as one of the best books ever written by a Hollywood insider.

In 2006, the year which marked the 100th anniversary of the actress' birth, Rizzoli published a gorgeous pictorial by Swiss film critic Peter Cowie, *Louise Brooks: Lulu Forever*. And in 2009 came *Dear Stinkpot: Letters From Louise Brooks*, by her long time friend Jan Wahl, the acclaimed children's book author.

Louise Brooks: Portrait of an Anti-Star was the first book about the actress. It was published in Paris in 1977, and later translated into English and published in the United States in 1986.

Portrait of an Anti-Star was edited by the noted French journalist Rolland Jaccard, and includes contributions by Jaccard, the acclaimed French-Morrocan novelist Tahar Ben Jelloun, and the celebrated Italian cartoonist / graphic novelist Guido Crepax. The latter's multi-part *Valentina* series, which started back in 1965 and was inspired by Brooks, was serialized in *Heavy Metal* magazine in the 1980s and has been issued in book form in both Europe and the United States; it is currently the subject of a major exhibit in Rome. (The newest issue of the Italian *Vogue* has a write-up on the exhibit which features many illustrations.)

Today, Jaccard continues to write about Brooks. His *Portrait d'une Flapper*, with Brooks on the cover, dates from 2007. And in May of this year, he and a few other authors, including American novelist Jerome Charyn, were involved with a French radio and web tribute to Brooks. It can be found here.

Author of Louise Brooks novel, *The Chaperone*, comes to Bay Area
This piece appeared on SFGate on June 22, 2012.

Laura Moriarty is a Kansas writer (not to be confused with the East Bay poet of the same name) whose just published novel, *The Chaperone*, has been enjoying a good deal of attention. A lot of the buzz has to do with the woman depicted on the book's cover, the luminous silent film star Louise Brooks.

The Chaperone is an engaging, tuned-to-the-times story of two women, separated by a generation, and the summer they spend together which changes them both. Based on an actual time in Brooks' life, *The Chaperone* tells the story of the woman who accompanies Brooks, an irreverent, 15 year old "budding bad girl," from Wichita, Kansas to New York City in 1922.

Only a few years before becoming a film star, Brooks left Wichita to study with the Denishawn Dance Company in the hopes of joining its ranks. Led by dance legends Ruth St. Denis and Ted Shawn, Denishawn was then the leading modern dance troupe in America; in 1922, its members included another young prodigy, Martha Graham. (All appear in the novel.)

Accompanying Brooks is her conservative middle-aged neighbor, the chaperone of the title, named Cora Carlisle.

Cora is the real star of Moriarty's story, and Brooks, though a larger than life personality is a supporting character. Despite differences in their ages and outlooks, this odd couple has more in common than they realize. Both are deeply wounded creatures in search of themselves.

Thoroughly researched, and drawing on facets of daily life in the early 20th century including orphan trains, the prohibition of liquor, changing sexual mores, and new opportunities and challenges for women—Moriarty's novel illustrates how quickly everything, from fashions and values to hemlines and attitudes, were changing—and what a profound effect these changes had on the lives of just about everyone, including Cora and Louise.

The Chaperone has been featured in *Oprah Magazine* as their #1 book for June, and both the *Christian Science Monitor* and *USA Today* picked it as their top novel of the summer. The *New York Times* has run three articles. Others have appeared in Moriarty's Kansas hometown newspaper, the *Lawrence World Journal,* and locally, in the *SFWeekly*. I penned a piece two weeks ago for the Huffington Post.

Actress Elizabeth McGovern (*Downton Abbey*) optioned the movie rights after having read the audio version of the book. Should a film go into development, Cora (her character in *Downton Abbey*) could end up playing Cora in a film version of *The Chaperone*. But who might play Louise Brooks is anyone's guess.

Recently, Moriarty took time to answer a few questions about her new book.

TG: How did you come to write *The Chaperone*? How did you come to discover the story of 15 year old Louise Brooks heading off to New York City in the company of a chaperone?

LM: I was browsing in a bookstore, and I came across the book *Flapper* by Joshua Zeist. He has a chapter devoted to Louise, and I'd always thought she was compelling. I started reading about her early life, and right there in the bookstore, I learned about the trip with the chaperone. Given what I already knew about Louise – that she was smart, self-directed, and temperamental – I knew this chaperone must have had her work cut out for her.

TG: What is it about their story that interests you?

LM: I'm always interested in inter-generational tension, and 1922 strikes me as a time when just a twenty-year gap in ages could make such a difference between two people. If the chaperone was 36 in 1922, she would have come of age during a time of corsets and covered ankles. The flappers with their bared knees – and all the changing social mores that fashion represents – would have been hard to get used to. So the chaperone might have been challenged by any forward-thinking adolescent, let alone the already sophisticated Louise Brooks. I was also intrigued by Louise's complicated personality and story. She was both smart and self-destructive, and I wondered about her sudden disappearance from Hollywood. One thing that impresses me about Louise is how authentic she was – she acted as she felt and she said what she thought. Hollywood wasn't the right place for her.

TG: Did writing *The Chaperone* involve much research? What were the challenges of writing about two historical figures – one of which we know a good deal about, the other obscure?

LM: I did a great deal of research for this book. Researching Louise was actually the easy part – I read her biographies and her autobiography, and I watched her films. I even looked at her old letters to see her handwriting. But I actually had to do more research for the chaperone, Cora, because even though she was invented, I wanted to make her a woman of her time, to make her someone who could have been thirty-six in 1922. But I really liked weaving Cora's imagined life into the real facts of Louise's.

TG: Were you a fan of Louise Brooks?

I knew who she was and I thought she was striking, but I wasn't a fan until I started reading about her. I'm certainly a fan now.

TG: When did you first encounter her? Is there anything you learned about Brooks that surprised you?

LM: I don't remember when I first learned who she was. I know I tried to copy her haircut back in my twenties, and it completely didn't work on me! But it wasn't until that day in the bookstore that I started learning about her life. As for surprises, there was an answer Louise gave to a question in her old age that I found really moving. LB fans will know, I think, what I'm alluding to, and I don't want to ruin it for people who haven't yet read her biography. But late in life, someone asked the hard and worn-down Louise if she'd ever really loved anyone, and her answer was pretty touching. I wish I could have been a fly on the wall when she was interacting with this person, the one person she could admit she loved.

TG: *The Chaperone* **has been described as "the best kind of historical fiction, transporting you to another time and place, but even more importantly delivering a poignant story about people so real, you'll miss and remember them long after you close the book." What's next?**

LM: Thanks! I really have liked writing historical fiction, and my next novel will be historical as well. I'm just starting the research now . . .

Downton Abbey – the Louise Brooks Connection

This piece appeared on the San Francisco Silent Film Festival blog on January 27, 2013.
In 2017, The Chaperone was made into a film by PBS Masterpiece; scripted by Julian Fellowes, the film is expected to air on PBS stations after its initial 2018 theatrical run. Elizabeth McGovern plays the title role of the chaperone, with Haley Lu Richardson set to play Louise Brooks.

If you are a fan of silent film and *Downton Abbey*, you may have noticed a scene where one of the downstairs help was spotted reading a vintage issue of *Photoplay* magazine with Mabel Normand on the cover. The connection the popular series has with the silent film era doesn't end there. The series, set in England in the early years of the 20th century, also has some rather interesting ties to Louise Brooks.

Back in November, a handful of English writers were asked by the *Guardian* newspaper which books had most impressed them during the course of the year. The piece was titled "Books of the Year 2012." The answer given by actor, novelist, screenwriter, director and *Downton Abbey* creator Julian Fellowes caused a bit of a stir, as the book her mentioned was published in 1989. Fellowes' answer reads this way.

"I suspect the book that has haunted me the most this year was the life of that queen of the silent screen, *Louise Brooks: A Biography* (University of Minnesota £17), by Barry Paris. I have seldom read so lyrical a tale of self-destruction. When she was a girl, my mother used to be mistaken for Louise Brooks and so I have always felt a sort of investment in her, but I was unprepared for this heartbreaking tale of what-might-have-been."

What an eloquent appreciation of Barry Paris' acclaimed biography of Louise Brooks.

One wonders if Fellowes knows that Shirley MacLaine, one of the stars of *Downton Abbey*, is also BIG fan of Louise Brooks. Over the years, MacLaine has said as much on in interviews, all the while expressing her interest in playing Brooks on screen. Additionally, one of the other stars of *Downton Abbey*, Elizabeth McGovern, has a similar interest in Brooks. After serving as the reader for the audio version of Laura Moriarty's 2012 novel, *The Chaperone*, McGovern snapped up the movie rights to the bestselling book, which tells a story centered around Brooks' time as an aspiring Denishawn dancer.

Inspired by historical facts, *The Chaperone* tells the story of a 36 year-old housewife from Wichita, Kansas who accompanies a neighbor's teenage girl to New York City in the summer of 1922. The neighbor is future silent film star and contemporary cult icon Louise Brooks, who only a few years before entering the movies left home at age 15 to study at a prestigious school of dance named Denishawn.

If, one day, Fellows directs a film version of *The Chaperone* with McGovern as the title character and MacLaine, possibly, as Louise Brooks' mother, just remember you saw it here first. But who will play the teenage Brooks?

Doctor Who and Louise Brooks

This piece appeared on the Louise Brooks Society blog on November 22, 2013, and was updated for this book in 2018. My interview with Paul McGann first appeared on SFGate on July 11, 2012.

The connections between Louise Brooks and *Doctor Who* are, to say the least, a bit unexpected.

According to some Doctor Who websites, the writers of the Eighth Doctor Adventures novels—a series of spin-off stories published by BBC Books in the late 1990s, modelled the appearance of Romana III (a companion Timelord) on Brooks.

In 2009, the actress appeared in the first issue in an ongoing series of Doctor Who comics. In "Silver Scream," the good Doctor travels to 1920's Los Angeles, where he encounters not only Hollywood stars but also aliens intent on doing harm. (Other prominent film stars in the issue include Charlie Chaplin, Pola Negri, Douglas Fairbanks Sr., Adolphe Menjou, Rudolph Valentino, Chester Conklin, and Buster Keaton.) As well, there is a reference to Lulu in "The Silent Scream," a Doctor Who audio drama from 2017.

But what's more, one of Brooks's biggest fans is an actor who once the played the Doctor himself!

To celebrate the 50th anniversary of Doctor Who, the Louise Brooks Society looks back to this 2012 interview with actor Paul McGann, who played the eighth Doctor.

McGann is, by his own admission, a BIG fan of Brooks. In 2007, the celebrated actor even wrote an article for the *Guardian* newspaper about the celebrated silent film star.

Who is Paul McGann? As an actor, he first made a name for himself in 1986 as the lead in a historical BBC drama set during WWI, *The Monocled Mutineer*. McGann is also known for his role in one of Britain's biggest cult films, the 1987 black comedy, *Withnail and I*. Other credits include *Empire of the Sun*, *Alien 3*, *Queen of the Damned*, and the BBC's *Our Mutual Friend* and *Hornblower* series.

McGann may be best known, at least to science-fiction fans, as the Eighth Doctor, a role he played in a 1996 made-for-television movie. Its story, of the Doctor's regeneration and attempt to save the earth, is set in San Francisco in 1999, on the eve of the millennium.

McGann is also a patron of Bristol Silents, a group formed to raise awareness and knowledge of silent film among the English film going public. He has interviewed Kevin Brownlow on stage, introduced screenings of films from the silent era, and written about them for newspapers including the *Guardian*; his aforementioned piece on Louise Brooks, with whom he shares a birthday, is well worth checking out.

McGann answered a few questions about his interest in the silent era and what he is looking forward to seeing at this year's San Francisco Silent Film Festival.

TG: When did you first get interested in silent film?

PM: About ten years ago after becoming a patron of Bristol Silents. I'd had a general interest since my student days in London, during which the restored *Napoleon* was premiered, Kevin Brownlow's *Abel Gance* and David Robinson's *Chaplin* were published, and Louise Brooks was being 're-discovered.'

TG: Tell me more about your involvement with Bristol Silents. How did that relationship come about?

PM: I supported one of their early events, I think it was a screening of *The Big Parade*, and met Chris Daniels [a founder of the group]. He's kindly involved me in quite a few of their projects since, each bigger and better by the year.

TG: Any favorite films? How about favorite directors or stars?

PM: The first director I worked with, Bruce Robinson, told me when we met that if I thought Jaws was the perfect movie I plainly hadn't seen *The Gold Rush*. So I did. He was right. I've been a fan of Louise Brooks since first seeing *Pandora's Box* on television. I remember thinking they must've had that girl playing Lulu parachuted in from the present.

TG: You've written and spoken about Louise Brooks, and introduced her films. What is it about the actress that attracts you?

PM: She appeared to find, if only briefly, the perfect working spirit. Matchlessly beautiful, fully intelligent and a total natural; most screen actors would kill to be so blessed.

TG: At this year's San Francisco Silent Film festival, you're narrating *South*, Frank Hurley's documentary of Ernest Shackleton's expedition to Antarctica. What can we expect?

PM: Musician Stephen Horne and myself will try to recreate at least a flavour of the public screenings Shackleton hosted at London's Philharmonic Hall in 1919 when he read from his memoir while Hurley's film played.

TG: Have you narrated the film before?

PM: Twice, in Bristol and Pordenone, Italy.

TG: Are there any films you're especially excited about at this year's Festival.

PM: Aside from the thrill of seeing a beautifully restored *Pandora's Box*, I'm really intrigued about *Little Toys* from China and *Erotikon* from Sweden.

TG: You played a Time Lord in *Doctor Who*. Were you to travel back in time and return to the silent era and be cast in a film, which film would that be?

PM: That's easy, Murnau's *Sunrise*. I'd gladly (my wife might say naturally) take over George O'Brien's duties as the man caught between Janet Gaynor and Margaret Livingston.

Loving Louise Brooks: A Student Film You Must Watch

This piece appeared on Huffington Post on July 23, 2010. It generated a bit of buzz. The following day, The Bioscope ran a piece about the film and referenced my article, as did MUBI, another film site. Some time later, when I went to Paris, I had the chance to meet Sébastien Pesle.

Normally, I'm not one to pay much attention to student films. They are what they are. Some are amusing, and some are interesting. And some are merely the work of beginners just learning their craft. But recently, I came across an 11 minute work which I think is so good it transcends the category of "student" work. Sure, it has flaws — but I find it so charming I want everyone to know about it.

It's called *Loving Louise Brooks*, and it's recently debuted on the internet. It's the work of Sébastian Pesle, an 18 year old recently graduated French high school student. He has crafted a very true film well worth watching.

It's a short work which speaks not only to the vagaries of young love, but also to cinematic obsession — and the times when those two forces collide. As a student effort, it is especially mature and rather impressive. It reminds me of the work of Woody Allen.

Loving Louise Brooks was made in late 2009 and early 2010. It is a wordless sound film, in effect a "silent film," and a homage to the filmmaker's own infatuation with the movies. There is a musical soundtrack.

The film has popped up on Daily Motion, and a few other video sharing sights. *Loving Louise Brooks* features Pesle as a young cineaste obsessed with the silent film star. In a couple of scenes, he is shown sitting in a movie theater watching the 1929 Brooks film, *Diary of a Lost Girl*. And in another scene, he can be spotted reading a soft cover edition of Brooks' memoir, *Lulu in Hollywood*.

His charming girl friend, longing for his affection, is played by Malvina Desmarest. In the end, she must effect Brooks' appearance (a la the character she played in *Diary of a Lost Girl*) to get his attention. Whether this ploy works or not, I won't tell. You will have to watch the film to find out. And by the way, the characters in this short work are themselves making a film. Also in the cast are Alexis Garin and Yannis Letournel. All are, or were, film students, I believe, at the Lycee Jean-Batiste Corot in France. The story is by Lauranne Launay.

Remembering Richard Leacock
This piece appeared on examiner.com on March 28, 2011.

The death last week of filmmaker Richard Leacock marks the passing of an important figure in not only the story of film, but also the story of Louise Brooks. Leacock was 89.

Leacock is best known as a documentary film maker and as one of the key figures in cinéma vérité. Born in 1921, Leacock's first efforts with a camera date to his teenage years. Three years as a combat photographer in World War II were followed by 14 months as cameraman assisting Robert Flaherty on *Louisiana Story* (1941).

Leacock worked on or directed dozens of films. A groundbreaking behind-the-scenes look at John F. Kennedy and the 1960 presidential campaign was followed by portraits of Duchamp and Stravinsky, a collaboration with Jean-Luc Godard, and the still screened *Monterey Pop!* (assisted by fellow cinéma vérité filmmaker D.A. Pennebaker).

In 1984, Leacock released *Lulu in Berlin*, a 50 minute filmed interview with Louise Brooks. Shot in 1974, it remains one of the very few interviews (filmed or otherwise) the actress ever gave. In it, the actress discusses her film career in the United States and Germany—as well as her disregard for Hollywood. *Lulu in Berlin* includes film clips, but was shot entirely "on location" in Brooks' small Rochester, New York apartment. The actress, dressed in a powder blue bathrobe, is seen seated at her kitchen table across from the documentarian.

Though rarely screened, *Lulu in Berlin* is likely familiar to film buffs and devotees of the actress. It was include as bonus material on the recently released DVD of *Pandora's Box* from the Criterion Collection. Excerpts have also been included in a number of documentaries and television programs.

Lulu in Berlin was screened in San Francisco in March, 2006 as part of a "Leacock / Pennebaker: Pioneers of Cinema Verite" series which took place at the M.H. de Young Museum. Leacock was present at that special screening, which I attended.

During the question and answer session after the screening, Leacock recounted the circumstances behind the making of the film, how much "fun" it was, and how much he adored Brooks, something which is evident in *Lulu in Berlin*. Leacock also recounted that after their filming was complete, the actress made an omlet, and ordered the filmmaker to go to the liquor store and buy a quart of gin.

According to Leacock, *Lulu in Berlin* was shown on the BBC in England (in the 1980s?), though with added dramatic parts depicting Brooks' life. Leacock said he had nothing to do with the added bits, and was dismayed that the BBC altered his film.

Interestingly, it should be noted that Leacock's *Lulu in Berlin* was not his first encounter with the Lulu character. In 1967, Leacock shot footage for a Chicago staging of Alban Berg's opera, *Lulu*. It's original production notes calls for a short filmed interlude. In the 1967 production, under the direction of conductor Sarah Caldwell, Andy Warhol associate Edie Sedgwick played Lulu.

During the question and answer session in 2006, Leacock also mentioned that he had completed a 400 page autobiography, which is so far unpublished. Presumably, something about his making of *Lulu in Berlin* would be contained in that book.

Obituaries of Leacock appeared in newspapers from around the world, including the *New York Times*, *Boston Globe*, *Washington Post*, and London *Telegraph*.

Louise Brooks stars in new music videos
This piece appeared on examiner.com on May 13, 2013.

Silent film star Louise Brooks (1906-1985) is featured in two new music videos from Europe. Three images of the bobbed hair screen actress can be seen in "Tangled Up," the stylish new video for the new single from Caro Emerald's new album, *The Shocking Miss Emerald*, which was released earlier this month. *The Shocking Miss Emerald* is the singer's second album.

In 2007, Emerald was asked to cut a demo, and recorded 'Back It Up'. When she performed the song on a local Dutch TV station a year later, the song exploded. Her debut album, *Deleted Scenes from the Cutting Room Floor*, was released in January, 2010 and immediately went to number one on the Dutch album charts. The album stayed number one for 27 weeks, an all time record, beating out Michael Jackson's *Thriller*, which spent 26 weeks at number one in 1983. *Deleted Scenes from the Cutting Room Floor* reached double platinum status in the Netherlands in July of 2010. In August of that same year it reached triple platinum, and by November it had gone quadruple platinum, before hitting platinum six times over by year's end. *Deleted Scenes From The Cutting Room Floor* would end up spending 104 weeks on the album charts, until it was removed because of a Dutch rule which stipulates that albums can't spend more than 2 years on the charts. The album has been released in over 40 countries.

"Tangled Up" has a deco-tango- Jazz Age atmosphere to it, both in the visual styling of the video and in the arrangement of the song itself. It is catchy jazz pop with a nostalgic beat. Gatsby fans and silent film buffs will also find an image of Charlie Chaplin in the video.

Curiously, and perhaps not coincidentally, the title of Emerald's new album brings to mind the title of the acclaimed memoir by Hollywood screenwriter Frederica Sagor Maas, *The Shocking Miss Pilgrim*. Fans will recall that Mass also penned the story for the Louise Brooks' 1927 film, *Rolled Stockings*. Louise Brooks is the star of a second new video from Europe, "Sur ma Serviette" ("On my towel") by Moussu T e lei jovents. The track is from this French group's new album *ARTEMIS*, their fifth, which was released in April on Manivette records/Le Chant du monde in France. It was recently reviewed in the *Guardian* newspaper in England.

Like Caro Emerald, Moussu T e lei jovents looks to the past for musical inspiration. The group takes its inspiration from Marseille in the 1930, a musical melting pot where Provençal songs could be heard alongside local operettas by Vincent Scotto or the black music coming onto the scene at the time (which includes blues and jazz as well as music from the West Indies and Brazil.

"Sur ma Serviette" is made up of scenes from Louise Brooks' one film made in France, the 1930 release *Prix de beauté*.

For more on the group, check out their website at http://moussut.ohaime.com/

Perhaps more popular today then she was in the 1920's, Brooks has been celebrated in song - and paid homage to - by a number of pop, jazz, and rock musicians. The short list of music referencing or alluding to the actress include the John Zorn / George Lewis / Bill Frisell album *News for Lulu* (1990), Orchestral Manoeuvres in the Dark's "Pandora's Box (It's a Long, Long Way)" (1991), Soul Coughing's "St. Louise Is Listening" (1998), Marillion's "Interior Lulu" (1999), and Rufus Wainwright's album *All Days Are Nights: Songs for Lulu* (2010).

Natalie Merchant's 'Lulu' Latest Pop Tribute to Silent Film Icon Louise Brooks
This piece appeared on Huffington Post on May 19, 2014.

Natalie Merchant was in London last week promoting the release of her new album. The singer-songwriter performed sold-out shows, appeared on the BBC, and joined author Alain de Botton on stage for a conversation about her latest record.

One of the songs from Merchant's self-titled album (on Nonesuch) is a homage to silent film star Louise Brooks. The song is titled "Lulu." During the event with de Botton, Merchant unveiled the video for "Lulu." It excerpts scenes from *Pandora's Box*, the once infamous, now famous 1929 silent film in which Louise Brooks played Lulu.

"By writing 'Lulu'," Merchant explained, "I tried to compress her colossal life into a few verses of a song. She was such an intelligent, sensuous woman, an intuitive artist born years before her time. She was hedonistic and unapologetic, headstrong and impulsive. She rose to dizzy heights of international stardom and fell into a life of hand to mouth subsistence and seclusion only to be rediscovered and revived again before her death."

Merchant's "Lulu" is the latest pop music tribute to Louise Brooks (1906-1985), a silent film star who suffered decades of obscurity and was reluctantly brought back into the limelight late in life. Today, with an ever-growing fandom, Brooks' reputation has gone from cult figure to 20th century icon.

Brooks has, along the way, also gathered a number of admirers in the world of music. Madonna, Siouxsie Sioux, and the country music star Lorrie Morgan have all name checked the actress and, at times, modeled their own look after the silent film star.

Also among Brooks' admirers is singer songwriter Rufus Wainwright. In 2010, he released *All Days Are Nights: Songs for Lulu* (Decca), his own tribute to the actress. Wainwright's interest in Brooks was widely written about at the time, including here on the Huffington Post. Earlier this month, in an interview with *Out* magazine, Wainwright explained the grip the actress holds on his imagination, "My spirit animal is Louise Brooks from *Pandora's Box*. That character she plays in the film, Lulu. That's why I wrote *Songs for Lulu*, she needed to be appeased."

Merchant and Wainwright are not the first well-known artists to pay musical tribute to the bobbed-hair silent star. Before them, Mike Doughty of the alt rock band Soul Coughing penned "St. Louise Is Listening," his own slacker jazz homage. The song appeared on Soul Coughing's seminal 1998 release, *El Oso* (Slash/Warner), and on Doughty's 2013 album of reimagined Soul Coughing songs, *Circles Super Bon Bon.....* Doughty, it should also be noted, sports a Brooks tattoo.

And before Soul Coughing, there was the new wave band Orchestral Maneuvers in the Dark, who's "Pandora's Box (It's a Long, Long Way)" was the second single from their 1991 album *Sugar Tax* (Virgin). Like Merchant's "Lulu," the official OMD video features clips from Brooks' famous film. The Andy McCluskey penned song made the top 20 in the United States, United Kingdom, Sweden, Germany, and Austria, and was even covered by an Estonian pop singer, Jüri Homenja, whose version is titled "Pandora laegas." Be sure and check out the more recent OMD concert video embedded below; it features huge projected images Brooks.

There are other notable pop and rock tributes. In 1993, Australian Jen Anderson was asked to compose music for a screening of *Pandora's Box*. Her original soundtrack included a vocal number, "Lulu the song." It's a lyrical piece, and was a hit down under. Just as poignant is "Lulu," from ex-Lowest of the Low front man Ron Hawkins. His "Lulu" appeared on *The Secret of My Excess* (Shake) in 1995, the first solo effort the Canadian indie rocker. There's also Ross Berkal's rock ballad "MLB (for Louise Brooks)," from 2010.

Other indie musicians who have recorded songs about or referencing the actress include Paul Hayes' "Louise Brooks," from his 2003 album *Vol.1: Love And Pain And The Whole Damn Thing* (Autocthonous Recordings), and Gosta Berling's "Berlin," from the San Francisco band's first EP, *Everybody's Sweetheart* (Baroquen Records, 2008). Sarah Azzara's terrific "Like Louise Brooks," from her 2000 album *Revenge of Dangergirl* (Latest Records), uses the actress' iconic image as a visual/cultural reference.

Marillion, a British band formed in 1979, are regarded as one of the most successful groups to emerge from the neo-progressive rock scene of the 1980s. They've sold 15 million albums worldwide. Their song "Interior Lulu," from 1999's *marillion.com* (Sanctuary), also references the actress.

Brooks may be more popular in France than just about anywhere. Among the French acts that have recorded tributes to the actress is the musette revival band Les Primitifs Du Futur (whose line-up includes cartoonist Robert Crumb); they reworked the haunting theme song from the 1930 Louise Brooks film, *Prix de beauté*, into "Chanson pour Louise Brooks." Their version appears on the 1999 album, *World Musette* (Paris Jazz Corner).

There are other musical tributes to the actress. A search through Spotify, CD Baby, Soundcloud, iTunes, Last.fm, ccmixter, and elsewhere will turn up a number of other examples about the "damned and beautiful" actress, as one lyric put it. See the slide show which accompanies this article for more tracks, including work by the trio of John Zorn / George Lewis / Bill Frisell, The Subterraneans, TIMELOCK, Lou Reed & Metallica, and others.

Most of the above mentioned tracks can also be heard on RadioLulu, my Louise Brooks-inspired, silent-film themed online station streaming music of the 20s, 30s, and today. It is hosted on live365.com. If you don't know Brooks' life story, and why so many musicians would record songs about her, be sure and check out Barry Paris' heartbreaking 1989 biography. It is available from the University of Minnesota Press.

Louise Rutkowski, Diary of a Lost Girl

This piece appeared on the Louise Brooks Society blog on May 26, 2014. Like other artists of her generation, Louise Rutkowski took inspiration from Louise Brooks.

A new album by Louise Rutkowski, titled *Diary of a Lost Girl*, was released on Jock Records in February of 2014.

Recently, I emailed the Scottish singer songwriter and asked if her album of ethereal electro pop had any relationship to Louise Brooks. She wrote back, "There is indeed a relation between my new album title and Louise Brooks. I have been a fan since I was a teenager."

Diary of a Lost Girl is the first solo album from Rutkowski, a former vocalist with the music collective known as This Mortal Coil, and an ambient band which acted as a kind of continuation of This Mortal Coil, The Hope Blister. Rutkowski signed with CBS

Records at age 19, recording three singles and an album. However, it's her work with independent label 4AD and the above named bands for which she is best known.

Funded through the direct-to-fan platform PledgeMusic, *Diary of a Lost Girl* has been described as "A truly haunting and beautiful album" and "Beautiful, stirring, and alive with emotion." The *Daily Express* called it "a gorgeous and simple album that highlights her powerful voice." While *The Scotsman* said it was "immaculately produced" and "elegantly accomplished." The Louise Brooks Society agrees.

Produced by Irvin Duguid, the album includes mixes by Calum Malcolm (The Blue Nile) and Steve Orchard (Paul McCartney, Peter Gabriel, U2); it also marks Rutkowski's return to writing original material—her first compositions since her music career began with the soul-influenced band Sunset Gun.

Rutkowski went on to note: "I first came across Louise Brooks when I was in my early 20s and in my first band. I saw a photograph of her and was totally enchanted by her look. I collected many photographs (two of which are still on my walls at home), I read Barry Paris' biography, and went to see her films at the Scala in London (now a music venue). Sadly, my book and photograph collection got destroyed in a house fire, but I still have a few things left. One is the *Diary of a Lost Girl* poster, which hangs in my flat. I also remember watching an interview with her when she was older? I have Kenneth Tynan in my head but not sure if that's correct."

"I also had my hair in a bob for many years! I was, and still am, inspired by her. It wasn't just her look, it was her acting and who she was as a person—so feisty and witty."

"As for the album title, I had been searching for a while for a suitable one, and found myself staring at the poster one night, realising 'that was it'! I chose it as it fitted perfectly with the feeling behind the songs as a collection. This is a very personal album, written mostly around the time of my mother's death (also a huge film fan and admirer of LB), and the word 'lost' rather fitted at that point. It has such a beautiful ring to it in any event."

A Glastonbury First
This piece appeared on Huffington Post (UK) on June 24, 2014.

Over the years, there have been great performances and historic moments at the annual Glastonbury Festival. This year should be no different.

Along with predictions of rain, there are rumours that Prince will make a surprise appearance. The five day festival, which runs through Sunday, June 29, features an eclectic line-up of musical acts; scheduled to perform are Arcade Fire, Lily Allen, Jack White, Robert Plant, Lana Del Ray, The Black Keys, Foster the People, Blondie, Yoko Ono, Dr. Feelgood, Dolly Parton, Nick Lowe, Suzanne Vega, and the tUnE-yArDs, among others.

One act breaking new ground are the Dodge Brothers, a five man quartet (I'll explain later) that play an exuberant, sometimes raucous hybrid of country blues, rockabilly, jugband and skiffle. Some have called what they play roots music, others call it Americana. Whatever it's called, it rocks.

On Saturday, June 28, the Dodge Brothers are set to become the first band to accompany a silent film at Glastonbury. The film is *Beggars of Life* (1928). Directed by William Wellman the year after he made *Wings* (the first film to win the Academy Award for Best Picture), *Beggars of Life* is a American drama about a lovely girl (the beautiful Louise Brooks) dressed as a boy who flees the law after killing her abusive stepfather. On the run, she rides the rails through a hobo underworld where danger is always close at hand.

Based on a novelistic memoir by hobo author Jim Tully, the film also features future Oscar winner Wallace Berry and the early African-American actor Edgar "Blue" Washington. Girls dressed as boys, race mingling, pastoral life gone wrong, and desperation among the glitz and glamour of the Twenties—there is a lot of friction in *Beggars of Life*. In her book, *100 Silent Films*, BFI curator Bryony Dixon calls it a movie to "wallow" in. *Beggars of Life* is rich with mood, tension, sentiment, harrowing danger, and beauty.

For the record, *Beggars of Life* is not the first silent film shown at Glastonbury. That honor belongs to *Metropolis* (1927), which was first screened in the 1980s. The Dodge Brothers, however, will be the first band to play live music to accompany a silent. It is something they've done before.

The Dodge Brothers are Mike Hammond (lead guitar, lead vocals, banjo), Mark Kermode (bass, harmonica, vocals), Aly Hirji (rhythm guitar, mandolin, vocals), and Alex Hammond (washboard, snare drum, percussion). Joining the band at Glastonbury and elsewhere when they accompany silent films is composer and silent film accompanist Neil Brand, a regular at London's National Film Theatre.

According to founder Mark Kermode, who doubles as film critic for *The Observer*, "all this started because Neil Brand approached us with the idea of playing to silents as they used to with local pickup bands. Neil can do this as he's a solo performer, but we were concerned about doing this as a band, and whether our music would fit with the films. He said 'Trust me - it'll work'. I've found that as long as I can see Neil's left hand I can follow what he's doing. The more we play silent films the less we use our cue sheets and the more we play to the film itself. This means that every performance is different."

Over the last few years, the Dodge Brothers have accompanied *Beggars of Life* around the UK, including well received gigs at BFI Southbank, The Barbican London, National Media Museum, and other venues. Aly Hirji, who performs under the name Aly Dodge, recently remarked "As we'd played to silent films all over the country, I thought it was time we took it to Glastonbury. I contacted the festival and they happened to be looking for something that would be different enough to draw an audience from the big music stages on Saturday night." Even if the band draws only a fraction of the estimated 175,000 people expected to attend the Festival, Glastonbury's Pilton Palais Cinema Marquee should prove their largest audience to date.

For those keeping track, the Dodge Brothers are not the only Glastonbury performer with a connection to Louise Brooks. (The silent film star is becoming something of a rock icon.) Also set to perform at this year's Festival on Sunday is Caro Emerald, whose 2013 "Tangled Up" video features three hard-to-miss images of the actress, one of which is the poster for *Pandora's Box* (1929). And then there is Metallica, who perform Saturday. In 2011, they collaborated with Lou Reed on *Lulu*, their oblique, noisy riff on the legendary character played by Brooks in the film version of *Pandora's Box*.

The Glastonbury Festival is a five day music festival that takes place near Pilton, Somerset, England. In addition to contemporary music, the festival hosts dance, comedy, theatre, circus, cabaret and other arts. More at www.glastonburyfestivals.co.uk

Rufus Wainwright pens tribute to silent film star Louise Brooks
This piece appeared on examiner.com on January 12, 2010.

It seems as though contemporary music is rediscovering silent film.

Tonight in San Francisco, Steven Severin, one of the founding members of Siouxsie and the Banshees, is giving a live performance of *Music for Silents*, which he wrote to accompany *The Seashell and the Clergyman* (1928) and other silent films.

And a few days ago, word got out that the acclaimed singer / songwriter Rufus Wainwright has recorded a new album called *All Days Are Nights: Songs for Lulu*. It's a tribute to the silent film star Louise Brooks and her best known role, that of Lulu in the German silent film *Pandora's Box* (1929). Wainwright's album, his sixth, is due in March.

To date, the Grammy-nominated Canadian-American musician has recorded five albums of original music, as well as EPs and tracks on compilations and soundtracks. Wainwright, who rose to fame in the mid- to late-1990s, is the child of famed folksingers Kate McGarrigle and Loudon Wainwright III. In 1998, Rufus Wainwright was named "Best New Artist" of the year by *Rolling Stone*.

An article by Ben Wener in Sunday's *Orange County Register* quotes Wainwright stating that *Songs for Lulu* were inspired by "any kind of reckless woman in your life, in your imagination … or in yourself." For Wainwright, that reckless woman has become Louise Brooks and the role for which she is closely identified.

Not much is so far known about *All Days Are Nights: Songs for Lulu*. A Wikipedia page already devoted to the forthcoming album reveals little beyond that the first part of the title, "All Days Are Nights," derives from William Shakespeare's "Sonnet 43" ("All days are nights to see till I see thee…"). Wainwright recently completed a theater project focusing on Shakespeare's sonnets with the avant-gardist Robert Wilson.

According to the Wikipedia entry on the album, when Wainwright was asked about the reference to Lulu, the musician stated in a November 2009 interview on radio station KUT in Austin, Texas that his Lulu is the " 'dark, brooding, dangerous woman that lives within all of us,' similar to the Dark Lady character in Shakespeare's sonnets."

During the KUT interview, Wainwright references both the actress the character of Lulu.

Like Andy McCluskey of Orchestral Manoeuvres in the Dark (OMD) with "Pandora's Box, It's a Long, Long, Way," Mike Doughty of Soul Coughing with "St. Louise Is Listening," and a number of other recording artists (The Green Pajamas, Paul Hayes, Sarah Azzara), Wainwright has turned his interest in one silent film star into music.

"I Am the Victim of Such a Lascivious Beauty" - Rufus Wainwright on Louise Brooks *This piece appeared on Huffington Post on August 5, 2010.*

"I have always wanted to be her" is the way Rufus Wainwright puts it, referring to Louise Brooks.

The iconic, long dead film star with the sharp black bob is best known for her riveting performance as Lulu in the 1929 silent film, *Pandora's Box*. Over the years, she has drawn a cult following of gay men and pop musicians. One of them is Wainwright, a singer praised by the *New York Times* for his "genuine originality."

"I've seen that film at least eight times. I watched it recently—we have it on the bus," Wainwright adds. And then, with equal parts seriousness and self-irony, the singer-songwriter declares, "I am the victim of such a lascivious beauty."

Wainwright is not only a self-described victim of the legendary femme fatale, he is also a fan—and a follower, of sorts, in her footsteps.

Wainwright's celebrated 2009 live album, *Milwaukee at Last!!!*, was recorded at the Pabst Theater in Wisconsin—the same stage where the teenage Brooks danced alongside Martha Graham, Ruth St. Denis, Ted Shawn and members of the famed Denishawn Dance Company. The Pabst is also one of three stops on Wainwright's current 16 city American tour which follow in the footsteps of Brooks' early years as a touring dance prodigy. Coincidence or some kind of fate?

These days, Wainwright is on tour to support *All Days Are Nights: Songs for Lulu*, his new CD. When asked about its allusive title, the singer-songwriter stated "I'm referring to Louise Brooks and the movie *Pandora's Box*, where she plays the character Lulu... What is fascinating about the character, the movie and the opera *Lulu* by Alban Berg—I have to admit I haven't yet read the [Frank Wedekind] play—is that she is pretty much an innocent. Yet, disaster reigns wherever she treads her little foot. For me, that is such a fabulous example of the nature of chaos—where terrible, terrible things happen and it has nothing to do with morality. It's a force of nature. Chaos happens in nature, and in mankind."

Long a fan of European cinema, the 37-year-old Wainwright discovered Brooks when he was 18 years old. And apparently, the lascivious beauty who left a trail of broken hearts on two continents made an impression. [For me] "she has always been a vision of the decadent, carefree, bohemian flapper who tears down the world where ever she goes, with a smile."

"She has become a kind of symbol of the dark world which I love so much—but can't really spend much time in," Wainwright adds, with a laugh. He's likely alluding to his own troubled past, which included widely-reported drug use, the pressures of celebrity pop-stardom and the recent death of his mother, acclaimed folk singer Kate

McGarrigle.

For Wainwright, Brooks' own chaotic life and the unfulfilled promise of her careers as a dancer and actress serve as a kind of warning shadow. "Every time I am a little bit vulnerable or under pressure or tired, I see her [Louise Brooks] as a vision, as a phantom, and I need to watch out—these new songs are a sacrifice to her spirit."

The new songs on *All Days Are Nights: Songs for Lulu* are, according to Wainwright, the "the toughest songs I have ever had to play and sing." For the musician, they represent a "mountain range of personal and artistic exploration" whose peaks and valleys are "grief and pain and also transcendence and also a certain spiritual knowledge."

Besides Milwaukee, Pittsburgh, Chicago, Denver and Los Angeles, Wainwright's tour also takes him to the San Francisco Bay Area, where he will be performing three dates in August. It's his longest stop in any one area—and a kind of coming home for Wainwright's muse. Frank Wedekind—the German playwright responsible for bringing Lulu to the world—was nearly born in the Bay Area.

How Wedekind (1864-1918) almost came be an American writer is a long story. It's a story which, someday, Wainwright might turn into another song, or an opera, or even a film score. When asked if he had ever thought about scoring a silent film, Wainwright answered in the affirmative, "that's a very interesting idea. Perhaps *Pandora's Box*."

Rufus Talks Lulu - Plays Denver August 17
This piece appeared on the Denver section of Huffington Post on August 17, 2010.

It's been three years since Rufus Wainwright played Denver. And in the meantime, a lot has happened.

The singer-songwriter, praised by *The New York Times* for his "genuine originality" and referred to by Elton John as "the greatest songwriter on the planet," has released a couple of albums, premiered an opera, acted in his third film, composed a musical adaptation of Shakespeare's Sonnets, and publicly and poignantly suffered the loss of his mother, the acclaimed folk singer Kate McGarrigle.

There have been many ups and downs, to say the least.

These days, Wainwright is in the middle of 16-city cross country tour in support of his new album, *All Days Are Nights: Songs for Lulu*. He's already played Boston, Philadelphia, Pittsburgh, and Chicago—and on August 17, he comes to Denver. The show, which had been set for the Paramount Theatre, has been moved to the Ogden Theatre for a reserved seated show.

Recently, Wainwright took time out of rehearsals to answer a few questions about *All Days Are Nights: Songs for Lulu*. His new album may be his best yet—and also his most revealing.

TG: You've mentioned five women were the muse for your new album. Who are they?

RW: Yes, there are five. I could start with the title, *Songs for Lulu*. I am referring to Louise Brooks and the movie *Pandora's Box*, where she plays the character Lulu. She has always been a vision of the decadent, carefree, bohemian flapper who tears down the world where ever she goes, with a smile. She has become a kind of symbol of the dark world which I love so much—but can't really spend much time in. Every time I am a little bit vulnerable or under pressure or tired I see her as a vision, as a phantom, and I need to watch out—these songs are a sacrifice to that spirit.

The next is Régine Saint Laurent, a character from my opera, *Prima Donna*. One of the arias from the opera is on the new album. She has been a character who has inhabited my life for four or five years. I've lived with her constantly - it's what one has to do to write an opera, inhabit the characters. Shakespeare's Dark Lady was wandering around as well. I'm working with Robert Wilson and the Berliner Ensemble on the Shakespeare sonnets project. The Dark Lady in Robert Wilson's version of the sonnets is really DEATH - she embodies death in that production. I have to say, if you ever have a chance to see it in Berlin, it is absolutely fantastic, and very effective.

The two other women are the most important women of my life, one being Martha—my sister, and the other being my mother Kate—who passed away. So it's quite a strong bunch—both mythical and real people.

TG: Archetypes?

RW: They are archetypes and also muses and foils.

TG: You said these songs were a "sacrifice." How so?

RW: You can look at this album as a kind of representation of grief and pain and also transcendence, and also spiritual knowledge—these are also the toughest songs I have ever had to play and sing—and they are matched with some of the simplest and purest melodies I have ever written. For me, it's been a mountain range of personal and artistic exploration, and with only two instruments, my voice and the piano. In a lot of ways it is a sacrifice. It takes a lot of energy. I have to be operating on all cylinders. I have to be totally true to myself when I perform.

TG: You mentioned Shakespeare's "Dark Lady." What does she mean to you?

RW: A lot of people ask me—or at least a lot of people talk about, they don't necessarily ask me—was Shakespeare gay? I don't think so, but I do believe he had sexual feelings for this young boy [referenced in the Sonnets]. That really took him off guard. So, I would say he was bisexual. The dark lady, on the other hand, is really his sexual drive. He is a kind of slave to this brooding attraction for this woman whom he wants to screw but is also screwed by. (Laughs) It's the tortuous nature of male and female relationships—the battle of the sexes. That is the impression I got.

TG: Your new album has been described as "stripped down." It's certainly the most revealing and personal of your recent projects.

RW: Recently, I said in an interview "if you wait, life will show you what's going on." That's the case with this album. Back when I released *Release the Stars*, there were rumblings of it being a kind of stripped down album. But I went full throttle the other way.

I knew at some point that I would have to make this kind of record. And now that I look back at it I see that it required many ingredients. One being a tragedy—my mother's passing, which was the toughest thing I have ever gone through. It needed that. It also needed some sort of reaction to these massive projects with huge orchestras—I'm talking about the opera. And the Robert Wilson project. And the Judy Garland show. So I needed some sort of yin to that yang, shall we say.

Also, to be frank, I am a strong believer that art is tied to the ways of the world. We are in a period of cutbacks and downsizing. So, there was also a very practical reason why I had to do it—I had to survive like everyone else in these challenging times.

Run You Luscious Lesbian
This piece appeared on exaimner.com on June 7, 2010.

Louise Brooks fan, and now recording artist The GrrrL (aka April Louise McLucas of Portland, Maine), has just released a rough-and-ready, do-it-yourself CD titled *Run You Luscious Lesbian*. It's a five track demo recording available for purchase online and through select brick-and-mortar locales.

The opening cut, "Black Is The Color (Louise Brooks Hair)," should appeal to the silent film star's many fans.

This is home-made music. Call it DIY if you must. To describe this disc as raw would almost be an understatement. It's that, but it's also closer to the bone and a lot more authentic and heartfelt *(that's not a bad word)* then a lot of music released today. This is outsider art. This is music which wears its heart on its sleeve.

When asked about her musical leanings, The GrrrL stated, "I'm heavily influenced by artists like PJ Harvey, Carla Bozulich, and Carla Kihlstedt. They all create unique music that resonates with me as an artist. While I consider myself an experimental rock musician, I would be the first to admit that I'm a non-musician because I don't really know the first thing about making music except that I like the sounds I produce. My motto is 'Anyone can make music if they have the passion for it'."

When asked about the impetus behind "Black Is The Color," the singer / songwriter noted, "*Pandora's Box* was the first Louise Brooks film I watched. It was soon after I started working at Videoport, an indie video store in Portland, Maine. I was drawn to the cover photo of Louise on the VHS box and took it home one day. That was the beginning of my love of Louise and of silent films. I now run a Silent Film Enthusiasts group here in Maine."

Run You Luscious Lesbian is The GrrrL's first solo project. She is also a member of two local bands in Portland, The Monster Demands A Mate and Ape vs Panda. The Grrrl project began in the winter of 2009, when McLucas recorded her first song, a lesbian take on the traditional song "Salty Dog Blues."

"Black Is The Color (Louise Brooks Hair)" also has its roots in traditional music. The GrrrL's version is a homage to the actress' famous bob. The song is a riff on "Black Is the Colour (of My True Love's Hair)," a traditional folk song, circa 1915, from the Appalachian Mountains region.

More about The GrrrL, including a few sample tracks, can be found on the artist's Myspace page at www.myspace.com/thegrrrlmusic.

Lou Reed, Frank Wedekind, Metallica and Lulu
This piece appeared on SFGate on July 25, 2011.

As great 20th century writers go, Frank Wedekind (1864-1918) is far from a household name. Once controversial and censored, this German-born playwright, poet, novelist and cabaret artist has long sat in the shadows of modern literature. What can critics do with a writer who once wrote "Search fearlessly for every sin, for out of sin comes joy."

Wedekind's obscurity may be coming to an end—if the music world has anything to do with it.** In 2006, Wedekind's first major play, *Spring Awakening* (1891), was adapted by Duncan Sheik and Steven Sater into a smash-hit rock musical on Broadway. It won eight Tony Awards and four Drama Desk Awards, while its London production garnered four Olivier Awards. Local productions of the musical continue to pop-up across the country.

Last year, acclaimed singer-songwriter Rufus Wainwright riffed off Wedekind's Lulu when he released *All Days Are Nights: Song for Lulu*. Wainwright admitted in an interview his song suite also owed a little something to his interest in the silent film star, Louise Brooks. She played Lulu in the 1929 film, *Pandora's Box*.

Word broke last month that former Velvet Underground front man Lou Reed has teamed up with local rockers Metallica on Reed's latest project, an adaption of the songs Reed wrote for Robert Wilson's recent avant-garde staging of *Lulu*—Wedekind's "monster tragedie," in Berlin.

In an interview with *New York* magazine, Reed stated "There are two stories Lulu's based on, and I rewrote Lulu from the get-go, taking the original plot—mostly *Earth Spirit*, not *Pandora's Box*—and followed it essentially from the point of view of Lulu and the various people who love her, until she gets involved with Jack the Ripper. The basics. So the Metallica version will have absolutely all of that and more. It'll probably come out by November."

We can only hope. Reed does not have a record deal, and Metallica are no longer on Warner Bros. "We are free to go wherever," Lars Ulrich said on David Fricke's blog on rollingstone.com. "I'm obviously psyched for people to hear this, in whatever way we feel is right." Metallica's James Hetfield had one condition. "I told Lou I want to be there when people hear it. . . . I want to see their faces."

Will *Lulu* end up on Broadway, like *Spring Awakening*? It's unlikely. "I don't think Metallica wants to be a band on Broadway!" Reed quipped in the *New Yorker* interview.

According to online reports, the as yet unnamed, 10 song Lou Reed / Metallica collaboration was completed at Metallica's studio north of San Francisco. That's appropriate, as Wedekind got "his start" here in the Bay Area.

As it turns out, Wedekind's parents were both German immigrants resident in San Francisco in the years following the Gold Rush. His father was a respected physician and progressive democrat whose participation in the Revolutions of 1848 in the German states led him to escape to America; his mother was a saloon entertainer, singer and actress twenty-three years his junior. (Some scholars have speculated that this unconventional relationship might have served as a model for the similar relationship between Dr. Schon and Lulu in *Pandora's Box*.)

A search of city directories for 1858, 1860, and 1862 reveals that the future playwright's Father, Friedrich Wilhelm Wedekind, had a medical practice at 136 and later 524 Montgomery Street in San Francisco. Doctor Wedekind was also a prominent member of the local German General Benevolent Society as well as President of the local German Club.

Friedrich Wedekind and Emilie Kammerer's second child—the future writer—was conceived in San Francisco, though born in what is now Hanover, Germany. Early in the pregnancy, the still patriotic couple decided to visit their native land. And that's where Benjamin Franklin Wedekind (named for the free-thinking American writer and revolutionary) was born in 1864.

And the rest, as they say, is history . . . a curious chain of events crisscrossing through time and place and literature and music.

** Of course, the first musical adaption of one of Wedekind's works was by composer Alban Berg, who fashioned his unfinished 1937 opera *Lulu* out of Wedekind's two Lulu plays, *Earth Spirit* (1895) and *Pandora's Box* (1904). In 1965, the San Francisco Opera staged the work's West Coast premiere. Berg's masterpiece was seen most recently in the Bay Area in 2003, as part of the San Francisco Opera's Femmes Fatales Festival.

Lou Reed and Metallica dream a nightmare called Lulu
This unpublished piece was written on November 2, 2011.

There are enough oblique allusions to Louise Brooks' life and career in the just released collaborative Lou Reed / Metallica album to lead me to think that the rock musician had the actress, at least partially, in mind when writing the material which became *Lulu* (Warner Bros.).

In the least, *Lulu* is a nightmare—a terrible, dark, painful dream. The question a listener, any listener, this listener, might ask is—who is the dreamer? Whose terrible, dark, painful nightmare are we listening to?

Is it Frank Wedekind's, the German playwright who penned the Lulu character? Is it Brooks', the small town American actress who played Lulu? (And somewhat in real life, as director G.W. Pabst said she would.) Is it Lou Reed's nightmare, channeled through persons and characters from the past? Or is it some messy, fluid combination thereof?

It's hard to say. And ultimately it may not matter. What remains is a 10 song musical slugfest.

Louise Brooks, William Kentridge and the Making of Lulu
This piece appeared on the Louise Brooks Society blog on November 3, 2015.

There is an old saying. Chance favors the prepared mind. There is another saying about being in the right place at the right time.

I love books. And have long been involved in various aspects of publishing. For two-and-a-half years I worked at Arion Press in San Francisco as its Director of Marketing and Sales. Arion Press, if you're not familiar, is one of the last letterpress publishers in the world. Begun more than 40 years ago, Arion makes extraordinary, limited edition, handmade books. Their *Moby-Dick*, with 100 wood engravings by Barry Moser, and their *Ulysses*, with 40 etchings by Robert Motherwell, are each legendary and sought after.

One day in 2013 at an Arion Press staff meeting, we were discussing upcoming projects. At the time, the press was looking for a new book to publish; the press was also wanting to work with artist William Kentridge—a proposed Flaubert project with Kentridge had stalled out. At the time, Kentridge was deep into his production of Alban Berg's opera *Lulu*, which was based on two plays by the German playwright Frank Wedekind.

I have always been an idea guy, and it was at that meeting that I suggested to Arion publisher Andrew Hoyem that the press pair Kentridge with Wedekind's two Lulu plays, *Earth Spirit* and *Pandora's Box*. I made the suggestion not long after having read in the *New York Times* that Kentridge himself was inspired by Brooks—the actress who played Lulu in the 1929 silent film, *Pandora's Box*. It seemed like a good fit.

Speaking to the *New York Times* in 2013, Kentridge explained "that his *Lulu* was being inspired by German Expressionism, Weimar cinema (including, of course, *Pandora's Box*, the G. W. Pabst version of the Lulu story starring Louise Brooks), Max Beckmann drypoints depicting brothels and the like...."

Not long after the staff meeting where I made my suggestion, Hoyem approached Kentridge with the idea of publishing the Lulu plays accompanied by artwork by Kentridge. After some back and forth, the project was a go.

Fast forward to 2015: Arion Press has just released its edition of Wedekind's *The Lulu Plays*, featuring 67 Kentridge drawings (printed by four-color offset lithography) bound into the book. The images are derived from brush and ink drawings for projections included in the artist's new production of Berg's opera, which opens at the Metropolitan Opera in New York on November 5. It looks to be a terrific production.

The role of Lulu is sung by the German coloratura soprano Marlis Peterson (a dirty blonde who wears her hair shoulder length); she is famed for the role, and in this production sports a dark bob *a la* Louise Brooks.

Those seeking a sneak peak of the visuals behind the opera should head over to the Marion Goodman Gallery in New York City, where "William Kentridge: Drawings for Lulu" is on display through December 19th. The exhibit presents the original 67 drawings by Kentridge used in the opera and the book, as well as a suite of four related linocut prints. The Arion Press edition of *The Lulu Plays* is also on display at the gallery, as well as at the IFPDA Print Fair in New York from November 4 through November 8.

The Arion Press edition of *The Lulu Plays* is a fine achievement. It's both handsome and sexy. Four-hundred copies were printed, each signed by the artist and numbered. The book is quarto format, measuring 13-1/2" x 10", and is printed by letterpress on luxurious creamy paper utilizing period type in fittingly black and red inks. The book is hand bound, and comes in a slipcase. Louise Brooks and her role in *Pandora's Box* is mentioned in the introduction.

To learn more about the new edition of *The Lulu Plays*, check there is a video from a Metropolitan Museum of Art on-stage conversation between Kentridge and Arion Press publisher Hoyem.

The Met's production of William Kentridge's staging of Alban Berg's opera will be streamed live into theaters across the country on Saturday, November 21st.

Lulu-mania Sweeps New York City
This piece appeared on Huffington Post on November 5, 2015.

Lulu, it seems, is everywhere.

Frank Wedekind's legendary femme fatale, who's beguiling behavior inspired nearly as many artists as Helen of Troy's beauty launched ships, can be found all over New York City.

Alban Berg's modernist opera, *Lulu*, which was based on Wedekind's two "Lulu" plays, *Erdgeist* (*Earth Spirit*, 1895) and *Die Büchse der Pandora* (*Pandora's Box*, 1904), has just opened a month-long run at the Metropolitan Opera. This new production stars the soprano Marlis Petersen and is directed by the South African artist William Kentridge, whose dynamic art for the staging of the opera proves as seductive and active as Lulu herself. The Met's new production of *Lulu* runs through December 3.

Meanwhile, across town, the Marion Goodman Gallery is showing "William Kentridge: Drawings for Lulu." This exhibit presents the original 67 Kentridge drawings used in the opera. Anyone who sees *Lulu*, who appreciates Kentridge's art, or who is inclined toward German Expressionism will want to see *and study* this must-not-miss show. "William Kentridge: Drawings for Lulu" is on display through December 19th.

Also on display at the Marion Goodman Gallery is a suite of four related linocut prints by Kentridge, as well as a new fine press edition of the Lulu plays which utilizes Kentridge's art. The book is from the San Francisco-based Arion Press, which has just released its edition of Wedekind's *The Lulu Plays* featuring the 67 Kentridge drawings (printed by four-color offset lithography) bound into the book.

The Arion Press edition of *The Lulu Plays* is a fine achievement. Four-hundred copies of this limited edition artist's book were printed by letterpress on luxurious creamy paper utilizing period type in fittingly black and red inks. The book, which is hand bound and comes in a slipcase, can be seen and no-doubt fondled at the Arion Press booth at the IFPDA Print Fair at the Park Avenue Armory through November 8.

It is on November 8 that a free screening of the 1929 silent film, *Pandora's Box*, starring Louise Brooks—the greatest Lulu of them all, will take place at Central Branch of the Brooklyn Public Library. The sensational G.W. Pabst directed film was drawn from the Wedekind play, and in turn contributed to Berg's realization of his opera (composed from 1929-1935, premiered incomplete in 1937) just a few years later.

If you are looking for a little background on Kentridge's art and its use in the new production of Berg's opera, as well as the Arion Press edition of *The Lulu Plays*, track down the video of a recent onstage conversation between Kentridge and Arion publisher Andrew Hoyem which took place last month at the Metropolitan Museum of Art.

Those in upstate New York who can't make it to NYC can look forward to seeing some of this work in the future. The newly renamed George Eastman Museum in Rochester recently announced that Kentridge has given the definitive collection of his archive and art—including films, videos and digital works, as well as his work for *Lulu*—to the museum. Founded in the 1940s, the museum has one of the world's largest and oldest photography and film collections. It was also the longtime home of Louise Brooks.

Lulu, who in Wedekind's play dies in London at the hands of Jack the Ripper, is very much alive these days in New York.

Opera with Louise Brooks inspired character debuts, and it's not *Lulu*
This piece appeared on Huffington Post on February 20, 2017.

The Invention of Morel, a new 90 minute opera with a Louise Brooks inspired character, has received its world premiere at the Studebaker Theater in Chicago, Illinois under the auspices of the city's Chicago Opera Theater. Additional information on the production can be found here.

The Invention of Morel is a music theater adaptation of the 1940 novella by Adolfo Bioy Casares. The score is by Stewart Copeland (the co-founder and drummer for the Police), with stage direction by the English actor-writer Jonathan Moore. Copeland and Moore collaborated on the libretto. The opera was commissioned by the Long Beach Opera and Chicago Opera Theater. (Excerpts from *The Invention of Morel* were performed as part of the New Opera Showcase, presented by OPERA America and NOVUS NY orchestra on January 18, 2016, at Trinity Wall Street.)

The opera features alluring Valerie Vinzant as Faustine, and Andrew Wilkowske as the Fugitive. Baritone Lee Gregory is the Narrator (the id of the Fugitive), and tenor Nathan Granner is Morel. Kimberly E. Jones plays Dora, Barbara Landis is the Duchess, Scott Brunscheen is Alec/Ombrellieri, and David Govertsen is Stoever.

The full opera debuted in Chicago on February 18th. In its reviews, the *Chicago Sun-Times* described the work as "the alternately unnerving nightmare and beautiful fever dream of a man on the run who sees no hope for his future until he conjures a relationship with an enigmatic woman," adding "*Invention of Morel* deftly balances period charm with a contemporary sense of artificial reality." The *Chicago Tribune* said it was "a brilliant piece of musical surrealism."

Casares' *La invención de Morel* is widely considered the first literary work of magical realism, predating the kindred fiction of Jorge Luis Borges, Gabriel Garcia Marquez, and others. It features a character named Faustine who was inspired by the author's long-time affection for Louise Brooks. Casares said as much in interviews in later years. Those facts are seemingly not lost on the designers of the opera, who have modeled their Faustine character after Brooks' appearance, especially her signature bob hairstyle.

Though not as well known as it should be, *The Invention of Morel* has had a unique, lingering resonance throughout the late 20th and early 21st centuries. Casares' book was made into a French movie called *L'invention de Morel* (1967), and an Italian movie called *L'invenzione di Morel* (1974). It is also believed to have inspired the Alain Resnais' film *Last Year At Marienbad* (1961), which was adopted for the screen by the French novelist Alain Robbe-Grillet. Brooks herself ended up on the cover of a recent edition of Casares' book, which in turn was given a shout-out on the television series *Lost* (2004–2010).

Notably, this is not the first time a contemporary opera singer has been modeled after Brooks. Witness William Kentridge's recent staging of Alban Berg's opera, *Lulu*, where the appearance of the Lulu character was meant to evoke the actress. The source material for both operas, of course, bear a relationship to Brooks as well, as Brooks starred as Lulu in a 1929 film adaption of Frank Wedekind's earlier play, *Pandora's Box*. [The Metropolitan Opera Orchestra staging of William Kentridge's production of *Lulu* was recently released on DVD / Blu-ray on the Nonesuch label.]

The *Chicago Tribune* noted: "As the Fugitive (forcefully sung and acted by baritone Andrew Wilkowske) falls desperately in love with a mysterious beauty who's one of Morel's guests, the symbolically named Faustine (a character inspired by the 1920s film star Louise Brooks), we see the Narrator (the excellent baritone Lee Gregory) pouring his confusion and fears into a diary. He tries to catch her attention and persuade her to return his longing, but she remains as remote as the rest."

About the opera, the Chicago Opera Theater stated on their website, "This world premiere opera is based on *La invención de Morel*, a 1940 novel by the influential Argentine author, Adolfo Bioy Casares. The story for this opera does not live within the classic constructs of time and space, but instead explores powerful driving forces of human emotion: love, desire, and sacrifice.... An escaped fugitive arrives on an isolated, strange island. While exploring his surroundings, he observes a group of tourists and quickly realizes something is not quite right in this paradise. Intrigued yet wary of these eccentric visitors, he begins to fall in love with one—a strikingly beautiful woman. He discovers these visitors are here at the invitation of Morel, a mad scientific genius, for the unveiling of his latest mysterious invention. When his heart pulls him helplessly toward this beautiful woman he must ask himself how much he is willing to sacrifice to be with her."

Chicago Opera Theater's world-premiere production of Stewart Copeland's *The Invention of Morel*, conducted by Andreas Mitisek, continues through February 26 at the Studebaker Theater, 410 S. Michigan Ave., in Chicago, Illinois.

Louise Brooks' Star Shines Brighter Than Ever
This piece appeared on Huffington Post on November 4, 2013.

More than 25 years after her death, Louise Brooks is more popular than ever.

The silent film star, famous for both her sleek dark bob and role as Lulu in *Pandora's Box*, is undergoing a revival. The actress—her image and legend, are seemingly everywhere.

On October 17th, bestselling author Donna Tartt (who also sports a stylish bob) told the *New York Times* that one of the books she's currently reading is Barry Paris' acclaimed biography of the actress. That book, first published in 1989, is considered one of the finest film biographies ever written.

The day before, the same newspaper suggested that South African artist William Kentridge had also been drawn to Brooks. Kentridge is staging Alban Berg's opera *Lulu* at the Met in 2015; he explained to the *New York Times* that "his Lulu was being inspired by German Expressionism, Weimar cinema (including, of course, *Pandora's Box*, the G. W. Pabst version of the Lulu story starring Louise Brooks), Max Beckmann drypoints depicting brothels and the like."

While the *New York Times* was giving shout-outs to the actress, a stage play about Brooks was running in London. Janet Munsil's *Smoking with Lulu* dramatizes an encounter between the older Brooks and the younger Kenneth Tynan, the English critic who had a lifelong erotic obsession with the actress. Munsil, a Canadian playwright, wrote *Smoking with Lulu* in 1995. Prior to its recent revival in London, *Smoking with Lulu* had been staged across the British Isles, Canada, and even once in Richmond, Virginia at a Louise Brooks-themed event called Lulupalooza.

Brooks' film career, which began in 1925, was brief. She appeared in 14 movies in the United States before heading to Europe where she starred in the three works on which her reputation rests, *Pandora's Box* (1929), *Diary of a Lost Girl* (1929), and *Prix de beauté* (1930). Upon her return the States, Brooks was reduced to small roles in largely B-grade films. By the mid-1930s, Brooks' film career was in shambles. Decades of obscurity would follow.

Beggars of Life (1928) is considered Brooks' best American silent. Directed by William Wellman shortly after he made *Wings*—the first film to win an Academy Award, *Beggars of Life* tells the story of a girl who dresses as a boy and goes on the run after killing her abusive stepfather. The film will be shown on November 10th in Pittsburgh, Pennsylvania at the Hollywood Theater. Brooks' biographer Paris is set to introduce, with live musical accompaniment provided by Daryl Fleming & the Public Domain.

Another Brooks' American silent, *A Girl in Every Port* (1928), will also be shown in the coming weeks. This Howard Hawks-directed buddy film, in which Brooks plays a gold digger, is considered the legendary director's best silent efforts. It screens at the Cinematheque at the University of Wisconsin in Madison on December 7th, with live musical accompaniment provided by David Drazin.

Elsewhere, in Europe on November 14 (Brooks' birthday), the Kino Ponrepo in Prague launches a month-long series highlighting the actress' best work. The Ponrepo is the National Film Archive of the Czech Republic, and they're set to show *Pandora's Box / Pandořina skříňka* (November 14th), *Diary of a Lost Girl / Deník ztracené* (November 21st), *A Girl in Every Port / Všude jiné děvče* (November 26th), *Beggars of Life / Žebráci života* (December 3rd), and *The Canary Murder Case / Případ zavražděného kanárka* (December 10th).

Brooks started as a dancer, worked as a showgirl and actress, and later while living in poverty and isolation developed her considerable talents as a writer. In 1982, she penned *Lulu in Hollywood*, a collection of highly praised autobiographical essays.

Though primarily a performer, Brooks has over the years acted as muse to various artists, including songwriters, novelists, poets, painters and fashion designers. There is a even a street named for the actress in the suburbs of Paris.

The Tiger Lillies are a British Grammy-nominated three piece band with a cult following who have toured the world with works of musical theatre including *Shockheaded Peter* and *The Gorey End*; they have also released nearly 30 CDs and been inspired by Brooks. Due out soon is *Lulu*, their homage to the actress and her role as Lulu in *Pandora's Box*.

The Tiger Lillies are currently touring the United States and Europe. Also on tour is Mike Doughty, a singer-songwriter and ex-front man for the band Soul Coughing. Doughty, who sports a Brooks' tattoo, is currently on tour playing "re-imagined" versions of songs by his former band, including the 1998 Brooks' homage "St. Louise Is Listening."

Another tribute comes from the fashion world. PerezHilton.com reported on November 1 that Rihanna is modeling a coat by designer Jean Paul Gaultier which bears a likeness of Brooks. This new design, it should be noted, is not Gaultier's first nod to Brooks.

Some 75 years after her last film, and some 25 years after her death, Louise Brooks' star shines brighter than ever.

Anthony Bourdain and Louise Brooks
This piece appeared on the Louise Brooks Society blog on June 11, 2018.

Anthony Bourdain had a thing for Louise Brooks. Over the years, he evoked her name time and again.

In the introduction to *My Last Supper: 50 Great Chefs and Their Final Meals* (2007), Bourdain was asked who he wished his dining companions might be at his last meal. His answer was telling. "Given that I'm ostensibly facing imminent death, I'd probably prefer being alone. But assuming heroic sangfroid, an eclectic bunch of dinner companions from times present and past might keep the conversation interesting: Graham Greene, Kim Philby, Ava Gardner, Louise Brooks, Orson Welles, Iggy Pop, Martin Scorsese, Gabrielle Hamilton, Nick Tosches, Muhammad Ali, and Carole Lombard."

That mention caught my attention, and when I met Bourdain—ever so briefly in 2008—I asked him about his interest in Brooks. He smiled, and asked "Wasn't she beautiful?"

The celebrated chef, author, television personality and travel documentarian—who took his own life on June 8th—was well known for his love of popular music. Less known was his love of world cinema and classic films, and Louise Brooks. In 2017, Bourdain was asked to name a few of his favorite films from the Criterion Collection. And among those he chose were works by John Huston, Orson Welles, and Stanley Kubrick. Another of Bourdain's picks was the only silent film to make his list, *Pandora's Box* (1929). Bourdain's brief comment on this pick amplifies his interest in the star of that classic silent film: "Two words. Louise Brooks. Never has a more beautiful, intelligent, quirky, sexy, uniquely commanding character graced the screen."

The "ideal dinner" or "last supper" question was one that Bourdain was asked with some regularity. And though his answer might vary, one name always was always present, Louise Brooks. Back in 2006, *Washington Post* readers put questions to the celebrated chef.

"Rockville, Md.: Looking back at all the places you've traveled and meals you've had, what would be your dream menu and who would you invite?

Anthony Bourdain: I would eat at the St. John restaurant in London. An all offal meal prepared by Fergus Henderson. Attending would be a young Ava Gardner, Louise Brooks, Kim Philby, Orson Welles, Richard Helms, Iggy Pop, Graham Greene and Martin Scorsese."

In 2008, www.seriouseats.com wrote. "When asked by the *New York Post*'s Page Six this weekend what his food fantasy would be, Anthony Bourdain replied: 'Chef Marco Pierre White and Keith Richards would be throwing something on the barbie in a backyard in Red Hook.' Attendees would include, among others, silent film actress Louise Brooks (allowed to speak, presumably) along with Orson Welles and the "CIA director of counterintelligence."

In 2013, Andrew Zimmern interviewed Bourdain for *Delta Sky* magazine. Bourdain named a few of his ideal dinner companions: "Orson Welles is there, for sure. Ava Gardner, Louise Brooks, Iggy, Marco Pierre White, my wife, she's funny. Daniel Boulud, Éric Ripert, that would be fun. Nigella, Bill Murray, Christopher Walken and Lidia Bastianich, because they're old friends. That would be a mother****ing dinner party right there. It would be an interesting and outrageous bunch."

In 2014, *Modern Luxury* magazine asked Bourdain which six iconic figures would be at his dream dinner party? His answer, "Orson Welles; actress Louise Brooks; British intelligence officer Kim Philby, who was actually a KGB spy; Ava Gardner; Iggy Pop; and movie director John Houston."

In 2016, Bourdain went on Reddit to answer questions, where he was asked if you could have dinner with any three people, alive or dead, who would they be? His answer, "Louise Brooks, Orson Welles, and James Angleton the former head of capital intelligence for the CIA. There's a couple of questions I'd like to ask him. They're all dead unfortunately."

In 2015, Bourdain visited my former place of employ, the Arion Press. He was there to check out the press—one of the last letterpress printers in the United States, but also to check out the Arion Press edition of the Lulu plays (the basis for *Pandora's Box*), as illustrated by artist William Kentridge. It was a book I suggested Arion publish, having known of the artist's interest in Louise Brooks as well as press' desire to work with Kentridge. It seemed a good fit. The result was one of the landmark letterpress editions of the early 21st century.

In a list of notable American memoirists, two names sit near one another under the letter B, Anthony Bourdain and Louise Brooks. Today, I think, they are likely sitting near one another in legend.

Interview with Thomas Gladysz

This interview was to appear on a film blog in late 2017, but was left on the cutting room floor.

BLOG: Where did you first come across Louise Brooks?

TG: This may date me, but it was back in the VHS era…. it must have been around 1990 or so. One Friday night, not having anything to do, I went to the video store to rent a movie. I didn't have a movie in mind, and so I wandered over to the classics section. *Pandora's Box* caught my eye. I had not heard of the film, and in fact, had only seen a few silent films at that time in my life. Nor was I familiar with Louise Brooks. I recall the VHS box said it was one of "the most erotic films of all time," or something like that. And so, it being a Friday night and me with nothing to do, I figure I would take a chance on this old "erotic" film.

BLOG: What attracted you to her initially?

TG: I was bowled over by Brooks. I watched the film that night, and got up the next morning and watched it again before I had to return the tape! I have never done that before or since; I simply had to come to terms with what I had seen – the miracle of Louise Brooks, as Lotte Eisner put it years earlier. Yes, I thought Brooks was beautiful, and erotic. But, there was something else about her, beyond the superficial. Since then, I have thought a lot about what it is about Brooks that I find so compelling. I don't know that I have come up with an answer.

For me, she is my It girl, and I am in love with the pursuit of her through watching her films and researching her life. Brooks is not a jealous mistress. I have other interests and cinematic crushes, like Clara Bow and Buster Keaton and Erich von Stroheim, but I always come back to Brooks. I founded the Louise Brooks Society in 1995 when I launched it online, and have been going ever since.

BLOG: Do you have a favorite film of hers?

TG: I guess *Pandora's Box* will always be my first love, but I am also very partial to *Diary of a Lost Girl*. I think it also a great film, perhaps the equal of *Pandora's Box* in ways. Also, *Prix de beauté*, the other film Brooks made in Europe, is very good. I have watched each a number of times. Among her American films, *Beggars of Life* is also a stand out, as is *The Show-Off* and *Love Em and Leave Em*. One of her American films which rank highly among critics and film historian is *A Girl in Every Port*. It's ok, but I don't get it.

BLOG: How do you think she is viewed today?

TG: That depends on who you ask, and when you ask it. In her day, Brooks was only a second tier star. With the coming of sound, her reputation plummeted and she shows up in those "trying to make a come-back" and "where are they now" articles. For a time in the 1940s and 1950s, she was largely forgotten. Today, however, she is as popular as her greatest contemporaries, Chaplin, Keaton, Clara Bow, Colleen Moore. I am not saying she is as great an actor as them, or was as accomplished. But today there is a still simmering cult around Brooks whereas some of her more celebrated contemporaries, like the Talmadge sisters, for example, are little remembered.

Among silent film buffs, Brooks is well regarded. The same among film historians. Today, Brooks is considered a Jazz Age icon. Which leads some to ask, why all the fuss over a "junior star"? The answer is *extra-cinematic*, if you will. She is beautiful, but so were many other stars of the silent era. The public's continuing attraction in Brooks has a lot to do with her story, her personality, her intelligence. Brooks had a remarkable life in many ways, and that's what makes her interesting to us in the 21st century. Brooks experienced a second act. She experienced a rise and fall and a resurrection that very few figures in history experience. That makes her unique.

After I first came across *Pandora's Box*, I was eager to find out more about this remarkable actress. And soon enough I made my way to Barry Paris' outstanding biography. Much of the continuing interest in Brooks can be traced back to this book. I have read many biographies and many film biographies. I don't think there has ever been a better book than Paris' Louise Brooks biography. It is so beautifully empathetic.

She rejected Hollywood and left for good, she seemed to despise everything there, didn't she?

TG: Yes. She hated Hollywood, and didn't care for the West Coast. She said so time and again in her writings, in letters, in interviews. She also hated herself for what she had become in Hollywood in the 1930s, a failed, forgotten actress. Wouldn't you be unhappy, even a little bitter, if the industry which made you now rejected you?

BLOG: You have written a book on her 1928 film *Beggars of Life*, it is a great film for a variety of reasons, directed by William Wellman off the back of the hugely successful *Wings*, staring the fantastic Wallace Beery and of course, Louise Brooks. What made this film, for you, one to study in detail?

TG: It started when Kino Lorber asked me to contribute an audio commentary to their new DVD / Blu-ray release of *Beggars of Life*. This is the second commentary I have done for them. (The first was for *Diary of a Lost Girl*.) I had already accumulated a bunch of material for a book I have long been working on *The Films of Louise Brooks*. When I sat down to do my audio commentary, I found I had more material than I could use for either project, so I decided to write a short companion book, perhaps 40 to 60 pages and formatted to rest on the shelf next to the DVD. By the time I finished, it was 100 plus pages. I am especially proud that I was able to uncover little known information and little seen images, and that William Wellman Jr. contributed the foreword. The book is titled *Beggars of Life: A Companion to the 1928 Film*. By the way, my wife designed the cover and I think it looks terrific.

Beggars of Life is a fascinating film. It was based on a bestselling book of the time by Jim Tully, a hobo author and a fascinating personality in his own right. As you mentioned, it was directed by William Wellman the year after he had directed *Wings*, the first film to win the Best Picture Oscar. And, the film stars not only Louise Brooks in her role and in her best American film, but also future Oscar winner Wallace Beery. Richard Arlen plays in support.

Beggars of Life was also the first Paramount film to include spoken dialogue, though the film's sound elements are thought to be lost. (There is also a story that Wellman "invented" the boom mic while shooting this film.) Later in life, Wellman declared *Beggars of Life* his favorite among his silent films.

My book has chapters on Tully (who visited the location shoot), Wellman and the making of the film, and Brooks (who penned an entire essay on the film). There is also a chapter detailing the other actors in the film, including the pioneering African American actor Edgar Blue Washington. I also look at what critics of the time thought of the film, its use of music and sound effects, and its depiction of trains and the hobo culture. The picture I found of Louise Brooks holding a sign decrypting "hobo code" is rather unusual. Film historian Frank Thompson, who has written about and knows an awful lot about Wellman, praised my book, saying he had learnt a great deal reading it. I was honored.

By the way, the Kino Lorber release print of Beggars of Life is outstanding, a huge improvement over the dreadful copies which have floated around the internet and on VHS for some time. This is the copy to get.

BLOG: Wellman was desperate to work with Brooks again, wasn't he? It almost happened in *The Public Enemy* in 1931, but of course the part went to Jean Harlow and Louise left Hollywood.

TG: Yes, he was. I tell the story in my book. Wellman and Brooks relationship got off to a rocky start. She thought he didn't like her. But over the course of working together on *Beggars of Life*, they came to respect one another. After Brooks returned from Europe, Wellman cast her in *The Public Enemy*. Wellman Jr. even speculates in his biography of his Father that he may have shot a few scenes with her, as there are handwritten notes on the shooting script to that effect. However, Brooks was her own best enemy. After accepting the role (and being announced as part of the cast), she decided she would rather go to New York City to hang around with her East Coast friends. What a missed opportunity! Had she played the part, her career might well have been revitalized.

BLOG: A lot has been made of her time with director G.W. Pabst in Berlin. He really seemed to understand what she had and utilized her like no one in Hollywood did. Would you say that Wellman saw this too and could have fulfilled her potential had she stayed in Hollywood? Or do you think she had to leave?

TG: Brooks had to leave. She did so after her contract wasn't renewed to her liking around the time she was making *The Canary Murder Case*. That was not long after she played in and got good reviews for *Beggars of Life*.

I think you make a good point. Pabst knew what to do with her, with her singular talent. The result is *Pandora's Box*, which is considered one of the great silent films; today, Brooks' reputation as an actress is based on what Pabst did with her in *Pandora's Box*.

I don't think Wellman could have single handedly revived her career. It's true to say that Brooks' suffered from self-defeating behavior. And, there were simply too many missed opportunities—from the first *Gentleman Prefer Blondes* and the Dixie Dugan / *Show Girl* films to the *Bride of Frankenstein*. What might have been!

BLOG: The character of Lulu in *Pandora's Box* is a huge part of German heritage, yet no German actress seemed to fit Pabst's vision of her. The casting reminds me of Vivien Leigh in *Gone with the Wind*.

TG: Yes, and like *Gone with the Wind*, there was a big fuss made over the casting of the "right" actress to play Lulu. The role almost went to Marlene Dietrich, who Brooks thought was too old and worldly for the part. This was back in 1928!

There is a belief that Pabst saw Brooks in the Howard Hawks' film, *A Girl in Every Port*, and decided to cast her as Lulu. Brooks said so, but only after George Eastman House film curator James Card said as much in the late 1950s. But I am not so sure. To me, the timeline doesn't fit. Though it was released in the United States months before work began on *Pandora's Box*, I wonder how Pabst could have seen *A Girl in Every Port* in Germany, where it didn't show until work on *Pandora's Box* was nearly done?

That *A Girl in Every Port* inspired Pabst is received wisdom. I think it was another film that intrigued the director, perhaps one of Brooks' lost 1927 films, like *The City Gone Wild*, where Brooks' plays a beautiful, hard-edged gangster's moll. I know my belief is film history heresy. But until I see some sort of record of Pabst saying it was *A Girl in Every Port*, then I will always be a doubting Thomas.

BLOG: One thing that interests me is the fact that she never read scripts, watched the daily rushes or the finished films, do you think the move to Berlin with Pabst was purely for the money as she had refused a contract renewal at Paramount, or was it a more artistic move, thinking that Berlin would suit her?

TG: I think her move to Europe was simply because she needed to work and somebody in Germany was willing to pay her way. Brooks didn't know anything about *Pandora's Box* or the Lulu character or Pabst, the film's director. She had been to England and France earlier (before she got into movies), so there was the allure of travel and adventure. Which Jazz Age twenty-something wouldn't want to go to Europe and party like its 1929? Berlin suited her, and she did have a good time.

Brooks was always a reluctant actress. She wasn't interested in the craft of acting and film until later in life. That's why she never watched many of her own films. She always remarked that she would rather have been a dancer. In fact, that's how she got started, as a member of the modern American dance company known as Denishawn. As a 15 year old, she was dancing alongside such dance greats as Martha Graham, Ruth St. Denis and Ted Shawn.

BLOG: She was a very liberated woman throughout her life. There are pictures of her at about five years old with the famous bobbed hair style, she always seemed to be a woman ahead of her time.

TG: I think Brooks was both a woman of her time and ahead of her time. She was born in 1906 in Kansas, and was certainly imprinted by that place and time. But, she always did her own thing. There is a fine novel about Brooks' early life called *The Chaperone* (by Laura Moriarty) which reflects her independent personality. So yes, she was liberated, or "modern," in a sense, but she wasn't a feminist as we think of feminism today. By the way, *The Chaperone* is going to be made into a feature film by PBS and the same team that made *Downton Abbey*. I am looking forward to it.

BLOG: Brooks is also a huge style icon—when you look at women's style today how much do you see her influence?

TG: Beginning in the 1970s and 1980s, Brooks has had a significant and continuing influence on fashion and style. Of course, there is her famous bob hairstyle. It wasn't a style or cut which she popularized. Go back to the 1920s, and you'll find Colleen Moore was more closely associated with that look. Bobbed hair is something Brooks wore pretty much all of her early life, even as a little girl when the look was known as a Pageboy or Dutch bob. Legendary hair stylist Sydney Guilaroff claimed that he shaped Brooks' bob into the distinct cut we know today. That was around 1925.

The Brooks' look shows up in film, from Cyd Charisse's character in *Singing in the Rain* to Liza Minnelli's Sally Bowles in *Cabaret* to Melanie Griffith's Lulu in *Something Wild*. There are others, as well. A handful of well known fashion designers have also acknowledged Brooks' influence. There is even a French perfume, Loulou, named after Brooks. And, you'll see pop singers and actresses and other personalities modeling themselves after Brooks' look. Kenneth Tynan, the famous English critic who was a big admirer of Brooks, once dressed up in drag like the actress for a costume party. And Linda Ronstadt, the singer, told me she has dressed as Brooks for Halloween. Ronstadt has worn her hair in a bob for the last few years.

BLOG: In her later life, Brooks became something of a film critic; her marvelous book, *Lulu in Hollywood,* is a must read for any film fan, but just how influential was she?

TG: *Lulu in Hollywood* is a slight book, a collection of autobiographical essays (many written for film magazines like *Sight and Sound* and *Film Culture*) on aspects of Brooks' life and film career. It is a smart, insightful book—and a good read. John Updike, the Pulitzer Prize winning novelist, once told me he thought Brooks was the finest writer to have ever come out of Hollywood. Roger Ebert also told me pretty much the same thing.

Lulu in Hollywood was influential as a book in bringing the reading public's attention to Brooks. It sold well. I don't think it had a big impact on film history, though you do sometimes see Brooks' observations on Pabst, Wellman, Bogart, Garbo and W.C. Fields showing up in other film books. After it was published, Lillian Gish (the subject of an essay in *Lulu in Hollywood*) wrote to Brooks and praised her work.

BLOG: It seems as if her legacy comes as a person rather than as an actress. She is someone who rejected Hollywood, yet who today is still one of the most celebrated silent actresses.

TG: That is true to a large degree. But still, without those handful of films behind it all—the European "trilogy" of *Pandora's Box*, *Diary of a Lost Girl*, and *Prix de beauté*—and her other surviving American films, like *Beggars of Life*, Brooks' personality would not be enough. In the end, the films are the basis for our interest today.

BLOG: I understand you were involved with the restoration of the recently found lost Louise Brooks film, *Now We're in the Air*.

TG: Yes, in a small way. Film preservationist Rob Byrne, who found the film in Prague, is a friend. He contacted me and asked if I would like to help with putting the fragments back together. My answer was yes! The film was incomplete, and in bad shape. As well, the inter-titles were in Czech. Thus, restoring what was found was something of a challenge, not only because foreign prints might differ from domestic prints, but because the translation of the inter-titles was more often an adaption then a literal translation. That was the case with the Czech print, whose surviving fragments were also out of order.

My wife and I drove down to Los Angeles, and visited the Margaret Herrick Library at the Academy. We found scripts, story drafts, plot summaries, and a continuity for the film. Between them, we were able to figure out what fragmentary material we had, its correct order, and most importantly, to provide the original English-language inter-titles. We were lucky. Had we not found all that material, the restoration would have been a lesser thing—and not as enjoyable as it turned out to be. My wife was also lucky in spotting a handwritten notation on the script wondering if some of the "leftover" aerial footage from William Wellman's *Wings* might be used in *Now We're in the Air*. When you seen the surviving material (about 22 minutes worth), you will see that it was! If your readers have a chance to see *Now We're in the Air*, then I would recommend they do so. It is amusing, and Brooks shines.

BLOG: Lastly, to anyone who doesn't know Louise Brooks, could you express what she means and has meant to you?

TG: I sometimes joke that my wife doesn't mind that I have a dead girlfriend.

5 THE SOCIETY

Sacramento • This week's library report • Notes from the library • Homage to Lulu: 100 Years of Louise Brooks • December Trip (parts one & two) • Interview: Thomas Gladysz, founder of the Louise Brooks Society • A Lost Girl, a Fake Diary, and a Forgotten Author • Thomas Gladysz's most treasured book • Reopening Pandora's Box in San Francisco • Louise Brooks Celebration in San Francisco • True Confession: I've Been Stalking Louise Brooks for 20 Years • Live365 is Dead, Long Live RadioLulu • RadioLulu Redux • CMBA profile: Louise Brooks Society

I launched the Louise Brooks Society in the summer of 1995, when I posted a few simple pages on the web. These first efforts were, in effect, a message to the world, "I like Louise Brooks. Here is some stuff I found. How about you?" I received messages in return, from fans, from Brooks' relatives, from students, film buffs, film scholars, and even a few celebrities. People from all walks of life were drawn to this singular silent film star. In fact, a few millions visitors have passed through the pages of the LBS. To date, I have communicated with individuals from 50 countries on six continents. Once, I even received a message from someone stationed in Antartica.

What started as a "virtual fan club" in cyberspace grew into something more. As individuals from around the world sent me clippings, images, translations and information, and my own research began to grow, so did my ambitions for the Louise Brooks Society.

About ten years ago, I created a mission statement: "The Louise Brooks Society is devoted to the appreciation and promotion of the life and films of Louise Brooks. The mission of the society is to honor the actress by stimulating interest in her life, films and writings, as well as her place in 20th century culture; by fostering and coordinating research; by serving as a repository for relevant material; and by advocating for the preservation and restoration of her films and other material.

The purpose of the LBS website is to promote interest in the actress by offering membership in a society; by serving as a focal point for related activities; by disseminating accurate information including scholarly texts and bibliographies; and by offering individuals a variety of materials to aid in their appreciation of the actress. Above all, the LBS encourages the viewing of Brooks' surviving films, and the fellowship of her admirers."

Through its website and use of social media, through scholarship and advocacy, and through publications, exhibits and events, I have sought to share my enthuisiasm for Louise Brooks with the world. The pieces which follow in this chapter detail some of my efforts.

Sacramento

This piece appeared on the Louise Brooks Society blog on May 29, 2005. At the time, I lived in San Francisco. It and the next two pieces are typical examples (albeit more interesting ones) of early entries on the LBS blog which recount my ongoing research.

Just back from Sacramento, and my research trip to the California State Library. I went through a few more reels of the *Daily Bruin*, the student newspaper at UCLA. Impressively, this college newspaper ran signed reviews by student-journalists of new films. These pieces were pretty good—extensive and thoughtful, and the equal of reviews found in many big city newspapers. I scavenged three reviews, as well as a smattering of articles on other films. About Louise Brooks, UCLA student Louise Kreisman declared "she excels in flippancy and heartlessness" in her write-up of *Evening Clothes*. Doris G. Taylor described the actress as sleek and graceful—but only adequate in her role of the Canary in the murder mystery based on the van Dine novel. And interestingly, the piece on *Now We're in the Air* has a bit of an interview with Wallace Beery about the role he plays in that film. Another curiosity I noticed was a May, 1931 advertisement for the nearby Beverly theater, which on a particular Saturday was running an odd double bill of *It Pays to Advertise* and *White Hell of Pitz Palu* (the German mountain film directed by G.W. Pabst featuring Leni Riefenstahl). Another curiosity was the fact that the great Jazz pianist Art Tatum was one of the opening stage acts for *When You're in Love*, the 1937 Grace Moore musical in which Louise Brooks had a bit part.

I also looked as the *Venice Evening Vanguard* (from Venice Beach), which proved to be a goldmine of articles, reviews and advertisements. I found something on every American Brooks' film from *The American Venus* (1926) to *It Pays to Advertise* (1931). There was a nifty caricature of the actress from *Love Em and Leave Em*, an article about director Alfred Santell which noted the recognition he received for his work on *Just Another Blonde*, an unusual staged portrait of Brooks, James Hall and Richard Arlen from *Rolled Stockings*, and an article about *Beggars of Life* which mentioned that live election results (for the 1928 Presidential race) would be announced during the screening. One other article I found was a ridiculous puff piece, "Miss Brooks Almost Inspiration for Popular Song," which tried to associate the actress with the song with the refrain "five foot two, eyes of blue, and oh, what those eyes can't do . . . ." The author of the article, however, admitted that Brooks' eyes were in fact dark brown.

Besides the *Daily Bruin* and *Venice Evening Vanguard*, I also continued my day-by-day look though the film and society columns of the *Hollywood Daily Citizen*. I managed to get through a few months, but didn't find anything mentioning Brooks—this time. I will continue my survey on my next visit to Sacramento. (Then, I also plan to tackle the Bakersfield newspaper and perhaps the Riverside newspaper.)

This week's library report

This piece appeared on the Louise Brooks Society blog on August 5, 2005. My "heretical" supposition as to how G.W. Pabst might have noticed Louise Brooks and cast her as Lulu, though mentioned elsewhere, made its first appearance here.

Three more inter-library loans were waiting for me at the San Francisco Public

Library. I went through microfilm of the *News-Sentinel* (from Ft. Wayne, Indiana) where I got some Denishawn material regarding their March, 1924 appearance. Along with a review, which referenced Louise Brooks, I found a earlier article which featured a group photo of the Denishawn dancers, including Brooks! I also looked through some later issues of *News-Sentinel*, where I found a rather nice advertisement for a screening of *Beggars of Life* dating from March, 1929 (some six months after it was released). And I found reviews and ads for *The Street of Forgotten Men* and *The American Venus* in the *Hartford Daily Courant* (from Hartford, Connecticut).

Another publication at I looked at was *Germania*, a daily newspaper from Berlin. Looking through microfilm of this publication was certainly the highlight of this week's trip, as the Berlin newspapers are difficult to get a hold of. I have been trying to find *Germania* for some time. My efforts paid off, as I found short reviews for *Blaue jungens, blonde Madchen*, *Die Buchse der Pandora*, and *Tagebuch einer Verlorenen*. These reviews got me to thinking.

It is commonly reported that G.W. Pabst cast Louise Brooks in *Pandora's Box* after having seen her in *Blaue jungens, blonde Madchen* (aka *A Girl in Every Port*). Looking at Brooks' list of films, this assumption makes sense, as the release of the Howard Hawks' buddy film (in which Brooks play a kind of temptress, not unlike Lulu) preceded the start of production on *Pandora's Box*. The Hawks' film was released in the United States on February 20, 1928. Pabst was attempting to cast Lulu in the Spring or Summer of that same year.

The claim that Pabst cast Brooks in *Pandora's Box* after having seen her in *A Girl in Every Port* was made by James Card in "Out of Pandora's Box: Louise Brooks on G. W. Pabst," an article published in 1956. And it was repeated by Brooks herself in the 1970's in filmed interviews. I wonder why? As newspaper reviews show, *Blaue jungens, blonde Madchen* didn't screen in Berlin until the first week of December in 1928, after production work on *Pandora's Box* was finished!

Could Pabst—largely an independent filmmaker—have seen the Hawks' film at a private screening? Or might Pabst have noticed Brooks through her roles in earlier, publically screened films such as *Die Schonste Frau der Staaten* (*The American Venus*), *Die Braut am Scheidewege* (*Just Another Blonde*), or *Ein Frack Ein Claque Ein Madel* (*Evening Clothes*)— each of which was shown in Berlin and received significant press coverage. It's a tidy assumption to believe Brooks' role in the Hawk's film struck Pabst's fancy. I wonder if it weren't another.

Tomorrow, I head over to the East Bay, where I will once again spend some time exploring the microfilm collection at the University of California, Berkeley. The microfilm collection at the Bancroft Library numbers in the thousands of rolls. Such riches! I've kept notes, and plan to pick-up where I left off last time.

This trip, I plan to look at some more South American and European newspapers. It's slow, tedious work —but I occasionally uncover a gem or two. (Like the review of *Pandora's Box* I found in a Buenos Aires newspaper from 1929; and the movie ads I found in newspapers from Mexico City, also dating from the 1920's; and the other clippings I uncovered in French, German, Polish and Russians newspapers and magazines from the 1920's and 1930's.) This is one of three or possibly four trips to Berkeley I plan to take this month before the microfilm collections is closed. The library is set to undergo a seismic retrofit. An article recently appeared in the *San Francisco Chronicle* about this historic library and the challenges it faces.

Notes from the library
This piece appeared on the Louise Brooks Society blog on October 28, 2005.
Years later, I came across a second reference to an Atlantic City beauty pageant short, this
time in a Santa Cruz, California newspaper; I have never been able to track down a copy of the film.

Earlier this summer, while looking through Neil Hamilton's scrapbooks at the New York Public Library, I ran across a 1925 clipping regarding *The Street of Forgotten Men*. (Actor Neil Hamilton—best known as Commissioner Gordon on the 1960's *Batman* TV series—was featured in *The Street of Forgotten Men*, which also happened to be Louise Brooks' first film!) And just now, at the end of October, I got around to borrowing microfilm of the *Wilmington Morning News*, the Delaware newspaper in which that clipping appeared. REMARKABLY, that Hamilton film was paired with a (unknown to me) non-fiction short about the then recent Atlantic City beauty pageant. Of course, as any Brooks' fan knows, that beauty pageant—one of the early Miss America contests—provided the background subject for the next Louise Brooks' film, *The American Venus*, which was released just a few months later.

This is exciting. Who knows what is on that short film—perhaps some brief footage of the making of the feature film? (I doubt that Brooks was present in Atlantic City. But who knows . . . .) I also ran across a brief article entitled, "Beauty Pageant Showing At Stanley Theatres." The article reads thus: "The thousands of Wilmingtonians who did not get the opportunity to be present in Atlantic City during the Beauty Pageant just completed there on Friday will see the principal scenes of the entire celebration in film at the Queen, Arcadia and Majestic Theaters beginning today. The scenes were especially 'shot' by the Stanley cameraman for the theaters of this organization." I'll pay anyone if they can provide me with a copy of that short film. I think it is titled *Atlantic City Beauty Pageant*.

Today, five inter-library loans were waiting for me. I also looked at some Denishawn material from the *New Haven Journal-Courier* (from New Haven, Connecticut) and the *Wisconsin State Journal* (from Madison, Wisconsin). Each yielded some long, detail-filled reviews and a few neat advertisements.

And, as well, I went through a number of months of two "other" American newspapers, the *Honolulu Star-Bulletin* (from the Territory of Hawaii) and the *Alaska Daily Empire* (also then a territory, pre-statehood). My search through the *Star-Bulletin* was based on my having earlier found film reviews in the *Honolulu Advertiser* (microfilm of which I came upon in Sacramento. The *Star-Bulletin* microfilm came on loan from the Library of Congress). I checked my *Advertiser* dates in the *Star-Bulletin* and came up with a couple of new reviews.

However, the *Alaska Daily Empire* (from Juneau) yielded nothing. I skimmed nearly six months of this newspaper, which ran only eight pages on a daily basis. I found advertisements and short, generic articles about films showing in town—but none featuring Louise Brooks. There were at least two or three movie theaters in Juneau in the late 1920's—and they showed motion pictures starring the likes of Buster Keaton and Erich von Stroheim. Apparently, Juneau didn't show many or any Paramount films. One day, I hope to find or acquire some Alaska citations for the LBS bibliographies. I have citations from almost every other state.

The search goes on.

Homage to Lulu: 100 Years of Louise Brooks

This piece appeared on the Louise Brooks Society blog on November 7, 2006. It begins with a press release for an exhibit mounted by the LBS. I was later told by a librarian at the SFPL that this exhibit was one of the more popular at the library that year.

"Homage to Lulu: 100 Years of Louise Brooks"
an exhibit at the San Francisco Public Library
November 4, 2006 through January 5, 2007
Main Branch, Fourth Floor, Steve Silver Beach Blanket Babylon Music Center

"Homage to Lulu: 100 Years of Louise Brooks" celebrates the centenary of the silent film star Louise Brooks (1906-1985). Now considered an icon of the Jazz Age, Brooks' popularity today rivals that of her more celebrated contemporaries. On display are dozens of vintage objects—including books, magazines, sheet music, postcards and related ephemera—which tell the story of her life and films.

Highlights include American and French photoplay editions (the movie tie-in editions of the 1920's), an editorial comic strip explaining the scandalous circumstances behind Brooks' affair with Charlie Chaplin, Brooks' inspired novels, a jumbo-size lobby card, and a full-page newspaper advertisement for *Show Girl*—the Brooks-inspired novel which became a hit stage play and the long-running comic strip "Dixie Dugan."

This exhibit—organized by Thomas Gladysz and the San Francisco-based Louise Brooks Society—coincides with many other events taking place around the San Francisco Bay Area and the world.

Here are some snapshots I took of "Homage to Lulu: 100 Years of Louise Brooks" —both as it was being installed and after it opened. Hopefully, this gives a sense of the scope of the exhibit, which is currently on display at the San Francisco Public Library. The hardest thing was figuring out what to include and what to leave out. There were some things that I was eager to share, like the full-page Sunday color comic of "Dixie Dugan," and the various compact discs, 45's and long playing records (LP's) I've collected over the years which feature an image of Louise Brooks.

December Trip (parts one & two)
This piece appeared on the Louise Brooks Society blog on January 21 & 28, 2007.

Last month, my wife and I took a trip to Detroit, Michigan. I spent time with my family (I grew up in the suburbs on the east side). I also had the opportunity to introduce *Pandora's Box* when it was shown at the Detroit Film Theater, which is part of the Detroit Institute of Arts. (The DIA is the fifth largest fine arts museum in the United States. It has a great collection of paintings, sculpture, and other works. Be sure and check it out if you're ever in the Motor City.)

I had intended to introduce the film three times, as it was being shown as many times over the course of the second weekend in December. A traffic jam on I-75, however, prevented me from making it to the Friday night screening. (I got there 15 minutes late, and the film started without my introduction.)

Nevertheless, I did make it to the Saturday evening and Sunday afternoon screenings. There was an article about the film in a couple of the local papers. More than 500 people were in attendance for each showing.

Here is a picture of me sitting in the DIA theater before the film was shown on Saturday night. As you can see, it is a splendid theater dating from the 1920's. I was told by one of the curators of film that this venue was the first museum theater in the United States to show films as "art." Screenings took place here before similar historic screenings at New York Museum of Modern Art.

My rambling six minute introduction spoke a little bit Louise Brooks, about the LBS, about various centenary happenings, about Brooks' connections to Detroit, and about the film we were about to see, *Pandora's Box*. I hope people liked what I had to say.

While in the Detroit-area, I took the opportunity to do a bit of research. I visited the Mount Clemens Public Library hoping to dig up something about Louise Brooks' 1935 dance engagement at the Blossom Heath Inn. (I spoke about this event in my introduction.) This one-time roadhouse is located in what is now St. Clair Shores, a suburb on the east side of Detroit. In the past, I acquired a few newspaper notices and advertisements in the major Detroit newspapers. Now, I thought I might look for additional material. As best I can figure, the only suburban newspapers covering this part of metro Detroit in the 1930's where those based in neighboring Mount Clemens. I looked through the *Mount Clemens Daily Leader* and *Mount Clemens Monitor* (a weekly), but found nothing. Happily though, the librarians in the local history room gave me a few suggestions, including a contact at the St. Clair Shores library. So, maybe something further will turn up. The search goes on.

###

From Detroit, my wife and I flew to Rochester, New York. As most readers of this blog know, Louise Brooks made her home in Rochester starting in the late 1950's. Rochester is also home to the George Eastman House, one of the largest motion picture archives in the world. My wife and I spent a full day at the GEH, mostly looking through clipping files and archival material related to the actress. We read letters both to and from Brooks, looked at vintage photographs she once owned, poured over many clippings about the actress, and examined other related documents such as manuscript pages, programs, and books. And of course, we took lots of notes.

While at the George Eastman House, we also took the opportunity to see the Louise Brooks exhibit, which was then on display. Here are a few snapshots taken in the museum. Anthony L'Abbate, the helpful curatorial assistant, took the picture of my wife and I.

As can be seen from these pictures, the Brooks exhibit at the GEH was a modest one. (The exhibit took up one room—with a few other pictures hanging in the adjoining hallway.) The exhibit mostly featured photographs, many of which were familiar, some of which were not. There were also a few related magazines, books, and other items, including a painting of two birds by Louise Brooks. The painting is something I had never seen before. (There is a similar piece of art depicted in the Barry Paris biography—see page 446.) I wonder how many such artworks Brooks completed?

It was thrilling to see this exhibit. And I am very glad we took the time to do so. My only regret is that we did not get into the GEH Dryden Theater. We saw it from the outside, but it would have been interesting to see it from the inside. Lastly, of note, there was a Brooks display in the George Eastman House gift shop. There were a few DVD's for sale. Peter Cowie's new book and the recently released *Pandora's Box* DVD from Criterion were each featured prominently.

While in Rochester, my wife and I also walked around the downtown. (Imagining Brooks herself walking these very streets in the 1950s or 1960's.) We also made a point of visiting the Rochester Public Library—which Brooks frequented—and took the opportunity to do some research.

We dug up articles, reviews and advertisements for the Denishawn Dance Company's two performances in Rochester during the years Brooks was a member of the troupe. We also scavenged some reviews and advertisements for Brooks' films when they were shown in the city in the 1920's. (Back then, Rochester boasted more than four city newspapers. And to date, I have only been able to get at a couple of them.)

We also copied more recent articles from the Rochester newspapers. For example, there were articles about the actress by Henry Clune, a local columnist. There was considerable coverage, including large headlines and front page articles, about the actress at the time of her death. And there were articles about the Louise Brooks biography by Barry Paris. All together, we gathered much new material. Citations for all that we found have been added to the LBS bibliographies.

Interview: Thomas Gladysz, founder of the Louise Brooks Society

This piece appeared on the SiouxWIRE website on April 5, 2007. The brief introduction was written by the editor of the SiouxWIRE.

The following is one of my favorite interviews from the Ramble Rocket era (2005). Thomas Gladysz created pandorasbox.com in 1995 and founded the Louise Brooks Society in 1994. He is a treasure trove of information and has been very generous with his time.

SW: Can you briefly explain to the uninitiated who Louise Brooks was?

TG: Louise Brooks was an actress whose greatest fame came during the silent film era. All together, she appeared in 24 films between 1925 and 1938. Today, she is best known for her 1929 role as Lulu—a singular femme fatale—in *Pandora's Box*. Some have called her one of the most beautiful women to have ever appeared in films. I agree. She is also a fascinating personality.

SW: How long have you been interested in Louise and what started this off?

TG: I have been interested—some would same obsessed—with Brooks for more than 12 years. My interest started after having seen her in *Pandora's Box*. It is a remarkable film, and Brooks herself is really quite stunning. Seeing that film led me to want to know more about the actress, which led me to the remarkable biography by

Barry Paris. Wanting to share my enthusiasm for the actress with others, I started the Louise Brooks Society. This year, the LBS celebrates 10 years on-line.

SW: Louise did a lot of work in Europe?

TG: Of her 24 films, Brooks only made three films in Europe. However, those three films are considered her very best. She went to Europe to play Lulu under the direction of G.W. Pabst, a great German director. Soon after, she made another film with Pabst, the equally acclaimed *Diary of a Lost Girl*. Her third European film, *Prix de beauté*, was made in France. It was based on a story idea by Pabst and Rene Clair, a great French director. European directors, European film critics, and European film lovers have long appreciated this Kansas-born actress. I suppose some would say that the "cult" of Louise Brooks was born in Europe. Today, Brooks is considered an important actress on the continent.

SW: She appeared with John Wayne in a "talkie" but then vanished. Why? What happened?

TG: Brooks' last film was *Overland Stage Raiders*, a B-western. After trying to re-establish her faltering career, Brooks came to the end of her days as an actress. John Wayne was at the beginning of his. (He would soon go on to star in *Stagecoach*.) Regarding *Overland Stage Raiders*, Brooks biographer Barry Paris wrote, "It is a dreadful film from start to finish, with every cliché known to Western man and western genre. Louise adored Wayne but could not stand the humiliation of the film. *Raiders* was the last straw. She never made another movie."

SW: About the members of *Pandora's Box*, is there a certain age group or geographical group that dominates? Any surprise fans from far off places?

TG: At last count, the 1000 members of the Louise Brooks Society hail from 46 countries on six continents! Members range in age from teenagers to computer savvy folks in their 50's and 60's. Members of the LBS include silent film fans, movie industry professionals, actors, poets, professors, artists, and other interested individuals from all walks of life. Lawrence Ferlinghetti, the well known Beat poet and publisher, is a member.

The majority of members come from the United States, and California is the state with the most members. Louise Brooks is also popular in Europe. There are numerous members from the British Isles—as well as France, Belgium, The Netherlands, Germany, Austria, Switzerland, Denmark, Norway, Sweden, and Finland. Fans of the actress also hail from the Czech Republic, Latvia, Hungary, Poland, Romania, Serbia, Croatia, Yugoslavia, Italy, Greece, Portugal and Spain (including a couple of members in the Canary Islands). Members of the LBS can also be found in Africa, Asia and across the Pacific Rim.

SW: What do you think the interest is in Louise Brooks? Do you think it will endure with a younger generation?

TG: I think different people are drawn to Brooks for different reasons. I know she is popular in the Goth community—where her perennially popular bob-haircut has become something of a fetish look. I know she is popular among film buffs, and those interested in the Jazz Age and flappers. I often receive email from students asking me about Louise Brooks and the 1920's. Seemingly, they have come across my web site while doing their homework.

SW: If I want to see her work, what can I do? Is there a way that my independent cinema can get hold of her films? Is her work available on DVD?

TG: Like so many movies dating from the silent film era, a number of Brooks' films are lost. Nevertheless, a handful are currently available on DVD, including her three European films as well as a few of her American flapper comedies. Other films can be found on video. A three-disc set of Brooks' films, with much bonus material, was recently released in France by Carlotta films. Brooks' films are also occasionally shown in theaters.

SW: What things have you learned while running the site? Did you acquire any interesting artifacts, stories, information?

TG: I have learned a lot about Louise Brooks by developing the website. I also learned a lot about web design and HTML! I am a self-taught web-designer and a self-taught film historian . . . . One of the most gratifying things about the LBS is the contributions and email I have gotten from fans around the world. Individuals have sent scans of rare pictures and articles about Brooks. Others have translated French or Russian or Swedish articles into English. Others have written to express their own enthusiasm for Brooks and their thanks for my efforts in keeping her legend alive.

SW: What other actors of the silent era do you admire? Directors? Writers?

TG: Where to begin? I adore Clara Bow. Garbo is remarkable. I am fascinated by Buster Keaton and Erich von Stroheim. Charlie Chaplin is great. I have a big interest in directors like G.W. Pabst and Fritz Lang. I am always reading something about early film, and right now I am reading a terrific biography of Marlene Dietrich. I recently read books about Valentino, Norma Shearer, Baby Peggy, and Ramon Novarro—all of which I enjoyed. And then there's Anna May Wong, Lon Chaney, Bela Lugosi, John Gilbert, Theda Bara, etc..... the silent film era is full of interesting personalities who made interesting films.

SW: What other artists (current/past) do you admire?

TG: I have had a long standing interest in modernism and many of its "isms"—symbolism, expressionism, and especially surrealism—both as a literary and visual art. Collage and montage, pulp culture, high / low culture, and the arts and culture of Eastern Europe all interest me. As do the Beats writers—poets like Allen Ginsberg. My short list of favorite writers would certainly include F. Scott Fitzgerald and Ernest Hemingway, as well as Jorge Luis Borges, Franz Kafka and Czeslaw Milosz. I also really love science fiction (both literature and movies), and my favorite sci-fi writers are Ray Bradbury, Neil Gaiman, China Mieville, Emil Petaja.

SW: If someone is interested and keen to learn more about films from the silent era, where would you suggest they start?

TG: Go to a movie theater showing a silent movie (especially if it has live musical accompaniment). Rent a DVD or video. Watch a Charlie Chaplin film. Fall in love with Clara Bow or Buster Keaton. Check out a biography of a silent film star or read a book about silent film history, like Kevin Brownlow's superb *The Parade's Gone By*. There are also a number of web sites, news groups and blogs devoted to early cinema. Just dive in. One thing will probably lead to another.

SW: Do you think that silent films have any advantage over "talkies" in any regard?

TG: In some ways, they are two different art forms. The best silent films are a kind of visual narrative, whereas sound films are more dependent on verbal narrative structure. I don't think silents are necessarily better than talkies, just different. I love silent film, and I love sound films. I have a growing interest in pre-code films

(American films of the early 1930's). I also enjoy contemporary films a great deal. *Somewhere in Time* is a film I have never been able to get out of my head. *Amelie* is divine. And I also enjoyed *Ghost World*. Those are a few that come to mind.

SW: What is your favorite Louise Brooks moment in her surviving films?

TG: The scene backstage in *Pandora's Box* where Brooks is fighting with Dr. Schon, her somewhat older patron and lover. He is struggling to kiss her. And suddenly the door opens, and they are caught by her lover's fiancé and his son. It is an electric moment. Brooks conveys so much through her body and face. She plays the scene perfectly. It is a scene that must be seen to be appreciated.

SW: Where would you like to see *pandorasbox.com* in another ten years?

TG: I would like to continue to develop the web site and expand the resources of the LBS. The site has been on-line for ten years, and has attracted more than one-million visitors. It has grown to become the largest & most comprehensive web site in the world devoted to any silent movie star. I would be proud if it could continue for another ten years. I guess that would be an accomplishment.

A Lost Girl, a Fake Diary, and a Forgotten Author

This piece appeared on Huffington Post on August 26, 2010. I wrote it after having edited, written the introduction, and self-published a long out-of-print book.

Recently, I self-published a book. Before you turn the page or double-click the next button, allow me to explain why.

What I actually did was self-publish a reprint of a long unavailable and little-known work. It has what some might call "cult appeal." The book has been out of print in the United States for more than 100 years. I wrote a long introduction and added illustrations and other material to my new edition.

Why did I do it? Simply put, because I believe in this book. It's a little gem, and a more than worthwhile work of literature. And what's more, there is a remarkable story behind it. I felt it needed a helping hand out of the obscurity into which it had fallen.

The book is called *The Diary of a Lost Girl*. It's by a turn of the last century German writer few today have heard of. Her name is Margarete Böhme.

What originally drew me to the book was the fact that it was the basis for the 1929 German film of the same name. That silent film stars Louise Brooks. She's an obsession of mine, as anyone who knows me is all too well aware. I'm always going on about her ... And I'm always looking into some facet of her life and career. I was curious about what seemed to me an otherwise obscure book. Why did the great German director G.W. Pabst make it into a film? What would he have seen in it?

Originally published in German as *Tagebuch einer Verlorenen*, the book was issued in England and then the United States as *The Diary of a Lost One*. A few years ago I tracked down an American first edition from 1908. There weren't many around, and I had to pay about $80.00 for a vintage copy.

The first time I read it, I thought it was just OK—an interesting period piece. However, there was something about it that stuck with me. I read it again. Its story, the story of a "lost girl" named Thymian, grew on me. I came to care about her character, and to feel drawn into her world. I was also curious about the author and the history of this, her best remembered work. What did others think about it, especially back then?

The more I searched, the less I found. Which is strange, because as I would discover, Böhme was, arguably, one of the more widely read German writers of the early 20th century—that's according to her near sole champion, Arno Bammé. (Without his pioneering efforts in Germany in the early 1990s, my reprint could not have been possible. Thank you fellow lover of little known literature.)

Böhme authored 40 novels, and in her day her work was compared to that of another prolific and bestselling author, Emile Zola. By the end of the Twenties, *The Diary of a Lost Girl* had sold more than 1,200,000 copies. It's ranked by literary scholars as among the best selling books of its time.

The Diary of a Lost Girl was more than a bestseller—it was a literary phenomenon. The book was translated into 14 languages, and was widely reviewed and discussed across Europe. There were even pirated versions in some countries. The book inspired a popular sequel (by Böhme, in response to a flood of letters from people of all walks of life), a controversial stage play banned in some German cities, a parody, lawsuits (Böhme herself was accused of being a prostitute—*how else could a woman have written such a book?*), two silent films, and *sui generis*—a score of imitators. Because of it all—and in spite of it all, the book remained in circulation for more than 25 years. It was finally driven out-of-print at the beginning of the Nazi era by groups seeking to suppress it.

That's pretty good for what some critics considered a mere "potboiler" or "tearjerker"—but had it been just that, it wouldn't have had the impact that it had. In 1907, for instance, the *New York Times* reported that *Dracula* author Bram Stoker would have wanted to ban it. In 1909, a newspaper in New Zealand called it "the saddest of modern books." In the 1920's, the philosopher and literary critic Walter Benjamin wrote about it; he described it as something like "a complete inventory of the sexual trade"—but it's not really that. And in 1956—despite its decade's long obscurity in the United States, the American novelist Henry Miller included it on his list of the books which influenced him the most.

The Diary of a Lost Girl was a book of its time, and ahead of its time. In some ways, it anticipates the work and themes of contemporary authors like Margaret Atwood and Mary Gaitskill and even J.T. LeRoy.

When first published in 1905, *The Diary of a Lost Girl* purported to be a genuine diary. It supposedly told the true-life story of Thymian, a young woman forced by circumstance and society into a life of prostitution. It was her means of survival. Her story goes something like this: raped by her Father's business associate, she conceives a child, is cast out of her home, is scorned by society, is forced to give up the child, and ends up in a reform school—from which she escapes and by twists of fate hesitantly turns to life as a high-class call girl. In 1907, the once popular English writer Hall Caine described the book as the "poignant story of a great-hearted girl who kept her soul alive amidst all the mire that surrounded her poor body." It's all very dramatic—and heady stuff for the time. There is even a delightfully morbid scene where Thymian hangs out at her own pre-purchased cemetery plot because she likes the view. (She traded for the plot after turning a trick.) There, she strikes up a friendship with an older, grieving widow. They enjoy talking.

However, this is more than a hooker with a heart of gold story. It's more sophisticated than that. The book subtly confronts its readers with the story of a likable young women forced from her home and happy life into one of tragic degradation. The complicity of her family—and by extension, society—is provocative. At the time, the book helped open a dialogue on issues around prostitution and the treatment of women. Thymian—a truly endearing character and a heroine till the end, refuses to be coarsened by her experiences or to be defined by the men in her life. She defines herself. I won't say how it ends.

Soon after publication, speculation arose as to its actual authorship, with the press and the public divided. Böhme claimed only to be the editor of the manuscript. And to help put it over, some early editions depicted diary pages said to be in Thymian's hand. A close reading of the text, however, suggests this wasn't the work of a doomed teenager but rather the work of a gifted and empathetic writer. Böhme and her publisher, it should be noted, always maintained their account as to the book's origins. One wonders why? Had there been a real Thymain? Some of those who wrote to Böhme asked after the character as if she were real.

Because of its subject matter and contested nature, the book was a sensation. It sold more than 30,000 copies within the first few months of publication. (That was a lot of books back then. That's a lot of books now.) Within two years, more than 100,000 copies were in circulation—there was even a special edition of the book issued to mark the milestone. *The Diary of a Lost Girl* continued to sell and sell and sell. Editions appeared in Poland and Russia and Sweden and Spain and elsewhere. A movie was made from its sequel, and there was even a French novelization (by another author) of the 1929 Louise Brooks film. Böhme's story resonated for decades.

Today, however, few have heard of *The Diary of a Lost Girl*, the now forgotten Margarete Böhme, or the controversy which once swirled around the book's authorship. Aside from my hope of selling a modest number of copies, I felt its story needed to be told once again. I wrote a 30 page introduction detailing what I think is the rather remarkable history of the book, as best I could figure it from across a century, a continent, and another language. I also added three dozen vintage images to put things in context. Louise Brooks as Thymian is pictured on the cover.

Last year, according to Bowker (a company that tracks publishing industry statistics), titles published outside of "traditional publishing and classification definitions" numbered 764,448. That's a lot of books. Chances are pretty good this self-published reprint of a century old work will get lost in the tide. But that's ok. I had to do it. I believe in this book.

"Thymian lives!"

Thomas Gladysz's most treasured book

This piece appeared in the San Francisco Chronicle on July 10, 2011.
For a time, this San Francisco newspaper ran short pieces in its book review called "Special edition: Most treasured book." Contributors, who included novelist Isabel Allende, actor Peter Coyote, science writer Mary Roach, linguist Geoffrey Nunberg, and other local luminaries, were given approximately 100 words to talk about their most treasured volume. Here is my contribution.

I'm passionate about the silent film star Louise Brooks, the actress with the dark bob who played Lulu in *Pandora's Box*. My obsession (there, I've said it) goes back to a book, *Louise Brooks*, an acclaimed biography of the actress by Barry Paris.

In 1995, my interest in all things Lulu led me to found the Louise Brooks Society, and later to mount a grassroots campaign to bring this exceptional biography back into print. A university press did so in 2000, and I was honored to be acknowledged in the new edition, which is still in print. My most treasured book is a copy that Paris signed for me. In it, he wrote, "For Thomas, who resurrected me and LB the way [Kenneth] Tynan did in the *New Yorker*."

Reopening Pandora's Box in San Francisco
This interview by Michael T. Toole appeared in Film International on August 22nd, 2012.

It was quite the celebration for both Louise Brooks fans and silent cineastes in general when the 17th Annual San Francisco Silent Film Festival presented a restored print of *Pandora's Box* last month. G.W. Pabst's ever engrossing and eminently stylish examination of pure sexuality and the uninhibited nature that can lead to personal ruination was a must see on everyone's list.

There were more than a few women holding onto their pearls like delicate essence and coiffing her signature black bob. Not noticing her devoted fan celebration at the festival is like saying you don't notice the neon lights when you go to Las Vegas. It's too palpable to ignore. But if any star deserved such allegiance, Brooks is at the top of the list. Only 21 at the time of filming, she gave a performance of such enigmatic maturity, free of campy stares and broad gestures, that her acting still looks contemporary. Also, the compilation of her essays *Lulu in Hollywood* just turned 30 this summer, yet it's still a captivating read for most film students today.

Not that you need to convince Thomas Gladysz much of this. As the Director of the Louise Brooks Society, an internet-based archive and international fan club devoted to the silent film star, Gladysz has contributed to numerous books on the star, organized exhibits and offered commentary in appearances on television and radio. Naturally, he was at the festival and sat down with us for a chat.

MTT: Tell us about your first attraction to Louise Brooks?
TG: I came across Brooks by accident in the early 1990s. It was a Friday night, and not having anything to do, I decided to rent a movie. I guess that dates this story? Well, anyways, I was browsing the classic films selection when I came across *Pandora's Box*. I hadn't heard of the film, let alone its star. I guess what caught my eye was the image of Louise Brooks on the cover. I thought she looked rather striking; and too, the cover of the VHS said something about it being an erotic film. I knew it couldn't be that sexy, since it was an old silent film. I figured I'd give it a chance. I watched *Pandora's Box* that night—and was wowed. So much so, I got up the next morning and watched it all over again. And, I was wowed again. Louise Brooks floored me. It is as simple as that.

There was something electric about her. Something singular. Something appealing. Something erotic. She had so much personality.

I had never seen anyone like her before on the screen. I had also never had such a strong reaction to a film—and I still haven't. It was like love at first sight. By the way, Video Wave—where I rented *Pandora's Box*, is still in business, and they still carry VHS tapes along with DVDs and Blurays. And, remarkably, they still have that tape on their shelves. That particular version of *Pandora's Box* has the Stuart Oderman accompaniment. It's my favorite soundtrack.

MTT: How did you get the ball rolling with the Louise Brooks Society?

TG: After having seen Brooks in *Pandora's Box*, I wanted to find out more, and just as importantly, I wanted to share my enthusiasm and talk to others about what excited me. I remember going to the library and looking through a directory of fan clubs, but found nothing for Brooks. For a few years, I had to be content with reading whatever I could find, like Brooks' own *Lulu in Hollywood*, and the outstanding Barry Paris biography. Back then, finding a new article, or a still, or even a reproduction lobby card was a big deal. All that changed with the internet. The world wide web was just getting going in 1995. That's when I started the Louise Brooks Society. I launched a website as a means of reaching out to others. I started a fan club—an international fan club actually, and started to gather material and form my own archive. Remarkably, individuals from all over the world started sending me material—like scans of articles and pictures and stills which I had never seen before. People wrote to me from Argentina and Australia, and from Singapore and Italy. Everywhere really. That's when I discovered just how big of a following Brooks has all around the world. I also heard from film scholars and film historians and family members of the actress, as well as poets and professors and rock stars.

MTT: What exceeded your expectations about the new print of *Pandora's Box*? Specifically, anything about the allure of Brooks or details that enhanced the narrative for you?

TG: I have seen *Pandora's Box*—either on the big screen or on VHS or DVD, numerous times. Nevertheless, I was looking forward to seeing this new restoration. I had not seen it prior to its showing at the San Francisco Silent Film Festival. After the film, a number of people came up to me asking what I thought. What I said then was that I had seen things in that print that I hadn't ever seen before, like the dark hairs on Brooks' arm, or the name on the drum kit of the jazz combo who played during Lulu's wedding reception. Those are just two small details among many. For me, this restored print was a revelation. More than ever before, *Pandora's Box* emerges as a visually rich film, full of symbolism. I was also able to better appreciate the film's consistently great cinematography. Before, one had to make allowances for certain lapses in the film. It now seems to hold together much better.

By the way, the restored version runs 143 minutes, some ten minutes longer than the Criterion DVD, for example. This restored version is not supposed to contain any new material, though it seems to. The longer run time is explained by those who did the restoration as being the result of a corrected projection speed.

MTT: What surprises you (or not) about the celebrity fans of silent films and to a specific extent, idols like Brooks?

TG: I think a lot of the celebrities who are fans of silent film, or of Louise Brooks, have been fans for a long time. But now, it's fashionable or popular to identify oneself with the great old movies. I recently happened to meet the English actor Paul McGann, whose best known for his roles in *Withnail & I* and *Doctor Who*. He was on hand to narrate a couple of films.

MTT: Did the SFSFF do the proper job of appealing to scholars and devoted fans of Brooks & Pabst with proper literature and introduction?

TG: I would have to say yes, in that I wrote the program essay on *Pandora's Box!* I also supplied the slides for the pre-screening slide show, which helped "set the stage" for what followed. Of course, a lot more could be said about *Pandora's Box*. It is a big film, with a long and complicated history. When I was given the assignment to write the program essay, I was asked to concentrate on the film's material history and critical reception—which meant delving into how the film was presented, censored, cut up and considered over the years. As one of the great films of the silent era, it deserves a book.

MTT: What is it about Brooks' that still fascinates us?

TG: That's a question I'm asked often. Its answer, I think, lies at the heart of the legend that has grown up around the actress. Its answer also lies in Brooks' own story—the story of her rise and fall and reemergence—not only within the annals of film history, but within popular culture and the even larger realm of public awareness. When Barry Paris wrote his outstanding 1989 biography of the actress, he originally titled it *Louise Brooks: Her Life, Death and Resurrection*. I think that title suggests something extraordinary and even mythic.

Today, I think it's fair to say Brooks is among the most popular silent film stars in the world. Her renown has even eclipsed that of many of her better-known contemporaries. I find those who don't know her name at least know her image, or the character she played in *Pandora's Box*, Lulu. Today, Brooks is better regarded than she was at the height of her fame.

MTT: The recent success of *The Artist* and *Hugo* has reignited interest in silent film. Do you see that interest spilling over onto your studies of Brooks and other silent stars?

TG: Yes, without a doubt. There seems to be growing interest in the silent era—both among the public and in the media. I see screenings and festivals popping up just about everywhere, and in unlikely places. With those screenings come newspaper and magazine articles which reference *The Artist* and *Hugo* to explain these old films to their readers.

On top of all that, there is a Pickford bio-pic in the works, and a Chaplin musical on Broadway, and a play about Buster Keaton in Los Angeles. One of the big books of this summer was *The Chaperone*, by Laura Moriarty. It told the story of the woman who chaperoned the 15-year old Louise Brooks to New York City in 1922. And too, I see a lot of buzz on the internet. There are new websites and blogs and Facebook pages and Twitter streams devoted to early Hollywood springing up all the time. It is all good.

MTT: What influence do you think Louise Brooks has had on contemporary cinema?

TG: That's an interesting question. I don't think she has had all that much influence—either on contemporary cinema or contemporary acting. Did Clara Bow, or Garbo for that matter? Not really. Each were singular personalities, and in the case of Brooks, she had been pretty much forgotten for decades. If anything, Brooks' influence has been in broader terms, as an icon or symbol of something extra-cinematic. And as such, she has been paid homage in many films, from *Singing in the Rain* to *Something Wild* and most recently, Martin Scorsese's *Hugo*.

MTT: Any tidbits on what's on the horizon for Brooks' fans?

TG: A couple of years back, the George Eastman House in Rochester, New York unlocked Louise Brooks' diaries. There's been speculation ever since about their publication. There is also talk about *The Chaperone* being made into a film. Elizabeth McGovern, who played Cora in *Downton Abbey*, reads the audio version of the book. According to author Laura Moriarty, McGovern loved it so much she optioned the film rights with the hope of playing the title character, who also happens to be named Cora. We'll see if it gets made, and who might play Louise Brooks! I have also heard of a couple of other proposed films, and a couple of novels in the works. There's talk, as well, about reviving Lulupalooza, the 2005 Louise Brooks film festival, which took place in Richmond, Virginia. If only one of these materializes, then it will be big news.

I am also working on a couple of books. One is *Louise Brooks A to Z*, an encyclopedia style work, and the other is a Louise Brooks' reader, an anthology of writings about the actress. And as well, I am revising my "Louise Brooks edition" of *The Diary of a Lost Girl*, from 2010. I plan on releasing it as an e-book.

Louise Brooks Celebration in San Francisco
This piece appeared on Huffington Post on November 13, 2015.

More than 20 years ago, I stepped into Video Wave, which was then on Castro Street in Noe Valley. It was a Friday night, and not having anything in particular to do, I thought I would rent a movie. Having seen many of the then new releases, I spent a few minutes browsing the classics section. One title caught my eye, *Pandora's Box*, a German film from 1929. I thought the actress on the cover was kind of hot.

I hadn't heard of the film—nor its star, Louise Brooks. What initially peaked my interest was the text on the back of the VHS tape, "censored because of its explicit sexuality." With it being a Friday night, and with me having nothing in particular to do, an erotic film—even though it was more than sixty years old and likely pretty tame — seemed like just the right thing. I took a chance.

I watched the film that night. And was stunned. I was blown away. Who was this Louise Brooks? And how had I never heard of her before? Dietrich, Garbo, the great sex goddesses I knew of. But not Brooks. I got up the next morning and watched *Pandora's Box* all over again. I simply had to, because I had to watch it again. I had to come to grips with what I had seen and experienced the night before. Like her victims in *Pandora's Box*, I was in the thrall of Lulu.

Thrilled by the movie and this actress "I had discovered," I asked everyone I could about Brooks. "She is beautiful. She has short dark hair like a helmet. She was in this silent film called *Pandora's Box*. She played Lulu. . . ." Friends, family, people I knew who were into film—no one really seemed to know much about her until a co-worker named Joan recalled there had been a biography. I tracked down the book at the San Francisco Public Library (back in the day when they still had wooden card catalogs) and set off on a quest to learn everything I could about the actress. I was hooked. On the few occasions when her films were shown at the Castro, I was among the first in line.

In 1995, the graphical world wide web was just getting started, as were companies like eBay and Amazon. The internet was starting to take off, and I had the idea to start a "virtual fan club in cyberspace" as a way to connect with others interested in what was quickly becoming my main passion in life.

I launched the Louise Brooks Society website in the summer / fall of 1995. I guess I was a pioneer of sorts. The LBS was the first site devoted to the actress, and one of the earliest film websites. Then, fandom had not moved from fan clubs and mimeographed newsletters to the digital wilds of the internet.

I remember the excitement I felt when my hit counter read triple digits. Soon, visitors were numbered in the thousands and then tens of thousands, and then hundreds of thousands. In 1996, *USA Today* named the Louise Brooks Society a "Hot Site," noting "Silent-film buffs can get a taste of how a fan club from yesteryear plays on the Web." A few years later, the *New York Times* described it as an "excellent homage to the art of the silent film as well as one of its most luminous stars."

The LBS was also singled out in the pages of *San Francisco Chronicle* and *San Francisco Examiner*, where it was named one of the best film sites on the web by Jeffrey Anderson. The local *Noe Valley Voice* also ran a feature on the LBS.

In 1998, the popularity of my virtual fan club in cyberspace got noticed by Turner Classic Movies. The cable station decided to commission a documentary on Brooks. "Fan Site Sparks Biopic", an article on *Wired* by San Francisco journalist Steve Silberman, quoted a TCM spokesman who said the level of interest in the Louise Brooks Society convinced the network to go ahead with the documentary. "The Web presence for Louise Brooks was overwhelming. It was definitely a driving force in convincing the network to produce this documentary."

Ten years ago, Leonard Maltin wrote "Not many sites of any kind can claim to be celebrating a tenth anniversary online, but that's true of the Louise Brooks Society, devoted to the life and times of the magnetic silent-film star and latter-day memoirist. Thomas Gladysz has assembled a formidable amount of material on the actress and her era; there's not only a lot to read and enjoy, but there's a gift shop and even a 'Radio Lulu' function that allows you to listen to music of the 1920s. Wow!"

It's been a wow, a blast, and a labor of love. The Louise Brooks Society has its own blog—2500 entries and counting, as well as its own online radio station, RadioLulu, which streams Louise Brooks and silent-film related music of the 1920's, 1930's and today. You'd be surprised by how many pop and rock songs there are about the actress, including a couple by local bands. Remember Rough Trade on Haight Street. That's where I bought the maxi-single of "Pandora's Box" by the English new wave group OMD.

The Louise Brooks Society website features a filmography which is the most comprehensive ever compiled on the actress. The site's annotated bibliographies, if printed, would run hundreds of pages. The LBS also tracks and promotes the many homage to the actress which have appeared in film, fiction, poetry, comics, music and the visual arts. I've seen Brooks graffiti in San Francisco. And I swear I didn't do it.

On Brooks' birthday Saturday, November 14th at 2 p.m., the Louise Brooks Society returns to Video Wave (now at 4027 24th Street and one of the last video rental shops in The City) to celebrate its 20th anniversary. This Louise Brooks Celebration is also a DVD / Blu-ray release party. I recently completed an audio commentary for the new Kino Lorber release of *Diary of a Lost Girl*, the film Brooks made with director G.W. Pabst just after she completed *Pandora's Box*. Louise Brooks, Lulu forever.

True Confession: I've Been Stalking Louise Brooks for 20 Years
This piece appeared on the Louise Brooks Society blog on December 12, 2015.

It all started more than 20 years ago on a Friday night at Video Wave in San Francisco. Not having anything in particular to do, I walked over to the local video store to rent a movie. There weren't any new releases that especially interested me. I had already seen most of what was then current. So, I spent a few minutes browsing the classics section. I am a film buff, and had seen much of what was on the shelves. One title, however, caught my eye, *Pandora's Box*, a German silent film from 1929. I thought the actress on the cover was kind of hot.

I hadn't heard of the film—nor its star. What peaked my interest was the text on the back of the VHS tape, "censored because of its explicit sexuality." With it being a Friday night, and with me having nothing in particular to do, an erotic film—even though it was from more than sixty years old—*seemed ok* to me.

I watched that film that night as if in a dream. Who was this Louise Brooks? And how had I never heard of her? The questions ricocheted through me. I couldn't believe what I was seeing. How could such an actress—such a woman even, be possible? I went to bed that night in a daze. And I got up the next morning and watched *Pandora's Box* all over again. I had to. The rental tape was due later that day, and, I really, really, really wanted to watch it again. Anyways, I simply had to come to grips with what I had experienced the night before. Like her victims in *Pandora's Box*, I was in the thrall of Lulu.

Excited by the movie and this actress "I had discovered"—*that was how I felt*, I asked everyone I could about Louise Brooks. "She is really beautiful. She has short dark hair, like a helmet. She was in this silent film called *Pandora's Box*. She played Lulu. . . ." Friends, family, people I knew who were into film—no one really seemed to know much about her until a co-worker recalled there had been a biography. A book. A place to start!

Long before the internet put a world of knowledge at our fingertips, I went to the library in search of information. Looking through the card catalog, I turned up a 1989 title, *Louise Brooks*, by Barry Paris. I hadn't heard of the book, but it looked substantial, and there was an especially alluring portrait on the cover, and even more tantalizing images inside. I devoured every page of that biography. It is the perfect book—the perfect match of subject and author. Its intelligence and especially its empathy, as well as its many citations and footnotes, fed my fascination with Louise Brooks. It became my Bible.

Aren't we all smitten with an actor or actress sometime in our life? Don't we all have a secret crush on some cute starlet or some handsome hunk? Don't we want to see every film starring our favorite? Haven't film buffs all saved a picture or magazine clipping for no particular reason known only to ourselves? I figured there must be others out there who appreciated Louise Brooks like I did. I was eager to talk with others about her. But who might they be? How could I find them? Was there a group?

I went back to the library and asked at the reference desk if there was a directory of fan clubs, and much to my surprise, there was. I scoured its many pages of small type. There were thousands of fan clubs: there were groups for Laurel and Hardy, Marilyn Monroe, John Wayne and for dozens of contemporary stars and entertainers I couldn't believe anyone cared about. Disappointed, I didn't find any for Louise Brooks.

All this—renting *Pandora's Box*, asking everyone I knew about Louise Brooks, finding the biography of the actress—took place when the world wide web was just getting started. Up until then, the internet was largely text and made up of places like Prodigy, The Well, UseNet groups, BBS and AOL. I had been online for a few years, and explored each. I once even telnet into the Berkeley Public Library. But now—around 1995, the web was going graphical, and anyone who could figure out HTML could make their own website.

That's when I had an idea. Why not make a webpage about Louise Brooks? Or better yet, why not make a multi-page website, and post some of the material about the actress I had started to gather. I might even "meet" others who shared my interest. That's when I decided to form the Louise Brooks Society, what I then called a "virtual fan club in cyberspace."

Thanks to my brother, who was a computer engineer at Hewlett Packard and who helped me figure out Hypertext Markup Language, I posted my first web pages. This was in the summer of 1995. The Louise Brooks Society had begun.

I did meet others—others passionate about the actress. Lots of others. They included distant relations of the actress, a couple of rock stars, a famous actress, an Academy Award winner, a Doctor Who, film historians, poets, novelists, and others from all walks of life. There is a fellow from Rome who is about as devoted to Louise Brooks as me and has his own website. We have exchanged countless emails. There are also new friends—some I have met, some not—in Wichita, Kansas and Rochester, New York and elsewhere. Some emailed me. Others I found by exchanging links on film websites, especially those devoted to silent film. It seems individuals interested in the silent era were among the first to colonize the web. There weren't many of us, I guess, and we wanted to find community.

Soon enough, the Louise Brooks Society started to take off. I remember being excited when my hit counter read triple digits. Quickly, visitors were counted in the thousands and then tens of thousands, and then hundreds of thousands. In 1996, *USA Today* named the Louise Brooks Society a "Hot Site," noting "Silent-film buffs can get a taste of how a fan club from yesteryear plays on the Web. The Louise Brooks Society site includes interviews, trivia and photos. It also draws an international audience." A few years later, the *New York Times* described it as an "excellent homage to the art of the silent film as well as one of its most luminous stars."

In 1998, the popularity of my virtual fan club in cyberspace got noticed by Turner Classic Movies. The cable station devoted to classic films decided to commission a documentary about Louise Brooks. An article on the *Wired* website, "Fan Site Sparks Biopic", quoted a TCM spokesman who said the level of interest in the Louise Brooks Society convinced the network to go ahead with the documentary and an evening of the actress' films. "The Web presence for Louise Brooks was overwhelming. It was definitely a driving force in convincing the network to produce this documentary."

I have always been the scholarly type, and long thought that I wanted the Louise Brooks Society to be more than just a fan club. I wanted to do something. I see the mission of the society as one of honoring the actress by stimulating interest in her life and films. To that end, I have compiled bibliographies on the actress and her films which if printed out would run hundreds of pages. I have also written a couple of hundreds articles and a couple of thousand blogs about Louise Brooks. In 2010, I wrote the introduction and edited the "Louise Brooks edition" of *Diary of a Lost Girl*, the once controversial novel that was the basis for the 1929 film. Co-published by the Louise Brooks Society, it was this significant book's first English publication in more than 100 years. Recently, I provided the audio commentary for the new Kino Lorber DVD & Blu-ray of *Diary of a Lost Girl*.

There's more. The Louise Brooks Society has its own online radio station, RadioLulu, which streams Louise Brooks and silent-film related music of the 1920's, 1930's and today. Musical purists have complained, but I can't help but include some of the contemporary rock and pop songs about the actress by the likes of Orchestral Manoeuvres in the Dark (OMD), Soul Coughing, Rufus Wainwright, Natalie Merchant, and others.

Something that the website does is track and promote the many homage to the actress not only in music but in movies, fiction, comic books, the visual arts and popular culture. Did you know there was a street named after Louise Brooks in Paris, as well as a French perfume? The current staging of Alban Berg's opera, *Lulu*, at the Met in New York City owes a little something to Louise Brooks.

Over the years, the Louise Brooks Society has sponsored exhibits and author talks and screenings. One of the group's great accomplishments took place in the year 2000. At the time, both Louise Brooks' own book, *Lulu in Hollywood*, as well as the Barry Paris biography which I loved, had fallen out of print. The LBS mounted a grass roots campaign to bring them back. And it worked. The University of Minnesota Press reissued both books, and acknowledged the LBS in each. At one point, a representative of the press told me those two books were among their bestsellers.

I didn't do it all by myself. The members of the Louise Brooks Society—which I number at about 1500 from 50 countries on six countries—have contributed in all manner of ways. Individuals from around the world have sent pictures and clippings, provided translations of non-English materials, and helped in other ways. In 2005, a fan in Virginia organized a Louise Brooks-themed festival called Lulupalooza.

Looking back, that chance encounter some 20 years ago with an old film started me off on a kind of journey into the heart of the Jazz Age, and also myself. I know that there are probably more than a few people who think I go on about her too much.

That's ok. I met my wife through the actress after hearing about this girl who not only had her own gramophone (how cool), but also a large poster of Louise Brooks. I had to see it.

I have wondered, and others have asked, why I am obsessed with Louise Brooks. I am not sure. At one point, I remember telling a friend that I was in love with this long dead movie star. My friend looked aghast. I was joking, of course. I am not really in love with Louise Brooks, appearances to the contrary.

There is a mystery at the heart of Brooks' story, and her attraction. It is a self-destructive rosebud, if you will. Though she left her mark on her time, Brooks always thought of herself as a failure. In his biography, Barry Paris quotes a letter the actress wrote to her brother, "I have been taking stock of my 50 years since I left Wichita in 1922 at the age of 15 to become a dancer with Ruth St. Denis and Ted Shawn. How I have existed fills me with horror. For I have failed in everything—spelling, arithmetic, riding, swimming, tennis, golf, dancing, singing, acting, wife, mistress, whore, friend. Even cooking. And I do not excuse myself with the usual escape of 'not trying.' I tried with all my heart."

Like Holden Caulfield in *Catcher in the Rye*, who wanted to rescue those children from going over the cliff, I think I somehow wanted to rescue Louise Brooks from something. From what, I am not sure. From being forgotten, perhaps. All I can do is try.

Live365 is Dead, Long Live RadioLulu

This piece appeared on Huffington Post on January 27, 2016. I wrote it after receiving notice that the streaming service that had long hosted RadioLulu would shut down.

Like others, I've long had the fantasy of being a disc jockey. As a DJ, I would share favorite music with listeners, introducing songs and artists with the occasional anecdote or bit of trivia only I might know. "Have you heard this rare recording by ...?" or "Did you know that this singer also performed on ...?" As a DJ, I imagined the pleasure others might take in hearing a performer or recording they, like me, especially enjoyed.

In 2002, I was able to turn my fantasy into reality thanks to Live365.com, the streaming radio service provider. A pioneer in the field since 1999, Live365 enables individuals like me the chance to program music which plays over the internet. It was simple. I paid a small annual fee, around $120.00, to cover music licensing fees and other costs associated with streaming content over the web.

But now, it's all over. Recently, Live365 announced that as of January 31, 2016 it will cease operations. As I understand it, it's shutting down is largely a result of actions by the Copyright Royalty Board, which raised rates for net broadcasters while special lower rates for smaller broadcasters (like me) were phased out. With the writing on the wall, Live365 laid off staff and investors pulled out.

As radio news sites have reported, the loss of Live365 is a tremendous blow to the diversity of internet radio—diversity made possible by thousands of niche broadcasters running their stations more as hobbies than businesses.

I was one of those hobbyists. And the station I created was called RadioLulu. It was named after Lulu, the character played by Louise Brooks in the 1929 silent film, *Pandora's Box*. RadioLulu plays Louise Brooks inspired and silent film themed music of the Twenties, Thirties and today. I think it is unique.

The station features rare recordings by early film stars (who knew Rudolph Valentino or Charlie Chaplin cut records?), as well as theme songs from silent films ("silent films were never silent"), early show tunes, dance bands, Jazz Age jazz, European rarities, novelty numbers, and more. There are hotel orchestras, crooners, torch singers and even a bit of contemporary rock and pop, the latter mostly tributes to Brooks by the likes of Orchestral Manoeuvers in the Dark (OMD), Natalie Merchant, Rufus Wainwright, and even avant-jazz instrumentalist John Zorn.

Back in 1995, I launched the Louise Brooks Society, a website which serves as home to an on-line archive and international fan club devoted to this singular silent film star. She is my passion. I have been collecting material, including recordings, related to the actress ever since. With Brooks, one thing would lead to another....

RadioLulu is a place where I was able to share my audio collection with others. Here, fans could hear all manner of rare recordings by Brooks' co-stars (Adolphe Menjou, Frank Fay, Joan Blondell, etc...) as well as her contemporaries (Clara Bow, Gloria Swanson, Joan Crawford, Jean Harlow, Barbara Stanwyck and others). RadioLulu also features music from five of Brooks' films—including the haunting themes from *Beggars of Life* (1928) and *Prix de beauté* (1930), as well as fan favorites like Maurice Chevalier's "Louise."

To give the music context, I added tracks from the times. Janet Gaynor and Charles Farrell can be heard singing the poignant 1929 hit, "If I Had a Talking Picture of You," one of a number of movie-related numbers on RadioLulu.

There are also numbers like "Hooray for Hollywood," "Take Your Girlie to the Movies," and "At the Moving Picture Ball," as well their downbeat flip-side, like Constance Bennett's rendition of "Boulevard of Broken Dreams," and the Alice White & Blanche Sweet number "There's A Tear for Every Smile in Hollywood" (from the soundtrack to *Showgirl in Hollywood*). Along with spoken word intros and miscellaneous snippets of dialogue, RadioLulu even featured regulations explaining proper radio station identification given by none other than Cary Grant, co-star of the 1937 romantic musical, *When You're in Love* (in which Brooks had an uncredited role). Grace Moore, Grant's co-star, is also featured.

It would be hard to list all the odd, interesting, and notable recordings on RadioLulu. Among the 432 tracks and nearly 23 hours of programming, I also included a few rare vintage songs about movie stars—Charlie Chaplin, Greta Garbo, Buster Keaton, Zasu Pitts, and Mickey Maus among them.

I am especially proud of having tracked down four different vintage recordings of the theme from Brooks' only French film, *Prix de beauté*. She didn't sing it—her role in this early talkie was dubbed; but who did has long been a matter of debate among fans. Some have even suggested Edith Piaf, but she hadn't. My four different vintage recordings solve the mystery. Each can be heard on RadioLulu along with the 2006 cover version they inspired, "Chanson pour Louise Brooks," by the French group Les Primitifs Du Futur, featuring the famed cartoonist Robert Crumb on mandolin.

My obsession with tracking down little known related recordings has even led to a discovery or two. One such discovery was figuring out who the jazz combo is seen playing at the wedding party in *Pandora's Box*. It turns out they were Sid Kay's Fellows, a popular dance band in Berlin in the late 1920s and early 1930s. They accompanied Sidney Bechet during his concerts in the German capitol, and during their heyday, released a number of 78 rpm recordings. When the Nazis came to power in 1933, the group-which included Jewish musicians—were forbidden to perform publicly. I managed to track down some of their early recordings, and today Sid Kay's Fellows can be heard once again on RadioLulu.

I also tracked down the musical group seen in Brooks' other great G.W. Pabst directed film, *Diary of a Lost Girl* (1929). That small combo was lead by the Spanish-born musician Juan Llossas, who would soon find fame for his Tangos. Did you know the Tango was once all the rage in Weimar Germany? RadioLulu features a few such recordings. One RadioLulu track I especially like is Marek Weber's "A media luz."

RadioLulu also features an unusual recording by Jaroslav Jezek, the "George Gershwin of Czechoslovakia." In 1929, the year that Brooks played Lulu in *Pandora's Box* and was suddenly famous all over Europe, Jezek wrote and recorded "Zasu," a memorable song whose sheet music depicts the actress! Coincidence? Not likely.

And speaking of Gershwin, my station also features a handful of songs penned by Gershwin, with whom Brooks had a flirtatious acquaintanceship. By the way, Brooks' favorite Gershwin song, "Somebody Love Me," can be heard on RadioLulu.

Though I hoped for acclaim, I knew would never reach a mass audience. Nevertheless, I love programming RadioLulu. It's the few listeners I reach that I aim to please. According to my monthly listener reports, at any one time dozens and sometimes even hundreds of individuals from around the world tune into RadioLulu. Over the years, a few thousand individuals have "liked" the station.

Occasionally, I do receive an email or a listener posted comment praising the station and saying how much they loved the Roaring Twenties or early jazz or old movies. On New Year's Eve, a woman named Theresa emailed. She wrote, "Wish I had discovered you earlier. Best station I've ever heard for old, unique style music of the 20's and 30's. Love hearing people I have only heard of but never actually heard like Josephine Baker, Ruth Etting, and so many movie stars not known for singing. So fabulous! Will you be able to keep going with licensing changes? This music and your station is a treasure."

That made me feel good. And so did film critic Leonard Maltin, who wrote a short piece about the Louise Brooks Society and pointed out my website even had its own radio station "that allows you to listen to music of the 1920s. Wow!"

Sometimes, recognition has come from unlikely places. There is a contemporary Spanish group named Rädio Lulú who play swing and retro pop music and may have taken their name from my station.

And sometimes, recognition comes from unlikely sources. A few years ago, I had the chance to meet the English actor Paul McGann, who starred in *With Nail and I* and played the eighth Doctor Who. Like me, he too is a devotee of early film. When we met, McGann had a quizzical look on his face before saying, "You're the guy that does RadioLulu. It's incredible. I listen all the time." The Pulitzer-Prize winning graphic novelist Art Spiegelman has told me he tunes-in as well, as has the award-winning science fiction writer Richard Kadrey.

Last November, I received an email from a listener named Nick. He is employed at the Vito Russo Library at the Gay Center in New York City; he wrote to say that RadioLulu is played at the library every Saturday, and that "Everybody loves it." That was gratifying as well. And that is why since 2002 I have pursued this labor of love called RadioLulu.

There is a lot of great music on Live365, as well as a lot of passion behind its many stations. I will miss the niche stations like mine and like those that play only Tiki music. I will miss the chance to discover new music. I will miss the opportunity to listen to favorites like Radio Dismuke (an amazing station featuring popular music of the 1920s & 1930s), Radiola! (another station featuring popular music of the 1920s & 1930s "guaranteed to wake up the mind and make it smile"), and Weimar Rundfunk (European Dance Orchestras and Hot Dance Bands). Each are longtime broadcasters. I am sure each will find a new home, if they haven't already.

There is a lot of great music on RadioLulu. Along with such famous names as Bing Crosby, Rudy Vallee, Benny Goodman, Tallulah Bankhead, Django Rheinhart, and Fred Astaire, there are as many less well known but just as deserving artists like the Eskimo Pie Orchestra, Scrappy Lambert, Hanka Ordonówna, Annette Hanshaw, Lee Wiley, Kiki of Montparnasse (Man Ray's muse), and Sidney Torch (the great British cinema organist). There is even a 1929 recording of the German dramatist Bertolt Brecht singing "Mack the Knife."

In 1940, Brooks self-published a now extremely rare booklet titled *Fundamentals of Good Ballroom Dancing*. I have a copy, and in it, the actress turned dancer recommended a few recordings with which to practice one's steps. I tracked down those recordings, and that's why you'll hear Xavier Cugat's "Siboney" and Wayne King's "I'm Forever Blowing Bubbles."

Here are some tracks you won't want to miss: "You Oughta be In Pictures" by Little Jack Little & His Orchestra, "Makin' Whoopee" by B.A. Rolfe & His Lucky Strike Orchestra, "Puttin on the Ritz" by Harry Richman, "The Vamp" by the Waldorf-Astoria Dance Orchestra, "Flapperette" by Nate Shilkret, and "I'm a Jazz Vampire" by Marion Harris. Oh, and don't miss "Lulu" by Twiggy (the 1960's supermodel). It is one of a couple dozen songs with "Lulu" or "LouLou" in the title.

I am not sure what will happen with RadioLulu. I am looking around for new streaming sites. I hope to continue sharing my collection of Louise Brooks inspired and silent film themed music with the world. How can I not?

RadioLulu Redux
This piece appeared on the Louise Brooks Society blog on December 26, 2017. It was written after I had reworked and relaunched RadioLulu.

Did you know that the Louise Brooks Society has its own online radio station? It's called RadioLulu. You can listen using the Tune-In app, Winamp or the Windows Media Player, or, you can even listen via the Tune-In app on ROKU on your television.

RadioLulu is a Louise Brooks-inspired, silent film-themed internet station streaming music of the 1920s, 1930s, and today. RadioLulu features vintage and contemporary music related to Louise Brooks as well as the silent and early sound eras. This is music you're not likely to hear anywhere else.

Launched back in 2002, this unique station now features vintage music from five of Brooks' films—the haunting themes from *Beggars of Life* (1928) and *Prix de beauté* (1930), as well as musical passages from *The Canary Murder Case* (1929), *Empty Saddles* (1936), and *Overland Stage Raiders* (1938). On RadioLulu, you'll also hear the familiar "Sidewalks of New York" (which was played on the set of *The Street of Forgotten Men*), as well as John Philip Sousa's seldom heard "Atlantic City Beauty Pageant" (which was written for the Miss America contest, as seen in *The American Venus*).

Vintage recordings by Brooks' screen co-stars are also featured on RadioLulu. Among them are Adolphe Menjou, Esther Ralston, Dorothy Mackaill, James Hall, Lawrence Gray, Noah Beery, Frank Fay, Joan Blondell, and Buck Jones. There is even a song by Blanche Ring, who appeared in *It's the Old Army Game* and was the aunt of Brooks' first husband, Eddie Sutherland. A few of Brooks' European co-stars are also represented, among them Siegfried Arno (*Pandora's Box*), Kurt Gerron (*Diary of a Lost Girl*), and Andre Roanne (*Prix de beauté*). Each is a rarity. As well, there are vintage tracks associated with Brooks' brief time with the Ziegfeld Follies, including a handful of recordings by performers who shared the stage with the actress, such as Ethel Shutta, Leon Erroll, and the great W.C. Fields.

RadioLulu includes a number of songs by Brooks' friends and acquaintances, as well as individuals she worked with over the years. Actress Tallulah Bankhead, chanteuse Lucienne Boyer, torch singer Libby Holman, bandleader Emil Coleman, and nightclub owner Bruz Fletcher can all be heard on RadioLulu. Other tracks associated with the actress and featured on RadioLulu include George Gershwin's "Somebody Loves Me"

(Brooks knew Gershwin, and this was her favorite Gershwin song), Xavier Cugat's "Siboney" (recommended by Brooks in her rare booklet, *Fundamentals of Good Ballroom Dancing*), and two numbers by Sid Kay's Fellows (the jazz band seen playing in the wedding reception scene in *Pandora's Box*).

All together, RadioLulu features more than 850 tracks! Notably, many of them come from rare 78 rpm discs you're unlikely to hear anywhere else. Of course, there's Maurice Chevalier's much-loved "Louise" as well as more than a dozen tracks with Louise, Lulu, or LouLou in the title. Among them is the Coon-Sanders Nighthawks' recording of "Louise, You Tease," as well as a number of different recordings of both "Don't Bring Lulu" and "Lulu's Back in Town".

Many contemporary tributes to the actress can also be heard on RadioLulu. These include songs by Natalie Merchant, Rufus Wainwright, Orchestral Manoeuvers in the Dark (OMD), John Zorn, and Soul Coughing. Famed cartoonist Robert Crumb is heard on "Chanson pour Louise Brooks". And there's Ross Berkal's tribute, "MLB (for Louise Brooks)." Berkal, who is mentioned in the Barry Paris biography and is a longtime member of the Louise Brooks Society, was acquainted with the actress later in her life.

Beyond songs related to Louise Brooks, RadioLulu also features hundreds of songs from the 1920s and 1930s (along with a smattering from the 1940s, 1950s, and 1960s). There is music from the movies aplenty, as well as rare recordings by early Hollywood stars and Jazz Age celebrities. There are tracks by the popular crooners and torch singers of the time, as well as little known numbers by regional dance bands and hotel orchestras. There are also early Broadway show tunes, early European jazz, popular vocal numbers, theme songs, and even a few novelty numbers.

Recordings by early Hollywood figures such as Charlie Chaplin, Buster Keaton, Lupe Velez, Clara Bow, Rudolph Valentino, Gloria Swanson and Joan Crawford are streamed. So are recordings by later stars Buddy Rogers, Claudette Colbert, Jean Harlow, Paulette Goddard, Barbara Stanwyck, and Dorothy Lamour. A few of the European actors and actresses heard on the station include Brigitte Helm, Camilla Horn, Anny Ondra, Conrad Veidt, Pola Negri, and Marlene Dietrich (notably, her early German-language recordings).

Among others, Janet Gaynor and Charles Farrell are heard singing the classic "If I Had A Talking Picture Of You," one of a number of movie-related songs. There's also "Take Your Girlie to the Movies," "At the Moving Picture Ball," and "Hooray for Hollywood," as well as rare vintage recordings about Chaplin, Garbo, Keaton, Mickey Mouse and Zasu Pitts. Be sure not to miss H. Robinson Cleaver's "Grace Moore Medley," Fred Bird & Luigi Bernauer's "Hallo Hallo Hier Radio," and Jack Hylton and His Orchestra's "My brother makes the noises for the talkies."

What else can be heard on RadioLulu? How about Constance Bennett singing "Boulevard of Broken Dreams," or Alice White & Blanche Sweet singing "There's A Tear For Every Smile in Hollywood" (from the soundtrack to *Showgirl in Hollywood*). The Waldorf-Astoria Dance Orchestra performs "The Vamp," Nate Shilkret plays "Flapperette," and Marion Harris sings "I'm a Jazz Vampire." Regulations explaining proper radio station identification are given by none other than Cary Grant, co-star of the 1937 Brooks' film, *When You're in Love*.

RadioLulu features many of the leading stars of the Jazz Age and Depression era— Rudy Vallee, Russ Colombo, Ben Selvin, Fred Waring, Ted Weems, Paul Whiteman,

Annette Hanshaw, Helen Kane, Mildred Bailey, Lee Wiley, Ruth Etting, Kay Thompson, and Frankie Trumbauer. There are recordings by such famous names as Duke Ellington, Fred Astaire, Bing Crosby and Benny Goodman, alongside rarely heard artists like the Eskimo Pie Orchestra and the Brox Sisters, as well as Scrappy Lambert, Fred Elizalde, and Dorothy Dickson! You never know who or what will turn up on this eclectic, always entertaining station.

And that's not all…. RadioLulu plays Ragtime, swing, standards, and some real hot jazz, including such popular hits as the "Charleston," "Black Bottom," and "Varsity Rag." There are vintage recordings of popular favorites like "Stardust" and "As Time Goes By," along with great, but little known works like James P. Johnson's "You've Got to be Modernistic." By the way, the single longest track is George Jessel's spoken word history "The Roaring Twenties 1920-1929."

Among the unusual European numbers on RadioLulu are little heard gems from the 1930s Polish chanteuse Hanka Ordonówna as well as the Gershwin of Czechoslovakia, Jaroslav Jezek; there's a stirring number by the great British cinema organist Sidney Torch; and even a 1929 recording of the German dramatist Bertolt Brecht singing "Mack the Knife." Along with lovely favorites by the likes of Josephine Baker, Django Rheinhart, and Mistinguett. Also heard are artist models Suzy Solidor and Kiki of Montparnasse. Both posed for the surrealist photographer Man Ray, an admirer of Louise Brooks.

Here are ten additional vintage RadioLulu tracks you won't want to miss: "Makin' Whoopee" by B.A. Rolfe & His Lucky Strike Orchestra, "Runnin' Wild" by Isabella Patricola, "The Sheik of Araby" by Fats Waller, "My Man" by Fanny Brice, and "Puttin on the Ritz" by Harry Richman, as well as "You Oughta be In Pictures" by Little Jack

Little & His Orchestra, "College Rhythm" by Jimmy Grier, "Singin' In The Rain" by Cliff Edwards (Ukulele Ike), "Slumming On Park Avenue" by Alice Faye, and "Ramona" by Dolores Del Rio.

And here are ten contemporary RadioLulu tracks you won't want to miss: "Lulu" by Twiggy (the 1960's supermodel), "Valentino" by Connie Francis, "Louise" by Eric Clapton, "Weight Lifting Lulu" by The Residents, "Interior Lulu" by Marillion, as well as "Marlene Dietrich's Favourite Poem" by Peter Murphy, "I'm In Love With A German Film Star" by The Passions, "Just Like Fred Astaire" by James, "Lulu Land" by Camper van Beethoven, and "Brandenburg Gate" by Lou Reed & Metallica (from their *Lulu* album).

Arguably, music has played a significant role in the life and films of Louise Brooks. I started RadioLulu as a means of sharing some of the many rare and related recordings collected by the Louise Brooks Society. Over the years, this unique, long running station has gained many fans and listeners. Famed film critic Leonard Maltin once rated it a "Wow." Likewise, Louise Brooks devotee and celebrated *Dr. Who* actor Paul McGann called it "incredible." The Pulitzer-Prize winning graphic novelist Art Spiegelman (author of *Maus*) has tuned-in on occasion, and told us so. As has the award-winning science fiction writer Richard Kadrey. And would you believe that a retro Spanish pop/swing/rock group named Radio Lulu named themselves after the station?

CMBA profile: Louise Brooks Society
This interview was published on the Classic Movie Blog Association (CMBA) website on February 15, 2018.

The CMBA profiles one of our classic movie blogs each month. This month we're featuring Thomas Gladysz, of the Louise Brooks Society.

The Louise Brooks Society is one of the most prolific and professional of the blogs in CMBA. Almost every day, there are updates on the site, and the writing and information is top-notch. It's a blog with a very specific focus—a silent film goddess with a short career but an iconic image. Author Thomas Gladysz has been running the society for over twenty years now, and he never seems to run out of things to say or images to share about Louise and her world. Thomas couldn't choose just one blog entry for you to look at, instead he advises you to "start with the most recent entry and simply scroll back words in time. If I have done a decent job, you will keep going." His blog can be found at louisebrookssociety.blogspot.com.

CMBA: What sparked your interest in classic film?
TG: I remember my father liking gangster movies of the 1930s, as well as Laurel & Hardy, so I suppose his tastes affected mine to some degree. However, as a young teen, I was a contrarian. And my tastes were formed by what I could see on television. My favorite films then were John Huston's *Moby Dick* (1956), Richard Lester's *A Hard Day's Night* (1964), and Francois Truffaut's *Fahrenheit 451* (1966). I grew up near Detroit, and I guess I was a bit idiosyncratic, as far as suburban kids were concerned. The first silent film I remember seeing was *Faust* (1926), which I picked up late one night on a UHF TV station out of nearby Canada. I was wowed. The scene where

Mephisto spread his cape over the city blew my teenage mind. Visually speaking, I hadn't seen anything like it before, and wouldn't again until college when I saw the dream cinema of Jean Cocteau.

I launched the Louise Brooks Society website in 1995. I did so after having seen Louise Brooks in *Pandora's Box* (1929). I was gob-smacked. I wanted to learn more about Brooks, to see every one of her films, and to meet others who shared by enthusiasm. I read everything I could get my hands on, and tracked down each of her available films. One thing leads to another…. Interest in G.W. Pabst – the director of *Pandora's Box* and *Diary of a Lost Girl* (1929)—led to an interest in his contemporaries, Lang and Murnau, as well as German Expressionism. Interest in the silent era and the Jazz Age led to an interest in flappers and F. Scott Fitzgerald and Clara Bow and Colleen Moore. My wife loves Buster Keaton and Ronald Colman and Erich von Stroheim, and I developed an interest in them as well. Louise Brooks, you might say, has been my education.

CMBA: What makes a film a "classic" in your opinion?

TG: A movie has to have a strong personality, or at least an alluring personality. Does that mean I follow the auteur theory? Perhaps so, but perhaps not. I was an English major in college, and I've always been drawn to films based on books. Another couple of longstanding favorites are Stanley Kramer's *Inherit the Wind* (1960) and David Lean's *Doctor Zhivago* (1965). I can't tell you how many times I've watched each of the various films (and the TV series) based on Dumas' *The Count of Monte Cristo*. I love that story. As a matter of fact, I love films about outsiders, loners, losers and those who are misunderstood or have been wronged. I guess that says more about me than about the classic status of a film. Obviously, some "classic films" are more successful than others as works of art. Individual films become classics for all manner of reasons. Some films considered great I find dull. Some films considered banal or silly I find enjoyable, like *My Man Godfrey* (1936) and *The Incredible Mr. Limpet* (1964). I know what I like.

CMBA: What classic film(s) do you recommend to people who say they hate old movies?

TG: That's a tough one. I would ask what contemporary films they like and try to think of a similar film from the past—provided the viewer can get past the technological hurdles, like black-and-white film, crude special effects, or the lack of spoken dialogue. Many of the Charlie Chaplin and Buster Keaton films and some of the pre-code films are classics because they transcend time. They are "universal." They still speak to a generation of viewers who've grown up on special effects.

If someone were to ask what Louise Brooks film they should watch, I would suggest *Diary of a Lost Girl* over *Pandora's Box*. Both are great films, but both are also problematic. Each is dark and a little depressing, which may turn-off some viewers. Also, both films were heavily censored, and what we have today is not quite complete, despite all the restoration work done on them. All-in-all, I would say *Diary* holds together a little better. Another recommended downer is *Beggars of Life* (1928). It's a terrific film. *Love Em and Leave Em* (1926) is a very different Brooks' film from those I just mentioned. It is fun, and a typical film of its time. I wish somebody would restore it.

CMBA: Why should people care about classic film?

TG: Kevin Brownlow once said: "Silent pictures show us how we lived and what our attitudes were. And as an art form, they can be wonderfully entertaining and often inspirational." I think that pretty much explains it.

CMBA: What is the most rewarding thing about blogging?

TG: Feedback. It is gratifying when readers post comments or show interest in what I've written. But I am not in it for the applause, because there is very little of that. Maybe I'm just talking to myself, but I started my blog as a form of dialogue with the world, with those who love watching, reading about, thinking about, and researching old movies. Classic film will never achieve a mass audience—just like my blog or the Louise Brooks Society website will never achieve a mass readership. But a few hundred or a few thousand are all right with me. I keep on. It's what I do.

I started the Louise Brooks Society blog in 2002, first on LiveJournal, and later I moved it to Blogger, where it now resides. A couple hundred have subscribed. I am a bit proud of the fact that I've kept it going all this time. Sometime this year, I will have posted for the 3000th time.

CMBA: What challenges do you face with your blog, and how do you overcome them?

TG: Despite the narrow focus of my blog—one film star with a short career—I seldom run out of things to write about. I've joked "all roads lead to Louise Brooks." And no matter how seemingly unrelated a topic might be, I always try to somehow relate it to Brooks or the silent era. (Trust me, I never stray that far.) The novelist Salman Rushdie once said, "To understand just one life, you have to swallow the world." That's my motto.

CMBA: What advice would you give to a new blogger?

TG: Be yourself. Your blog can be anything you want it to be. Don't imitate others, but also, importantly, don't be ignorant of what others have done. Check out other bloggers! A good novelist is someone who reads lots of fiction. And a good blogger is someone who reads other blogs. Who knows? Other bloggers might well have done something that inspires or informs what you are trying to do.

Bring the real world into this digital medium. Read print books! Research something you are curious about. Visit a library or archive or historical museum to find out more about your subject. *Explore your local connection.* If you like Jean Harlow or William Powell or Esther Ralston, find out where their films where shown in your town... and what the local critics thought of them. Did your favorite star ever visit your town or city? There are a million angles.

Also, take advantage of all that the internet has to offer to enrich your blog—like newspaper and magazine archives, audio sources like SoundCloud, social media (it pays to get the word out), and the "community" of other film lovers. Your blog is a journey. Be open to possibilities. Explore. Have fun.

CMBA: What is one blog post that you would like to share on your profile—and why?

TG: That too is a difficult question to answer. I have recently gone back and read some of the posts from the early years of my blog, and admittedly, I found them wanting. Many of them were rather slight. These days, I try to be more substantial, and not just write a sentence or two and post a bunch of pictures. That's never really been my style. Anyone reading this interview who intends to check out my blog might start with the most recent entry and simply scroll back words in time. If I have done a decent job, you will keep going, at least for a wild.

6 RELATED READING

Walter Benjamin, His and This Arcades Project • Remembering Bruce Conner, a fave rave • The San Francisco origins of Lulu • Lulu's debut... on this day in 1905 • Danger and Desire: 6 Great Lulus • Marlene Dietrich and Louise Brooks • Louise Brooks art #2 • Louise Brooks, Modernism, the Surrealists, and the Paris of 1930 • Louise Brooks and The Invention of Morel, by Adolpho Bioy Casares • Divine Dancer • Atlantic City Pageant March • Lee Miller and Louise Brooks • Louise Brooks and F. Scott Fitzgerald - a connection • Evelyn Brent revealed in new book • Rolled Stockings screenwriter Frederica Sagor Maas dies at age 111 • A Jim Tully Revival: Hobo Author Back in Print • Canary Murder Case author featured in new book • Celebrating G.W. Pabst • Daisy D'Ora, one-time German actress, dies at age 97 • Discovering a Polish Lulu • Who was Margarete Bohme? • Long before Three Cups of Tea • Piracy and The Diary of a Lost Girl • How many silent films were based on Diary of a Lost Girl? • The Diary of a Lost Girl: A brief history of a banned book • The Diary of a Lost Girl, the research continues • The Holocaust, Heinrich Himmler, Jodi Picoult, and The Diary of a Lost Girl • Sigmund Freud, John Huston, and Louise Brooks (& not Ghoulardi) • Louise Brooks and the Maltese Falcon • King of Gamblers star subject of new book • Louise Brooks and Bruz Fletcher: Camped, Tramped & Riotous Vamps • A Louise Brooks / Ed Wood / Elvis Presley connection • Theodore Roszak (1933-2011) • An encounter with a curious character • Lee Israel, writer who forged Louise Brooks letters, has died • Remembering Roger Ebert (a fan of Louise Brooks) • Jan Wahl Through a Lens Darkly • Talking to the Piano Player • In celebration of Stuart Oderman (1940-2017) • David Levine, painter and illustrator, has died • Bill Berkson, In Memoriam (1939-2016) - poet and Louise Brooks devotee • John Ashbery & Louise Brooks encounter in Paris • Homage to George W. Lighton of Kentucky, idealistic silent film buff who perished in the Spanish Civil War

The writer Salman Rushdie once said, "To understand just one life you have to swallow the world." I say, "All roads lead to Louise Brooks."

The nexus of interests and passions which arose around my "falling in love" with Brooks (aka my "discovery" of the actress) led me to explore not only the films of the 1920s and 1930s, but also all manner of related and not-so-related books, authors, art, and music.

Which is another way of explaining how one thing leads to another. And how these pieces of related reading came about.

The pieces gathered here follow tangential threads of interest, from Walter Benjamin's arcades project (a kind of rambling model for this chapter, and even this book) to a brief look at John Philip Sousa, F. Scott Fitzgerald, and Heinrich Himmler as well as longer considerations of an Argentian novelist, a gay nightclub singer, and an obscure Kentucky film-buff who died in the Spanish Civil War.

Each has a connection, sometimes slight, to Louise Brooks.

Walter Benjamin, His and This Arcades Project

This piece appeared on the Louise Brooks Society blog on March 11, 2010. I hadn't read or thought about it until I selected it for inclusion in this collection. Its subject and rambling nature serves as a model for this chapter of related reading, and perhaps even for my approach to Louise Brooks and her career.

The other day, I picked up a copy of *The Arcades Project*, by Walter Benjamin. I got it because I had noticed (*via* Google book search) that Margarete Böhme is mentioned in this massive, posthumously published work. I am doing a bit of research on Böhme and her books for a project I am working on.

Who is Margarete Böhme, you may ask? And who is Walter Benjamin? And what do they have to do with Louise Brooks? Let's take a stroll through the glass covered shops in the passage way of the 20th century. . . .

Böhme (1867-1939) was a turn-of-the-last century German writer whose sensational 1905 book, *Tagebuch einer Verlorenen*, was the basis for the 1929 film, *Diary of a Lost Girl*, starring Louise Brooks. Though little known today, *Tagebuch einer Verlorenen* was described in one scholarly work I recently examined as one of the best selling autobiographical narratives of the 20th century. And, in fact, by the time G.W. Pabst made his film of the book with Louise Brooks, Fritz Rasp, and Valeska Gert, sales of this controversial title in Germany had reached more than 1,200,000 copies! That's a lot.

Benjamin (1892-1940) was a German-Jewish philosopher, literary critic, theorist, essayist and translator of Charles Baudelaire. Benjamin knew and was friends with seemingly everyone from Rainer Maria Rilke (lover of Lou Andreas Salomé, who was the possible inspiration and namesake of Lulu) and Bertolt Brecht (who attended Frank Wedekind's funeral) and Theodor Adorno (who essayed Alban Berg's unfinished opera, *Lulu*). Benjamin also knew Georg Lukács, Georges Bataille, Hannah Arendt, Hermann Hesse, Kurt Weill and others remembered today. Tragically, and desperately, Benjamin killed himself while fleeing the Nazi invasion of France. According to Wikipedia, "Over the last half-century the regard for his work and its influence have risen dramatically, making Benjamin one of the most important twentieth century thinkers about literature and about modern aesthetic experience."

Benjamin's *The Arcades Project*, begun in 1927, is a monumental study on which he continued to work until his death. At one point, the manuscript was destroyed and thought lost forever. However, a second copy was found and later published. Unfinished, it is a mass, a mess, a conglomeration of notes and considerations concerning European and French bourgeois life in the 19th and early 20th centuries. If you will, it is an intellectual ramble down a collective memory lane.

The Nobel Prize winning South African novelist J. M. Coetzee, writing in the *Guardian* newspaper, described the work this way. "[*The Arcades Project*] suggests a new way of writing about a civilization using its rubbish as materials rather than its artworks: history from below rather than above. . . . What does *The Arcades Project* have to offer? The briefest of lists would include: a treasure hoard of curious information about Paris, a multitude of thought-provoking questions, the harvest of an acute and idiosyncratic mind's trawl through thousands of books, succinct observations, polished to a high aphoristic sheen, on a range of subjects . . . . and glimpses of Benjamin toying with a new way of seeing himself: as a compiler of a 'magic encyclopedia'."

It was into this bound labyrinth—into this unfinished attempt to liberate the suppressed "true history" of the 19th and 20th centuries—that I strolled in search of Böhme. I found a single reference, a single line of text on page 559 couched between similarly brief jottings on the nature of Jugendstil (the German name for Art Nouveau). The single line read:"Segantini and Munch; Margarete Böhme and Przybyszewski."

Come on Walter, give me something more to work with than just mere juxtaposition. For Christ's sake! Or was it for the sake of something else. . . . I wondered, and looked things up.

Giovanni Segantini (1858-1899) was an Italian painter of the Symbolist persuasion. Same with Edvard Munch (1863–1944), the famous Norwegian painter and printmaker.

Böhme, as mentioned above, was German novelist whose brand of melodramatic realism could be toned grim. As in *Tagebuch einer Verlorenen*, she often wrote about the lives of young women, and prostitutes. Stanisław Przybyszewski (1868–1927) was a Polish novelist, dramatist, and poet of the "decadent naturalistic school." He is also associated with the Symbolist movement, which was a considerable force in Middle Europe at the turn of the last century. It's been noted that Przybyszewski's fascination with the philosophy of Nietzsche and Satanism plunged him into a bohemian lifestyle.

I wondered, did Benjamin mean to suggest he saw Böhme as a Symbolist?

What did Segantini-Munch & Böhme-Przybyszewski have in common? Certainly there was the shared theme of the troubled/in trouble young women. Above is Munch's 1894 painting, "Ashes." It's one of a number of works by this artist which depicts distressed young female. Other examples can be found at the bottom of his Wikipedia page. There, don't fail to note the painting called "Vampire," which also depicts a young women embracing her lover.

Böhme's fiction made a specialty of sympathetically portraying the lives of troubled young women. That's the story of Thymian Gottebal, the lost girl or "lost one" whose story is told in *Tagebuch einer Verlorenen*—and portrayed by Brooks in *Diary of a Lost Girl*. When Böhme's book was released in England in 1907, it even carried an endorsement from Hall Caine, a then well known man of letters to whom Bram Stoker's novel, *Dracula*, was dedicated. His blurb read in part, "It is difficult for me to believe that a grown man or woman with a straight mind and a clean heart can find anything that is not of good influence in this most moving, most convincing, most poignant story of a great-hearted girl who kept her soul alive amidst all the mire that surrounded her poor body."

Just two years after it was first issued in Germany, Böhme's publisher put out a special edition to commemorate the printing of the 100,000th copy of the book. I happen to have one of those vintage editions. Here is a scan of its rather striking cover.

And yes, that is a Medusa-haired Devil holding up a the dead baby.

Whether Benjamin read this book isn't known. But considering it popularity and controversial nature in Germany and even across all of Europe (it was translated into 10 languages and published in Poland, Finland, Russia, etc...), and considering he name checks the author in *The Arcades Project*, it seems somewhat likely. How could he have missed it? It seems right up his alley/arcade.

Which then raises the question, did Benjamin seen the 1929 G.W. Pabst film? That is also not known, though the always on the move Benjamin was known to be in Berlin in 1929, the same year *Diary of a Lost Girl* and the earlier *Pandora's Box* premiered in the German capitol.

I was curious. Had Benjamin mentioned Wedekind in *The Arcades Project*? The answer is yes. He does so twice on page 492, in the course of a passage.

Wedekind, of course, was the similarly controversial German playwright whose works include the still popular and still performed *Frühlings Erwachen* (*Spring Awakening*, 1891) and *Die Büchse der Pandora* (*Pandora's Box*, 1904). Like Böhme, he too wrote about troubled youth. Lulu—whose archetype may be traced back to Lilith and forward to Lola-Lola in the *Blue Angel* and even to Lolita (penned by another late 1920's Berlin resident) —is Wedekind's most famous character.

In *The Arcades Project*, Benjamin writes, "On what is 'close' (Veuillot: 'Paris is musty and close') in fashion: the 'glaucous gleam' under the petticoats, of which Aragon speaks. The corsets as the torso's arcade. The absolute antithesis to this open-air world of today. What today is derigueur among the lowest class of prositutes—not to undress —may once have been the height of refinement. One liked the women *retroussee*, tucked up. Hessel thinks he has found here the origin of Wedekind's erotics; in his view, Wedekind's fresh-air pathos was only a bluff. And in other respects?"

Again, I am left uncomprehending. I look up Hessell (there is a handy "Guide to Names and Terms" in the back of the book) and find out that he is Franz Hessell (1880-1941), a German writer and translator. And interestingly, with Benjamin he produced a German translation of Marcel Proust's *À la recherche du temps perdu* (in English translation, *In Search of Lost Time* or *Remembrance of Things Past*). That's interesting, because Proust may well have been Brooks' favorite writer. In an article titled "Books that Gave Me Pleasure" published in the *New York Times* on December 5, 1982 Brooks is quoted as saying "I have been reading Proust all my life, and I'm still reading him."

What I also learned about Hessell is that he was one of the first German exponents of the French idea of flânerie, and later published a collection of essays on the subject related to his native Berlin, *Spazieren in Berlin*. He was also the inspiration for the character of Jules in Henri-Pierre Roche's celebrated novel *Jules et Jim*, the same book which became the François Truffaut film. (The possible real life inspiration for the young woman between Jules and Jim was the artist Beatrice Wood, whom I met late in her life. She must have been nearly 100 years old at the time. Ever flirtatious, she kissed me on the cheek. But that's another story.) However, others think the young woman at the heart of the triangle may have been Hessel's wife, Helen.

The one other reference to Wedekind in *The Arcades Project* comes in the editor's notes. Entry three in section C [Ancient Paris, Catacombs, Demolitions, Decline of Paris] reads thus (please buckle up, it's chunky):

"Certain of these muses of Surrealism can be identified more precisely: Luna, the moon; Kate Greenway (1846-1901), English painter known for her illustrations of children's books; Mors, death; Cleo de Merode (1875-1966), French dancer who epitomized the demimonde; Dulcinea, the beloved of Don Quixote and the image of idealized woman; Libido, an allusion to Freud; Baby Cadum, publicity and advertising; Frederike Kempner (1836-1904), German poet and socialite. A comparison with the two other 'catalogues of muses' reveals that Dulcinea is a variant of Ibsen's Hedda Gabler and that Benjamin thought of adding the painter Angelika Kauffmann (1741-1807), a friend of Goethe's. Another list, presumably the earliest, is found in 'The Arcades of Paris'."

And here is where it gets interesting. The note continues, "Countess Geschwitz, a lesbian artist, is a character in Frank Wedekind's *Erdgeist* and *Die Büchse der Pandora* plays which inspired Berg's unfinished opera *Lulu*. The identity of Tipse remains a mystery. When Benjamin writes that the mother of Surrealism was *eine Passage*, he plays on the feminine gender of the noun in German." That's right, he does.

Geschwitz, played by Alice Roberts, is pictured here dancing with Lulu, played by Louise Brooks, as her new husband Dr. Schon, played by Fritz Kortner, looks on. Could Walter Benjamin have envisioned himself as Schon? Perhaps.

And perhaps it is helpful to mention, in reference to Goethe, that as early as 1935 (according to Barry Paris' sublime biography of Louise Brooks), director G.W. Pabst was intent on making a film of the poet's *Faust*, "whose dream cast was clearly fixed in his mind. Pabst's *Faust* would star Greta Garbo as Gretchen and Louise Brooks as Helen of Troy." I can't imagine it. . . .

Also worth noting was Brooks' own fictionalized account of her life called *Naked on My Goat*. Its title derived from *Faust*. [The rare 1952 clipping pictured here references the book, though you will have to use an magnifying glass to read the fine print. Brooks destroyed the manuscript by throwing it down an incinerator. Into the flames of hell it went, in a sense, and there it remains one of the *great* lost books—great in the sense of all that it would have revealed. I was once told that a few pages of it, along with this clipping, were once found in the back of a Kansas closet. Who knows?]

I can't imagine *Naked on My Goat* would have been a very satisfying read. Brooks' style as a writer had not yet formed, and her earliest efforts, as when she wrote the September 17, 1925 *New York Times* review of *No, No Nanette* assigned to journalist Herman Mankiewicz, were saturated with purple prose. Mankiewicz, you see, was drunk, and Brooks, the brainy showgirl, was game. It would takes years of practice later in life to achieve her style. She did it by literally rewriting her favorite authors— Brooks copied passages over and over again from favorite books in her distinct longhand, until she could do so no longer.

Why did she do it? What was she searching for? What did she hope to find? What was Brooks' Rosebud?

According to acclaimed composer David Diamond (again via BP), a Rochester, New York friend of the actress, one of Brooks' cherished books was *The Journal of Eugenie de Guerin*. Its author was a brilliant, pessimistic, obscure French diarist (1805-1848). One of Brooks' favorite passages was this " . . . This globe is an abyss of misery and all we gain by stirring its depth is the discovery of funereal inscriptions and burying places. Death is at the bottom of everything and we keep continually digging as though we were seeking for immortality."

This passage and its archeological allusions evokes, for me, *The Arcades Project*— which reads as an unearthing, an unburying of some lost or repressed ideas, or even feelings, a welling up to the unconsciousness and intellect. Was *The Arcades Project* the primordial example of archeologicalism? It makes me wonder, what was Walter Benjamin's Rosebud?

Well, enough of this. I spent far too long on this rambling blog. I had meant to do some more background research on Margarete Böhme but got lost in the arcades. This afternoon, I had meant to watch a DVD documentary on Theda Bara—there may still be time—and look at Bram Dijkstra's two brilliant books, *Idols of Perversity* and *Evil Sisters*. I had better get on with it.

If anyone is interested, Walter Benjamin's *The Arcades Project* is available for purchase on-line or through better independent bookstores. And for kicks, here are a couple of illuminating excerts from the book's many reviews, as well as a scan of Louise Brooks' personal bookplate. It looks somewhat Jugendstil to me.

"A painstaking act of literary reconstruction has fleshed out Walter Benjamin's lost masterpiece. . . . We may consider here Benjamin's wonderful remark that 'knowledge comes only in lightning flashes. The text is the long roll of thunder that follows.' *The Arcades*

Project is the reverberation of that thunder in a thousand different directions. . . . This posthumous volume suggests that, in its incomplete and fissiparous state, his reflections are themselves an unflawed mirror for the world which he was attempting to explore. He seems to have retrieved everything, and anticipated everything." - Peter Ackroyd, *The Times of London*

"The Arcades Project is truly a kaleidoscopic montage of a dream of the meanings of society, a dream deferred by the advance of Nazis into Paris. In 1940, when Benjamin fled, he left behind the sprawling, incomplete masterpiece he had begun in 1927. But by then, it had already become, he wrote, 'the theater of all my struggles and all my ideas'." - Forrest Gander, *Providence Journal-Bulletin*

The San Francisco origins of Lulu
This piece appeared on the Louise Brooks Society blog on February 24, 2010.

On Monday, I wrote a piece for examiner.com about researching local history online. My local library, the San Francisco Public Library, recently announced on one of its blogs that a number of city directories and other old books and records had been uploaded to the Internet Archive.

To see a list of these newly available documents and other content scanned from the SFPL, follow the link archive.org/details/sanfranciscopubliclibrary. These newly available documents join a number of other works of interest at the Internet Archive. As one can guess, these directories are a great source of historical and genealogical information. Looking around as I love to do, I came across some interesting and obscure information regarding the origins of "Lulu."

Did you know that the German playwright Frank Wedekind has San Francisco roots? Wedekind, of course, is the author of both *Spring Awakening* (the basis for the popular Broadway rock musical) and *Pandora's Box* (the basis for both the 1929 Louise Brooks silent film, as well as Alban Berg's 1937 opera).

During the early years of his life, Wedekind's father served as physician. A progressive democrat, he also participated in the 1848 Revolution, and next year escaped to America, where he made a small fortune in land speculation. In San Francisco, he married Emilie Kammerer, a singer and actress twenty-three years his junior. (Some scholars have speculated that this relationship might have served as a kind of model for the relationship between Dr. Schon and Lulu in *Pandora's Box*.)

A search of the newly available city directories for 1858, 1860, and 1862 reveals that the future playwright's Father, Friedrich Wilhelm Wedekind, had a medical practice at 136 and later 524 Montgomery Street in San Francisco. Doctor Wedekind was also a prominent member of the local German General Benevolent Society as well as President of the local German Club.

Friedrich Wilhelm Wedekind and Emilie Kammerer's second child—the future writer, was likely conceived in San Francisco—though born in Hanover, Germany. Early in the pregnancy, the patriotic couple decided to return to their native land. And that's where Benjamin Franklin Wedekind (named for the free-thinking American revolutionary—and later known simply as Frank) was born in 1864.

Lulu's debut... on this day in 1905
This piece appeared on the Louise Brooks Society blog on May 29, 2014.

On this day in history, Lulu made her debut in Vienna.

The premiere of Frank Wedekind's *Die Büchse der Pandora (Pandora's Box)*, a restricted performance due to difficulties with the censor, had already taken place in Nuremberg in 1904. A second staging, in Vienna, was arranged at the instigation of the critic and satirist Karl Kraus. This second stage production took place at the Trianon Theater in Vienna, Austria on May 29, 1905.

The production was notable, as was the cast. It featured dramatist Frank Wedekind as Jack the Ripper, Tilly Newes (Franks Wedekin's wife, Tilly Wedekind) as Lulu, Arnold Korff as Dr. Hilti (Korff also played the Elder Count Osdorff in the 1929 film, Diary of a Lost Girl), and Irma Karczewska as "Bob." The play's producer, Karl Kraus, played Kungu Poti.

Who was Irma Karczewska? By all accounts, she was a striking personality and noted beauty who was involved in an erotic triangle with Kraus and Sigmund Freud's first biographer, the pioneering psychologist Fritz Wittels. Read all about it in *Freud and the Child Woman: The Memoirs of Fritz Wittels*, edited by Edward Timms, published by Yale University Press in 1995.

According to the publisher, Yale University Press, "In his memoirs, Wittels writes frankly and vividly about the erotic subculture of fin-de-siècle Vienna, early controversies within the Psychoanalytic Society, and the interactions between the two. Freud himself plays a crucial role in the story, and the erotic triangle in which Kraus, Wittels, and Irma Karczewska were involved is shown to have impinged directly on the activities of the famous Society."

One wonders who else might have been in the audience on that historic day. Perhaps Sigmund Freud? If not, I wonder if he was aware of or had read Wedekind's *Lulu* plays?

Also, on this day in 1967, G.W. Pabst, who directed Louise Brooks in *Pandora's Box* and *Diary of a Lost Girl*, died in Austria. Strange how points in history intersect.

Danger and Desire: 6 Great Lulus
This piece appeared on Huffington Post on November 5, 2015.

Although she died countless times on stage and on film, Lulu still lives.

Frank Wedekind's immortal character—the great *femme fatale* of the 20th century—first appeared in his once controversial, now celebrated "Lulu" plays, *Erdgeist* (*Earth Spirit*, 1895) and *Die Büchse der Pandora* (*Pandora's Box*, 1904).

In the years that followed, Lulu was reborn in other art. Wedekind's plays were the basis for two great silent films in the 1920s, as well as Alban Berg's masterful opera of the 1930s. The plays and their stage performances, the films, and the opera all influenced one another. It is known, for example, that Berg saw G.W. Pabst's 1929 film *Pandora's Box* while composing his great modernist opera, as did his great champion and correspondent Theodor Adorno, who wrote that he was profoundly affected by Lulu.

There have been other later film adaptions, poems, paintings and drawings, comic books, and even erotica inspired by the character of Lulu, as well as a few rock and pop recordings like Rufus Wainwright's *All Days Are Nights: Songs for Lulu* (2010) and the Lou Reed / Metallica collaboration *Lulu* (2011).

Her origins remain obscure. Did Wedekind base the character on Lou Andreas-Salomé and his own frustrated relationship with the vivacious intellectual (who preferred the company of Nietzsche, Freud, and Rilke)? Or did Wedekind base Lulu on his mother, a one-time showgirl in Gold Rush San Francisco? She married Wedekind's father, an older and respectable professional, not unlike Dr. Schön in the plays.

Or, was Wedekind—a rogue in his youth—smitten with Lulu, a popular circus performer in Paris in the 1890s? We do know that Wedekind was inspired by the circus as well as Félicien Champsaur's 1888 circus pantomime, *Lulu*. In the prologue to *Earth Spirit*, the characters are introduced by an Animal Tamer as if they are creatures in a traveling circus. Lulu herself is described as "the true animal, the wild, beautiful animal" and the "primal form of woman."

Over the years, actresses from Eva Gabor to Judy Davis have played Lulu on stage and in film, while many others have sung the role in opera. Here is a shortlist of six great, memorable Lulus. Each has shaped the way we see the character today.

Marlis Petersen: It would be something of an understatement to say there is great anticipation around the new production of Alban Berg's *Lulu* that opens at the Metropolitan Opera in New York. The excitement building over this new Lulu stems not just from the fact that artist William Kentridge is behind the staging of this modernist masterpiece, but that Marlis Peterson will be singing the role of Lulu. The riveting German soprano (a blonde who sports a dark bob *à la* Louise Brooks) is appearing in her 10th and just announced final production of the opera. As an interpreter of *Lulu*, few have made the role so much their own. No wonder Peter Gelb, the Met's general manager, calls her "the leading Lulu of the day." *Lulu* opens at the Metropolitan Opera on November 5 and continues through December 3. On November 21, *Lulu* will be live streamed to theaters across the United States.

Marlis Petersen   PHOTO: Kristian Schuller/Metropolitan Opera

Louise Brooks: The best known Lulu may well be Louise Brooks, the bobbed-hair, Kansas-born silent film star called to Germany to play Lulu in the G.W. Pabst directed film, *Pandora's Box*. Movie-goers at the time were dismayed. They asked, how could an American play what was an especially German character? Though she claimed not to know what it was all about, or even to have read Wedekind's text until years later, Brooks so convincingly inhabits the character of Lulu that any actress or singer playing the role is hard pressed to ignore her. In a recent piece, critic Graham Fuller suggests that Brooks the actress and not Pabst the director is the film's real *auteur*. It's not a new notion, but still a provocative one.

Fritz Kortner and Louise Brooks in a scene from *Pandora's Box*.

Asta Nielsen: The first film Lulu was Asta Nielsen, the great Danish actress, who played Lulu in *Earth Spirit* (1923). One of the early international movie stars, she was noted for her large dark eyes, mask-like face, and androgynous figure. (Famously, she played Hamlet in 1921.) About her, the French poet Apollinaire once exclaimed, "She is everything! She is the drunkard's vision and the lonely man's dream." Be that as it may, Nielsen often and movingly portrayed strong-willed, passionate women trapped by tragic consequences. Due to the erotic nature of her performances, Nielsen's films were censored in the United States, and her work to this day remains obscure to American audiences.

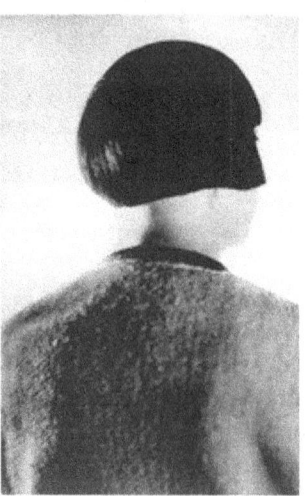

Asta Nielsen in 1913, as Lulu in 1923, and turned from the camera in 1930.

Kyla Webb: Back in 2005 and 2006, the then newly formed Silent Theatre Company of Chicago staged a brilliant and singular adaption of the Lulu plays. Taking their cue from the silent cinema, this Lulu was performed without words. The intent was to say what words often cannot express—here, gesture and body language did all the talking. At the heart of *Lulu: a black and white silent play* was an immensely talented young actress, Kyla Webb (pictured right), in the title role. Webb was Lulu incarnate—throwing her affections and body about with abandon on a razor's edge of danger and desire.

Tilly Newes: The second actress to play the role on stage was Tilly Newes. *Pandora's Box* was first staged in Nuremberg in 1904, but was banned by the German censor. Austrian writer Karl Kraus produced a private performance in Vienna the following year, and cast Newes, an

Austrian actress, as Lulu. Newes and Wedekind, who played Jack the Ripper, had an affair, and after the playwright insulted her, the actress threw herself into a river. Wedekind rescued her, and soon proposed. Despite a difference of 22 years, they remained together until Wedekind's death in 1918. In 1969, she published an autobiography, *Lulu—the role of my life*.

(L) Tilly Newes and Frank Wedekind in *Pandora's Box*.
(R) Tilly Wedekind as Lulu in *Earth Spirit*.

Melanie Griffith: Though she didn't play Wedekind or Berg's Lulu, Melanie Griffith was Lulu to a generation of moviegoers. In Jonathan Demme's 1986 thriller, *Something Wild*, Griffith is given the character's name and unpredictable persona, as well as Brooks' trademark hairstyle. Though a stylistic gloss on some of Wedekind's more profound themes, *Something Wild* remains a clever, layered, Hitchcockian take on the nature of desire and uncertainty.

Melanie Griffith   PHOTO: Metro-Goldwyn-Mayer

Marlene Dietrich and Louise Brooks

This piece appeared on the Louise Brooks Society blog on May 3, 2004. The day before, I posted a couple of paragraphs on Steven Bach's Marlene Dietrich: Life and Legend, which I had just finished reading. I enjoyed that book a good deal, and, it got me thinking about the similarities between the two legendary actresses, including the fact that later in life both scrubbed floors in atonement for past sins, and both actively sought to shape their legacies.

A few years back, I came across an obscure drawing by the Polish writer Bruno Schulz (1892-1942) which I believe depicts Louise Brooks and Marlene Dietrich. If it is not them, then it bears a rather striking resemblance to the two great cinematic femme fatales, Lulu and Lola.

Schulz is best known for his short stories, and he is considered one of the great Polish writers of the 20th century. His brief literary career ended during the second World War when Schulz was gunned down by a German officer. John Updike, an admirer, has described the author as "one of the great transmogrifiers of the world into words." [Schulz's most famous work, *The Street of Crocodiles* (1934), was itself transmogrified into a stunning 1986 film by the Brother's Quay. It is extraordinary—one of the most memorable and poetic films I have ever seen.]

Schulz was also gifted artist. The drawing I came across, which dates from 1930 but is now lost and only exists in reproduction, does seem to depict Brooks and Dietrich. In the title of the drawing, the two women are termed "temptresses." The standing Brooks figure is garbed in showgirl attire, a la *Pandora's Box*, while the Dietrich figure is seated with legs crossed, a la *The Blue Angel*. Perhaps I am wrong, but this image seems another link between the mythic characters Lulu and Lola.

Louise Brooks art #2

This piece appeared on the Louise Brooks Society blog on April 13, 2010.

This is the second installment of an irregular series of posts highlighting "Louise Brooks art"—paintings, drawings, photographs, collages, cartoons, sculpture, etc . . . . all featuring the silent film star Louise Brooks or at least in some way inspired by the actress.

"Profil en face" by Herbert Bayer.

I used to work as a syndicated art critic, and in my day I have looked through a lot of art books—both old and new. My favorite period is the early 20th century. Thus, I thought this entry in the series would focus on a couple of kindred historic examples.

The first is a 1929 photomontage by Herbert Bayer (pictured above) titled "Profil en face." Brooks' likeness is a dominant element in the work. This obscure piece has been reproduced in at least a couple of books including *the way beyond 'art' – the work of herbert bayer* (Wittenborn, Schultz), from 1949.

Bayer (1900–1985) was an Austrian-born graphic designer, painter, photographer, sculptor, interior designer and architect associated with the Bauhaus. His best known work may be "Lonely Metropolitan" (which depicts a pair of hands, eyes inset their palms, floating before the facade of a building).

The second example of Brooks in a early 20th century piece of art is by Edward Burra. The piece is titled "Composition Collage," and dates from 1929 / 1930. This equally little known piece also includes the face of the actress (far right), as well as that of Lon Chaney. I am sure the female face to the far left belongs to someone I have seen before, but just can't recall at this time.

"Profil en face" by Herbert Bayer.

Edward Burra (1905–1976), whose work is pictured above, was an English painter, draughtsman and print maker, best known for his depictions of the urban underworld. To my eyes, his work, or at least this piece, has a decidedly expressionist feel.

Do you know of other early 20th century art which includes a likeness of Louise Brooks? Perhaps some collage or montage by a Czech surrealist? If so, I would love to hear from you. Maybe, if there were enough of it, we could create a secret museum devoted to the actress.

Louise Brooks, Modernism, the Surrealists, and the Paris of 1930
This piece appeared on the Louise Brooks Society on August 25, 2016.

Louise Brooks has long been popular in France, and in Paris in 1930, she must have seemed to be *everywhere*.

At the time, much of Brooks' celebrity stemmed from the fact that she was starred in an important French production, *Prix de beauté*, around which there was considerable interest. It was big news that a popular American actress was featured in an important

French production, which was also one of the earliest French talkies. Consequently, articles about the actress and the film appeared in many of the newspapers published in City of Lights. Over the years, I have collected dozens of such clippings, along with a number of magazines which picture the actress on the cover.

Brooks' image was nearly ubiquitous. There is a even picture from the time, shown above, of the actress' portrait on display in the window of a photographer's studio.

Brooks' popularity in France peaked around the time she was in Paris making *Prix de beauté*, which was in production between August 29 and September 27, 1929. The press recorded her arrival in the city (see clipping), and a steady stream of news about the making of the film followed.

Prix de beauté debuted at the famous Max-Linder Pathe on May 9, 1930. Sheet music and a half-dozen different 78rpm recordings of the film's popular theme song were issued.

Prix de beauté was a success, enjoying a three month continuous run in various Parisian theaters. After two months at the Max-Linder (during which it also played for a few weeks at the historic Lutetia-Pathe to accommodate demand), the film

G.W. Pabst, en arrivant dernièrement à Paris, fut reçu par Louise Brooks, qu'il eut pour interprète dans *La Boîte de Pandore*. Notre photographie, prise à la gare du Nord, montre la jolie vedette et son metteur en scène.

moved to the Folies Dramatiques, where it was advertised as an "immense success" and played nearly a month more. This extended run took place at a time when most films played only a few days or a week. In fact, advertisements from the time show that *Prix de beauté* would be revived again and again over the next few years.

(Remarkably, *Prix de beauté* was not only popular, but also inspirational. A novelization of *Prix de beauté* was published in 1932, two years after its debut in Paris. And in 1933, a short story by the noted French writer Leon Bopp was published which describes a character in love with Louise Brooks.)

While *Prix de beauté* was enjoying its successful run in Paris, another of Brooks' films—the German production *Diary of a Lost Girl* (in French *Trois Pages D'un Journal*), was also playing in the French capital at the Au Colisee. Like today, films were advertised in the newspaper, and on one occasion, the two film's respective advertisements sat side-by-side. A popular film, *Trois Pages D'un Journal* was later shown at the Rialto and Splendide theatres in Paris. As was *Beggars of Life (Les mendiants de la vie)* at the Clichy-Palace in March of the same year.

Like *Prix de beauté*, *Diary of a Lost Girl* continued to be shown on and off in Paris in 1930. The French, it seemed, could not get enough of its pathetic story. A novelization of the film was also published which depicted Brooks on the cover. In November, the film was shown at the famous Ursulines theater as part of a trippple bill which included G.W. Pabst's *Joyless Street*, Howard Hawk's *A Girl in Every Port*, and Pabst's *Diary of a Lost Girl*.

A Girl in Every Port (which the famed French writer Blaise Cendrars deemed "the first appearance of contemporary cinema") debuted at the Ursulines, which according to Wikipedia was "one of the oldest cinemas in Paris to have kept its facade and founder's vision" as a "venue for art and experimental cinema." The film, which was one of the few American films to retain its American title in France (a fact noted at the time by the *New York Times*), proved popular and was revived time and again in Paris in the 1920s and 1930s and later. [On of their first dates, Jean-Paul Sartre took Simone de Beauvoir to one of its showings.]

The Ursulines, a small theater which showed a number of Brooks films, opened in 1926 with a program of films by André Breton, Man Ray, Fernand Léger, René Clair and Robert Desnos. In 1928, it premiered the first film by Germaine Dulac, *The Seashell and the Clergyman*, based on a story by Antonin Artaud.

Remarkably, a number of now-classic films also premiered at the theater, such as René Clair's *Le Voyage Imaginaire* and Erich Von Stroheim's *Greed*. At the beginning of the sound era, the premiere of Josef von Sternberg's *Blue Angel*, starring Marlene Dietrich, took place there. In December 1930, *Diary of a Lost Girl* and *Blue Angel* even shared the bill.

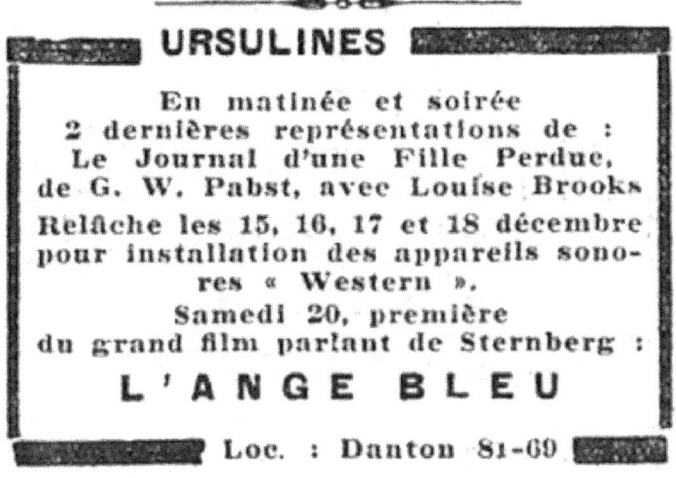

The remarkably history of the Ursulines theatre, a kind of cinematic home to Surrealist cinema, got me thinking about the affection at least some of the surrealists had for Brooks. Philipe Soupault, the great French Surrealist poet, mentioned the actress in his journalism and even reviewed *Diary of a Lost Girl*. (A couple of images of the actress adorn the poet's later collected writings on the cinema, *Ecrits de cinema 1918-1931*.)

It's also known that Man Ray, the great surrealist photographer, was smitten with the actress. Years later, in 1958, the photographer and the film star met in Paris, with Man Ray recounting how he had seen Brooks image everywhere in Paris so many years before. Man Ray was fond enough of Brooks that he sent her a small painting in memory of their meeting and in memory of his memory.

Perhaps Man Ray had also seen one or two of Brooks' films. Earlier, in 1928, *A Girl in Every Port* shared the bill with a short Man Ray film, *L'Etoile de Mer*, at the Ursulines during the months of October, November, and December. *L'Etoile de Mer* (*The Starfish*) was scripted by the surrealist poet Robert Desnos; the film itself "stars" Desnos and Alice Prin. Better known as Kiki de Montparnasse, Prin (who was Man Ray's one-time paramour) famously sported Brooks-like bobbed hair and bangs.

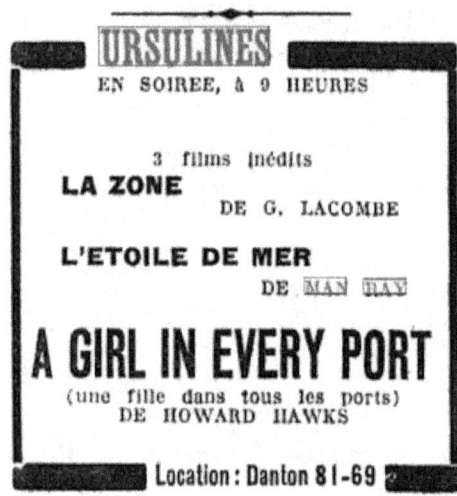

Of course, one might also add Lee Miller to this story. She had an interest in the actress. Miller, a sometime Surrealist photographer and a one-time paramour of Man Ray, is known to have seen Brooks dance in Poughkeepsie, New York long before Brooks became a film star and Miller a Surrealist....

Lee Miller and Louise Brooks
This piece appeared on the Louise Brooks Society blog on January 17, 2006.

Lately, I've been paging through *Lee Miller: A Life*, a new biography by Carolyn Burke. I was drawn to the book because of my interest in Surrealism, especially the work of Man Ray. For those who may not know, Lee Miller and Man Ray—both photographers—had a brief, but significant and tempestuous affair around 1930. They also influenced each other's work.

In the introduction, Burke writes: "Mesmerized by her features, we look at Lee Miller but not into her. We think of her as a timeless icon. To this day, her life inspires features in the same glossy magazines for which she posed—articles explaining how to re-create her 'look.' This approach turns the real woman into a screen on which beholders project their fantasies. Looking at her this way perpetuates the legend of Lee Miller as 'an American free spirit wrapped in the body of a Greek Goddess' .... In Lee Miller's time, her admirers were equally spellbound by her beauty, but they also saw her as an incarnation of the modern woman—in the United States of the twenties, as a quintessential flapper; in the Paris of the thirties, as a subversive *garçonne* or a maddeningly free *femme surréaliste*—one who sparked creativity in others but played the role of muse only when it suited her, and sought, despite her lovers' objections, to keep her energy for herself."

I was struck by how applicable this text is to Louise Brooks—and the way we think about her today. While reading the introduction, I was surprised, as well, to soon come across Louise Brooks herself. Burke writes: "Breaking free of conventional roles for women, whether in traditional or avant-garde circles, Lee Miller stired up trouble for herself and for those who loved her. Like screenwriter Anita Loos and actress Louise Brooks (whose careers she followed), she helped reshape women's aspirations through her embrace of popular culture. . . ." Checking the index, I found this is one of nine references to the actress in the book! Who would have thought? Though near contemporaries, I don't think the two ever met—nor does the biographer suggest it—though Miller, apparently, attended a Denishawn performance which included Brooks in Poughkeepsie, New York in January, 1923.

There are other fascinating similarities between the two women, who were born only a year apart. I won't go into them, except to add that I am really looking forward to finish reading this book soon. (Does the biographer know, I wonder, that Man Ray was also taken with Brooks? According to Brooks' biographer Barry Paris, "[Man Ray] lived in Paris and was struck by Brooks's face when he saw it in the magazines during the *Prix de beauté* filming. He never forgot her and in the late fifties sent her one of his abstract paintings, which hung thereafter on the wall of her bedroom.")

Louise Brooks and *The Invention of Morel*, by Adolpho Bioy Casares

This piece appeared on the Louise Brooks Society blog on February 29, 2016. Brooks' appearance on the cover of a 2003 edition of The Invention of Morel *was inspired by the LBS. Before publication, the publisher contacted me regarding the actress and an appropriate image.... After publication, a stream of articles noting the connection between the novel and the film star began to appear. In 2017, an opera based on the book debuted. Its female lead sported bobbed hair.*

Back in 1997 or so, I ran across a tantalizing review of Adolfo Bioy Casares' memoirs, *Memorias: Infancia, adolescencia y como se hace un escrito*. In a short write-up, a scholar mentioned the Argentine author's affection for Louise Brooks. This excited me, as I had been aware of Bioy Casares and his work through his friendship with Jorge Luis Borges, a favorite author. Always on the look-out for references to Brooks, my favorite film star, I set to find out more; I couldn't imagine how these two interests could be linked.

What I found, remarkably, is that Louise Brooks stands at the heart of one of the most important works of 20th century literature. *The Invention of Morel* is not only an oblique homage to the actress, a small town girl, but also a means to preserve, in writing, the memory of a writer's desire for an elusive star.

Today, Adolpho Bioy Casares (1914–1999) is considered one of the great authors of the 20th century. In fact, he is thought by some to be a near equal of his great friend and sometime collaborator Jorge Luis Borges. Bioy Casares authored short stories as well as novels, including *A Plan for Escape* (1945), *The Dream of Heroes* (1954), *Diary of the War of the Pig* (1969), and *Asleep in the Sun* (1978), each of which have been translated and published in English. Bioy Casares also collaborated with Borges on the seminal *Anthology of Fantastic Literature*, as well as a series of satirical sketches and detective stories written under the pseudonym H. Bustos Domecq. Late in his career, Bioy won several important awards including the Gran Premio de Honor of SADE (awarded in 1975 by the Argentine Society of Writers), the French Legion of Honor (awarded in 1981), and the Miguel de Cervantes Prize (awarded in 1991).

Bioy Casares is best known for his 1940 novella, *La invención de Morel* (*The Invention of Morel*). It has been described variously, as both a stoic love story and a metaphysical mystery. It tells of a man who, evading justice, escapes to a mysterious island. A group of travelers arrive, and the fugitive's fear of being discovered means he must keep his distance from one of the travelers, a woman named Faustine, with whom he falls in love. The fugitive desires to tell her his feelings, but an anomalous phenomenon makes their meeting impossible. Struggling to understand why everything seems to repeat, the fugitive realizes that the people he sees on the island are nothing more than recordings made with a special machine invented by a scientific genius named Morel; this machine is able to project not only three-dimensional images, but also voices and scents, making everything indistinguishable from reality. In fact, the fugitive is the only real person on the island.

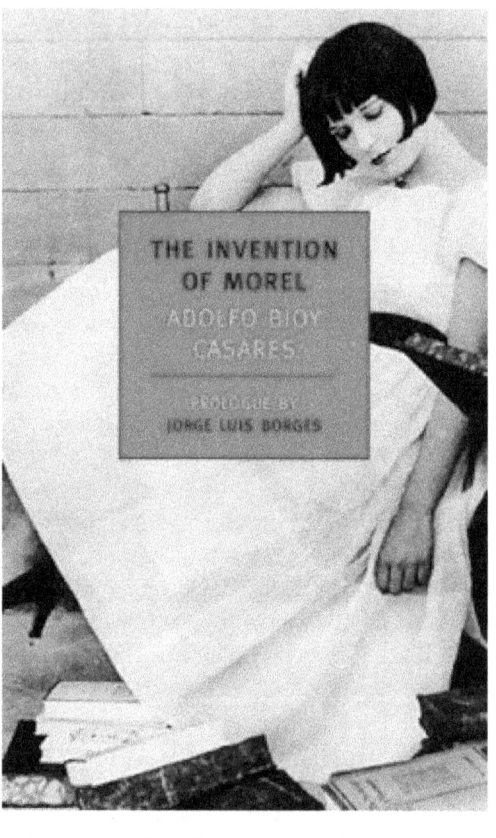

One recent review noted, "Though it was published in 1940, the book's continuing relevance was recently proven when it was featured on *Lost* — a cameo many viewers perceive as a key to that TV show's plot. Just know that *Morel* is a poetic evocation of the experience of love, an inquiry into how we know one another, and a still-relevant examination of how technology has changed our relationship with reality."

The Invention of Morel mixes realism and metaphysical fantasy with elements of science fiction and the Gothic to create what is widely considered the first work of "magical realism." It prefigured the boom in Latin American literature, and proved to be Bioy Casares' breakthrough effort when it won the First Municipal Prize for Literature of the City of Buenos Aires in 1941. Despite it being his seventh book, Bioy Casares considered *The Invention of Morel* to mark the beginning of his career as a writer.

Borges wrote a prologue to the *The Invention of Morel* in which he placed the book alongside Henry James' *The Turn of the Screw* and Franz Kafka's *The Trial* as examples of works with "admirable plots." Borges also termed it a work of "reasoned imagination," linking it to the philosophical romances of H. G. Wells, notably through its title, which alludes to *The Island of Doctor Moreau*.

In his prologue, Borges also stated "I have discussed with the author the details of his plot; I have reread it; it seems to me neither imprecise nor hyperbolic to classify it as perfect." The Mexican Nobel Prize winning poet Octavio Paz echoed Borges' assessment, "*The Invention of Morel* may be described, without exaggeration, as a perfect novel." Other well known Latin American writers also expressed their admiration for the book, among them the Colombian Nobel Prize winner Gabriel García Márquez, the Argentine writer Julio Cortázar, the Cuban writer Alejo Carpentier, and Uruguayan novelist Juan Carlos Onetti.

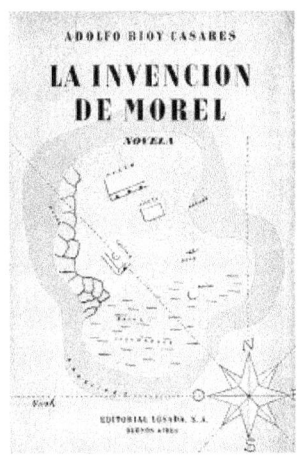  

The first edition of *La invención de Morel* featured cover art and interior illustrations by Norah Borges de Torre, sister of Jorge. Call me crazy, but I think it somewhat significant that Faustine is depicted with short bobbed hair not unlike the trademark style worn by Louise Brooks.

In his memoirs, Bioy Casares wrote of his disillusionment over the decline of the screen career of one of his favorite actresses, Louise Brooks. After *Memorias* was published, the book and the passage on Brooks was called to the attention the Argentinian magazine *Film*. In their July, 1995 issue, Fernando Martin Peña and Sergio Wolf published an interview with Bioy Casares in which he expanded upon some of the points he made in his memoirs. What follows is an excerpt (in translation) from the 1995 interview.

QUESTION: You said that the inspiration for *La invención de Morel* came to you, at least partially, from the vanishing of Louise Brooks from the movies. What happened with you and Louise Brooks?

ADOLFO BIOY CASARES: I was deeply in love with her. I didn't have any luck, because she disappeared quickly. She went to Europe, she made a film with Pabst, and then I didn't like her so much as when she was in Hollywood. And then, she vanished too early from the movies.

QUESTION: Could she be seen as one of the characters in *La invención de Morel*?

ADOLFO BIOY CASARES: Yes, she would be Faustine.

QUESTION: It's funny, because everybody falls in love with Louise Brooks through her German films.

ADOLFO BIOY CASARES: Well, I didn't.

Bioy Casares loved film, and once wrote, "I want to wait for the end of the world on the seat of a movie theater." Bioy Casares also loved the stars of his youth, and named names. In the above mentioned interview, Bioy Casares goes on to say that when he was young he went to the movies all the time, and also had a liking for Marion Davies and Anna May Wong. He also liked Garbo, though only in the light-hearted *Ninotchka*. Bioy Casares didn't care for horror films, though he mentions in the interview that Borges was a big fan of *The Bride of Frankenstein*. I wonder if Bioy Casares would have liked that film more had director James Whale cast Brooks, his first choice, in the role of the bride, instead of Elsa Lanchester.

What follows is the passage from Bioy Casares' memoirs in which he discusses Brooks and his love of early film. With the help of the web and an Argentine friend, I have attempted a translation of the above passage and have come up with something inelegant, but still interesting.

Over time, I fell in love with movies, I became a regular viewer and now I think I want to wait for the end of the world on the seat of a movie theater..

I fell in love, simultaneously or successively, with the film actresses Louise Brooks, Marie Prevost, Dorothy Mackaill, Marion Davies, Evelyn Brent and Anna May Wong.

Of these impossible loves, I was most passionate about Louise Brooks, and it made me miserable. I hated that I could never know her! Worse, one never saw her again. This is exactly what happened. After three or four movies, I was spellbound, and Louise Brooks disappeared from the screens of Buenos Aires. I felt that disappearance, first, as a tearful break; then as a personal loss. Had she been better liked by the public, I feel Louise Brooks would not have disappeared. The truth (or what I felt) is that she was little known to the public, and also to people I knew. Granted she was cute – rather 'pretty' – though others complained she was a bad actress; if they found her a clever actress, they regretted that she was not more beautiful. Just like before the defeat of Firpo [the Argentine boxer who lost to Jack Dempsey], I proved that reality and me disagreed.

Many years later in Paris, I saw a movie (I think by [Alain] Jessua) in which the hero, like me (when I was wrote *Heart of a Clown*, one of my first literary attempts), took everything as a joke and consequently was hated by the woman he loved. That character, like me, admired Louise Brooks. Lately, here in Argentina and elsewhere, there is a renewed assessment and growing admiration for the actress, which is deserved. I read admiring and intelligent articles about her in the *New Yorker* and the *Cahiers du Cinéma*. I also read *Lulu in Hollywood*, a diverting memoir, written by Louise Brooks.

In 73 or 75, my friend Edgardo Cozarinsky asked me one afternoon in a cafe in the Place de l'Alma in Paris if I know a girl who would play Louise Brooks in a film which was in preparation. I was the expert who was to say if the girl was acceptable or not for the role. I said yes, not only to help the possible actress. Clearly, if I had been asked the question during my anguished passion, perhaps the answer would have been different. To me, no one seemed to be Louise Brooks.

In the passage above, Bioy Casares seems to suggest that he tried to write a short story called, "Heart of a Clown," featuring a character like himself similarly in love with Brooks. However, I am told it is not so. Reportedly, Bioy Casares tried to write such a story to impress someone when he was young, but only got as far as an idea and a title. . . . I don't know what became of the proposed film featuring a Brooks-like character mentioned in the last paragraph. Bioy Casares' friend, Edgardo Cozarinsky, is no doubt a kindred soul. In 1994 he completed the documentary, *Citizen Langlois*, about the famous film archivist and key figure in Brooks' life.

Boiy Casares' book was made into a French movie called *L'invention de Morel* (1967), and an Italian movie called *L'invenzione di Morel* (1974). Faustine was played by Anna Karina in the latter. Sometime in the late 1980s or early 1990's, the Quay Brothers also hoped to turn Boiy Casares' book into a film, but were unsuccessful in their pursuit of the rights.

It is thought, by some, that Boiy Casares' book inspired Alain Resnais' sur-real film *Last Year At Marienbad* (1961), which was adopted for the screen by the French novelist Alain Robbe-Grillet. The case for lineage is loosely made by Thomas Beltzer in his essay, "Last Year at Marienbad: An Intertextual Meditation." Beltzer's argument largely hinges on information found on a later-day dust jacket for Boiy Casares' *A Plan for Escape*. Beltzer's case is called into question (though not entirely refuted) by Dan DeWeese in his essay, "The Invention of Marienbad." Both pieces are worth reading.

What is known is that Boiy Casares' *The Invention of Morel* echoes through the television series *Lost* (2004–2010). The popular and critically acclaimed show follows the survivors of a passenger jet crash on a mysterious tropical island somewhere in the South Pacific. Like *The Invention of Morel*, the show contains science fiction and supernatural elements while messing with perceived reality. During season four, one of the show's main characters is seen reading the 2003 NYRB edition of *The Invention of Morel* (shown here).

Thanks to Argentians Diego Curubeto and Erica Füsstinn for supplying and translating some of the information found on this page. Here is some further reading:

"Memorias: Infancia, adolescencia y como se hace un escritor," by Melvin S. Arrington Jr. *World Literature Today*, Winter, 1995.
— the review of Bioy Casares memoirs that brought to light the author's fondness for Brooks

"*Last Year at Marienbad*: An Intertextual Meditation," by Thomas Beltzer. *Senses of Cinema*, November 2000.
— essay that builds the case for the influence of *The Invention of Morel* on *Last Year at Marienbad*

"*The Invention of Morel*, Reading Group Guide." New York Review Books, 2003.
— a concise summary on the novella, with study questions

"Interview with the Brothers Quay." Electric Sheep. March 4, 2007.
— Quay Brothers discuss their 2005 film *The Piano Tuner of Earthquakes* and it's relationship to *The Invention of Morel*

"A Different Stripe: Playing in Peoria: *The Invention of Morel*." Typepad, August 10, 2007.
— NYRB blog post

"*The Invention of Morel*," in *The Facts on File Companion to the World Novel: 1900 to the Present*, by Michael Sollars. Facts on File, 2008.
— analysis of the Bioy Casares novel

"The Invention of Marienbad," by Dan DeWeese. *Propeller Magazine*, February, 2014.
—questions the linking of *The Invention of Morel* and *Last Year at Marienbad*

"Time and the Image: *The Piano Tuner of Earthquakes*," by Arturo Silva. *Bright Lights Film Journal*, January 28, 2016.
— Analysis of the Quay Brothers' *The Piano Tuner of Earthquakes*, with a look at it's relationship to *The Invention of Morel*

Divine Dancer
This piece appeared on the Louise Brooks Society blog on December 23, 2004. I wish someone would make an American Masters-style documentary on Ruth St. Denis. She is significant enough to warrant one.

 Finished reading *Divine Dancer: A Biography of Ruth St. Denis* by Suzanne Shelton. I really liked this book, and would recommend it to anyone interested in Denishawn or early 20th century cultural history. Shelton's book is certainly is one of the most enjoyable biographies I have read in some time. It is well written, well researched, and full of interesting information.
 St. Denis had an incredible life, and was acquianted with, or knew, many of the leading personalities of her day. St. Denis once performed on the same bill as W.C. Fields, danced for the painter John Singer Sargeant, and was friendly with the Nobel Prize winning Indian poet Rabindranath Tagore. Rodin once sketched her, and she danced for King Edward VII. St. Denis had "special relationships" with the architect Stanford White (famous for his own special relationship with Evelyn Nesbit), the showman David Belasco, and the German writer Hugo von Hofmannsthal. It was also rumored she had an affair with the painter Egon Schiele. In 1906 (the year Louise Brooks was born), St. Denis toured Germany, where she met the dramatist Frank Wedekind, author of the Lulu plays!
 All of that is background to her incredible achievements as a dancer. She was a contemporary of (and personally knew) Isadora Duncan, Anna Pavolva, Maud Allan, and Loie Fuller. Both as a solo artist and as a founding member of the Denishawn dance company, St. Denis—perhaps more than anyone else—helped introduce modern dance to America. Her's was a truly singular life.
 A footnote: my copy of *Divine Dancer* had belonged to the composer and musician Lou Harrison (who I once met and even saw perform). Like St. Denis, Harrison had a

great interest in Asian culture. Whereas St. Denis was drawn to Indian dance (her nautch dance was well known), Harrison was drawn to the music of the Indonesian gamelan. I do not know that St. Denis and Harrison ever met, but I would not be surprised if they had, as their circles of friends may well have overlapped. Besides his considerable accomplishments as a composer, Harrison was also a music critic and calligrapher. My copy of *Divine Dancer*, which I purchased after Harrison's death when his possessions were being dispursed, bears the composer's calligraphic ownership signature.

Atlantic City Pageant March
This piece appeared on the Louise Brooks Society blog on January 10, 2006.

I just got a CD (on the NAXOS label) of John Philip Sousa's music for wind bands. The disc contains a track of interest, "The Atlantic City Pageant March" (1927). According to the linear notes, "During Sousa's final years, beginning in 1926, the band often played summer engagements at Atlantic City's Steel Pier. *The Atlantic City Pageant March* was written at the request of the city's mayor, and honoured the famous Atlantic City Beauty Pageant." That's only two years after Louise Brooks and Famous Players-Lasky were in Atlantic City filming *The American Venus*, whose story centered on the famed beauty contest.

Curiously, this is not the first time I have come across an instance of Sousa "shadowing" Brooks . . . . I recently noticed—while looking in the *Independence Daily Reporter*—that Sousa and his band performed in Independence, Kansas just a week or so after Brooks and Denishawn had danced in the city in January, 1924. (The paper reported that the band concert was the next big happening in town after the dance recital.) Another time, I came across a screening of *Evening Clothes* in Chicago. And at that 1927 event, Sousa's band performed onstage prior to the film being shown.

Louise Brooks and F. Scott Fitzgerald - a connection
This piece appeared on the Louise Brooks Society blog on August 27, 2015. Though Fitzgerald was smitten with actresses Lois Moran and Colleen Moore—and even wrote about each, Louise Brooks (or at least the image of Brooks) has become increasingly linked to the life and works of the Jazz Age author. The Kindle edition of Fitzgerald's Flappers and Philosophers, for example, features Brooks on the cover, as do a few other editions of Fitzgerald's books.

I recently came across a review of an intriguing book, *The Perfect Hour: The Romance of F. Scott Fitzgerald and Ginevra King, His First Love*, by James L.W. West III. The book was published by Random House in 2005. The review, by Fitzgerald scholar/biographer Scott Donaldson, reveals what *The Perfect Hour* only hints at—a previously unknown link between actress Louise Brooks and author F. Scott Fitzgerald.

Louise Brooks first encountered F. Scott Fitzgerald in Hollywood. According to the Barry Paris biography, they first met in 1927 in the lobby of the Ambassador Hotel. In letters and in interviews, Brooks recounted their one or two additional meetings over the years. What Fitzgerald and Brooks shared was a dislike of Hollywood. Despite its reputation as a dream factory, both the writer and the actress were profoundly unhappy during their tenures in Tinseltown.

The publisher description of *The Perfect Hour* summarizes the book this way: "In *The Perfect Hour*, biographer James L. W. West III reveals the never-before told story of the romance between F. Scott Fitzgerald and his first love, Ginevra King. They met in January 1915, when Scott was nineteen, a Princeton student, and sixteen-year-old Ginevra, socially poised and confident, was a sophomore at Westover School. Their romance flourished in heartfelt letters and quickly ran its course—but Scott never forgot it. Ginevra became the inspiration for Isabelle Borgé in *This Side of Paradise* and the model for Daisy Buchanan in *The Great Gatsby*. Scott also wrote short stories inspired by her— including "Babes in the Woods" and "Winter Dreams," which, along with Ginevra's own story featuring Scott are reprinted in this volume. With access to Ginevra's personal diary, love letters, photographs, and Scott's own scrapbook, West tells the beguiling story of youthful passion that shaped Scott Fitzgerald's life as a writer. For Scott and Ginevra, "the perfect hour" was private code for a fleeting time they almost shared and then yearned after for the rest of their lives. Now West brings that perfect hour back to life in all its freshness, delicacy, and poignant brevity."

Being a Fitzgerald devotee, I purchased a copy of *The Perfect Hour* and read it and liked it. If you have an interest in Fitzgerald, you should check it out!

What West reveals is that in the mid-Teens, while being courted by Fitzgerald, Ginerva King was infatuated with a "Chicago boy" by the name of Deering Davis, with the two suitors aware of one another. What Scott Donaldson reveals is that Deering Davis is the same Chicago (play)boy who married Brooks in 1933.

Of course, it is known that Brooks had met Scott and Zelda Fitzgerald at a Hollywood party. Brooks described meeting the Fitzgeralds at the Ambassador hotel in Los Angeles in 1927. "They were sitting close together on a sofa, like a comedy team, and the first thing that struck me was how small they were." Brooks "had come to see the genius writer," adding, "but what dominated the room was the blazing intelligence of Zelda's profile… the profile of a witch."

What we don't know is whether or not Deering Davis (Brooks' second husband) ever revealed his earlier courtship of Fitzgerald's "first love" to Brooks. I suppose it's unlikely, as the Davis-King romance was one of youth and had taken place nearly 20 years earlier. It has always been a mystery to me as to what Brooks saw in Davis. Was it the fact he was tall, dark, and "handsome"? To me, Fitzgerald is handsome, Davis not so. I don't think Davis photographed all that well, and he always seemed to have dark rings under his eyes. Ginevra King thought him a very good dancer, as did Brooks, who formed a dance team with Davis for a short time in the early 1930s.

What we do know is that Davis had a reputation as a Chicago playboy, and romanced many women. Evidently, he had what it took. Above is a little known clipping depicting Deering Davis and Louise Brooks.

Evelyn Brent revealed in new book
This piece was published on examiner.com on October 7, 2010.

Evelyn Brent should be well known to fans of Louise Brooks. The two actresses had a lot in common.

Each starred in *Love Em and Leave Em* (1926), the story of two sisters. The film was something of a hit, and should be considered among Brooks' better American silent films. Brent also had a role in another film in which Brooks was cast, the neglected

1937 crime picture, *King of Gamblers*, directed by Robert Florey. (Brooks' role in this latter film was cut.)

As Brooks enjoyed only a brief career in Hollywood, any actor or actress who can claim more than one appearance in a Brooks' film is something of a rarity. Nevertheless, their encounters made an impression. In 1975, Brooks wrote a short appreciation of Brent published in the bulletin of the *Toronto Film Society*.

Though Brent's reputation has languished in the annals of film history, she is now the subject of an excellent new biography which should go a long way in reviving interest.

Like Brooks, Brent had an interesting career, and in the 1920s and 1930s appeared in a number of notable films. She worked alongside actors still remembered today (William Powell, George Bancroft, Emil Jannings), as well as under the direction of some of the leading filmmakers of her time (Tod Browning, Josef von Sternberg, Frank Tuttle). Brent was also an interesting if not enigmatic personality, and her life story contains a number of twists and turns which should keep even the casual film buff or student of human nature interested.

All of this comes through in Lynn Kear's *Evelyn Brent: The Life and Films of Hollywood's Lady Crook* (McFarland, 2009). The book, with contributions by James King, features a foreword by Kevin Brownlow. The acclaimed film historian writes, "Brent's story, a fascinating one with ups and downs, is a cautionary tale of fame, fortune, choices, and Hollywood."

In his review of this new book, film historian Anthony Slide evokes Brooks' reputation in relation to Brent's. In reviewing the book, Slide states that this new book ". . . looks at the career of one of the most coldly beautiful and very up-to-date in terms of her good looks and restrained performances of silent actresses. No, I am not talking about Louise Brooks. The latter is not quite frankly as talented an actress, and certainly does not boast a career as long as that of the lady to whom I refer."

Anyone familiar with the up and down trajectory of Brooks' life and career will feel on familiar ground in reading Kear's new book.

Brent (born 1899) moved from modeling in New York City to small roles in films while still a teenager. Her debut (actually her second film) came in 1915 with *The Shooting of Dan McGrew*. Brent also worked on the British stage and in British silent films. In 1922, she was "discovered" by Douglas Fairbanks and Mary Pickford. A year later, Brent was selected a WAMPAS Baby Star.

By the end of the Twenties, Brent was an established veteran who had already appeared in a string of well regarded roles in films like *The Dangerous Flirt* (1924), *Silk Stocking Sal* (1924), and *Love Em and Leave Em* (1926). Brent had sultry good looks which were popular with fans on both sides of the aisle.

In 1928, following her divorce from producer Bernard Fineman, Brent was happily living with writer and film critic Dorothy Herzog. By then, this tiny brunette who had wowed fans and critics alike in *Underworld* (1927) and *The Last Command* (1928) was approaching major stardom. She'd also been something of a sensation in Paramount's first dialogue film, *Interference* (1928), and appeared in the all-star revue *Paramount on Parade* (1930).

However, around this time (and like Brooks), Brent was headed into a personal and professional downward spiral ending in bankruptcy and only occasional work in films for poverty row studios.

In the Thirties, Brent toured vaudeville and found work as a bit player in B-list films like *Hopalong Cassidy Returns* (1936) and *King of Gamblers* (1937). After performing in more than 120 movies, the still alluring actress retired in 1950. She worked for a number of years as an actor's agent. Brent died in 1975.

Throughout her life—and despite her successes, something always seemed to be holding Brent back—as with Brooks. What happened to the largely unfulfilled promise of her career is in the words of Kear "a complicated story laced with bad luck, poor decisions, and treachery."

Film scholar Kear has published two well-received volumes on the life and career of Kay Francis. *Evelyn Brent: The Life and Films of Hollywood's Lady Crook* is half biographical study and half filmography. It's packed with details, and a few images. Any fan of Louise Brooks will want to check it out—as it does contain a good number of references to Brooks and the two films Brooks and Brent made together. The only complaint one might have against the book is that there isn't enough of it. This 300 page book is about evenly divided between biography and an extensive and detailed filmography. The 119 pages of biographical material reads quick and leaves you wanting more. It is an engaging and well researched work which includes 36 photos, appendices, and bibliography.

Brent fans will have a chance to see the actress on the big screen when the Niles Essanay Silent Film Museum in Fremont, California screens the 1926 romantic comedy, *Love Em and Leave Em*, on October 9th. Showtime for this rare 16mm screening is 7:30 pm.

Recently, two silent film masterpieces starring Brent and directed by Josef von Sternberg, *Underworld* and *The Last Command*, were released on DVD through the Criterion Collection. Lynn Kear's *Evelyn Brent: The Life and Films of Hollywood's Lady Crook* (McFarland) is available through the McFarland website as well as amazon.com and select independent bookstores.

Rolled Stockings screenwriter Frederica Sagor Maas dies at age 111
This piece appeared on the Louise Brooks Society blog on January 7, 2012.
It was adapted from a piece published the day before on examiner.com.

Silent era screenwriter Frederica Sagor Maas, who penned a handful of Jazz Age comedies and dramas including the 1927 Louise Brooks film, *Rolled Stockings*, died on January 5th at age 111.

The former La Mesa, California resident and "supercentarian" was among the last surviving personalities from the silent film era, and perhaps the last individual closely associated with one of Brooks' silent films. Maas was also considered the second (or third according to some reports) oldest person in California.

As a woman, Maas was often assigned work on flapper comedies and light dramas. Her first big success, *The Plastic Age* (1925), was a smash hit for Clara Bow, the "It girl." Maas' screenwriting and story efforts—sometimes credited, sometimes not – include other Bow films like *Dance Madness* (1926), *Hula* (1927), and *Red Hair* (1928), two films featuring friend Norma Shearer, *His Secretary* (1925) and *The Waning Sex* (1926), the Garbo noted movie *Flesh and the Devil* (1926), and the now lost Brooks film *Rolled Stockings* (1927).

Rolled Stockings is a romantic drama set among carousing college students. It was one of a number of similarly-themed films aimed toward the youth market. To add a bit of verisimilitude, *Rolled Stockings* was filmed largely on and around the campus at the University of California, Berkeley. Local papers of the time reported on the arrival and activities of the film crew and cast.

The Richard Rosson-directed film was made for Paramount, and features the Paramount "junior stars." Besides Brooks, its cast includes then up-and-comers Richard Arlen, James Hall, Nancy Phillips, and El Brendel. *Rolled Stockings*, adapted from an original story idea by Frederica Sagor, proved popular in the summer of 1927—and not only in the United States. It also played across Latin America and Europe.

In its review, the *New York Morning Telegraph* wrote, "Freddy Sagor has written quite a nice little story," while Robert E. Sherwood, writing in *Life* magazine, called *Rolled Stockings* "a surprisingly nice comedy . . . the characters are of importance, and they are nicely represented by the adroit Louise Brooks."

The critic for the *Ann Arbor Times News*, a college town newspaper, appreciatively stated "The three stars, Louise Brooks, James Hall and Richard Arlen are so thoroughly likeable and the story so different from the usual line of college bunk, that *Rolled Stockings* proves to be a delightful bit of cinema entertainment."

In 1999, at the urging of film historian Kevin Brownlow, Maas published her autobiography, *The Shocking Miss Pilgrim: A Writer in Early Hollywood* (University Press of Kentucky). Maas was 99 at the time. In the book, which features an introduction by Brownlow, she recalled her life both in and out of Hollywood—as well as her remembrances of *Rolled Stockings* and impressions of Brooks.

I first met Frederica Sagor Maas in May of 1999 at a lunch held in her honor at Musso & Frank's restaurant in Hollywood. At the time, I was attending the national booksellers convention in Los Angeles while scouting film books for the San Francisco Silent Film Festival. At the publisher's booth I spotted an advance copy of her book, and queried about the author. Learning of her connections to silent Hollywood, I managed to get myself invited to the lunch being held the following day. That night, I stayed up late reading her engaging memoir. And that's when I discovered she had penned the story to one of Brooks' films. (Subsequently, I had the chance to read the manuscript of that story, which is held at the Margaret Herrick Library in Burbank.)

My meeting with Frederica at the annual booksellers convention led to a July event at the San Francisco bookstore where I was then working. At the time, Maas was nearly blind and frail, and at this—her first ever bookstore author event—she agreed to be interviewed about her remarkable life. I sat with her and asked questions about the many remarkable personalities she had known—Brooks, Clara Bow, Norma Shearer, Erich von Stroheim and others.

During that memorable evening, Maas told many stories, including one about Joan Crawford, who was then known as Lucille LeSueur and was just starting out in the movies.

As an experienced Hollywood insider, Maas was assigned by her studio to greet the young actress at the train station. She did so, but found the young actress rather uncouth. LeSueur, seeing Maas as a person of experience and sophistication, nevertheless asked the well-dressed scriptwriter to help build her wardrobe and shape a more glamorous image. Maas agreed, but found the experience challenging. Maas added that she thought Crawford a "tramp." The assembled crowd howled with laughter.

The next day, Maas appeared at the San Francisco Silent Film Festival, where she addressed a crowd of more than 1000, drew a thunderous round of applause, and signed copies of her book—which quickly sold out.

Over the years, I kept in sporadic contact with Maas' guardians. I remember when she turned 100. And then 110. And then 111. I still have my autographed copy of her memoir—as well as a rare autographed photoplay edition of *The Plastic Age* which Frederica signed especially for me. Both are treasured, and memory evoking keepsakes.

Frederica Sagor Maas with Thomas Gladysz & Christy Pascoe
at the Castro Theater in San Francisco in 1999.

A Jim Tully Revival: Hobo Author Back in Print
This piece appeared on the Huffington Post on December 8, 2010.

In the 1920s and 1930s, Jim Tully was something of a household name.

His writing—his singular brand of rough and tumble realism—was both popular and critically acclaimed. In his heyday, Tully's books appeared on bestseller lists, were adapted for the stage, made into movies, and got both good and bad reviews in major publications across the country. One of his controversial books was even banned, and a large part of its first edition destroyed.

Despite his past celebrity, few today have heard of Jim Tully. In the years following WWII, his reputation waned—but not because he was considered out-of-date. If anything, Tully was ahead of his time.

Some consider Tully a precursor to the "hard-boiled" school. In the Twenties, Tully wasn't writing about the glitz and glamour of the Jazz Age. Rather, his sometimes muscular prose concerned petty criminals, addicts, hoboes and other misfits of society.

Charles Willeford, one of the leading hard-boiled crime fiction writers, has praised Tully and written of his influence.

Over the last year and a half, the Kent State University Press in Kent, Ohio (Tully's one-time home) has begun reissuing this forgotten writer's long-out-of-print books. So far, they've released *Circus Parade* (with a foreword by the late comix artist Harvey Pekar), *Shanty Irish* (with a foreword by film director John Sayles), *The Bruiser* (with a foreword by critic Gerald Early), and Tully's breakthrough work and what's likely his best remembered book, *Beggars of Life* (with an introduction by series editors Paul Bauer and Mark Dawidziak).

Next year will see the release of Bauer and Dawidziak's biography, *Jim Tully: American Writer, Irish Rover, Hollywood Brawler*. That book will include a foreword by documentary film maker Ken Burns, who has called it a "wonderful, hugely important biography." All together, these forewords by so many celebrated contemporary figures suggest this little remembered author has a still strong following, at least among the cognoscenti.

Born near St. Marys, Ohio in 1886, Tully experienced an impoverished childhood. After the death of his mother in 1892, Tully's Irish immigrant ditch-digger father sent the boy to an orphanage in Cincinnati. He remained there for six years until the misery became more than he could bear. Tully ran away though he was only a teenager.

Thereafter, what education this wild boy of the road received largely came in hobo camps, railroad yards, and public libraries scattered across the country. Tully is known to have stolen books by favorite writers (such as Dostoyevsky) from the local libraries in which he often found shelter.

After moving to California, Tully began writing in earnest. He also became one of the first free-lance writers to cover Hollywood. His journalism and celebrity portraits appeared in *Vanity Fair* and other leading magazines of the day, from *Scribner's* to *True Confessions*. He was highly paid for his no holds barred accounts.

Tully wrote about Hollywood celebrities (including Charlie Chaplin, for whom he had once worked) in ways that the studios and the stars did not always find agreeable. For these pieces, Tully became known as the most-hated writer in Hollywood. It was a title he relished.

His first book, *Emmett Lawler* (1922), was originally composed as a single paragraph of 100,000 words. In an autobiographical statement published in 1933, Tully wrote "My first book was bad, and is now forgotten. I found myself, I think, in *Beggars of Life*, which I wrote in six terrifying weeks, while living with a bootlegger." The book was "intended as a compilation of dramatic episodes in the life of a youthful vagabond, which I was for seven years."

Published in 1924, *Beggars of Life* was the first of five autobiographical books Tully regarded as part of a larger single work. His "Underworld Edition" included *Circus Parade* (1927), "a series of none too happy and often ironical incidents with a circus," *Shanty Irish* (1928), "the background of a road-kid who becomes articulate," *Shadows of Men* (1930), "the tribulations, vagaries, and hallucinations of men in jail," and *Blood on the Moon* (1931). Of his books, these autobiographical works were the closest to his heart.

Tully also wrote celebrated novels about Hollywood, *Jarnegan* (1926), boxing, *The Bruiser* (1936), and the down-and-out, *Laughter in Hell* (1932). Shortly after publication, a novel about prostitutes set in Chicago, *Ladies in the Parlor* (1935), was seized by the police due to claims it was obscene. Most copies were destroyed and today it is a prized rarity.

Tully's last book, *A Dozen and One* (1943), includes an introduction by Damon Runyon. It features biographical portraits of 13 famous people Tully encountered during his life including Chaplin, H.L. Mencken, Jack Dempsey, Clark Gable, Diego Rivera and others.

With the May, 2011 publication of their long-in the-works biography, Bauer and Dawidziak will take to the road and revisit some of the cities and towns the hobo author once stopped-in decades earlier. They even plan on visiting a local jail where Tully was incarcerated for vagrancy.

Whether or not Tully's work will strike a chord with contemporary readers remains to be seen. It could take time, as Tully is an acquired taste. Certainly, readers of Jack Kerouac, Charles Bukowski, William Vollmann, or Stephen Elliott will find something of interest in Tully's stories and prose.

His champions Bauer and Dawidziak have described Tully as "the greatest long shot in American literature." Considering his ramshackle life, it is a miracle he wrote at all. If you're a sucker for neglected books or lost classics, the work of this "literary bum" is worth a gamble.

Canary Murder Case author featured in new book
This piece was published on examiner.com on December 30, 2010.

The 1929 Louise Brooks film, *The Canary Murder Case*, is based on bestselling book of the same name by the pseudonymous S.S. Van Dine, a once-popular and critically esteemed author of detective fiction.

Though little read today, Van Dine is considered an important early figure in the development of the modern detective story. Many of his books were bestsellers, and many were turned into popular films and radio programs.

Van Dine is one of three writers featured in a new book, *Making the Detective Story American: Biggers, Van Dine and Hammett and the Turning Point of the Genre, 1925-1930* (McFarland), by J.K. Van Dover. This 221 page study also examines the fiction of Earl Derr Biggers and Dashiell Hammett during a crucial five year period when these three authors helped transform the detective story into the genre we know today.

The characters they created, including Philo Vance (Van Dine), Charlie Chan (Biggers), and the Continental Op (Hammett), represented a new style of detective— each solving crimes in innovative and decidedly American ways. Together, the collective successes of these three authors helped push crime and detective fiction away from earlier European models and into territory which was fresh and exciting.

Van Dine was born Willard Huntington Wright in 1888. He studied art in Europe, and eventually found work as a critic for various magazines and newspapers (including the *Los Angeles Times*), and served as the editor of *The Smart Set*. (Notably, during his tenure with *The Smart Set*, Wright was the first to publish the work of Frank Wedekind in the United States.)

Wright also wrote a novel and short stories, a book on Nietzsche, and a book on art and aesthetics. (His brother was the noted modernist painter Stanton Macdonald-Wright.)

Wright continued as a journalist and critic until 1923, when he reportedly became ill due to exhaustion from overwork; in reality, his ailment was a secret drug addiction. Wright's doctor confined him to bed (supposedly because of a heart ailment, but actually because of cocaine dependency) for more than two years. In frustration and boredom, Wright began reading and studying thousands of volumes of crime and detective fiction. In 1926, thinking he could do better and hoping to make a little money, he published his first S. S. Van Dine novel, *The Benson Murder Case*. It was a success.

The Canary Murder Case followed in 1927. It was the first Van Dine book to be filmed. Released by Paramount in both silent and sound versions, *The Canary Murder Case* premiered in February, 1929 and starred William Powell as Philo Vance and Louise Brooks in the title role of the blackmailing showgirl who is murdered. The film was a popular success, and helped focus even more attention on Van Dine and his exceptional modern detective, Philo Vance.

Though he was personally conflicted about the worth of his genre work (hence his pseudonym), Van Dine gave detective fiction a good deal of thought. He also wrote two important essays on the subject and compiled an anthology. But what's more, he got readers thinking about the form and rules and merits.

J.K. Van Dover has written an admirable book because it reminds us of the rich and vital history of a genre which is assuming its own place on the shelves of literature—witness the recent publication of Hammett's works in the Library of American series. *Making the Detective Story American* is well written, thoroughly researched, and an interesting read.

Celebrating G.W. Pabst
This piece was published on examiner.com on July 14, 2010.

G.W. Pabst stands alongside Fritz Lang and F.W. Murnau as one of the three great directors working in Germany during the silent film era. Pabst, however, has not always gotten the attention paid to his more celebrated colleagues.

A month-long film series at Bard College in New York may help turn the tide of critical thinking. "The Best of G.W. Pabst" includes seven films by the Austrian-born director. It features his celebrated and often revived masterpieces *Pandora's Box* (1929) and *Diary of a Lost Girl* (1929), each of which star Louise Brooks, as well as *The Threepenny Opera* (1931), which stars Lotte Lenya and is based on the musical theater of Bertolt Brecht and Kurt Weill.

Though Pabst is sometimes tagged as an expressionist, his films range from drama and social criticism to satire, melodrama, comedy and historical epics. And that may have been his problem. Pabst may have been a little too varied for his own good.

Also on the schedule of the Pabst festival, which kicks off July 15, are the psychoanalytic thriller *Secrets of a Soul* (1926), the provocative *The Loves of Jeanne Ney* (1927), the bleak plea for peace *Westfront 1918* (1930), and the socialist-toned *Kameradschaft* (1931). Not on the bill are two other notable works, *Joyless Street* (1925), which helped make Garbo a star, and *The White Hell of Pitz Palu* (1929), one of the so-called "mountain films" popular at the time. This latter work starred Leni Riefenstahl.

Why has Pabst not received the critical and popular attention given Lang and

Murnau? Some have argued that Pabst was never a true *auteur* like other better remembered directors, nor did he make the number of great films as did Lang and Murnau and their contemporary, Ernst Lubitsch.

In his day, Pabst's films were also on the receiving end of a fair amount of critical disdain—and even official censorship. The recently released *Concise Cinegraph: Encyclopedia of German Cinema*, which depicts Pabst and Brooks on the cover, notes "Pabst's films, which comprise some masterpieces of Weimar cinema, often revolve around themes of poverty, extravagance, sexuality and violence, and frequently caused problems with censors, meaning many of his films were released in only an abridged form."

The other problem with Pabst's reputation is the fact that he spent the war years in Austria and Germany. Unlike the three previously named directors, Pabst didn't leave for a career in Hollywood. According to his wife, Pabst planned to emigrate, but was trapped on the continent when the war broke out. There is evidence to support this claim, but the fact remains he is the only important German director of the pre-war era to make films under the Nazis.

Pabst, however, was no friend to Nazism. His left leanings were well known (he was even called "Red Pabst"), and the Nazis hated his decadent Weimar era films like *Diary of a Lost Girl*. Nevertheless, Pabst's reputation—which could have been made in the post-WWII era when Lang and Murnau rose through the ranks—has never really recovered from the unfair taint of collaboration.

Lee Atwell, the author of one of two English-language books on Pabst, stated in 1977, "Pabst's strength as a director was not ideological and, second, that while pursuing a new vein of realism, he remained temperamentally still profoundly romantic."

Like Hitchcock, Pabst's other strength was his direction of women—Garbo, Asta Neilsen, Henny Porten, Bridgette Helm, Reifenstahl, and especially the American-born Louise Brooks. Pabst brought the then little-known actress to Germany to play in two films which are now considered his best, *Pandora's Box* and *Diary of a Lost Girl*. They are also the Pabst films most often revived.

On July 17th, *Diary of a Lost Girl* will be shown in San Francisco as part of the San Francisco Silent Film Festival. And on the same day in Berlin, the same film will be shown as part of the "Berlin Babylon - Silent Film Festival." One week later, the Babylon Kino in Berlin will also screen *Pandora's Box*.

Will there be a Pabst's revival? It's hard to tell. Reputations, it seems, rise and fall.

Daisy D'Ora, one-time German actress, dies at age 97
This piece was published on examiner.com on June 26, 2010.

Daisy D'Ora, a German actress whose brief film career included a role in the 1929 Louise Brooks' film *Pandora's Box*, has died. D'Ora was 97 years old, and was considered one of the last surviving German actresses from the silent era. It is also believed that D'Ora was until her death the oldest living Miss Universe contestant. In 1955, *Time* magazine described her as "one of the more curvesome ornaments of Germany's silver screen."

D'Ora was born in 1913 in Potsdam, Germany and died in Munich on June 19,

2010.

D'Ora was a baroness named Daisy Baroness von Freyberg-Eisenberg. She came from impoverished nobility, and out of necessity, went to work as a teenager. According to some accounts, she had always longed to be a movie star. However, because work in show business was considered unseemly for a member of the upper classes, she acquired a stage name.

D'Ora was discovered at the age of 15 by director G.W. Pabst, who noticed her in a cosmetics advertisement. Her role in *Pandora's Box* was her first film. She was only 16 years old when the film debuted in February, 1929.

Pandora's Box is widely considered one of the great films of the silent era. In it, D'Ora plays Charlotte, the youthful fiancée of the respected and older Dr. Schon, played by Fritz Kortner. In one of the most famous scenes in the film, Charlotte together with Schon's son (played by Francis Lederer) discovers Dr. Schon and Lulu (played by Brooks) in a compromising position backstage.

Despite her renowned beauty, D'Ora appeared in supporting roles in only a few more films in 1929 and 1930. In 1929, she appeared in *Der Mann, der nicht liebt* with Gustav Diessel (Jack the Ripper in *Pandora's Box*) and in *Es flüstert die Nacht* (*Hungarian Nights*), with Lil Dagover. Her last film, in 1930, was *Nur am Rhein*, and starred bobbed Truus Van Aalten.

After the movies, D'Ora married a career diplomat, Oskar Schlitter. D'Ora's uninhibited ways and outspoken comments often got her and her husband into trouble. According to the profile of D'Ora published in *Time* magazine in 1955, at a formal reception at the German embassy in Madrid she greeted the ex-Kaiser's grandson, Prince Louis Ferdinand, with a whoop and a holler and a lusty "Hi there, Lulu!" Schlitter was transferred to another post.

However, other faux pas followed. In 1955, while her husband was stationed in Britain, the freewheeling D'Ora made headlines around the world when she referred to England as an "enemy country." Schlitter was recalled and offered to resign. A spokesman claimed she meant to say "foreign country."

Between her career in the movies and her life as the wife of a diplomat, D'Ora was also a model and beauty contestant. By chance, she met the famous writer Erich Maria Remarque, who was judging a fashion show in which D'Ora participated at the luxurious Hotel Eden in Berlin.

The author of *All Quiet on the Western Front* persuaded her to take part in a beauty contest. She won, and as a result, was sent as "Miss Germany" to the United States for a Miss Universe contest held in Galveston, Texas. D'Ora, as Daisy Freyberg, placed fourth in 1931. Screen beauty Dorothy Lamour was among the semi-finalists that year.

D'Ora's beauty was of such renown that a famous vocal group of the time, the Comedian Harmonists, even referenced her in a song. "Hello, what are you doing today, Daisy" can be found on the group's greatest hits CD.

Discovering a Polish Lulu

This piece was published on examiner.com on August 2, 2010.

For those interested in film history, in silent film, and in Louise Brooks—Marek Haltof's *Polish National Cinema* (Berghahn Books) offers a little something for everyone.

It's a groundbreaking work well worth checking out.

Haltof's 300-page survey is also the first comprehensive English-language study of Polish filmmaking and film culture from the end of the 19th to the beginning of the 21st century.

The first two chapters, "Polish Cinema before the Introduction of Sound" and "The Sound Period of the 1930s," are each fascinating and detailed accounts of the origins and development of a national cinema before and just after the time when the Polish state gained independence. Buffeted as it was between Germany and Russia and the more dominant film industry's found in each of those countries, Polish cinema was, naturally, influenced by its neighbors.

German and Russian as well as French and American films showed in Poland—and each left their mark. It's known, for example, that at least a few of Louise Brooks' American silent films as well as her German-made movies were shown in Warsaw—the capitol of both Poland and the Polish film industry. *Pandora's Box*, retitled *Lulu*, opened at the Casino Theater in Warsaw at the end of May, 1929. It ran for a couple of weeks, and was well received. Adam Furmanskiego, a noted conductor, led the orchestra at the Polish premier.

One striking example given by Haltof of the German influence on Polish cinema is noted in the book's second chapter, on the films of the 1930s.

Haltof writes, "The treatment of women in Polish melodramas oscillates between presenting them as femme fatales in the tradition of Pola Negri's silent features made for the Sfinks company, and as vulnerable figures at the mercy of the environment. The former representation, which is not very popular in Polish cinema, can be seen in *Zabawka* (*The Toy*, 1933), directed by Michal Waszynski. The title refers to the female protagonist Lulu (Alma Kar), a Warsaw cabaret star, who is invited to a country manor by a wealthy landowner. The landowner's son and local Don Juan both fall in love with Lulu and pay for it. The name of the protagonist and the theme of the film suggest G.W. Pabst's influence (Louise Brooks as Lulu in *Pandora's Box*, 1929), and this inspiration has been emphasized by one of the scriptwriters of the film."

Haltof, a Polish-born scholar, is now resident in the United States where he teaches Film in the English Department at Northern Michigan University. Via email, he confirmed the influence of the one film on the other. He also supplied a photocopy of a page from a hard-to-find Polish work, *Historia filmu polskiego* (1988), which he cites in his own book. It quotes coscriptwriter Andrzej Tomakowski from the 1930s on the influence of *Pandora's Box* on *Zabawka*.

A viewing of *Zabawka* confirms the influence. The character, played by the charming Alma Kar, is named Lulu and is like Pabst's Lulu, a showgirl desired by many (including a Father and his son) with disastrous results. In one early scene, this Polish Lulu is surrounded by a line of chorus girls each wearing a sharp bob haircut like that worn by Brooks in *Pandora's Box*—except each of these 1930s Polish chorines are blonde.

The only other book which covers similar material in Polish film history is *The Law of the Looking Glass: Cinema in Poland, 1896-1939*, by Sheila Skaff. It, however, does not include material on *Zabawka*.

Who was Margarete Böhme?
This piece was published on examiner.com on September 30, 2010.

The recent publication of my new "Louise Brooks edition" of *The Diary of a Lost Girl* has led some to enquire about the book's little known author. Fans have asked, "who was Margarete Böhme?"

Böhme (1867-1939) was, arguably, one of the most widely read German writers of the early 20th century. She authored 40 novels—as well as short stories, autobiographical sketches, and articles. Today, however, she is little known—even in her native Germany.

The Diary of a Lost Girl, first published in 1905 as *Tagebuch einer Verlorenen*, is her best known and bestselling book. It was translated into 14 languages, and inspired a sequel, a play, a parody, controversy, lawsuits, two silent films, and a score of imitators. By the end of the Twenties, the book had sold more than 1,200,000 copies, ranking it among the bestselling books of its time. One contemporary scholar has called it "Perhaps the most notorious and certainly the commercially most successful autobiographical narrative of the early twentieth century."

Böhme began writing early. At age 17, she published her first story, "The Secret of the Rose Passage," in a German newspaper. She then went on to place her work in weekly magazines, both under her own name and under a pseudonym. Some of her early novels were serialized in periodicals, while others were issued in book form by various German publishers. At first, Böhme wrote what would today be termed popular fiction—but as her work matured, she turned to more serious themes.

Beginning in 1903, Böhme wrote six novels in the span of two years. Few of them, however, met with much success. With the publication of *Tagebuch einer Verlorenen* in 1905, the author's fortunes changed. The book was an overnight success, and Böhme's reputation was secured. Her succeeding books were met with serious consideration, translated into other languages, and widely reviewed. At the time, Böhme's work was favorably compared to that of the French writer Émile Zola. An American literary review described Böhme as "One of the leading novelists of the younger realistic school in Germany."

Dida Ibsens Geschichte (*The History of Dida Ibsen*), from 1907, is a kind of sequel to *The Diary of a Lost Girl*. As Böhme states in the forward, the book was written in response to a flood of letters she received regarding her earlier book. People from all walks of life had written to the author. Some wrote to say they had cried over the book. Others, wanting to pay their respects, even enquired as to whereabouts Thymian's grave!

Critics consider *W.A.G.M.U.S.*, the story of a department store, to be Böhme's best work. This 1911 novel chronicles the growth of a colossal business which crushes its smaller competitors by systematically underselling them. The book touches on emerging modern business methods, the treatment of employees, and issues around commerce and consumerism. Shoplifters, then a new phenomenon, also come into the story. *W.A.G.M.U.S.* was published in America, where one leading review called it "a distinctly remarkable book."

Böhme was a progressive minded author, and most of her later work was concerned with the everyday lives of women. Much of her later fiction also has a strong social message. For example, *Christine Immersen*, from 1913, concerns the harsh working conditions faced by female telephone operators (then also just coming onto the scene).

Despite her considerable European reputation, only two of Böhme's books would find their way into English. They are *Tagebuch einer Verlorenen* as *The Diary of a Lost One* in 1907, and *W.A.G.M.U.S.* as *The Department Store* in 1912. Each was first issued in Great Britain and then the United States. They were, in all likelihood, also distributed around the English-speaking world. In 1909, a newspaper in New Zealand referred to *The Diary of a Lost One* as "The saddest of modern books."

Böhme continued to publish throughout the Teens and Twenties. In 1933, *Tagebuch einer Verlorenen*, still considered a controversial book, was again the subject of attack. An attempt was made in the early days of the Nazi-era to ban Böhme's book. It was deemed trash, and its author considered suspect (and possibly even Jewish). Though an official decree was never issued, *Tagebuch einer Verlorenen* was finally driven from print more than a quarter-century after it was first published.

By 1937, Böhme's name had disappeared from annuals devoted to German literature. With a changing century and the cultural chaos preceding the coming war, Böhme's books fell out of print and faded from view. The author died on May 23, 1939 at the age of 72. Like her famous heroine and the book which tells her tragic tale— Böhme became an author lost to history.

There is little in English about Margarete Böhme. I will be discussing the author and her best known book at the San Francisco Public Library on November 14th. My talk will be followed by a screening of the 1929 Louise Brooks film. The Louise Brooks edition of *The Diary of a Lost Girl* is available online and through select independent bookstores.

Long before Three Cups of Tea
This piece appeared on Open Salon on April 21, 2011, and was a Salon editor's pick.

Before Greg Mortenson and *Three Cups of Tea*, before James Frey and *A Million Little Pieces*, and long before Clifford Irving and his *Autobiography of Howard Hughes*, there was Margarete Böhme and *The Diary of a Lost Girl*. If you haven't heard of it, you're not alone.

The book, of course, should be familiar to fans of the silent film star Louise Brooks. It served as the basis for one of her best films, G.W. Pabst's *Diary of a Lost Girl*, from 1929.

Despite its present-day obscurity, *The Diary of a Lost Girl* has some claim to being the Mother of all modern literary hoaxes. Like the above mentioned titles, this now little known 1905 book was a contested bestseller in its day. One contemporary scholar has called it "Perhaps the most notorious and certainly the commercially most successful autobiographical narrative of the early twentieth century."

The Diary of a Lost Girl purportedly told the true-life story—in diary form—of a young woman named Thymian forced by both circumstance and society into a life of prostitution. The book went on to sell more than 1,200,000 copies—a remarkable number for the time. And like the above mentioned titles, its authenticity came into question. Some thought it an outright hoax.

Today, *The Diary of a Lost Girl* is accepted as a work of fiction. But when it was first published, it was said to be the genuine diary of a young girl. Böhme claimed only to be its editor. As "the editor" states in her forward, she was given the manuscript and intended to rework it into a novel. But, on the advice of her publisher, she instead presented it as an authentic diary.

The book's publication and rapid success quickly led to all manner of speculation as to its authorship—with readers, critics, and the press divided. To lend its story credence, some early editions of *The Diary of a Lost Girl* even depict manuscript pages said to be in Thymian's hand.

Both the author and her publisher, it should be noted, always maintained their account as to the origins of the diary. According to the forward of a 1988 German reissue, Böhme would forgo any claims as author as late as 1935—a few years after the book had been driven out-of-print by conservative groups seeking to suppress it. Belief in its authenticity continued in some quarters for decades, even into the 1970's.

Why Mortenson did what he did has yet to be explained. Why Jones and Frey did what they did—passing off fiction as memoir—has been revealed. The motives of Clifford Irving and J.T. LeRoy and other hoaxers have come to light. But why Böhme presented her book as genuine isn't really known.

Some have suggested that the author, facing the double standard of the day, realized the personal and professional consequences she would suffer for having published a novel about the demimonde. Böhme, it should be noted, was then a struggling writer as well as a divorced woman and a single mother.

Others have speculated that the book's claim to be an actual diary was a literary ploy to put over its provocative subject matter. Back then it wasn't considered acceptable for a woman to write about such things. At one point, Böhme herself was accused of being a prostitute—the thinking being *how else could a woman have written or even edited such a book?*

The Diary of a Lost Girl is a knowing work. The literary critic Walter Benjamin, who wrote about it, described it as "A complete inventory of the sexual trade." In America, it was referenced in scholarly works on sexuality and criminal behavior.

In its 1907 review, the *Manchester Guardian* noted "It professes to be an authentic document, the actual diary of the woman it describes, unaltered save for the excision of some passages and the suppression of real names. There can be no doubt this is not the case. It is a careful narrative, directed toward a distinctly moral purpose. The psychology of it is arresting and unmistakably founded upon experience."

To the attentive reader—the force of its narrative, its detailed realism, its references to the literature of prostitution, and its psychological observations all betray a literary sophistication beyond that of a teenage girl.

Admittedly, there is a whiff of melodrama about the book; a newspaper in New Zealand once called it "The saddest of modern books." Ultimately, however, it is the book's subtle literary achievement which betrays its claim to be an authentic diary.

There have been many literary frauds and hoaxes over the years. Today, most of them have been forgotten. What makes *The Diary of a Lost Girl* stand out is its remarkable history, of which its contested origins are only the beginning. *Dracula* author Bram Stoker, for example, was said to be in favor of banning it. American novelist Henry Miller claimed it as one of his favorite books.

Within a few years of publication, *The Diary of a Lost Girl* had sold hundreds of thousands of copies and was translated into 14 languages. It was reviewed and discussed across Europe, and the book was said to have had some small influence on German social policy. Because of its popularity, there were even pirated versions in Poland and The Netherlands.

The book inspired a bestselling sequel (by Böhme in response to a flood of letters), a controversial stage play, a parody, lawsuits, two films, and *sui generis*—a score of imitators. There was also a film of the sequel, and even a French novelization of the 1929 German film made from the book. Because of it all—and in spite of it all, *The Diary of a Lost Girl* remained a steady seller for more than 25 years. It had a long run. The book was eventually driven out-of-print in Germany at the beginning of the Nazi era.

Last year, after being out-of-print in English for more than 100 years, I brought this noteworthy book back into print. I added a few dozen images (of the author, of earlier editions, of scenes from the films), and wrote an introduction detailing the book's remarkable and contested history.

Why did I do it? Because I think it is a worthwhile book, a neglected gem, and a good read.

Piracy and *The Diary of a Lost Girl*
This piece appeared on the Louise Brooks Society blog on June 4, 2010.

Today, the pirating of movies, music, and even books is a major concern. But back in the early years of the 20th century, when Margarete Böhme wrote the book which became the 1929 Louise Brooks film, *Diary of a Lost Girl*, piracy was also a problem.

Böhme's book was a huge bestseller in Germany—a phenomenon really. It sold more than 100,000 copies in less than two years. It was so popular that it was translated into 14 languages and published across Europe—from England and France to Hungary and Russia. There was such demand for the book that there were even pirated editions in at least two countries, The Netherlands and Poland.

In The Netherlands, the book was retitled and published as *Thymian*, the name of the "lost girl" and the character played by Louise Brooks. This unauthorized translation was issued by Albert de Lange, an otherwise reputable publisher. From what I was able to find, the translation was by the noted poet Hillegonda van Uildriks, alias Gonne Loman-van Uildriks (1863-1921). Remembered primarily as a translator, Uildriks was the first to translate Jane Austen into Dutch. She would also translated Robert Louis Stevenson and H.G. Wells, among others.

Böhme's book was published in Dutch as *Thymian*, with the subtitle "From the life of a fallen woman." The cover pictured here (courtesy of Digitale Bibliotheek voor de Nederlandse Letteren.) is unusual in its visual representation of the book's heroine.

Böhme's book was also published in Poland in both authorized and unauthorized editions. I was able to uncover an interesting advertisement for the authorized translation which references the pirated version.

The book was issued in Poland under the title *Pamiętnik Kobiety Upadłej*. This 1906 advertisement notes, "Every mature man or women should read this book." Also, it warns against the unauthorized edition, and notes that the book is available in all bookshops. The authorized Polish edition was translated by Felicya Nossig, who would later translate Selma Lagerlöf, Josef Conrad, and other writers of note. Nossig is noted in the advertisement. (For those keeping track, the unauthorized translation was titled *Pamiętnik Uwiedzionej*.)

If any readers of this blog have any early editions of Böhme's book in any language other than German, I would appreciate hearing from you. The information in this post comes from my introduction to the new "Louise Brooks edition" to *The Diary of a Lost Girl*.

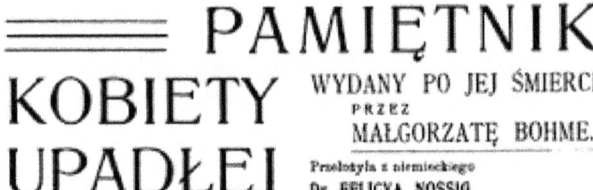

How many silent films were made based on *Diary of a Lost Girl*?
This piece appeared on the Louise Brooks Society blog on June 23, 2010.

How many silent films were made based on Margarete Böhme's 1905 book, *Tagebuch einer Verlorenen*, or *The Diary of a Lost Girl*. There were at least two, and possibly three.

The first was directed by Richard Oswald and was based on his adaption of Böhme's book. This 1918 film starred Erna Morena as Thymian, with Reinhold Schünzel as Osdorff, Werner Krauss as Meinert, and Conrad Veidt as Dr. Julius. As a film, this version of *Tagebuch einer Verlorenen* was well reviewed, but the demands of the censor at the time led to cuts and even a change in its title. Once censorship was lifted after the end of WWI, scenes thought too provocative or critical of society were restored and its famous title restored.

The cast and crew of the first version was indeed a remarkable assembly. Oswald went on to direct many films including the sensational *Different from the Others* (1919). Together, Krauss and Veidt achieved cinema immortality in *The Cabinet of Dr. Caligari* (1920). Schünzel would also write and direct; his best known work is the seminal *Viktor und Viktoria* (1933). Pictured here are Veidt and Morena in a scene from *Tagebuch einer Verlorenen*.

In 1929, Böhme's book was made into a film for a second time. G.W. Pabst's version of *Tagebuch einer Verlorenen* came on the heels of his now classic *Pandora's Box*, a film based on the similarly controversial Lulu plays authored by Frank Wedekind. Both of these films starred Louise Brooks. Also appearing in Pabst's *Diary of a Lost Girl* is Fritz Rasp as Meinert and the dancer Valeska Gert as the sadistic reform school disciplinarian. The well known character actor Kurt Gerron also has a role in this second adaption.

However, in researching my introduction to the just issued new edition of *The Diary of a Lost Girl*, I found that some film databases, such as filmportal.de and IMDb, list a 1912 German production titled *Tagebuch einer Verlorenen*. It was directed by Fritz Bernhardt and produced by Alfred Duskes. Little else is known of the film, which is presumably lost. Likewise, its relationship to Böhme's book is uncertain. The question remains, how many silent films were made based on *Diary of a Lost Girl*?

The Diary of a Lost Girl: A brief history of a banned book
This piece appeared on the Louise Brooks Society blog on October 2, 2012.

Every year since 1982, the American reading public observes Banned Books Week. This year, as in the past, hundreds of libraries and bookstores draw attention to the ongoing problem of censorship by hosting events and by creating displays of challenged works. It's about creating awareness.

In 2010, the Louise Brooks Society did its part by helping bring a once censored work back into print. The book is *The Diary of a Lost Girl*. It's by a turn-of-the-last-century German writer few today have heard of, Margarete Böhme. Her book, a once-controversial bestseller, had been out of print in the United States for more than 100 years.

Though little known today, *The Diary of a Lost Girl* was a literary phenomenon in the early 20th century. It is considered by scholars of German literature to be one of the best-selling books of its time.

The Diary of a Lost Girl is an unlikely work of social protest. It's also a tragedy. In 1907, the English writer Hall Caine described it as the "poignant story of a great-hearted girl who kept her soul alive amidst all the mire that surrounded her poor body." In 1909, a newspaper in New Zealand called it "the saddest of modern books." Years later, a contemporary scholar called it "Perhaps the most notorious and certainly the commercially most successful autobiographical narrative of the early twentieth century."

The book tells the story of Thymian, a young woman forced by circumstance into a life of prostitution. Her story goes something like this. Seduced by her Father's business associate, the teenage Thymian conceives a child which she is forced to give up; she is then cast out of her home, scorned by society, and ends up in a reform school—from which she escapes and by twists of fate hesitantly turns to life as a high-class escort. Prostitution is the only means of survival available to her. If its story sounds at all familiar, it's likely because the book was the basis for the 1929 German movie of the same name. That silent film, still shown in theaters around the world, stars Louise Brooks.

The author of *The Diary of a Lost Girl*, Margarete Böhme (1867-1939), was a progressive minded writer who meant to expose the hypocrisy of society and un-Christian behavior of some of its leading members. She also meant to show-up the double standards by which women of all ages suffer. Böhme's frank treatment of sexuality (by the standards of the day) only added fuel to the fire of outrage which greeted the book in some quarters.

First published in Germany in 1905 as *Tagebuch einer Verlorenen*, Böhme's book proved an enduring work—for a quarter century and despite ongoing attacks by critics and social groups. The book was translated into 14 languages, and was reviewed and discussed across Europe. It inspired a popular sequel brought about by a flood of letters to the author, a controversial stage play banned in some German cities, a parody, lawsuits, two silent films—each of which were censored, and a score of imitators.

The book confronts readers with the story of a likeable young women forced into a life of degradation. The complicity of her family—and by extension society—in her downward turn is provocative. However, Thymian—an endearing character and a heroine till the end, refuses to be coarsened by her experiences. She also refuses to let others define her—she defines herself. At the time, Böhme's book helped open a dialogue on issues around the treatment of women.

In 1907, when the book was translated into English, its British publisher placed an advertisement in newspapers. The ads proclaimed Böhme's work "The Book that Has Stirred the Hearts of the German People," but somewhat defensively added "It is outspoken to a degree, but the great moral lesson it conveys is the publishers' apology for venturing to reproduce this human document."

In response to a review of the book in the *Manchester Guardian*, the Rev. J.K. Maconachie of the Manchester Association Against State Regulation of Vice wrote a surprising letter to the editor. He stated, "The appearance in Germany of this remarkable book, together with the stir it has made there and the fact that its author is a woman, betoken the uprising which has taken place in recent years amongst German women against the evils and injustice which the book reveals.... It may be hoped that discriminating circulation of *The Diary of a Lost One* will help many here to realize, in the forceful words of your reviewer, 'the horror of setting aside one section of human beings for the use of another.'"

The Diary of a Lost Girl, editions then and now

Back in Germany, the same sorts of groups which objected to the book also objected to the two films made from it. The first, from 1918, is considered lost, but we know from articles of the time that it was withdrawn from circulation because of its controversial story. The second film, which starred Louise Brooks, has survived only in censored form.

As records from 1929 show, various groups including a German morality association, a national organization for young women, a national organization of Protestant girl's boarding schools, and even the governor in Lower Silesia all voiced their objections to aspects of the film. As with the book, these groups objected to various key scenes. Each found the work to be demoralizing.

At the end of the Twenties, *The Diary of a Lost Girl* was still in print and was still being reissued in countries across Europe. It had by then sold more than 1,200,000 copies—ranking it among the 15 bestselling books of the era. Twenty five years after it was first published, however, Böhme's "terribly impressive book, full of accusations against society" was still considered a provocation. That's why, just a very few years later at the beginning of the Nazi era, conservative groups still unsettled by its damning indictment deliberately drove it out-of-print.

In 1988, after decades of obscurity, a facsimile of the special 1907 edition was published in Germany. It was followed in 1995 by a small paperback which featured Louise Brooks on the cover. The recent "Louise Brooks edition" reprint of the original English language translation, also with Brooks on the cover and with some 40 pages of introductory and related material, appeared in 2010.

The impetus behind publishing a new edition of *The Diary of a Lost Girl* was about creating awareness. More importantly, it gives voice to a story which critics had long tried to silence.

The Diary of a Lost Girl, the research continues
This piece appeared on the Louise Brooks Society blog on March 9, 2013.

Lately, I have been working on a revised 2nd edition of my Louise Brooks edition of *The Diary of a Lost Girl*, by Margarete Böhme. (Böhme's book was the basis for the 1929 film by G.W. Pabst.) Someday, I plan on incorporating much of my new research into an expanded e-book. Notably, I have uncovered a bunch of interesting new material, including, even, a connection to Sigmund Freud! I also uncovered what I think was the very first newspaper review of *The Diary of a Lost One* in the United States, while finding out that the book was banned in Canada.

One of the things I have also been tracking is the influence Böhme's book had on subsequent literature. In Germany, it brought about not only a popular sequel, a controversial stage play, a parody, and two (or three) silent films—but a score of imitators as well. There was also a movie made from the book's sequel; and in France, a novelization of the 1929 film with Louise Brooks was issued.

In England, Böhme's book lingered in the British imagination for some time. It went through at least three printings. It was also referenced in a few literary works from the time—one in 1909, another in 1917. It also inspired another. That latter book, from 1931, was titled *No Bed of Roses: A Pathetically Realistic Story of a Woman of the Underworld*.

When *No Bed of Roses* was advertised in England it was described as "The Diary of a Lost Soul" (which also was the original advertised English-language title of *The Diary of a Lost One*). In not unfamiliar language, an ad for *No Bed of Roses* stated "These are the actual diaries of a prostitute and dope fiend. They form one of the most important human documents uncovered in our time."

No Bed of Roses was followed by *God Have Mercy on Me*. Like *The Diary of a Lost One*, this sequel (with an equally lurid cover) was edited from the reportedly real life diaries of a wayward, nearly anonymous woman named O.W.

The Holocaust, Heinrich Himmler, Jodi Picoult, and *The Diary of a Lost Girl*
This piece appeared on the Louise Brooks Society blog on May 28, 2014.

I am continuing to research *The Diary of a Lost Girl*, Margarete Böhme's controversial 1905 novel which served as the basis for the equally controversial 1929 film starring Louise Brooks. I plan on issuing a revised and expanded print edition of my 2010 "Louise Brooks edition" of *The Diary of a Lost Girl* which will include new findings. Among them are these two items.

Heinrich Himmler, one of the most powerful men in Nazi Germany and one of the individuals most directly responsible for the Holocaust, is known to have read Böhme's novel in 1920, 15 years after it was first published and three years before he joined the Nazi party. That's according to two books on Himmler which I have just come across.

Both Bradley F. Smith's *Heinrich Himmler: A Nazi in the Making* (Hoover Institution Press, 1971) and Peter Longerich's *Heinrich Himmler* (Oxford University Press, 2012) record that the then 20 year old student read Böhme's *The Diary of a Lost Soul* (its alternate title). Himmler kept a record of his reading, and notes having read Böhme's book in March 1920, while residing in Munich and Ingolstadt. At the time, according to Longerich, Himmler's reading was largely novels and stories "concerned with love, erotic attraction, and the battle of the sexes."

According to Smith, *The Diary of a Lost Soul* caused Himmler to "reexamine his attitudes" and doubt "the scorn he usually poured on those who had wandered from the path of virtue." It was a book, Himmler noted, "that offers insight into dreadful human tragedies and makes one look at many a whore with different eyes." Afterwords, he went on to read other works including Henrik Ibsens's *A Doll's House*.

I also just recently learned that *The Diary of a Lost Girl* received a shout-out in *The Storyteller*, a 2013 novel from author Jodi Picoult. *The Storyteller*, a #1 *New York Times* bestseller, is based on an incident which took place during the Holocaust. In one scene, a key character is preparing to flee, and is gathering important possessions.

I contacted Picoult, and asked about her character's mention of *The Diary of a Lost Girl*. Picoult wrote back, "I was looking for a book of the time period that would have been something Minka might have read—so I did a little digging for some popular titles of the time!"

> It was the call to action that we needed. My father began rummaging through the drawers of the server, and then he started to move books from shelves and reach into jars in the kitchen cabinets, collecting money that I had not known was hidden there. My mother settled Majer in his bassinet although he was screaming, and began to collect winter coats and woolen scarves, hats, and mittens, warm clothing. I flew into my parents' bedroom and took my mother's jewelry, my father's tefillin and tallith. In my own room, I looked around. What would you grab, if you had to pack up your life in only minutes? I took the newest dress I owned and its matching coat, the one I had worn for the High Holy Days last fall. I took several changes of underwear and a toothbrush. I took my notebook, of course, and a stash of pencils and pens. I took a copy of *The Diary of a Lost Girl* by Margarete Böhme, in its original German—a novel I had found at a secondhand store and had hidden from my parents because of its racy subject matter. I took an exam upon which Herr Bauer had written "Exceptional Student" in German.

Picoult's choice is apt. Böhme was an especially popular author, especially with women, and apparently with somewhat curious males like Himmler.

From the time it was first published in 1905, *The Diary of a Lost Girl* continued to sell and remained in print in various editions all the way into the early 1930's, when it was driven out of print by right wing German groups deeply upset with its story. (Himmler read an edition published in 1917.) Along with the anti-war novel *All Quiet on the Western Front* and works by Thomas Mann, Böhme's *The Diary of a Lost Girl* was one of the dozen bestselling books in Germany in the period from 1900 to 1939. It is believed to have sold more than 1.2 million copies. The book is back in print in Germany and the United States.

Sigmund Freud, John Huston, and Louise Brooks (& not-Ghoulardi)
This piece appeared on the Louise Brooks Society blog on June 15, 2016.

Here's an odd one. . . . While doing some Louise Brooks research I came up with one of the strangest finds I have ever stumbed across, linking Sigmund Freud, director John Huston, and the 1929 Louise Brooks' film, *Diary of a Lost Girl*.

The Academy of Motion Picture Arts and Sciences contains many documents, among them a batch of correspondence related to the John Huston Film, *Freud* (1962), starring Montgomery Clift in the title role. The correspondence comes from the Freud estate, and from those involved in the film's production. Among them was one Ernie Anderson, who sent a letter on November 24, 1961 explaining that Freud had no direct involvement with two earlier G.W. Pabst films, *Secrets of a Soul* (1926) and *Diary of a Lost Girl*.

Anderson was a long-time assistant to Huston (and not, apparently, the cult figure "Ghoulardi," the father of contemporary director Paul Thomas Anderson). To me, what's odd is why Huston would have been curious about *Diary of a Lost Girl*, which was then quite obscure, having been seldom screened in the United States and even less written about in film histories.

Louise Brooks and the *Maltese Falcon*
This piece appeared on the Louise Brooks Society on December 13, 2016.
Interstingly, in August of 1930, Brooks attended a party at the Los Angeles home of composer
Dimitri Tiomkin at which Dashiell Hammett was also present, as was Humphrey Bogart.

For the longest time, I have believed that a photograph seen in the 1931 Warner Bros. version of *The Maltese Falcon* was that of Louise Brooks. Now, I am not so sure. This first adaption of the famed Dashiell Hammett story, directed by Roy Del Ruth, stars Ricardo Cortez as private detective Sam Spade and Bebe Daniels (shown below) as Ruth Wonderly.

I have seen this film twice before at theaters in San Francisco (the setting of the film), and each time I spotted the image and said to myself "That's Louise Brooks." I guessed it was one of her French portraits, taken while she was in Paris filming *Prix de beauté*. It certainly looks like one of the images taken by the Studio Lorelle, though it doesn't match any of them.

The image in question is seen twice in the film. The first time is early on, about 30 minutes into the story. The second time is somewhat near the end. In this later scene, Spade places a telephone call from his apartment. And hanging on the wall near the phone is a picture of a woman we assume to be his sweetheart. That woman, I have long thought, is Brooks. But now, I am not so sure.

Or might it be someone else, a bit of random set decoration? I've wondered why was it there? I haven't been able to find any connections between Brooks and the film, except that in 1931, Brooks appeared in one Warner Bros. movie, *God's Gift to Women*, and was considered for another, *The Public Enemy*. Each was released around the same time as *The Maltese Falcon*. Might an extra publicity photo around the studio account for why an image of the Brooks was included in this latter production?

If it isn't Brooks, might anyone know who it is? I can't decide.

King of Gamblers star subject of new book
This piece was published on examiner.com on November 24, 2010.
I own a grey market copy of King of Gamblers, and think it one of the better B-movies I've seen.

King of Gamblers was one of the last films in which Louise Brooks had a role. Unfortunately, her small part—as the fiancé to a character played by Lloyd Nolan—was cut at the time of the film's release.

Nevertheless, this 1937 Paramount drama—an underworld crime story about a slot-machine racket and the crusading reporter who uncovers it—is a terrific "B" movie given "A" treatment at the hands of noted director Robert Florey. Should you ever have a chance to see it, you won't be disappointed.

The film stars Akim Tamiroff as a syndicate boss. However, it's the crusading reporter in *King of Gamblers*, played by Nolan, who steals the show.

Nolan, a venerable character actor whose career spanned 50 years, is the subject of a new book by broadcaster Joel Blumberg and writer Sandra Grabman. The 294-page *Lloyd Nolan: An Actors Life With Meaning* has just been published by BearManor Media. It is a quick read, and includes a foreword by the well known critic Jeffrey Lyons.

Nolan (1902–1985) was born in San Francisco, California. He began his career on the local stage in the Bay Area, enjoyed some success in New York City, and was soon lured to Hollywood. *King of Gamblers* was made near the beginning of Nolan's long movie career.

Nolan started in films in 1935 with *"G" Men*, and over the years played detectives, doctors, and police officers in numerous crime stories, westerns, and dramas heavy on action.

Today, the best remembered of his many films are *The House Across the Bay* (1940), *A Tree Grows in Brooklyn* (1945), *Lady in the Lake* (1947), *Peyton Place* (1957), *Airport* (1970), and Woody Allen's *Hannah and Her Sisters* (1986). Many of the films Nolan appeared in were "B" movies, including the Michael Shayne detective series. Nolan also turned-up in a number of television shows in the 1950s and 1960s, and won an Emmy.

This versatile average Joe could play any character in any genre, and was believable to each role. Nolan was someone you could relate to—one often got the feeling that he was regular fellow who stumbled into a picture with a group of actors.

Nolan's off-screen life is also revealed in *Lloyd Nolan: An Actors Life With Meaning*. The actor was devoted to his autistic son, and when he died in an accident 2500 miles away, Nolan channeled his grief into action.

For the rest of his life, this well known Hollywood actor did everything he could to better the lives of those affected by autism; he even led the charge in 1974 for the creation of the first public education law for austic children in the United States.

Lloyd Nolan: An Actors Life With Meaning is the story of two lives—a prolific on-screen life familiar to moviegoers and television fans alike—and an off-screen life that has affected many throughout the country.

Louise Brooks and Bruz Fletcher: Camped, Tramped & Riotous Vamps
This piece appeared on examiner.com on December 16, 2010.

Chances are, even the most ardent Louise Brooks fan will not have heard of Bruz

Fletcher. However, a first ever book on this 1930's recording artist and nightclub entertainer should go a long way toward helping reestablish his mercurial reputation.

And oh, what a reputation he had and deserves to have. *Bruz Fletcher: Camped, Tramped & a Riotous Vamp*, by Tyler Alpern, tells the story of this multi talented performer, composer, novelist, and artist (1906-1941). Fletcher was queer—an entertainer associated with the Pansy Craze of the pre-WWII era—and about as out as one could be in the 1930s.

He was also friends with Louise Brooks. The two performed on the same bill for a few weeks running at a Palm Beach, Florida nightclub in 1935. Brooks was also known to frequent Fletcher's performances in Hollywood a few years later.

In fact, in the late 1930s, Fletcher was a fixture on the Hollywood scene. His name regularly shows up in society and gossip columns of the time. As a popular local nightclub act, many film world celebrities saw him perform at the Club Bali, where his campy, coded routine was showcased. According to newspaper accounts, Brooks saw Fletcher perform on at least five different occasions in 1937 and 1938. The well known costume designer Travis Banton, who was also gay, was Brooks' companion on at least two of those outings.

Brooks' plays only a small role in Flether's story, though their connections go beyond social encounters. Earlier on in 1929, for example, Fletcher appeared on stage with Brooks' *American Venus* co-star Esther Ralston. Fletcher wrote her act, his partner Casey Roberts designed her gowns, and together they played to packed houses in Los Angeles, Chicago, New York and elsewhere. Fletcher also wrote songs for Peggy Fears, another one-time friend and fellow performer of Brooks (in the Ziegfeld Follies). Over the years, Fletcher would write material and sometimes tour with other silent era films stars.

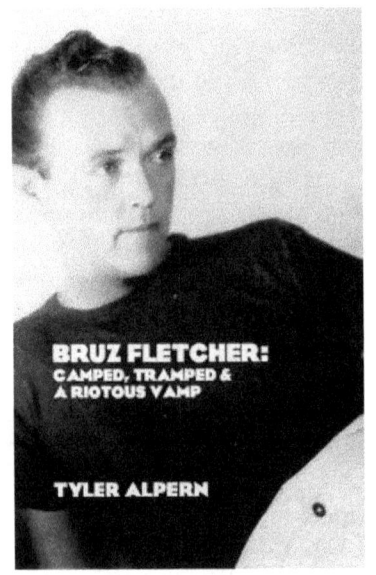

Brooks' sexual orientation—and attitude towards gays and lesbians—is a debated issue. In her apparent friendship with Fletcher, we find yet one more example of a homosexual with whom Brooks associated.

Bruz Fletcher: Camped, Tramped & a Riotous Vamp, issued by Blurb Books, pieces together the story of how Fletcher came to associate with early Hollywood stars—and how he came to enjoy a celebrated, years-long run at the Club Bali. It would prove to be the pinnacle of his career.

Fletcher was born to one of the wealthiest and most dysfunctional families in Indiana. It's said that Booth Tarkington's *The Magnificent Ambersons* was inspired, in part, by the Fletcher family. Fletcher's Aunt married the Pulitzer Prize winning novelist.

Fletcher's father lost the fortune his family had built over generations, only to became an elevator operator. (At one time, American currency bore their family name. An antique ten dollar bill with the name of the Fletcher National Bank of Indianapolis is depicted in the book.)

Fletcher ran away from home at age 8, and later attempted suicide as a teen. While home from school for the holidays, his mother and grandmother drank poison in committing a double suicide. His older sister escaped family life and lived as a man, joined a Broadway show, then went to Germany where she was jilted by a count. Later, she was committed to an asylum and was arrested for attacking a fraudulent Lady Bathurst before dying at age 24.

In his short life, Fletcher would twice live a rags-to-riches experience. As an entertainer, he overcame it all and sparkled as he performed nightly in glamorous high society nightclubs, delighting his often well-known patrons with his witty, sophisticated and often risqué songs.

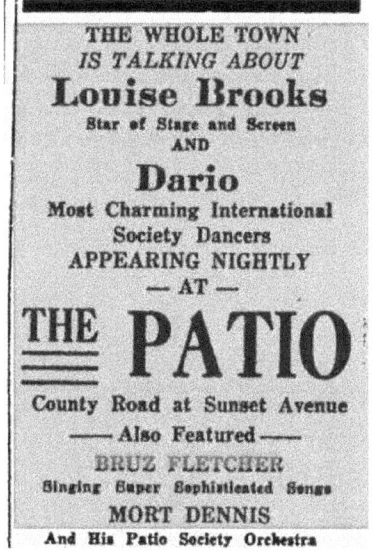

Though he killed himself at age 34 in 1941, Fletcher left behind three albums of remarkable songs and two novels that give colorful and candid glimpses into his world—a world populated by society dowagers, misfits, celebrities, addicts, servants, lovers and eccentrics that covered a variety of sexualities and mores.

The genesis of Tyler Alpern's book about Bruzz Fletcher is his fascinating website about the entertainer, which can be found at www.tyleralpern.com/bruz.html.

Six years in the making, *Bruz Fletcher: Camped, Tramped & a Riotous Vamp* tells the story of one of a forgotten, pre-Stonewall artist whose story has only recently come to light. It is heavily illustrated, and contains lyrics to most of Fletcher's songs, contributions from family members, collectors, and fans. *Bruz Fletcher: Camped, Tramped & a Riotous Vamp* is a remarkable book because it tells such a remarkable story.

Besides his new book, Alpern helped compile a compact disc of Fletcher's rare recordings from the 1930s. Originally issued by the independent Liberty Music Shop label, Fletcher's cosmopolitan recordings—the same ones Brooks heard, can now be found on *Drunk with Love*. It is available through CD Baby, and is also well worth checking out.

A Louise Brooks / Ed Wood / Elvis Presley connection
This piece appeared on the Louise Brooks Society blog on October 28, 2009.
In 2018, I found that Pandora's Box had made its West Coast debut in Los Angeles just a few days prior to it being shown in Monterey.

This falls into the category of "believe it or not" or "six degrees of separation" or "shook the hand that shook the hand." But whatever the case may be, it's true.

Recently, while researching a historic 1962 screening of *Pandora's Box* in Monterey, California, I came across an amusing, somewhat curious and admittedly tenuous connection between Louise Brooks and Ed Wood—and by extension, Elvis Presley! I know it's more than a bit of a stretch, but here goes.

The 1962 screening was part of a film seminar organized by a young curator named

Philip Chamberlin. By invitation, James Card attended the event and brought along a print of *Pandora's Box*, where the German film was shown on the West Coast for the very first time! Pauline Kael was also there, as was the poet Jack Hirschman, as well as other significant figures in the film world of the 1960s.

As it turned out, Chamberlin later moved to Los Angeles, where he founded the film series at LACMA, and was a producer, archivist, etc.... He also eventually married the one-time actress and songwriter Dolores Fuller. Anyone who knows the story of Ed Wood and his attempts at film making knows her name. Fuller and Wood were romantically involved, and Fuller appeared in a couple of Wood's films. After Fuller left Wood, she turned to songwriting, and contributed a number of songs to various Elvis Presley films. A few of her songs were even minor hits.

That's it. A Louise Brooks / Ed Wood / Elvis Presley connection—*of sorts*. I know it's a stretch—and really falls into the category of "six degrees of separation" (a la Kevin Bacon), but there you go. And just in time for Halloween, which is just a few days off.

I think Ed Wood would have approved.

Theodore Roszak (1933-2011)
This piece appeared on SFGate on July 9, 2011.

Theodore Roszak, a Berkeley writer who coined the term "counter culture," has died. He was 77.

Roszak was a social critic, cultural historian and author. He was also a novelist and taught history at Stanford and San Francisco State University before joining the faculty at California State University, Hayward.

Roszak first came to national prominence in the 1960s with the publication of *The Making of a Counter Culture*. That book chronicled and gave explanation to the youth-movements of the time.

Roszak's book captured a large audience of youthful dissenters, dropouts and Vietnam War protesters—as well as their baffled elders. *The Making of a Counter Culture* found common ground between student radicals and hippie dropouts in their mutual rejection of what he called "technocracy"—the regime of corporate and technological expertise that dominates industrial society. His was a thinking man's take on the year of the young rebels.

Writing in the *San Francisco Chronicle* in 1969, Alan Watts noted, "If you want to know what is happening among your intelligent and mysteriously rebellious children, this is the book. The generation gap, the student uproar, the New Left, the beats and hippies, the psychedelic movement, rock music, the revival of occultism and mysticism, the protest against our involvement in Vietnam, and the seemingly odd reluctance of the young to buy the affluent technological society—all these matters are here discussed, with sympathy and constructive criticism, by a most articulate, wise, and humane historian."

Roszak's humanity and deep level of understanding is a defining characteristic of his multi-genre writings. Though topical and published more than 40 years ago, *The Making of a Counter Culture* is still in print through the University of California Press.

Roszak was a Guggenheim Fellow and was twice nominated for the National Book

Award. Among his other books are *The Dissenting Academy* (1968), *Masculine/Feminine: Readings in Sexual Mythology and the Liberation of Women* (1969), *Where the Wasteland Ends* (1972), *Unfinished Animal: The Aquarian Frontier and the Evolution of Consciousness* (1975), *The Cult of Information* (1986), *The Voice of the Earth* (1992), *The Gendered Atom* (1999), and, as coeditor, *Ecopsychology: Restoring the Earth, Healing the Mind* (1995).

In *The Making of an Elder Culture: Reflections on the Future of America's Most Audacious Generation* (2009), Roszak sought to remind baby boomers of the creative role they once played in society and of the moral and intellectual resources they need draw upon in their later years in order to once again effect change.

As a thinker, Roszak was also a kind of cultural archeologist whose digs into our collective past and present took the form of fiction. I saw Roszak read from his work in local bookstores, and I put on an event for his last novel, a satire on New Age religion, *The Devil and Daniel Silverman* (2003).

The Memoirs of Elizabeth Frankenstein (1995) was a gender twisting take on the Frankenstein story. In its review, *Publisher's Weekly* wrote, "How ironic that a woman who wrote as a man should, after nearly 200 years, be given such ardent voice by a man writing as a woman. Roszak, author of the seminal nonfiction work *The Making of a Counterculture* and several previous novels including *Flicker*, risks much and achieves all in this richly imagined, frankly erotic homage to Mary Shelley."

The Memoirs of Elizabeth Frankenstein won the James Tiptree, Jr. Award, an annual literary prize for science fiction or fantasy that expands or explores our understanding of gender. The award is named for Alice B. Sheldon, who wrote under the pseudonym James Tiptree, Jr.

I came to Roszak's fiction through *Flicker*. It is a remarkable novel which Roszak described to me (and others) as "a secret history of the movies." Robert Regan, a film historian with a penchant for literature, recently stated on Facebook "Roszak and DeLillo are the only writers to create credible fictional filmmakers and their works."

The description for *Flicker* goes like this: "Jonathan Gates could not have anticipated that his student studies would lead him to uncover the secret history of the movies—a tale of intrigue, deception, and death that stretches back to the 14th century. But he succumbs to what will be a lifelong obsession with the mysterious Max Castle, a nearly forgotten genius of the silent screen who later became the greatest director of horror films, only to vanish in the 1940s, at the height of his talent. Now, 20 years later, as Jonathan seeks the truth behind Castle's disappearance, the innocent entertainments of his youth—the sexy sirens, the screwball comedies, the high romance—take on a sinister appearance. His tortured quest takes him from Hollywood's Poverty Row into the shadowy lore of ancient religious heresies. He encounters a cast of exotic characters, including Orson Welles and John Huston, who teach him that there's more to film than meets the eye, and journeys through the dark side of nostalgia, where the Three Stooges and Shirley Temple join company with an alien god whose purposes are anything but entertainment."

Roszak loved old movies and old movie stars. Louise Brooks (my favorite silent film star) or at least a character based on Brooks plays a part in *Flicker*. Roszak told me he was a fan of the actress, and had seen her surviving films.

If *Flicker* sounds weird and strange and wonderful and would make a good movie, you're right. At one point, Darren Aronofsky (*Black Swan*) was backing a production of a movie version of the book. However, like so many worthwhile projects, this one seems to have come to a halt.

Go discover *Flicker* for yourself, or check out *The Making of a Counter Culture*, or one of Roszak's other books. They are sure to shake your psyche.

An encounter with a curious character
This piece appeared on Open Salon on September 14, 2010, where it was a Salon editor's pick.

In June, the 59 year old writer F. Gwynplaine MacIntyre took his own life. He set his book and paper-filled New York City apartment on fire and died in the resulting blaze. It was an ugly ending to what was certainly a sad, even tormented life.

On Sunday, the *New York Times* ran a long article on the enigmatic, Scottish-born author. Little is known about him, except that at one point, in order to escape his past, he changed his name to "Fergus MacIntyre." According to Wikipedia, the allusive author acknowledged he took the middle-name of "Gwynplaine" from the protagonist of *The Man Who Laughs*, the memorable novel by Victor Hugo turned into an equally memorable 1928 film starring Conrad Veidt. In those works, Gwynplaine was the disfigured, always smiling malcontent who later inspired "The Joker" character in *Batman*.

MacIntyre was best known as a genre author whose sporadic output included science fiction, fantasy, horror, and mystery stories, as well as a science fiction novel and a book of light verse and miscellaneous humorous pieces. He was once praised by Isaac Asimov and Ray Bradbury. Reportedly, a number of unpublished manuscripts were burned in his apartment fire.

MacIntyre also authored newspaper articles and book reviews, and ghost authored and contributed to other works. Again according to Wikipedia, MacIntyre "contributed substantial script material" to a 2006 documentary on the silent film actress Theda Bara, *The Woman with the Hungry Eyes*. It was directed by Hugh Munro Neely, who also directed *Louise Brooks: Looking for Lulu*.

MacIntyre's reputation in the film community (which is curiously not addressed in the *New York Times* article) rests on his having written reviews of long lost films which he sometimes claimed to have seen. These reviews appeared on IMDb and film message boards, where they live-on to this day.

Such claims, made convincing through MacIntyre's skills as a writer, drove film historians to distraction. To many in the online film community, he was little more than a prankster playing with the facts while playing a joke on serious film enthusiasts. MacIntyre's claims to have seen lost films included at least one featuring Louise Brooks, *A Social Celebrity* (1926).

In the spring of 2006, I emailed MacIntyre regarding his 2002 IMDb review of that lost Brooks film. Not then knowing his reputation, I wrote "I am preparing a book on the films of Louise Brooks, and noticed your thoughtful comments on *A Social Celebrity* on the IMDB website. I am wondering if you ever saw the film? (The last known copy of *A Social Celebrity* was lost in a disastrous nitrate fire at the Cinémathèque Française in the late 1950s.) If you have in fact seen the film, I would be very curious to know when and where."

MacIntyre responded the next day.

"Greetings to Thomas Gladysz (do you pronounce it Gladdish?) from Fergus (F. Gwynplaine) MacIntyre, whom you contacted regarding the film *A Social Celebrity*.

Although I've read your IMDb review of *Looking for Lulu*, and your email address is an obvious tribute to Brooks, I'm surprised to learn that you're writing a book about her. Surely every possible fact about Louise Brooks has long since been unearthed?

I wish you good luck with your book, and I encourage you to avoid the cliche which several other authors (including Brooks herself) have perpetrated when writing about her: please do not refer to Brooks as 'Lulu'. Lulu was one of the characters she played onscreen. Louise Brooks was a far more fascinating and complex person than Lulu was.

To answer your question: yes, I have seen a print of *A Social Celebrity*. It was a 'flash print', meaning that it possessed the original (Paramount) intertitles, but they ran for only a few frames each; the print was intended for distribution in a non-Anglophone market, and the local exhibitor was supposed to use the flash titles as a guide for translations, which would occupy more footage than the flash versions and be onscreen longer. I viewed this print more than ten years ago, and it was already slightly deteriorated due to nitrate instability.

This print is (or was) in the personal collection of a private film collector in Europe, who does not wish to be publicly identified. He owns several original nitrate prints of films that were released in the 1930s and earlier. I was given some limited access to some of the films in his collection, solely in order to examine their physical deterioration, and to advise him as to which reels of film in his collection were most urgently in need of restoration or duplication to acetate safety stock. Normally, when a reel of film has deteriorated to the point where I'm unwilling to subject it to the vagaries of a motorised projector, I will inspect the footage through a hand-held Steenbeck viewer. Several reels of the *A Social Celebrity* print had begun to decompose, so I Steenbecked them rather than running them through a projector.

I have offered to put this collector into contact with several professional film restorers in Europe and Britain, and it is my understanding that he will eventually have most of the nitrate films in his collection converted to acetate stock. I have very little ability to influence his actions in this matter.

This collector is a private individual who only very rarely grants access to his film collection. I was given very limited access to his collection, solely in order to inspect his films as physical artefacts in need of restoration. I do not have direct contact with this gentleman; I contact him only through his attorneys, who are strongly inclined to refuse all requests for access to his collection. He has made it clear that he will not grant public access to his collection. As this gentleman has been helpful to me in my own business endeavours, I must respect his privacy.

Thank you for reading my IMDb reviews. I'm not an employee of IMDb, and they don't pay me for my reviews. I'm a full-time journalist and author. If you log onto www.amazon.com and go to their Books section, then key a search for my by-line "F. Gwynplaine MacIntyre", you'll see the covers of two books that I wrote and illustrated. One of these is my Victorian erotic horror/romance novel: *The Woman Between the Worlds*, featuring Conan Doyle, Aleister Crowley, GB Shaw, WB Yeats, Arthur Machen, Sir William Crookes and several other eminent Victorians united to aid an invisible she-alien during an invasion of London by alien shape-changers. This novel got rave reviews from Harlan Ellison on his Stateside cable-tv show. I'm also the author and illustrator of a humour anthology which was praised by Ray Bradbury and other authors: *MacIntyre's Improbable Bestiary*, likewise available on Amazon, which contains some original material I wrote about Lon Chaney and silent films.

To whet your appetite, here's the cover (my artwork and typography) of my anthology: http://images.amazon.com/images/P/1587154722.01.LZZZZZZZ.jpg

I took some notes while I was Steenbecking *A Social Celebrity*. If you have any specific questions about the content of this film, I will gladly try to answer them for you, but I must decline any request to give you access to the print.

Straight on till mourning, Fergus (F. Gwynplaine MacIntyre)."

Could it be true? I wondered. In my naiveté, I hoped it would be. I responded immediately and pressed MacIntyre for details, sent him specific questions, but didn't hear back. I am sure I came off as too eager, and MacIntyre wasn't willing to go extra innings.

A few days later, I wrote MacIntyre again. "I am not sure you received my email. I am glad to know that a copy of *A Social Celebrity* still exists in some form—even if that copy is unattainable—and may one day be given to a public archive. I shall await that day!" I never heard from him again. And as time passed, I began to feel this curious character with unsubstantiated claims had been pulling my leg.

The *New York Times* noted MacIntyre worked night jobs in order to spend his days at the New York Public Library researching things which interested him. Those subjects included early films, of which he was by all accounts knowledgeable. Undoubtedly, he relished their depictions of days gone by—and of a world, made safe through the passage of time, which no longer existed.

MacIntyre was something of a pastiche artist—witness his own description of his sole published novel, *The Woman Between the Worlds*. His reviews of silent films he couldn't have seen read like a kind-of critical pastiche of reviews found in the old film periodicals housed at the New York Public Library. That occurs to me now when I reread his IMDb review of *A Social Celebrity*. Its last line, "Louise Brooks is as seductive as usual, but she has very little to do here," strongly echoes the kind of observation made by film critics in the 1920's.

It's hard to know why MacIntyre claimed to have seen *A Social Celebrity* and other lost films—and thereby muddied the historical record. He must have known it irritated others. Perhaps it was a game. Perhaps it was one way of getting attention. Perhaps it was his way of asserting control over a world in which he felt increasingly out-of-sorts. We'll never know.

MacIntyre was an enigmatic, intellectual loner. He once wrote, "I collect the fragments of time that other people throw away, and I put these to good use." The *New York Times* article on F. Gwynplaine MacIntyre can be found at www.nytimes.com/2010/09/12/nyregion/12froggy.html.

Lee Israel, writer who forged Louise Brooks letters, has died

This piece appeared on the Louise Brooks Society blog on January 8, 2015. In 2018, a film based on Lee Israel's book was released.

Lee Israel, a writer and biographer who forged a series of letters from Louise

Brooks and others, has died. She was 75 years old. The *New York Times* has an extensive obituary.

Earlier in her career, Israel had published a popular biography of the actress Tallulah Bankhead, but as a writer, fell on hard times. She turned to forging letters from famous personalities, including actors, entertainers and writers such as Humphrey Bogart, Ernest Hemingway, Eugene O'Neil, and Louise Brooks.

The *New York Times* noted, "In the early 1990s, with her career at a standstill, she became a literary forger, composing and selling hundreds of letters that she said had been written by Edna Ferber, Dorothy Parker, Noël Coward, Lillian Hellman and others. That work, which ended with Ms. Israel's guilty plea in federal court in 1993, was the subject of her fourth and last book, the memoir *Can You Ever Forgive Me?*, published by Simon & Schuster in 2008." Brooks' name, x'ed out, appears on the cover.

After her memoir was published in 2008, Israel turned to selling her forged letters (as such) on eBay. As I noted on this blog at the time: "The eBay description reads, 'Lee Israel, author of the recently published *Can You Ever Forgive Me? Memoirs of a Literary Forger*, which The *New York Times* called 'pretty damned fabulous,' is offering several letters for sale—the hilarious forgeries that experts from coast to coast could not distinguish from the extraordinary letters written by the silent film star. These are the letters Lee Israel had not yet sold when the FBI came knocking at her door. $75 each, suitable for framing to bamboozle your literary friends. Letters of inauthenticity provided."

I didn't buy any of Israel's forgeries, but I did email her. We exchanged a couple of notes, but all-in-all, she was reticent to talk about what she did. Earlier, Israel was interviewed in *Vice* magazine:

VICE: Well, it could've been that they didn't fuss because you went to such great lengths to make the content of the letters believable and entertaining.

LEE ISRAEL: Yes. For instance, my Louise Brooks letters were based on her actual letters. In the beginning, I spent weeks reading these fabulous letters by her in the library. I got into her soul and her sensibilities and gained lots of knowledge about her life. So when I sat down to do the forgeries, I was just taking baby steps. In the beginning those letters were mostly Louise's words with a bunch of stuff just changed around. But when they started to sell like hotcakes, I got surer of myself and moved farther and farther away from the model. The Noël Coward and Dorothy Parker and Edna Ferber stuff was not even based on real letters. I was using things written in other forms and incorporating them into my work.

Remembering Roger Ebert (a fan of Louise Brooks)
This piece appeared on the Louise Brooks Society blog on April 4, 2013.

I'll never forget the first time I met Roger Ebert, which was more than a few years ago, as this snapshot testifies.

I introduced myself as the director of Louise Brooks Society. Roger and I had the chance to chat for a bit, and he told me how much he enjoyed visiting my Louise

Brooks Society website, and how, on a few occasions, he had used the site while looking things up about the actress and her best known film, *Pandora's Box*. I was pleased. Roger was encouraging, and he also told me of his own affection for and interest in Louise Brooks.

I encountered Ebert a few more times over the years, and continued to read his articles and columns. Ebert wrote about Louise Brooks a few more times, while praising both *Pandora's Box* and *Diary of a Lost Girl* as great films. If you haven't already read his glowing reviews of those two films, then search them out. They have, in the past, been found on his website, as well as in his books, *Great Movies* and *Great Movies II*.

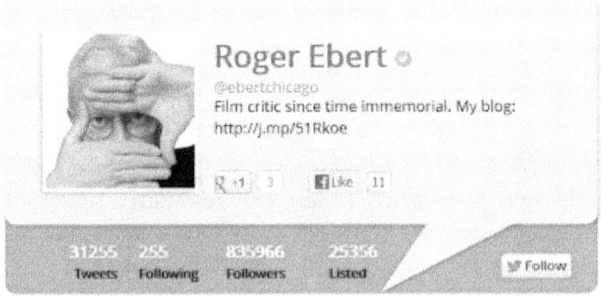

The birthday of Louise Brooks. My Great Movies review of "Pandora's Box," a film any serious film lover should know: http://t.co/53Xrr1Mw

Ebert has also tweeted about Louise Brooks and her two famous films. And a little more than a year ago, Ebert tweeted three times about the actress and *Diary of a Lost Girl*.

@ebertchicago: My Streamer of the Day. "Diary of a Lost Girl," a silent masterpiece with the immortal Louise Brooks. on.fb.me/GH64U0

@ebertchicago: New in my Great Movies Collection: Louise Brooks in Pabst's "Diary of a Lost Girl." Remorseless. On Netflix Instant. bit.ly/GHbzQK

@ebertchicago: The latest review in my Great Movies Collection: Louise Brooks in the unforgettable "Diary of a Lost Girl." bit.ly/GHbzQK

Ebert has also written about another Brooks' film, *The Show-Off*, in his "Ebert Club Newsletter." In 2010, Ebert wrote "Notice that whenever Louise Brooks is on screen, you simply can't focus on anyone else..."

I was also honored when Ebert tweeted about some of my own writings about Louise Brooks, mentioning and linking to stories I had written for the Huffington Post on *Beggars of Life* and on the Brooks' journals for examiner.com. Today, the world lost a great champion of the movies. And as well an admirer of Louise Brooks.

Jan Wahl Through a Lens Darkly
This piece appeared on examiner.com on August 13, 2009.

Jan Wahl has led a charmed, almost storybook life. He has followed his interests and passions with zeal. He has gone places and done things most of us only dream of.

Part of his good fortune has to do with his talents as a writer, his artistic sensibility and appreciation for great and fine things. Some of it has to do with being in the right place at the right time. But then, chance favors the prepared mind.

Wahl is well regarded as a children's book author, with more than 100 works to his credit. His first book, *Pleasant Fieldmouse* (1964), featured illustrations by Maurice Sendak! In a long and distinguished career, Wahl has also worked with such well-known children's book illustrators as Mercer Mayer, William Joyce, Erik Blegvad**,** and Garth Williams.

Wahl has also been a life-long film buff. His interest in and passion for the movies have brought him into contact with a number of greats—as fan and enthusiast, as a writer, and as a film collector. Those encounters, and more, are related in an enjoyable new book of essays, *Through a Lens Darkly* (BearManor Media).

The chapter titles tell the story: "Conrad Veidt Slept Under the Bed," (about the author's youthful adoration of the actor), "Gloria Swanson Wore a Funny Hat," "The Day I Almost Killed Garbo" (a commonplace anecdote with mystical overtones), "Glamour Pusses Up Close: Mae West, Marlene Dietrich, Dolores Del Rio and Rita Hayworth," and "Postcards from Leni." The latter relates Wahl's consideration of and correspondence with the German filmmaker, Leni Riefenstahl.

Of special interest are two chapters, "A Cup of Coffee for Carl Th. Dreyer" and "Quick Comet in the Sky: Louise Brooks." The first tells the story of how Wahl came to work for and befriend Carl Th. Dreyer, the great Danish director whose few works include two cinematic masterpieces, *The Passion of Joan of Arc* (1928) and *Vampyr* (1932). Wahl recounts his participation in the making of Dreyer's second from last film, *Ordet*, in 1955.

Wahl enjoyed—and at times probably didn't enjoy—a 20 year friendship with the legendary silent film star, Louise Brooks. Wahl writes, "I feel lucky to have known her. Yet she was not easy to know. Without a doubt, she was the most complex, most baffling, the brightest person I have known. She may have shared intelligent and sparkling insights, but she could be fiercely angry and sharp tongued. Then, just perhaps, apologetic. If I look at her movies, mostly *Beggars of Life*, *Pandora's Box*, *Diary of a Lost Girl* or *Prix de beauté*, I marvel at what she suggested onscreen—despite a disappointing life."

In the book's most sustained chapter, Wahl details how he came to know the actress while a student in Copenhagen in the 1950's. A telling photograph shows Brooks, James Card and Wahl at the Danish Film Museum in 1957.

Over the next two decades, Wahl received more than 100 letters from "Brooksie" or "Loulou"—as well as the occasional "excellent homemade fudge." Those letters (which would certainly make a great book) reveal Brooks intense isolation, her coming to terms with her past, and her struggle to become a writer. It was a dream the older Brooks and the young Wahl shared.

Early on, Wahl helped Brooks with her own writing. And over the years, through their correspondence and meetings, the young fan became the fallen star's champion. In *Through a Lens Darkly*, Wahl tells sobering stories of Brooks' later years.

Other film world folk with whom Wahl crossed paths include Myrna Loy, Jackie Coogan, the legendary European silent film star Asta Nielsen, and even Ernest Thesiger, Dr. Pretorious in James Whale's *Bride of Frankenstein*. And there is the widow of avant-garde filmmaker Oskar Fischinger's, Elfriede. (Fischinger is a great favorite of Wahl's.) And film archivists too, preservationists and historians such as David Shepard, James Card of the George Eastman House, and Berkeley's own Russell Merritt.

Through a Lens Darkly also relates stories about other acquaintances and friends in the arts. There are encounters with the legendary dancers Paul Swan and Ruth St. Denis, crooner Bing Crosby (who sings the aspiring author "Happy Birthday"), the poet and poetic filmmaker James Broughton, writers Ivy Compton Burnett, Katherine Anne Porter, Dylan Thomas, and Vladimir Nabokov (Wahl's instructor at Cornell), as well as the great Danish writer Isak Dinesen (author of *Seven Gothic Tales* and *Out of Africa*, etc…), among others. It's a mixed lot, and Wahl drops a lot of names, but it is oh so much fun.

"The Baroness Tossed Me Out" is devoted to Dinesen, for whom Wahl—then a graduate student—came to work for after receiving a summoning cablegram, "Am dying. Wish to dictate last tales. Please come. Karen Blixen." He did just that—acting as recording secretary and companion to the then elderly writer.

The problem with *Through a Lens Darkly* is that there's not enough of it. As a reader, I have a hundred questions. I want to know more. Were you surprised when the King of Denmark showed you the chrysanthemum tattoo on his back? And do you still have the antique silver piece actor Broderick Crawford bought for you as a thank you gift for showing him around Copenhagen? And do you regret not accompanying Dinesen to Russia after she was invited by the author of *Doctor Zhivago*, Boris Pasternak?

Nevertheless, *Through a Lens Darkly* is a good read. Wahl's conversational style also makes it a fast read. In the words of Ray Bradbury, "If you love films, Jan Wahl's book is the perfect book for you. *Through a Lens Darkly* is right-on. Get it!"

**They say there's nothing like a good book...
also from Jan Wahl and BearManor Media:**

Adventures with
Louise Brooks,
Lillian Gish,
Dolores Del Rio,
Jackie Coogan,
Leni Riefenstahl,
Rita Hayworth,
Robert Mitchum,
Mae West,
Carl Th. Dreyer,
Isak Dinesen
and others!

"If you love films, Jan Wahl's book is the perfect book for you. Through a Lens Darkly is right-on. Get it!"
– Ray Bradbury

"A lively and funny book."
– Julie Harris

"The problem with Through a Lens Darkly is that there's not enough of it."
– Thomas Gladysz

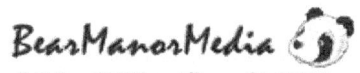

P O Box 71426 • Albany, GA 31708
Phone: 760-709-9696 • Fax: 814-690-1559
Book orders over $99 always receive FREE US SHIPPING!
Visit our webpage at www.bearmanormedia.com for more great deals!

Talking to the Piano Player

This piece appeared on examiner.com on November 23, 2009. Nine years earlier, Oderman and I exchanged a phone call and letters. He thanked me for having read his then new book on Lillian Gish, and noted that he had worked with Gish, Gloria Swanson, and Louise Brooks in 1967. He thought each of them "outspoken women who fought to survive in what was essentially a man's world."

Stuart Oderman is an unsung hero of the silent cinema.

For more than 50 years, Oderman has accompanied silent films in venues across the United States (including San Francisco). And for 40 years, he has served as the official pianist at screenings of silent films at the Museum of Modern Art in New York. A well travelled virtuoso, Oderman has also in the last half-century performed in theaters and universities in Canada and Europe. A long time friend and correspondent of Lillian Gish, Oderman has also played for her films with the actress in attendance on more than a few occasions

Oderman's accompaniment to silent films can be heard on various VHS and DVD releases. Of them, one stands out. This reviewer considers Oderman's accompaniment to the Home Vision Cinema release of *Pandora's Box* one of the finest soundtracks of all time.

More than a musician, Oderman is also an author—and a champion of the actors and actress of the silent and early sound era. Though born well after the advent of talkies, Oderman is still partial to silent film. He considers it "pure film." The pianist has published articles chronicling the artists important to the time, and has turned his enthusiasms and knowledge into five books.

Those books are *Roscoe "Fatty" Arbuckle: A Biography of The Silent Film Comedian, 1887-1933* (McFarland), *Lillian Gish: A Life on Stage and Screen* (McFarland), *The Keystone Krowd* (BearManor), and *Talking to the Piano Player* (BearManor). This later book contains reminisces of encounters and friendships with Colleen Moore, Douglas Fairbanks, Jr., Anita Loos, Marlene Dietrich, Frank Capra, Jackie Coogan, Madge Bellamy, Aileen Pringle, Allan Dwan, Adela Rogers St. Johns, Betty Bronson, Lois Wilson, Constance Talmadge and others.

Oderman's latest is *Talking to the Piano Player 2* (BearManor). This new book is a second collection of profiles and reminisces—or what the author terms personal interviews. His subjects are prominent past personalities from music and film including Joan Blondell, Lita Grey, Louise Brooks, Joseph L. Mankiewicz, Tallulah Bankhead, Artie Shaw, Harry Richman, Ann Miller, Veronica Lake, Marie Windsor, Vivian Blaine, and others.

One of the most poignant profiles is of Harry Richman (1895-1972), the popular American entertainer of the 1920s and 1930s. Oderman encountered the then retired bandleader, singer and actor in Santa Monica in 1970.

As he tells it, Oderman came across Richman's out-of-print autobiography in a thrift store for 50 cents, and the clerk who rang the sale mentioned the book's author lived nearby and sometimes went to the "House of Pies or to Zucky's Delicatessen late at night by himself."

Finding Richman in the phone book, Oderman telephoned and was invited to the entertainer's tiny white bungalow. They spoke at length on a few occasions, with Oderman mentally recording their conversations while noting the impoverishment of the singer who made "Puttin on the Ritz" a smash hit. On top of Richman's piano, we are told, were signed vintage glossies of Lenore Ulric, Clara Bow, and Jean Harlow—three women with whom the entertainer was once romantically involved.

Similar circumstances brought Oderman and Veronica Lake (1922-1973) together. By chance, Oderman encountered the film noir femme fatale with the peek-a-boo hairstyle early one morning in 1963. Long out of the public spotlight and trying to make end's meet, Lake was bartending at the Martha Washington, a women's residence hotel in New York City.

Ever the plucky though sincere fan, Oderman approached Lake and asked her to breakfast. "We order coffee and juice, and the Early Breakfast Special: eggs, home fries, and toast." "She wants to speak for no other reason than to dispel any myth that she is an easy pickup who waits for film buffs to list her credits, although I tried not to say. . . ." Oderman's observations depict an actress with a keen mind coming to terms with her past.

Another once forgotten actress Oderman encountered was Louise Brooks (1906-1985). The pianist met her in 1967 after a screening of *Pandora's Box* at the George Eastman House in Rochester, New York.

Oderman's six page portrait of Brooks includes her observations on not only aspects of her own life and career (the Ziegfeld Follies, G.W. Pabst, Marion Davies, Charlie Chaplin, etc…), but also contemporary figures (Grace Kelly, and Paul Newman and Elizabeth Taylor in *Cat on a Hot Tin Roof*). It complements the portrait of the actress in her later years as revealed in Jan Wahl's recent book, *Dear Stinkpot: Letters from Louise Brooks*.

Along with other often poignant and revealing profiles, *Talking to the Piano Player 2* includes photographs taken at the time Oderman became acquainted with his subjects, as well as other rare photographs from the author's personal collection. All together, it is interesting and enjoyable read.

In celebration of Stuart Oderman (1940-2017)
This piece appeared on the Louise Brooks Society blog on August 2, 2017.

As I type this blog, I am listening to one of my very favorite film soundtracks—Stuart Oderman's piano accompaniment to *Pandora's Box*. It was Oderman's exceptional, romantic pastiche of classical piano music that helped me fall in love with Louise Brooks—and helped open up a world of music by the likes of Debussy, Satie, Rachmaninoff, Brahms, and others. Thank you Stuart Oderman.

Back in the late 1990's, I was so desperate to re-enter Oderman's moving score that I made a tape cassette recording of the VHS soundtrack by placing my recorder next to my TV set. Despite its aural limitations, I have played it many times since—almost to the point of it wearing out. Admittedly, it was a crude recording, and the fidelity was poor. Once, when I enthusiastically played it for a friend, a pianist, I could sense the look on her face was one of bewilderment. She likely only heard musical noise. I heard scenes from the film.

Stuart Oderman, one of the finest silent film accompanists, died on July 28 at the age of 77. The Louise Brooks Society mourns his passing.

Oderman was many things. Besides a pianist, he was also a writer and film historian. Oderman was the author of five books, including titles on Roscoe "Fatty" Arbuckle, Lillian Gish, and the Keystone Cops.

He also authored two volumes of memoirs called *Talking to the Piano Player*. The first volume includes interviews with some of the most important people of a bygone film era: Marlene Dietrich, Frank Capra, Colleen Moore, Jackie Coogan, Madge Bellamy, Aileen Pringle, Allan Dwan, Adela Rogers St. Johns, Douglas Fairbanks, Jr., Anita Loos, Leatrice Joy, Dorothy Davenport (Mrs. Wallace) Reid, Patsy Ruth Miller, Ann Pennington, Claire Windsor, Betty Bronson, Minta Durfee, Lois Wilson and Constance Talmadge.The second volume featured interviews with Artie Shaw, Lita Grey, Joseph L. Mankiewicz, Harry Richman, Veronica Lake, Marie Windsor, Joan Blondell, Gloria DeHaven, and Tallulah Bankhead.

Significantly, for more than 53 years, Oderman accompanied and composed music for silent films at the Museum of Modern Art in New York City, as well as at theaters, museums and universities across the United States, Canada, and Greece. His scores appear on VHS / DVD releases of *Pandora's Box*, the Charlie Chaplin documentary *The Eternal Tramp*, and the Harry Houdini film, *The Master Mystery*.

Television audiences may be familiar with his Laurel and Hardy series, and his work for the Comedy Channel.

Oderman came to his calling in a special way. While still in high school, the young movie buff used to cut classes in order to see whatever silent films were playing locally. In 1954, he snuck off to the Museum of Modern Art in New York to see the Lillian Gish film *Broken Blossoms*.

A lady sitting next to him took notice and said, "You belong in school." His response was, "I want to play piano for silent films." The woman turned out to be Gish. She took him by the hand down to the piano, Oderman later recounted, and introduced him to Arthur Kleiner, the celebrated silent film pianist.

Kleiner became his teacher and Gish his point-of-entry to the silent era. "She gave me a life," he says of the actress some consider the finest of the era. "I owe her."

I owe Stuart Oderman.

David Levine, painter and illustrator, has died
This piece appeared on the Louise Brooks Society blog on December 29, 2009.
In 2018, I was fortunate enough to acquire two original ink drawings of Brooks by Levine, including the oft-reproduced image shown below.

The *New York Times* reports that David Levine, "a painter and illustrator whose macro-headed, somberly expressive, astringently probing and hardly ever flattering caricatures of intellectuals and athletes, politicians and potentates for nearly half a century" died Tuesday in Manhattan. He was 83 and lived in Brooklyn."

To fans of Louise Brooks, Levine is well remembered as the creator of an especially charming and pointed caricature of the silent film star and memoirist. He drew her for the *New York Review of Books* at the time *Lulu in Hollywood* was published. That likeness, among Levine's finest, was reproduced countless times on the subscription cards inserted into thousands and thousands of newsstand copies of the publication.

Levine's likeness of Louise Brooks was also reproduced on the cover a book of postcards of the illustrator's art which was published a few years back.

Levine's reputation is high. According to the write-up in the *New York Times*, "Mr. Levine's drawings never seemed whimsical, like those of Al Hirschfeld. They didn't celebrate neurotic self-consciousness, like Jules Feiffer's. He wasn't attracted to the macabre, the way Edward Gorey was. His work didn't possess the arch social consciousness of Edward Sorel's. Nor was he interested, as Roz Chast is, in the humorous absurdity of quotidian modern life. But in both style and mood, Mr. Levine was as distinct an artist and commentator as any of his well-known contemporaries. His work was not only witty but serious, not only biting but deeply informed, and artful in a painterly sense as well as a literate one. Those qualities led many to suggest that he was the heir of the 19th-century masters of the illustration, Honoré Daumier and Thomas Nast."

As a book lover and longtime reader of the *New York Review of Books*, I saw many of Levine's caricatures. They stood out. They were distinct..His caricature of Brooks is one of my favorites. I am even fortunate enough to own a signed limited edition print of the image, which I obtained from the artist. It can be seen in the image below. Brooks is just over my right shoulder, along with a few other treasures at "LBS headquarters."

Remembering Bruce Conner, a fave rave
This piece appeared on the Louise Brooks Society on November 18, 2016.

Bruce Conner was born on this day in 1933 in McPherson, Kansas, and raised in Wichita, Kansas.

This American artist, who passed away in 2008, is still renowned for his work in painting, drawing, sculpture, assemblage, collage, photography, and performance, among other disciplines. Though primarily a visual artist, Conner is perhaps best known for his work as a film maker. His short 16mm and 35mm experimental films like "Report" (1963-1967), "Breakaway" (1966), and "Crossroads" (1976) are each a mini *tour-de-force*. And so is his first work in the field, a 16mm non-narrative short titled "A Movie" (1958). In 1991, it was selected for preservation by the United States National Film Registry at the Library of Congress.

Conner is currently the subject of a major retrospective exhibit at the San Francisco Museum of Modern Art (through January 22, 2017). The exhibit, "Bruce Conner: It's All True," opened at the New York Museum of Modern Art, where it received a rave review in the *New York Times*, which called it an "extravaganza" and "a massive tribute." *Times* critic Roberta Smith called Conner a "polymathic nonconformist" who was "one of the great outliers of American Art" and who "fearlessly evolved into one of America's first thoroughly multidisciplinary artists." After having seen the exhibit in San Francisco, I wrote about it in the Huffington Post.

It's worth noting that Conner had a not uncritical nostalgic affection for old Hollywood. He obliquely appropriated imagery and themes from pulp and pop culture. Witness the works in "Bruce Conner: It's All True" with titles like "St. Valentine's Day Massacre / Homage to Errol Flynn" (1960), "Homage to Mae West" (1961), "Homage to Jean Harlow" (1963), and "Son of the Sheik" (1963), as well as others not includes in this retrospective. Granted, these works are not "about" the movie stars or films they reference, but that doesn't mean they are not an intentional oblique nod.

Conner also had a lifelong interest in his fellow Kansan, Louise Brooks. He told me so on more than one occasion. Both grew up in Wichita. Conner was also familiar with the biography of the actress by Barry Paris.

Back in 1997, I mounted a small exhibit about Louise Brooks at a small neighborhood cafe here in San Francisco. Conner, who lived in the next neighborhood over, read about it in the local paper and visited the exhibit. (So did the artist known as Jess.) Conner must have appreciated my little exhibit, which was made up of film stills, vintage magazine covers, sheet music, and other ephemera I had collected. Conner even wrote a note in the guestbook. I was wowed, and flattered, to say the least, as I had long been interested in Bruce Conner's art. (I can't really fix a date on the beginning of my deep interest in the artist, but it could date to around the time I read Rebecca Solnit's 1990 book, *Secret Exhibition: Six California Artists of the Cold War Era*.)

Sometime later, Conner and I got in touch, at first by phone and then in person. Eventually we met, and he had me over to his San Francisco home, where at his kitchen table and in between phone calls from friends like Dennis Hopper, Conner told me of his "near encounter" with Brooks. Conner also told me of his involvement with early showings of her films in San Francisco. It was information, it seemed to me, he was desirous to pass on.

I wanted to take dancing lessons from Louise Brooks when she moved back to Wichita, Kansas in the 1940's. My parents wouldn't let me. They spoke to each other about her "scandalous" relationship to her young male students.

Bruce Conner

Their near encounter took place around 1942 (as best I can date it), after Brooks left Hollywood and returned to Wichita, where the one time world famous film star moved back in with her parents. It was not a harmonious scene, as Brooks was flat broke and the world (including gossiping locals) had deemed her a failure.

As a former Denishawn dancer and Ziegfeld showgirl, Brooks knew how to move with grace, and so, she opened a dance studio in downtown Wichita in what amounted to a half-hearted attempt to earn some money. Conner, still just a boy, was aware that a movie star was in town (there were articles in the local paper), and he told me he took to keeping on eye on her dance studio. Conner admitted to spying on the studio, watching Brooks come and go. Conner even drew a map of the area, marking the location of Brooks' studio in the Dockum Building on East Douglas and its relationship to the theaters where Conner would go to the movies.

Conner also told me how, at one point, he wished to take dancing lessons from Brooks, but his parents would not allow it. Conner told me that it was because of Brooks' scandalous reputation, something no doubt talked about by neighbors. If I recall, he also told me that his parents and other neighbors or friends knew Brooks' and her family, and that this social circle of friends and acquaintances once encountered one another at a Wichita party, and a punch was thrown. Conner himself never got up the nerve to make contact with Brooks, telling how he once almost rang her doorbell.

via wichitaksdailyphoto.blogspot.com

In 2006, the Louise Brooks centenary was celebrated by the San Francisco Silent Film Festival when they showed a restoration of Louise Brooks' most celebrated film, *Pandora's Box*. I was asked to introduce the film, and to introduce Bruce Conner; the artist spoke about what the actress meant to him and his near encounter with this singular film star. Somewhere, there is video of this occasion at the Castro Theater in San Francisco before a sold-out audience of more than 1400 people. Here, at least, is a photograph.

Bruce Conner is one of the great outliers in contemporary art. And in a sense, Louise Brooks is one of the great outliers in film history. Her films, like the art of Conner, have touched many. John Lennon, a kindred spirit, once wrote to Conner, "You don't know me but I know you and you are my fave rave." Happy birthday Bruce Conner.

Bill Berkson, In Memorium (1939-2016) - poet and Louise Brooks devotee
This piece appeared on the Louise Brooks Society bog on June 16, 2016.

Bill Berkson, acclaimed poet and and friend to the Louise Brooks Society, passed away early today (June 16th). Berkson was a writer, art critic and curator of considerable accomplishment. He was also a big fan of Louise Brooks.

I had the pleasure of having put on an event with Berkson some years ago, as well as visiting Bill at his book and art filled San Francisco apartment, where we talked about our favorite silent film star and the time that he and his good friend, the poet Frank O'Hara, attended a 1961 screening of *Prix de beauté* in New York City. Afterwords, both O'Hara and Berkson wrote poems inspired by the actress.

O'Hara wrote "F.Y.I. (*Prix de beauté*)," which references the actress. It was first published in a small literary journal, and later collected in *The Collected Poems of Frank O'Hara*, to which Berkson wrote the footnote and explained its inspiration.

Berkson ending up writing "Bubbles," which was based on essays Brooks was publishing in film journals in the 1960s. "Bubbles" was likewise published in a small press magazine and later collected in the book *Lush Life* (1984).

In 1997, Berkson allowed me to print the poem as a broadside. It was one of a small series of poems inspired by / or in homage to the actress which I've desktop published in small autographed editions of 25 copies. A scan of the broadside—which depicts an image of the actress floating beneath the text of the poem—is shown here.

Bubbles

I was a bathing beauty in THE AMERICAN VENUS.
My dream of becoming a great dancer: How sweet he was then,
a brilliant, laughing young man of the world, his heart
so tender: "Get married!" I cried, bursting into fresh black
tears: Glittering white sequins: I put no value on my beauty.
Somedays I thought I would run away from Hollywood forever –
to Miami to Havana to Palm Beach to Washington D.C. no less!
Now we are in the air, warriors of the sky, burning the beans
and WANTED FOR MURDER: No rehearsal, no retakes:
His actors cry real tears: He wanted Dick to cry too and
Dick was not a spontaneous weeper: Breaking out of his grasp,
I grabbed a shotgun and killed him with dramatic swiftness.
That developed his character: Stars shimmering by beasts
in the black sky: His jaw muscles hunched closer to deliver
his monolog: "You're a lousy actress and your eyes are
too close together." I shoved him away, saying "Are you
trying to make love to me?" "Why not?" he said furiously,
jumping up and backing away to the door to make his exit.
"You go to bed with everyone else – why not me?"

Bill Berkson

John Ashbery & Louise Brooks encounter in Paris
This piece appeared on the Louise Brooks Society blog on September 4, 2017.

The American poet John Ashbery has died. He was 90 years old. Ashbery was a writer of considerable accomplishment, and the first living poet to have a volume published by the Library of America dedicated exclusively to his work. But more than that, his 1975 collection, *Self-Portrait in a Convex Mirror*, was the only winner of the American book world's unofficial "triple crown": the Pulitzer Prize, the National Book Award, and the National Book Critics Circle prize. In 1985, Ashbery was named a MacArthur "genius," and in 2011, he was given a National Humanities Medal and credited with changing "how we read poetry."

Ashbery was born in Rochester, New York, in 1927. He attended Harvard, and long lived in New York City. He is grouped with Frank O'Hara and Kenneth Koch as part of the avant-garde "New York School" of poets, although Ashbery believed what they really had in common was living in New York.

I met him once, when he did a rare drop-by book signing at the bookstore I once worked at. (He signed more than a dozen books for me, including his translations of a few of the surrealist writers.)

It was then that Ashbery told me of his encounter with Louise Brooks, in a Paris hotel lobby in the late 1950s. As Ashbery explained, the hotel manager noticed that the poet was from Rochester, New York—and that was where Brooks was then living. (It's likely both registered as being from the city in upstate New York.) And so, they were introduced..

I can't remember how the subject of Louise Brooks came-up (though I suppose I am always talking about the actress), but it might of had to do with Ashbery's friends, the New York poets Frank O'Hara and Bill Berkson. Both had written poems "about" Louise Brooks, and both were "fans" of the actress' films. Ashbery, as it turned out, also had an interest in the actress. (Interestingly, Frank O'Hara's roommate at Harvard was the illustrator / artist Edward Gorey, another admirer of Louise Brooks.)

It seems New Yorkers love Louise Brooks, just as she loved New York.

Homage to George W. Lighton of Kentucky, idealistic silent film buff who perished in the Spanish Civil War
This piece appeared on the Louise Brooks Society blog on June 29, 2016. It is one of my favorites. Regrettably, it was also the subject of a number of acrimonious remarks from a politically conservative film scholar who criticized my sympathic portrait of Lighton, an idealistic leftist.

I continue to find fascinating bits about Louise Brooks and her times. . . . Earlier today, for example, I came across a letter to the editor published on January 2, 1931 in a Louisville, Kentucky newspaper. The letter, of all things, mentions the 1929 Louise Brooks' film, *Pandora's Box*. To me, that is fascinating—because the film was then little known in the United States. Its only recorded showing prior to 1931 was a two week, December 1929 run at an art house in New York City which was reviewed in the local newspapers and nationally in a handful of trade publications. One wonders how a movie goer outside of NYC might have known of the film?

The letter to the editor was penned by George W. Lighton, a 20 year old Louisville resident and obvious film buff with a preference for the silent cinema. Lighton wrote his letter in response to a December 21, 1930 piece by Louisville film critic Boyd Martin naming what he considered some of the best films of the year. They include *All Quiet on the Western Front*, *Hell's Angels*, *The Love Parade*, and others.

Boyd was a thoughtful and prolific newspaper critic for the *Louisville Courier Journal*. (His reviews of earlier Brooks' films are in the Louise Brooks Society archive.) And Lighton, one would guess, was a regular reader. Within just a few days, the young film buff mailed his response to Boyd's column. It is copied here.

In his letter, Lighton all but admits to having *not* seen most of the films he sets out to call to the public's attention. Perhaps he was just showing off his knowledge of foreign cinema, or perhaps he was hoping an exhibitor might take notice and screen these films in Louisville. It's hard to say. Nevertheless, it is a remarkable list—full of German and Soviet classics, and one which holds up to the test of time.

Who was George W. Lighton? I haven't been able to find out much about him except that he was born in 1911 and was a bright kid who seemed to be reader and film buff and someone very curious about the world. In 1933, a couple years after his letter was published, he was lecturing in Louisville on the subject of "The Movies— Our Newest Art." His talk, which followed one by Boyd on the subject of "Current Plays on Broadway," was sponsored by the Division of Adult Education at the University of Louisville.

George William Lighton.

Lighton, I think, was also an idealist and a wanderer. According to the 1938 article, when money ran out after his first year in college, Lighton took "hobo trips" around the country, venturing as far as Canada and Mexico. In the midst of the Depression, he spent five years bumming around and recording his observations in a notebook. "He kept an extensive journal of his experiences, his impressions of cities and people and his reactions to works of art in museums all over the country. He wrote about being robbed by a one-legged man in Chicago and about the plight of the Harlan County miners and about being stranded when a 'too cheap' bus abandoned its passengers enroute to California." "He looked up people who interested him and recounted conversations he had with Theodore Dreiser, John dos Passos, and Eisenstein and others. He had an article published in *Cinema* and hoped to take up a literary career."

Lighton rambled around until he was convinced by the head of the University of Louisville English department to return to school and get his degree. He did so, and graduated in June 1937 from the University of Louisville, where he was the only student to ever be awarded honors in both sociology and humanities. Discouraged by not being able to find a job, he took off for Chicago in August of that year.

EUROPEAN FILMS.

To the Editor of The Courier-Journal.

In last Sunday's Courier-Journal Mr. Boyd Martin selected what he considered the ten best motion pictures of the year 1930. His judgment was necessarily limited to American-made talkies in general and those exhibited in Louisville in particular. For the sake of orientation and to give a sense of the cinema's world perspectives I should like to submit a selection of films from the world's production for 1930:

1. "Arsenal." Russian silent film, directed by Alexandre Dovzhenko. Technical resourcefulness and dramatic sense; use of symbolism.
2. "Old and New." Russian silent film, directed by Sergei M. Eisenstein. Development of a cinematic language. Step from synthesis to analysis.
3. "Westfront, 1918." German talkie, directed by G. W. Pabst. Sound as connected with visual motion. Creative experiment.
4. "Applause." American talkie, directed by Rouben Mamoulian. Creative intelligence frees the U. S. cinema from the fetters of sound recording. Use of the mobile camera; subordination of dialogue.
5. "Pandora's Box." German silent film, directed by G. W. Pabst. Cinema at its most naturalistic. From Frank Wedekind's story. The film reaches its most adult stage.
6. "The Blue Angel." German talkie, directed by Josef von Sternberg. Employed true technique of screen with minimum of actual dialogue, although with an accompaniment of sound.
7. "Soil." Russian silent film, directed by Alexandre Dovzhenko. Philosophical meditative film that approaches poetry.
8. "The China Express." Russian silent film, directed by Illy Trauberg. Tremendous power of imagery and movement.
9. "Morocco." American talkie, directed by Josef von Sternberg. Technically the most advanced talking picture yet made in America. A silent picture with incidental dialogue.
10. "All Quiet On the Western Front." American talkie, directed by Lewis Milestone. Among the most devastatingly potent moving pictures ever made. Shows Russian influence.

Other worthwhile silent pictures of 1930 were "The Wonderful Lies of Nina Petrova," "White Hell of Pitz Palu," "Cain and Artem," "Asphalt," and "City Girl," a part-talkie that was essentially silent film in its technique. Other European talkies of note are "The Tiger of Berlin," "Murder," "Atlantic," "Two Hearts In Waltz Time," and "The Last Company." While it is very improbable that these pictures of European make will ever be shown in Louisville, American-made movies following in their beaten path and utilizing their technical achievements will be exhibited here in the coming year. And it is best that the public know something of European films in order that it should not be led again into attributing originality and artistic direction to a film that is merely an imitation, as was the case with "The Patriot" in 1927.

GEORGE W. LIGHTON.
Louisville.

In September 1937, his Mother received a letter from her son, who was then in Paris, mentioning that he would be going to Spain to fight against Fascism. Another letter followed. "I am now in Spain as a member of the International Brigade of the Loyalist Army. I had not been in Paris more than two days when I enlisted as a volunteer." Many more letters followed, detailing daily life and his movements around Spain. Lighton's last letter was sent on Christmas day, 1937.

Despite no additional letters, and despite reports of the deaths of American volunteers in Spain, Lighton's mother continued to believe he was still alive. She held onto her belief until one of her son's friends in Spain wrote to say he had been killed, but where and when was uncertain. Also lost was the journal Lighton kept in Spain. Lighton's friend wrote "telling of the pact he had had with George to recover his note book in the event of his death." "On my return to the company I tried, but failed to obtain possession of George's journal," the friend wrote.

There is little found online except for the few clippings mentioned above, and a page on the Abraham Lincoln Brigade Archives website. There are also passing mentions in a couple of contemporary books, *Letters from Barcelona: An American Woman in Revolution and Civil War* (2009), and *A History of Education in Kentucky* (2011). In the former, Lighton is described as a "idle dreamer and griper" by the subject of the book, who appears to have been acquainted with many participants in the Spanish Civil War, including George Orwell. In the latter, Lighton is made out to be an internationalist apart from his fellow students, most all of whom were then staunch isolationists.

I would be interested in reading Lighton's contribution to *Cinema*. There was one journal by that name published in New York, and one in London, during the early 1930's. I wonder if there is an index for either periodical?

Show Girl
in Hollywood

By J. P. McEvoy

Have been trying for months now to get my feet in some trough but all I get is the run around.

You're too pretty to be writing for a living.

I say to myself Pritzie I'm just what your osteopath ordered to stop that pain in your head.

You remember Dixie Dugan, Show Girl!

Dixie made her debut in the pages of LIBERTY. She took the country by storm! Newspapers from coast to coast reprinted her story. Hollywood filmed it, and filled the movie houses. When printed as a $2.00 book, it became a best seller. SHOW GIRL was translated into German, Danish, Swedish, French. Ziegfeld is producing it on Broadway.

And still America demands: "More Dixie Dugan!" LIBERTY will meet the demand.

DIXIE DUGAN, high-stepping, wise-cracking as ever, has crashed the gilded gates of Hollywood . . . Dixie is strutting her stuff for the speakies . . . worrying her pretty head over contracts and options . . . quarreling with her true love Jimmy Doyle, now scenario writer for Colossal Film Corporation . . . fighting with callous-hearted picture executives.

DIXIE, in brief, is having one high time in Hollywood—the new Hollywood, filled with sound and plenty of fury . . . filled with Broadway actors and playwrights . . . with high brow authors doing scenarios for Rin Tin Tin . . . with Broadway song writers thinking up theme songs in three by six bungalows . . . doll-faced stars with limping larynxes fading into oblivion . . . great big technical men from Rochester and Schenectady . . . Wall Street money men, merging . . .

And does Dixie find adventure? Well—we're telling you to read this new LIBERTY feature!

Popular as SHOW GIRL was, we believe this is even brighter, gayer, more glamorous, louder and funnier. With telegrams, letters, diary extracts, press clippings and what have you, McEvoy weaves a great story around this sparkling show girl. It will be quoted from Park Avenue to Sunset Boulevard. Don't miss it if you want to stay smart! It starts in the issue of LIBERTY on sale June 15—a week from next Saturday.

Maybe I could get a job posing.

What do I want with a screen test? Suppose it turned out good? I'd have to leave New York and go to Hollywood and make pictures.

Watch for the start of this new LIBERTY feature!

8 FURTHER READING
ABOUT LOUISE BROOKS & THE LBS

My interest in Louise Brooks turned me into a bibliographer. It was something that happened out of necessity.

For more than a decade beginning in the late 1990s, I was quite nearly obsessed with tracking down every book, every article, every review, every mention or printed reference to the actress. I visited every public and university library within driving distance of my home in San Francisco, and put through literally hundreds of inter-library loan requests for material I couldn't obtain locally. I also took the opportunity to visit libraries and archives whenever I travelled, in New York City, Washington D.C., and Los Angeles, as well as in Chicago, Detroit, and Rochester, even Paris and London. I wanted everything.

This obsessive hunt for material led to a number of minor discoveries, but it also necessitated that I organize what became an ever growing mass of material. I had accumulated four large filing cabinets of photocopies (there was one long drawer devoted just to Denishawn), as well as a dozen additional boxes of vintage clippings, pamphlets, magazines and other printed material. And then there were the thousands of digital files on my computer, yet more material found scouring the internet and its various databases. When last measured, my digital archive contains at least ten gigabytes.

As a means to organize and track this material, I created more than three dozen thematic bibliographies which I posted the Louise Brooks Society website. There were primary and secondary bibliographies, a bibliography for each film, different bibliographies devoted to Brooks' efforts as a dancer and showgirl, bibliographies covering each decade of Brooks' life, etc…. I discovered my calling as a compiler, and adding to them became an incremental pleasure. When printed out, they filled two rather thick binders.

Reproducing my bibliographies is beyond the scope of this book. Instead, offered here are two of them – one featuring books about the Brooks and her films, and the other highlighting some of the press the Louise Brooks Society has received over the years.

I have always thought bibliographies are interesting things in-and-of themselves. They are one of the first things I look at when reading a new biography or work of history. They are like road-maps the authored travelled, and which you may as well.

If you are anything like me, they may lead you to something new and interesting and even suprising.

FURTHER READING ABOUT LOUISE BROOKS

Along with Brooks' own memoirs, *Lulu in Hollywood*, what follows is a checklist of key books about the actress and her films. Not cited are other works, some significant, which are only in part about Brooks.

Pabst, G. W. *Pandora's Box (Lulu): A Film by G.W. Pabst*. New York: Simon and Schuster, 1971.
—the first study of of the silent film masterpiece

Jaccard, Roland. *Louise Brooks: portrait d'une anti-star*. Paris: Editions Phébus, 1977.
—original French edition

Roland Jaccard. *Louise Brooks: Portrait of an Anti-Star*. New York, NY: New York Zoetrope, 1986.
—subsequent English-language edition

Paris, Barry. *Louise Brooks:* New York: Knopf, 1989.
—reissued by the University of Minnesota Press in 2000.

Cristalli, Paola and Donne, Valeria Dalle. *Louise Brooks: l'européenne*. Paris: Transeuropa, 1999.
—multi-lingual collection of essays on *Die Büchse der Pandora, Das Tagesbuch einer Verlorenen*, and *Prix de beauté*.

Brooks, Louise. *Lulu in Hollywood*. Minneapolis: University of Minnesota Press, 2000.
—expanded and revised edition

Krenn, Günter, and Karin Moser. *Louise Brooks: Rebellin, Ikone, Legende*. Wien: Verlag Filmarchiv Austria, 2006.
—a significant, German language work

Cowie, Peter. *Louise Brooks: Lulu Forever*. New York: Rizzoli, 2006.
—a coffee-table picture book

Rocco, Vanessa. *Louise Brooks and the "New Woman" in Weimar Cinema*. New York: International Center of Photography, 2007.
—exhibit pamphlet

Böhme, Margarethe. *The Diary of a Lost Girl*. PandorasBox Press, 2010.
—the "Louise Brooks edition" of the book which was the basis of the 1929 film; edited, and with an introduction by Thomas Gladysz

Wahl, Jan. *Dear Stinkpot: Letters from Louise Brooks*. Albany, GA: BearManor Media, 2010.
—hopefully, the first collection of Brooks' letters

Graves, Tom. *My Afternoon With Louise Brooks*. Memphis, Tennessee: Rhythm Oil Publications, 2011.
—short e-book later expanded, in part, in the print book, *Louise Brooks, Frank Zappa, & other charmers and dreamers* (DeVault-Graves Digital Editions, 2015).

Lafayette, Maximillien de. *Louise Brooks: Her men, affairs, scandals and persona*. New York: Times Square Press, 2012.
—utterly worthless book only included here for the sake of completeness; its errors and many bad reviews speak for themselves

anonymous. *Louise Brooks Photo Book*. Japan: City Lights Publishing, 2013.
—negligible e-book included here for the sake of completeness

Jaccard, Roland. *Portrait d'une flapper*. Paris: P.U.F, 2014.
—French language study from the author of *Louise Brooks: portrait d'une anti-star*.

Gladysz, Thomas. *Beggars of Life: A Companion to the 1928 Film*. PandorasBox Press, 2017.
—with a foreword by William Wellman Jr.

Gladysz, Thomas, and Robert Byrne. *Now We're in the Air: A Companion to the Once "Lost" Film*. PandorasBox Press, 2017.
—with a foreword by Robert Byrne

Hutchinson, Pamela. *Pandora's Box*. London: British Film Institute, 2018.
—a significant study

FURTHER VIEWING ABOUT LOUISE BROOKS

Film Firsts: Louise Brooks (1960) - television short
Lulu in Berlin (1985)
Jacumba Hotel (1985)
Arena: Louise Brooks (1986) - television
Louise Brooks: Looking for Lulu (1998)
E! Mysteries & Scandals: Louise Brooks (1999) - television
Louise Brooks - Cinq pas vers le mythe (c. 2004)
Naked on My Goat (2014)
Documentary of a Lost Girl (forthcoming)

FURTHER VIEWING RELATED TO LOUISE BROOKS

The Love Goddesses (1965)
Memories of Berlin: Twilight of Weimar Culture (1976)
Hollywood ["Star Power" episode] (1980)
Cinema Europe: The Other Hollywood [parts II and VI] (1996)
Icons: Louise Brooks (2001) - BBC television short

This LBS advertisement appeared in 2015.

FURTHER READING ABOUT THE LOUISE BROOKS SOCIETY

Launched in 1995, the Louise Brooks Society was one of the first websites devoted to silent film or a silent film star. Only a few pages at first, the LBS has grown over the years, and so has its acclaim as a resource for fans of Louise Brooks and early cinema. The LBS has been mentioned in a handful of books, as well as on websites and in newspapers, magazines and other publications from all over the world. Here is a select, chronological checklist of material about or referencing the LBS.

Meddis, Sam Vincent. "Net: New and notable." *USA Today*, May 23, 1996.
—"Silent-film buffs can get a taste of how a fan club from yesteryear plays on the Web. The Louise Brooks Society site includes interview, trivia and photos. It also draws an international audience." (This piece also ran in *Florida Today*.)

anonymous. *Net Directory*, issue 7, 1996.
—the LBS is named one of five best sites devoted to actresses in this UK computer magazine

Paracchini, Fabio. *Cybershow: cinema e teatro con Internet*. Milano: Ubulibri, 1996.
—brief mention in Italian book

C. J., "NB." *Times Literary Supplement*, March 14, 1997.
—referenced in English literary journal

Anonymous. "Louise Brooks Society." *Microtimes*, issue 170, 1997.
—brief write-up

Roberson, Fontaine. "Flapper Has 'Virtual' Fan Club in Noe Valley." *Noe Valley Voice*, September, 1997.
—article in San Francisco, California monthly

Silberman, Steve. "Fan Site Sparks Biopic." *Wired News*, April 10, 1998.
—article on *Wired* magazine website

Farrant, Darrin. "Programs - Sunday." *Melbourne Age*, April 16, 1998.
—referenced in Australian newspaper: "The Louise Brooks Society has an exhaustive web site about this fascinating siren."

Bentley, Rick. "Ahead of Her Time." *Fresno Bee*, April 30, 1998.
—article in Fresno, California newspaper. "Internet users have embraced the actress for years. Web pages and various sites have dealt with this actress, whose fame started in the silent films era and exploded in the information age. Her career and her life off the set have become a source of interest unparalleled by many other film stars. And those bits and bytes of information were a catalyst for this TV special."

Evenson, Laura. "Lovely Lulu Lives Again." *San Francisco Chronicle*, May 3, 1998.
—article in California newspaper

anonymous. "NetWatch." *Atlanta Journal and Constitution*, May 5, 1998.
—mentioned as exemplary website in Georgia newspaper

E! Entertainment. "Louise Brooks" episode. *E! Mysteries & Scandals* (TV Series), November 16, 1998.
—biographical program with Hugh Hefner, Roger Ebert, film historian Frank Thompson, and Thomas Gladysz (as Director of the LBS)

Bennett, Graham (editor). *Directory of Web Sites*, Chicago: Routledge, 1999.
—brief write-up

anonymous. "Fan Site Profiles." bLink. February, 1999.
—article in magazine for Earthlink subscribers

Malcolm, Derek. "GW Pabst: Pandora's Box." *Guardian* Unlimited, July 22, 1999.
—referenced on English newspaper website

Krenn, Günter and Paolo Caneppele. *Film ist Comics: Wahlverwandtschaften zweier Medien ; die Projektionen des Filmstars Louise Brooks in den Comics von John Striebel bis Guido Crepax*. Wien: Filmarchiv Austria, 1999.
—footnotes to and brief mention of the website in this Austrian book

Forestier, Katherine. "Private Icon." *South China Morning Post*, December 1, 1999.
-- "The voiceless Internet has been the perfect medium for reviving the image of one of the greatest icons of the silent movie era. Louise Brooks, with her trademark raven 'helmet' hair style, adorns many a Web site. The renewed interest in her, fueled by the cyberspace Louise Brooks Society, prompted Turner Classic Movies to fund the television profiule *Louise Brooks: Looking for Lulu* (World, 10 pm)."

Garner, Jack. "Movie buffs can find trivia, reviews online." *Rochester Democrat & Chronicle*, September 12, 2000.
— mention in New York newspaper: "A fine example of a fan page, a thoughtful, artful site devoted to the life and times of a fabled silent movie legend, with rare articles from the '20s and superb photos." (This syndicated piece appeared in newspapers across the country including the *Asbury Park Press, Burlington Free Press, Cincinnati Enquirer,* Louisville *Courier-Journal*, Nashville *Tennessean* and elsewhere.)

Douglas, John. "Online with you." *Grand Rapids Press*, March 26, 2001.
—mention in Michigan newspaper: "There has never been a more interesting actress in the history of movies or a more beautiful woman than Louise Brooks, who made a name for herself in American and German films. This Web site at pandorasbox.com, created by The Louise Brooks Society, is crammed full of photos of the lady with the page boy bob. It also has biographical material and still shots from her movies plus posters and links to other Brooks' sites. It also tells which of her films are available on video and DVD."

Anderson, Jeffrey M. "Thirteen great film sites." *San Francisco Examiner*, November 29, 2001.
— "This San Francisco-run site pays tribute to one of the greatest and most under-appreciated stars of all time, Louise Brooks, who played numerous bit parts and starred in only two films during the silent era. It contains tons of info, pictures and history."

Aimeri, Luca, and Dario Tomasi. *Internet per il cinema: tecniche, generi, cinematografie, autori*. Torino: UTET libreria, 2001.
—mention in Italian book

l., tk. "Ins Netz gegangen Pandora Brooks." *Stuttgarter Zeitung*, July 14, 2002.
—mention in newspaper from Stuttgart, Germany

O'Connell, Pamela Licalzi. "Dreaming Celebrities and the Earth's Eye Candy." *New York Times*, August 29, 2002.
—"The Louise Brooks Society (www.pandorasbox.com) is an excellent homage to the art of the silent film as well as one of its most luminous stars."

Pattenden, Mike. "An era of glamour." London *Sunday Times*, April 27, 2003.
—"With her sculpted dark bob and rebellious lifestyle, Louise Brooks was perhaps the ultimate flapper icon. A screen star to rank with Bacall and Hepburn, Brooks' career straddled the silent era and early talkies. She bucked the system to make movies in Europe, notably *Pandora's Box*, which lends its name to www.pandorasbox.com, dedicated to her remarkable life and including some of her more risque poses—a reminder that the 1920s were as much about sex and style as any era since."

Blackberry Cat. "Louise Brooks: Actress and Writer." BBC, November 12, 2004.
—mention on English news site

Dufour, Nicolas. "Louise Brooks, l'adoration perpétuelle." *Le Temps*, December 23, 2004.
—referenced in French newspaper

Melton, Wayne. "That '20s Girl: Lulupalooza celebrates the work of a screen goddess." *Style Weekly*, July 20, 2005.
—referenced in Richmond, Virginia weekly

Caloudas, Constantine. "Louise Bobs Her Hair." *Washington City Paper*, July 22, 2005.
—referenced in Washington, D.C. weekly

Maltin, Leonard. "Links We Like: Louise Brooks Society." *Leonard Maltin's Movie Crazy*, August 1, 2005.
—"Not many sites of any kind can claim to be celebrating a tenth anniversary online, but that's true of the Louise Brooks Society, devoted to the life and times of the magnetic silent-film star and latter-day memoirist. Thomas Gladysz has assembled a formidable amount of material on the actress and her era; there's not only a lot to read and enjoy, but there's a gift shop and even a 'Radio Lulu' function that allows you to

listen to music of the 1920s. Wow!"

Matheson, Whitney. "Happy birthday, Louise!" *USA Today*, November 14, 2006.
—"My favorite Louise Brooks site belongs to the Louise Brooks Society, a devoted group of fans that even keeps a blog. There, you can find just about everything about the actress: articles, filmography, photos, links and more."
SiouxWire. "Interview: Thomas Gladysz, founder of the Louise Brooks Society." SiouxWire, April 5, 2007.
—interview on website

Stinnett, Chuck. "Louise Brooks had beauty that was decades ahead of its time." *The Gleaner*, September 22, 2009.
—"Brooks remains a focus of remarkable interest...." - mention in Henderson, Kentucky newspaper

"Louise Brooks." KRPS, November ?, 2009.
—radio program about the actress with Thomas Gladysz, director of the Louise Brooks Society, on National Public Radio affiliate in Pittsburg, Kansas

Couch, Christina. "Silent films get a new life online, but not everybody's celebrating." *Time Out Chicago*, August 25, 2010.
—mention in article on Louise Brooks, *Pandora's Box*, and the internet

Blackburn, Gavin. "Forgotten book by Margarete Boehme to be revived in US." *Deutsche Welle*, November 3, 2010.
—article on English-language German news site

K., A. "Stoletni dnevnik prostitutke, oče avtobiografskih izmišljotin?" RTV Slovenia, November 4, 2010.
—article on Slovenian news site

LaSalle, Mick. "*Diary of a Lost Girl* to be screened at main library." *San Francisco Chronicle*, November 12, 2010.
—referenced in California newspaper

Rombeck, Terry. "A cut above: Local author's novel generates national buzz." *Lawrence News-Tribune*, June 10, 2012.
—referenced in Kansas newspaper

Toole, Michael T. "Reopening *Pandora's Box* in San Francisco." *Film International*, August 22, 2012.
—interview in film journal

De Jesus, Janice. "Orinda author turns fascination into novel." *San Jose Mercury News*, February 26, 2014.
—referenced in California newspaper

Wellman, William A. *Wild Bill Wellman: Hollywood Rebel.* New York : Pantheon Books, 2015.
—brief mention in biography of the director

Smurthwaite, Nick. "The Archive: Louise Brooks – something of an enigma." *The Stage*, September 1, 2015.
— referenced in UK publication: "One of the most luminous stars of the silent era, Louise Brooks has been all but erased from cinema history. Only a handful of movie buffs keep her memory alive, mostly through the 20-year-old Louise Brooks Society, whose aim is to honour the charismatic actor and stimulate interest in her life and work."

Mack, Megan. "Connections: The Rise, Fall, and Resurrection of Louise Brooks." WXXI, December 2, 2015.
—radio interview with Thomas Gladysz, documentarian Charlotte Siller, and film critic Jack Garner on National Public Radio affiliate in Rochester, New York

Tanner, Becky. "Wichita's silent movie star is subject of upcoming documentary." *Wichita Eagle*, April 3, 2016.
—"Even today, Brooks has a devout following that includes the Louise Brooks Society, which promotes her life as a star and dancer." -- referenced in Kansas newspaper

Frumkes, Roy. "BEGGARS OF LIFE (KINO/Lorber)." *Film in Review*, August 9, 2017.
—"The recently recorded score by the Mont Alto Motion Picture Orchestra is often lovely and rarely distracting, and there are two commentaries, one favoring Ms. Brooks (by the founding director of the Louise Brooks Society) and another by William Wellman Jr. for balance."

Garner, Jack. "Silent film Beggars of Life with legendary Brooks out on Blu-ray." *Rochester Democrat & Chronicle*, August 20, 2017.
—article in New York newspaper

Weissberg, Jay. "*Now We're in the Air.*" Pordenone / Le Giornate del Cinema Muto, 2017.
—"Louise Brooks Society founder Thomas Gladysz found evidence that William Wellman was also attached at some point, which makes quite a bit of sense, but by June the studio revealed that the director for *Now We're in the Air* would be Frank R. Strayer, a considerably lesser talent than the original three choices."

Wilson, Andrew. "St. Marys author celebrated in book." *Evening Leader*, September 2, 2017.
—article in St. Marys, Ohio newspaper

Classic Movie Blog Association. "CMBA Profile: Louise Brooks Society," February 15, 2018.
—interview on film website

Brady, Tara. "Louise Brooks: 'I was always late, but just too damn stunning for them to fire me'." *Irish Times*, June 2, 2018.
    -- "She has super-fans. An online tribute site, the Louise Brooks Society, contains an extraordinary day-by-day chronology of her life."

ABOUT THE AUTHOR

Thomas Gladysz is the Director of the Louise Brooks Society (www.pandorasbox.com), which he founded in 1995. He is the author of hundreds of articles on early film, most of which were written for online publications. He has also contributed program essays to the San Francisco Silent Film Festival, Syracuse Cinefest, Telluride, and Ebertfest. In 2004, Gladysz contributed the entry on Louise Brooks to the *Encyclopedia of the Great Plains* (University of Nebraska Press). He also edited and wrote the introduction to the "Louise Brooks edition" of Margarete Böhme's *The Diary of a Lost Girl* (2010), and authored *Beggars of Life: A Companion to the 1928 Film* (2017), and *Now We're in the Air* (2017). His audio commentaries for *Diary of a Lost Girl* (2015) and *Beggars of Life* (2017) appear on the Kino Lorber DVD / Blu-rays. More at www.thomasgladysz.com

www.ingramcontent.com/pod-product-compliance
Lightning Source LLC
Chambersburg PA
CBHW080456110426
42742CB00017B/2904